HINDU

Covering the earliest Sanskrit rulebooks through to the codification of "Hindu law" in modern times, this interdisciplinary volume examines the interactions between Hinduism and the law. The authors present the major transformations to India's legal system in both the colonial and postcolonial periods and their relation to recent changes in Hinduism. Thematic studies show how law and Hinduism relate and interact in areas such as ritual, logic, politics, and literature, offering a broad coverage of South Asia's contributions to religion and law at the intersection of society, politics, and culture. In doing so, the authors build on previous treatments of Hindu law as a purely text-based tradition and, in the process, provide a fascinating account of an often neglected social and political history.

Timothy Lubin is Professor in the Department of Religion, and Lecturer in Law and Religion in the School of Law at Washington and Lee University. His publications concern classical Hindu ritual and doctrine, and their relation to legal precepts and practices in India.

Donald R. Davis, Jr., is Associate Professor in the Department of Languages and Cultures in Asia at the University of Wisconsin, Madison. His previous publications include *The Spirit of Hindu Law* (2010) and *The Boundaries of Hindu Law: Tradition, Custom and Politics in Medieval Kerala* (2004).

Jayanth K. Krishnan is Professor of Law and the Charles L. Whistler Faculty Fellow at Indiana University, Bloomington, Maurer School of Law. Krishnan's academic interests focus on the legal profession and law-and-globalization, with a special emphasis on how these areas intersect in India. His publications on these subjects have appeared in reputed law reviews and peer-reviewed journals.

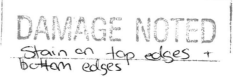

HINDUISM AND LAW: AN INTRODUCTION

EDITED BY

TIMOTHY LUBIN

Washington and Lee University

DONALD R. DAVIS, JR.

University of Wisconsin, Madison

JAYANTH K. KRISHNAN

Maurer School of Law, Indiana University, Bloomington

CAMBRIDGE
UNIVERSITY PRESS

CAMBRIDGE UNIVERSITY PRESS
Cambridge, New York, Melbourne, Madrid, Cape Town, Singapore,
São Paulo, Delhi, Dubai, Tokyo, Mexico City

Cambridge University Press
The Edinburgh Building, Cambridge CB2 8RU, UK

Published in the United States of America by Cambridge University Press, New York

www.cambridge.org
Information on this title: www.cambridge.org/9780521887861

First published 2010

Printed in the United Kingdom at the University Press, Cambridge

A catalog record for this publication is available from the British Library

Library of Congress Cataloging in Publication data
Hinduism and law : an introduction / [edited by] Timothy Lubin, Donald R. Davis, Jr.,
Jayanth K. Krishnan.
p. cm.
ISBN 978-0-521-88786-1 (hardback)
1. Hindu Law. 2. Hindu law – History – Sources. 3. Law – India – History.
4. Hinduism. I. Lubin, Timothy, 1964– II. Davis, Donald R., Jr., 1970– III. Krishnan,
Jayanth K., IV. Title.
KNS122.H564 2010
349.54–dc22
2010015147

ISBN 978-0-521-88786-1 Hardback
ISBN 978-0-521-71626-0 Paperback

Contents

List of contributors

EDITORS

TIMOTHY LUBIN is Professor in the Department of Religion, and Lecturer in Law and Religion in the School of Law at Washington and Lee University. His publications concern classical Hindu ritual and doctrine, and their relation to legal precepts and practices in India. He is at work on a volume entitled *Authority, Law, and the Polity in Premodern India.*

DONALD R. DAVIS, JR., is Associate Professor in the Department of Languages and Cultures in Asia at the University of Wisconsin, Madison. His previous publications include *The Spirit of Hindu Law* (2010) and *The Boundaries of Hindu Law: Tradition, Custom and Politics in Medieval Kerala* (2004).

JAYANTH K. KRISHNAN is Professor of Law and the Charles L. Whistler Faculty Fellow at Indiana University, Bloomington, Maurer School of Law. Krishnan's academic interests focus on the legal profession and law-and-globalization, with a special emphasis on how these areas intersect in India. His publications on these subjects have appeared in reputed law reviews and peer-reviewed journals.

CONTRIBUTORS

WHITNEY COX is Lecturer in Sanskrit at the School of Oriental and African Studies, University of London. His research interests include Sanskrit and Tamil literature and literary theory, and the history of Śaivism. He is at present working on a reinterpretation of the accession of the Cola emperor Kulottuṅga I.

RICHARD H. DAVIS is Professor of Religion and Asian Studies at Bard College. His most recent books are *A Priest's Guide for the Great*

Festival: Aghorasiva's Mahotsavavidhi (2009) and *Global India circa 100* CE*: South Asia in Early World History* (2010).

LAURA DUDLEY JENKINS is Associate Professor of Political Science at the University of Cincinnati. Previous publications include her book on affirmative action, *Identity and Identification in India: Defining the Disadvantaged* (2003, 2009), as well as articles on religious freedom and conversion, competing minorities' claims for affirmative action, colonial and contemporary government anthropology, the role of social science in anti-discrimination law, and reserved legislative seats for women.

ADITYA MALIK is Associate Professor/Reader in Indian Religions in the School of Social and Political Sciences at the University of Canterbury, New Zealand. His publications on pilgrimage, oral narratives, and ritual performance in Rajasthan and Uttarakhand include *Nectar Gaze and Poison Breath: An Analysis and Translation of the Rajasthani Oral Narrative of Devnarayan* (2005).

LAWRENCE McCREA is Assistant Professor of Sanskrit Studies at Cornell University. His research focuses mainly on traditional Indian poetics, hermeneutics, and language theory. He is the author of *The Teleology of Poetics in Medieval Kashmir* (2008) and (with Parimal Patil) of *Buddhist Philosophy of Language in India: Jñānaśrīmitra's Monograph on Exclusion* (2010).

AXEL MICHAELS is Professor of Classical Indology in the South Asia Institute, Heidelberg University. His publications include *Hinduism: Past and Present* (2004), *The Price of Purity: The Religious Judge in 19th Century Nepal* (2006), and *Śiva in Trouble: Rituals and Festivals at the Paśupatinātha Temple of Deopatan, Nepal* (2008).

SMITA NARULA is Associate Professor of Clinical Law at New York University School of Law. She is Faculty Director of the law school's Center for Human Rights and Global Justice and its International Human Rights Clinic. Narula has published extensively on human rights issues in South Asia, with a special emphasis on caste-based discrimination and the rise of Hindu nationalism.

PATRICK OLIVELLE is Professor in the Department of Asian Studies at the University of Texas at Austin. His focus in recent years has been the early textual development of the Dharmaśāstras. Besides the four early Dharmasūtras, he has critically edited and translated the Dharmaśāstras of Manu and Viṣṇu. He has also completed a new translation of Kauṭilya's *Arthaśāstra.*

ROSANE ROCHER is Professor Emerita of South Asia Studies at the University of Pennsylvania. Many of her publications concern the intellectual exchange between India and the West in the late eighteenth and early nineteenth centuries. They include analytical articles and three biographies (the most recent in press) of British Indologists.

RACHEL STURMAN is Assistant Professor of History and Asian Studies at Bowdoin College. Her work focuses on the history of law, political economy, and affective relations in colonial and postcolonial India. She has recently completed a manuscript entitled "The Properties of Subjects: Economic Governance and the Family in Colonial India."

ANANYA VAJPEYI teaches South Asian history at the University of Massachusetts, Boston. She was educated at the Jawaharlal Nehru University, Delhi, at Oxford University, where she read as a Rhodes Scholar, and at the University of Chicago. Her first book, *Righteous Republic: The Political Foundations of Modern India*, is in press.

RINA VERMA WILLIAMS is Assistant Professor of Middle Eastern and South Asian Languages and Cultures, and of Studies in Women and Gender, at the University of Virginia. Her research interests focus on the politics of women and gender, religion, law, and nationalism in South Asia and comparative contexts. She is the author of *Postcolonial Politics and Personal Laws* (2006).

ROBERT YELLE is Assistant Professor in the History Department and in the Honors Program at the University of Memphis. He earned a JD with Honors from the University of California at Berkeley and a PhD from the University of Chicago. He received a Guggenheim Fellowship for work on his second book, tentatively entitled *Modernity and Disenchantment: Christianity and the Secularization of Colonial India.*

Acknowledgements

This volume would not have been possible without the support of many institutions and individuals. The editors' home institutions, Washington and Lee University, the University of Wisconsin, Madison, and Indiana University, Bloomington, have provided funds and other resources, and have allowed us to try out early drafts of some chapters in the classroom.

A Fulbright-Hays grant from the CIES allowed the first editor to carry out the last phase of work in India, under the auspices of the Institut français de Pondichéry.

The University of Wisconsin, Madison provided the means and the venue for a workshop, convened by Donald Davis in October of 2007, which brought together many of the contributors at an early stage in the process. John Stavrellis gave the script a very thorough final read through, and made useful suggestions.

The editors also collectively wish to thank their editors at Cambridge University Press, especially Kate Brett who initially proposed the idea for the book and shepherded it along as it took shape. Laura Morris, Joanna Garbutt, and Rosina Di Marzo ably guided it through the production process, with meticulous copyediting by Leah Morin.

Chronology

c. 3rd century BCE	Rock and Pillar Edicts of King Piyadasi (Aśoka Maurya); *Āpastamba Dharmasūtra*
early 2nd century BCE	*Gautama Dharmasūtra*
mid–late 2nd century BCE	*Baudhāyana Dharmasūtra* (i.e., "Proto-Baudhāyana," namely the early part consisting of the first and most of the second book)
1st century BCE	*Vasiṣṭha Dharmasūtra*
from early CE	South Indians involved in maritime trade settled on the coasts of Sumatra and Cambodia, and along the Straits of Malacca
c. 150	Sanskrit inaugurated as cosmopolitan language; incorporation of *artha* into Dharmaśāstra texts and the concomitant incorporation of regional legal norms into the early *smṛti*s (*dharmaśāstra*s)
c. 2nd century	*Mānava Dharmaśāstra* (*Manu Smṛti*)
c. 4th–5th century	*Yājñavalkya Smṛti*
c. 400–700	Inscriptions begin to indicate strong presence of corporate groups; production of *smṛti*s with more detailed and pronounced sections on legal procedure
c. 5th–6th century	*Nārada* and *Bṛhaspati Smṛti*s
c. 7th century	*Viṣṇu Smṛti*
c. 7th–8th century	*Kātyāyana*, *Parāśara*, *Vaikhānasa Smṛti*s
c. 700–900	Temple building increases; earliest commentaries
c. 900–1200	Monumental temples built by regional rulers; earliest digests

c. 1200	Delhi Sultanate introduces state administration of law in Persian
13th–early 16th century	Spread of South Asian populations in Indonesia
c. 1300	Vernaculars begin to be used for legal documentation
c. 1365–1445	*Prāyaścittaviveka*
1500	First European colonial presence; formalization of vernacular government documents
c. 1510–80	Raghunandana Bhaṭṭācārya
c. 1540–80	*Divyatattva*
1772	Judicial Plan of Warren Hastings, governor of Bengal; colonial administration becomes the central force in law; "personal law" institutionalized
1776	Publication of *A Code of Gentoo Laws*
1794	Publication of Jones's translation of the *Laws of Manu*
1798	Publication of Colebrooke's *A Digest of Hindu Law on Contracts and Successions*
1810	Publication of Colebrooke's *Two Treatises on the Hindu Law of Inheritance*
1829	Abolition of suttee (*satī*)
1830	English replaces Persian as the administrative and diplomatic language
1833	Slavery Abolition Act passed (in the UK), ends slavery throughout most of the British Empire, leading to an increase in indentured servitude that encourages the spread of South Asians to Mauritius, Guyana, Surinam, Trinidad, Jamaica, South and East Africa, and Fiji
1850	Caste Disabilities Removal Act
1856	Hindu Widows Remarriage Act
1859	Code of Civil Procedure
1860	Indian Penal Code; Code of Criminal Procedure

1864	Pandits cease to be employed as law officers to the courts
1891	Age of Consent Act
1899–1902	Boer War in South Africa
1906	Zulu Rebellion
1923	Publication of *Hindutva: Who is a Hindu?* by Vinayak Damodar Savarkar (alias "Mahratta")
1937	Hindu Women's Right to Property Act ("Deshmukh Act")
after 1945	postwar diaspora of South Asians to the UK, the USA, Canada, Australia, New Zealand, continental Europe, and the Persian Gulf nations
15 August 1947	India becomes independent
1950	Constitution of India enacted
1952–5	"Hindu Code" debates
1955–6	"Hindu Code" Bills enacted
1955	Hindu Marriage and Divorce Act
1956	Hindu Succession Act
1956	Hindu Minority and Guardianship Act
1956	Hindu Adoptions and Maintenance Act
1985	Shah Bano decision
1986	Muslim Women (Protection of Rights on Divorce) Act
mid-1990s	The "Hindutva Cases"
1992	Destruction of the Babri Masjid (mosque) in Ayodhya as part of a campaign to reclaim the site for a temple commemorating the Hindu god Rāma's birthplace

Abbreviations

ABBREVIATIONS OF INDIC TEXTS

ĀpDhS	*Āpastamba Dharmasūtra*; ed. and trans. Olivelle (2000).
ArthaŚ	*Arthaśāstra* of Kauṭilya; ed. and trans. Kangle (1969).
BDhS	*Baudhāyana Dharmasūtra*; ed. and trans. Olivelle (2000).
BSm	*Bṛhaspati Smṛti*; ed. Rangaswami Aiyangar (1941a).
DhDN	*Dharma Dwaita Nirṇaya*; ed. Gharpure (1943).
DhK	*Dharmakośa*; ed. Joshi (1937–41).
DT	*Divyatattva* of Raghunandana Bhaṭṭācārya; ed. and trans. Lariviere (1981a).
GDhS	*Gautama Dharmasūtra*; ed. and trans. Olivelle (2000).
Kāvyādarśa	*Kāvyādarśa;* ed. Thakur and Jha (1957).
LDhP	*Laghudharmaprakāśikā*; ed. and trans. Unni (2003).
LP	*Lekhapaddhati*; ed. and German trans. Strauch (2002); English trans. P. Prasad (2007).
MA	*Mulukī Ain*; ed. Sarkāra (1965); ed. Fezas (2000).
MDh	*Mānava Dharmaśāstra*; ed. and trans. Olivelle (2005a); with the commentaries of Medātithi, Sarvajñanārāyaṇa, Kullūka, Rāghavānanda, Nandana, and Rāmacandra: Mandalik (1886); with the commentary of Medhātithi and trans. G. Jha (1920–9); with the commentary of Kullūka: Vidyasagara (1874).
MīmS	*Mīmāṃsāsūtra* with Śabara's *Mīmāṃsā Bhāṣya*; ed. Abhyankar and Joshi (1970–7).
NirSindhu	*Nirṇayasindhu* of Kamalākarabhaṭṭa; ed. Acharya (1991).
NSm	*Nārada Smṛti*; ed. and trans. Lariviere (1989a).
Pāṇini	*Aṣṭādhyāyī* of Pāṇini; ed. Kielhorn (1880–5).
Patañjali	*Vyākaraṇa Mahābhāṣya* of Patañjali; ed. Kielhorn (1880–5).
PSm	*Parāśara Smṛti*; ed. Tarkalankara (1893).

SmC — *Smṛticandrikā*; ed. Srinivasacharya (1914–21); trans. Gharpure (1948).
TĀ — *Taittirīya Āraṇyaka*; ed. Mahadeva Sastri and Rangacarya (1985).
TMB — *Tāṇḍya Mahābrāhmaṇa*; ed. Chinnaswami Sastri (1936).
TV — *Tantravārttika* of Kumārilabhaṭṭa; ed. Abhyankar and Joshi (1970–7).
VDC — *Vikramāṅkadevacarita* of Bilhaṇa; ed. Bühler (1875).
VDh — *Vaiṣṇava Dharmaśāstra* (*Viṣṇu Smṛti*); ed. Jolly (1881); ed. Olivelle (2009); ed. with the *Keśavavaijayantī* commentary of Nandapaṇḍita: Krishnamacharya (1964).
VDhS — *Vasiṣṭha Dharmasūtra*; ed. Olivelle (2000).
YSm — *Yājñavalkya Smṛti*; ed. Stenzler (1849); with the *Mitākṣarā* commentary of Vijñāneśvara: Pandey (1967); with the *Balakrīḍā* commentary of Viśvarūpācārya: Ganapati Sastri (1921–2).

EPIGRAPHICAL PUBLICATION SERIES WITH ABBREVIATIONS

(citations by volume and record number)

CII — *Corpus Inscriptionum Indicarum*, Archaeological Survey of India.
EI — *Epigraphia Indica*, Archaeological Survey of India.
SII — *South Indian Inscriptions*, Archaeological Survey of India.

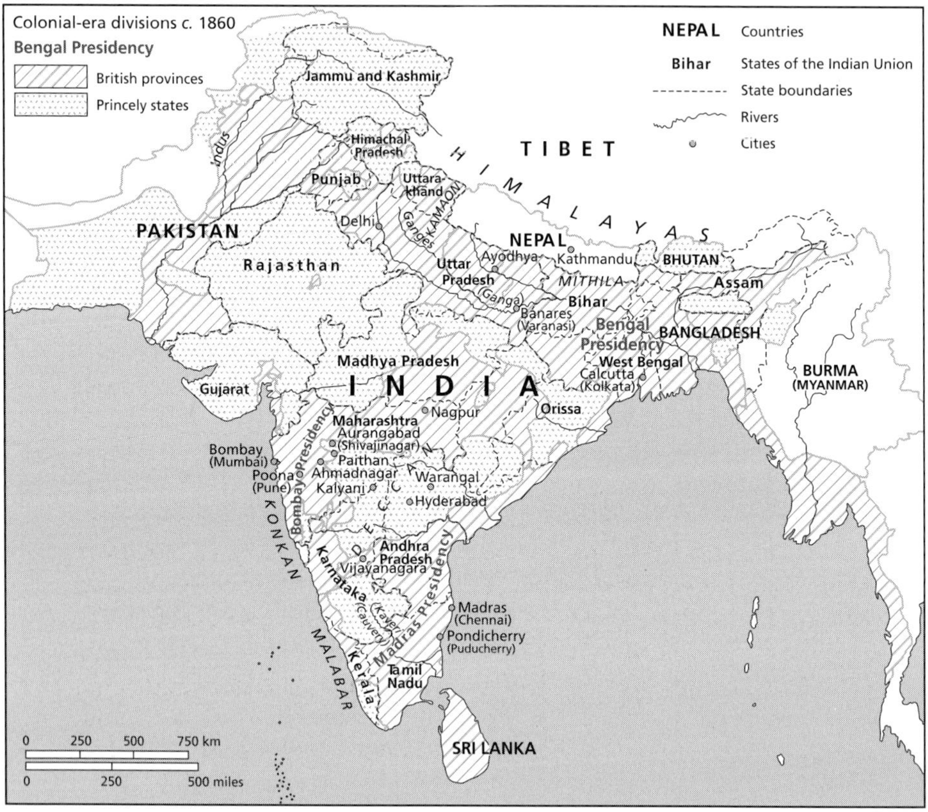
Colonial-era divisions c. 1860
Bengal Presidency
British provinces
Princely states
NEPAL Countries
Bihar States of the Indian Union
State boundaries
Rivers
Cities
TIBET
HIMALAYAS
Jammu and Kashmir
Indus
Himachal Pradesh
Punjab
Uttara-khand
KAMAON
Ganges
Delhi
PAKISTAN
Rajasthan
NEPAL
Ayodhya
Kathmandu
BHUTAN
Uttar Pradesh
(Ganga)
MITHILA
Assam
Bihar
Banares (Varanasi)
Bengal Presidency
BANGLADESH
West Bengal
Calcutta (Kolkata)
Madhya Pradesh
INDIA
BURMA (MYANMAR)
Gujarat
Nagpur
Orissa
Maharashtra
Aurangabad (Shivajinagar)
Bombay (Mumbai)
Paithan
Poona (Pune)
Ahmadnagar
Warangal
Kalyani
Hyderabad
Bombay Presidency
KONKAN
DECCAN
Andhra Pradesh
Vijayanagara
Karnataka
Madras Presidency
Madras (Chennai)
(Kaveri) (Cauvery)
Pondicherry (Puducherry)
MALABAR
Kerala
Tamil Nadu
SRI LANKA
0 250 500 750 km
0 250 500 miles

South Asia: political divisions *c.* 1860 and today

Introduction

Timothy Lubin, Donald R. Davis, Jr., and Jayanth K. Krishnan

Law and religion have much in common as social institutions and as historical phenomena. Broad areas of overlap and even broader areas of complementariness between these spheres have been observed in Roman, Judaic, Christian, and Islamic societies, and have generated a vast literature. There is also a rich ethnographic literature on law in nonliterate societies, emphasizing dispute resolution, informal legal process, and cultural context. Yet India's potential contribution to this field has remained almost completely unnoticed, despite both the fact that the Hindu and Buddhist religions have produced vast and highly refined legal literatures, and the fact that the Hindu religious texts and Indian legal practices became the focus of intense scrutiny by European scholars during the centuries of colonial administration. This volume is intended to begin to rectify this oversight by offering an up-to-date and accessible analysis of the main features and periods of what has conventionally been called Hindu law, and of the interrelations between law and Hinduism more broadly, up to the present day. Furthermore, several of the chapters break new ground in developing interdisciplinary approaches to the study of Hinduism and law – for example, in examining the literary articulations or the ritual dimensions of law in Hindu contexts.

"HINDUISM"

Numerous stumbling blocks lie before the readers of this book. Its title itself displays two of them: "Hinduism" and "law." The term "Hinduism" is of modern coinage, and was not used by any Hindus themselves as a religious category until the middle of the nineteenth century, when they began to appropriate it from European usage. "Hindu" was initially more an ethnic label than a religious one. The Persians, and then the Greeks, used it to refer to the peoples living around and beyond the Sindhu River (which they pronounced "Hindu"; "Indus" and its derivate "India" reflect the Latinized form of the Perso-Greek name). Indians (of whatever religion) do not seem to have applied the label to themselves until after Turkic rulers had established Persianate Islamic kingdoms in several parts of India, especially after 1206; late medieval works speak of "Turaka" or "Turuṣka," which designated ethnic Turks and Arabs, and only secondarily Muslims in general, much as in earlier centuries "Yona" (or "Yavana") was applied not merely to Ionians but to any denizen of "the West" (i.e., Persia and beyond). Vis-à-vis the "Turaka," "Hindu" meant simply Indian.

The period of British rule coincided with the emergence of the modern comparative study of religions, and consequently the classification of non-Christian religions into various "isms": Judaism, Muhammadanism, Buddhism, animism, and so on. In the seventeenth and eighteenth centuries, the adherents of India's indigenous religions were called "Gentoo," based on the Portuguese for "gentile," i.e., pagan idolator. But by the early nineteenth century the ethnonym "Hindu" (in use since the 1660s, spelled variously) had supplanted it, yielding the umbrella term "Hinduism." As the Victorian age progressed, Indians came increasingly to reflect on what made their religious culture distinctive in comparison with Christianity and Islam, and in so doing came to adopt the name Hindu and to reflect on what the name "Hinduism" might properly or essentially refer to. During the last quarter of the nineteenth through the middle of the twentieth century, a reformist, modernizing view of Hinduism dominated the discourse, particularly among Anglophone Indians. At the same time, certain elements of traditional piety were celebrated as central to Hindu cultural, social, and civic life, and thus as the natural foundation and justification for an independent Indian polity.[1]

As a result, although it has become commonplace for historians to speak of "Hinduism" as a purely modern conception (or "invention"), there are at least two ways – one "emic" and one "etic" – in which it makes sense to retain the label. First, for all the diversity of beliefs and practices among Hindus, the notion of a unifying core or thoroughgoing thread has ancient roots (including careful philosophical justification), and the idea has increasingly been embraced and appropriated by Hindus over the last two centuries. Today, many self-described Hindus bristle at the suggestion that Hinduism is a modern contrivance or an artificial amalgamation. This is a justification based on contemporary self-perceptions among Hindus, but, even from the perspective of the detached outsider, there are reasons to

[1] "The result of contact with foreigners has always been a revival of Hinduism" (Burnell 1878: 604).

accept (with appropriate caveats) the heuristic utility of the concept of "Hinduism." Even if the religious traditions grouped under this name lack a consistent minimal set of shared distinctive features, a cluster of "family resemblances" is discernable: assertion of the existence of divine persons, in many cases said to emanate from a single supreme unity (or pair), more abstractly conceived; techniques of mental or spiritual culture commonly involving the repetition of mantras, fasting, and meditation; worship involving offerings of food and other prestations before a physical embodiment of the deity (although a few movements have rejected or criticized image-worship); allusion to or citation of authoritative texts in Sanskrit (even if those texts are not the central focus) – the juristic literature going by the name of Dharmaśāstra is an example; and more generally a distinctive range of styles of devotion and expression quite unlike that of other religions found in India. These family resemblances may be enough to justify our speaking of the family as "Hinduism."

One problem that remains is that other religions originating in India share many of these traits to almost the same degree, notably: Buddhism (almost extinct in India by the nineteenth century, but now represented by some modern converts and by immigrants such as refugees from Tibet) and Jainism. Sikhs, practicing a tradition that arose out of the religious ferment of broadly Hindu devotionalism in sixteenth-century North India, adamantly claim the status of a distinct religion, and several movements with similar origins are inclined to do the same. Some low castes have on principle rejected the "Hindu" label because they see it as inseparable from Brahmanical (Sanskrit) doctrine, which they regard as oppressive and corrupt.[2] (Indeed, acceptance of the authority of the Veda and respect for the religious prerogatives of Brahmins used commonly to be cited even by scholars as the single unifying feature of Hinduism.) In any case, it is still possible to find local religious communities, unheeding of cosmopolitan discourse – and conversely, learned reformers and spiritual guides – who prefer to describe their religion as Vaiṣṇava or Śaiva, or Ārya or Sanātana-Dharma, rather than Hindu. For legal purposes under the Indian Constitution, all of these groups count as Hindu today, which only helps blur the elusive, shifting boundary between "Hindu ethnicity" (or "culture" or "nationality") and "Hindu religion."

[2] Throughout this volume, the terms "high" and "low" in reference to caste are used heuristically, that is, as reflecting their conventional usage in both popular and official discourses. There is no intention to endorse their normative values or the theological doctrines that legitimize them. The same goes for other caste descriptors that impute inherent purity or impurity to particular groups.

Thus, the name "Hinduism" today covers a large number of historically related but often emphatically distinct traditions and offshoots. One of the common points of reference for most of these – whether they accept its authority or reject it – is the Sanskrit literary and scholastic (*śāstra*) tradition, which is the forum in which most classical religious expression appeared. Sanskrit textual production, spanning three millennia, has produced a vast body of works in many fields, religious (Hindu, Buddhist, and Jain) and secular. Such works were produced almost exclusively by members of the Brahmin caste or other elite groups such as courtiers or learned monks. As a result, the interests and concerns of such groups are disproportionately represented: Much of the religious and cultural life of other elements in society is either ignored or represented from an outsider's point of view, and much simply went unrecorded. For our purposes, this means that much of the legal affairs of Hindus (or of Indians in general) cannot be recovered.

Hence, in spite of both emic and etic defenses of Hinduism as a coherent tradition, the risk is great that "Hinduism" will remain a catch-all concept, by which any religious idea, practice, or institution that one cannot place in another tradition gets classified as Hindu by default. We feel that it makes sense to recognize that, for all the pluralism and regionalism of Hindu religious and legal life, widespread learned traditions – and Dharmaśāstra in particular – have wielded tremendous systematizing force and myriad forms of indirect influence that have defined the most widely recognized conceptions of Hindu orthodoxy and orthopraxy. This circumstance encourages us to seek a greater incorporation of law and legal studies into the study of Hinduism as a way of adding clearer contours to the discursive uses of the term "Hinduism."

DHARMA AND LAW

What we do have, and have in plenty, is scholastic material on law, most of which belongs to the field of Dharmaśāstra, augmented by Kauṭilya's *Arthaśāstra* (a second-century treatise on politics and civil administration, including legal procedure) and some literary passages depicting legal process or discussing *dharma*.

The word *"dharma"* is sometimes translated as "law," but this can be misleading. Both terms in fact have broad semantic ranges that overlap only in part. When we speak of law in premodern India, we face not merely a terminological problem but a conceptual one: Are the Indic phenomena to be discussed as law of the same basic sort as the phenomena included under that category in the West today? The English word "law" has several senses, but the basic ones in *legal* usage are: (1) a body of rules considered binding on a particular political or social unit, and the principle of justice underlying it ("the law" = *ius, Recht, droit, diritto*, archaically, the "Right"),[3] or one of the individual rules thereof ("a law" = *lex, Gesetz, loi, legge*); (2) a code or canon of such rules, including constitution, charters, statutes, and decrees, but also documents such as contracts and deeds conforming to legal principles, and jurisprudence; (3) institutions and practices for the creation and application of such rules, and for the adjudication of disputes.

In the West, legal rules have come about in various ways, taking various forms. Some begin as divine commandments, embodied in scripture, especially the "Law of Moses" or "Jewish law," or the "Old Testament," and elaborated into a code (such as Talmud or canon law) through exegesis and authoritative pronouncements. This notion of law has since been extended to apply to the rules and codes of other religions. Apart from such elements of sacred law, legal rules may be instituted through legislative acts and institutions of a state (civil law), or they may emerge as more or less explicitly formalized standards derived from the customs or usages of a society or particular groups therein (common law), standards that may often remain unwritten but are no less binding for that.

Hindu India has known all three sorts of legal institutions, and all three came into play in legal practice at least up to the colonial period. *"Dharma"* is the term most closely associated with sacred law, both as an abstract notion of righteousness or justice, and in more concrete terms as the collective name for specific rules of social conduct and ritual action laid down in (or considered to be implicit in) revealed scripture ("the Veda"). Although it is part of the "*dharma* of the king" to enforce such laws, the ultimate sanctions and rewards entailed by such rules transcend all human agency: the impersonal law of karma, and the possibility of divine interventions. The legal institutions of premodern Indic states include the facilitation of legal process (*vyavahāra*) and the judgments and ordinances (*śāsana*) of the king. Customary law (*ācāra*), mostly unwritten, was probably the legal regime that governed the majority of the population, and both the Dharmaśāstra and royal inscriptions recognize the broad validity of customary law, at least within its proper jurisdiction. Indeed, the Dharmaśāstra explicitly encompasses all of these spheres of law, subordinating all elements to the transcendent standard of *dharma*. And although in principle the chief source (or "root," *mūla*) of *dharma* is supposed to be the sacred words (*śruti*)

[3] Thus Lord Coke declared that "when an act of parliament is against common right or reason ... the common law will controul it and adjudge such Act to be void" (1777, vol. VIII, 118a).

of the Veda, in practice the system relies mainly on *smṛti*, the collective remembrance of Vedic *dharma* embodied in the teachings of the great sages, and the customs (*ācāra*) of properly trained upper-caste Hindus – together constituting something quite like the rabbinic notion of "Oral Torah."

"HINDU LAW" VERSUS "HINDUISM AND LAW"

Having considered the separate terms of our title, we now turn to their juxtaposition. By "Hindu law," we refer primarily to both the theoretical and the practical law described in Dharmaśāstra literature. By this definition, Hindu law is a system of religious law, analogous to other traditions such as Jewish, Islamic, or canon law. Religious legal traditions have a textual canon, often relatively open, and a scholastic commentarial tradition, which together serve a remarkably stable religious vision and support a distinctively religious understanding of law's purpose, form, and content. Hindu law would have been just one of several coexisting legal or normative orders at any given place and time in India. To characterize any historical legal system or order as an instance of Hindu law requires a demonstration of its connection to the Dharmaśāstra tradition as its scriptural foundation. Such a connection to Dharmaśāstra is the *sine qua non* of categorizing a legal system or legal order as *Hindu*.

By "Hinduism and law," in contrast, we seek to erect the framework of a new field of study on the model of other work in law and religion that focuses on the mutual connections between particular religious traditions and particular legal systems.[4] Hinduism, despite being notoriously difficult to define or circumscribe, is a sufficiently cohesive and identifiable religious tradition that exhibits both the influences of and the influences upon legal orders and systems of several kinds. Abstract juxtapositions such as law and Hindu theology or law in Hindu epic literature are, in this view, both possible and academically sound, as are more concrete comparisons such as Hinduism and old Javanese law or Hindu temples and modern Indian law. Also possible, of course, is an investigation of Hindu law and Hinduism. The point here is that it is imperative that we attend to the possibilities opened up by examining Hinduism's relationship to legal ideas, institutions, and practices as a separate, or at least separable, matter from any examination of Hindu law.

4 See, for example, Witte (2008) for an exploration of the impact of Christian ideas and institutions on the development of the Western legal system.

The structure and organization of this volume reflect this important conceptual distinction that we make throughout, namely to differentiate the narrower tradition of Hindu law and jurisprudence from the larger historical and thematic connections of Hinduism and law. Part I of the volume is devoted to Hindu law. The contributions trace both the history of the practice of Hindu law and the development of its textual foundations. Parts II and III are devoted to Hinduism and law, with the first focused on premodern sources and the latter on colonial and postcolonial materials.

OVERVIEW OF THE PARTS

Part I

Accordingly, the first part of the volume presents a detailed chronological survey of Hindu law in various phases: from its early origins and the formation of the Dharmaśāstra canon, its recanonization under the British, and its partial survival in contemporary Indian "personal law." In the first chapter, Donald Davis offers a comprehensive overview of the history of the practice of Hindu law, considering the important political, religious, economic, linguistic, and literary changes that have affected it from the fourth century BCE until the present. By design, the chapter looks beyond textual developments in Dharmaśāstra, both because those are discussed in the next chapter and because a concern with practical law forces us outside these texts. The idea is to offer a way of describing Hindu law in general terms that can be substantiated through an examination of historical change, drawing on evidence from both within and beyond Dharmaśāstra.

In Chapter 2, Patrick Olivelle turns our attention to the classical literature of Dharmaśāstra, characterizing the various genres that emerged – the aphoristic *sūtra*s, the verse *śāstra*s, and the medieval commentaries (*bhāṣya*) and anthologies – and identifying conceptual and legal trends that appear in them. He notes the contributions, at an early stage, from the tradition of political science, especially parallels with the *Arthaśāstra* of Kauṭilya (second century CE). Axel Michaels, in Chapter 3, follows this up by assessing the sorts of materials available for documenting legal practice in South Asia prior to the sweeping changes that came with the advent of the colonial powers. This evidence includes inscriptions recording the edicts and rulings of kings, decisions of Brahmin or other caste councils, endowments, and legal titles; legal formularies (e.g., the *Lekhapaddhati*); and court records of the Maratha state. The royal legal codes of Rāṇa-period (nineteenth century) Nepal and French colonial records of the Tamil choultry courts (eighteenth to nineteenth century) are considered as two examples of Hindu law in transition as European models of law transform traditional patterns.

The fourth and fifth chapters trace the reconfiguration of Hindu law under British colonial administration. Rosane Rocher first describes the creation of "Anglo-Hindu Law." In its formative period, *c.* 1772–1815, the British attempted, with the guidance of Orientalist scholars, to identify and translate fundamental treatises of Dharmaśāstra. In this effort, the aid of traditionally trained Brahmin scholars (pandits) was enlisted to bring authoritative native expertise. Rocher shows how the colonial decision to administer Hindu law was the mainspring for Sanskrit studies by Westerners, and how, from the 1770s to the 1820s, the search for consistency in law decisions moved away from reliance on pandits as sources and custodians of Hindu law, first to trust in foundational texts, then to Orientalist authority in the field, and finally to adherence to a system of case law based on precedents.

Rachel Sturman's chapter, "Marriage and family in colonial Hindu law," examines how and why issues relating to marriage, gender, and the family came to form the core of colonial Hindu law, both in the everyday adjudication of the courts and in the heated public debates concerning the morality of Hindu practices that marked the late nineteenth and early twentieth centuries (for example, on the issue of child marriage and the age of consent). Highlighting the colonial treatment of Hinduism as a legal system, Sturman explains the relationship between colonial Hindu law (which formed a branch of civil law) and secular civil and criminal law. Finally, she considers the implications of the colonial system of Hindu law both for creating a secular legal system and for the lives of Hindu families.

The first part closes with Rina Verma Williams's study of the reformulation of Hindu law in independent India ("Hindu law as personal law"). The creation of independent India as a secular state required a reform of the colonial-era "personal laws" (those applicable to such matters as marriage, adoption, and succession). Ultimately, this process detached the legal category of "Hindu law" from its traditional roots in Dharmaśāstra. Williams analyzes the 1950s Hindu Code Bills debates to trace two interrelated transformations: Gender became the site *on which* modern Hindu law (as personal law) has been constructed; and the modern state became the institution *through which* modern Hindu law (as personal law) must be negotiated. As the links to classical/textual Hindu law receded, Hindu law as personal law became progressively more embedded in discourses of community, identity, and modern state power.

Part II

The second part of the volume examines the relation of Hinduism and law in premodern historical periods from two perspectives. First, this section addresses cases in which Dharmaśāstra has had an impact on, or been impacted by, other Hindu traditions such that legal ideas and institutions are connected to Hindu ideas and institutions and vice versa. Second, the section shows how Hindu expressions of legal norms may be approached in theoretically novel ways. The purpose of Part II is thus to open new lines of thought within Hindu studies that point to the crucial role played by law in the tradition, but also to propose new ways of understanding Hindu law by viewing it through distinct theoretical lenses.

Contributions to this section further point to a new academic horizon, namely the possibility of legal studies of Hindu traditions that move beyond Dharmaśāstra. While each chapter still engages directly or indirectly with this hegemonic textual genre of Indic law, the very possibility of "law and hermeneutics," "law and literature," "law and performance," or even "law and religion" in premodern India outside Dharmaśāstra suggests perspectives on a whole range of social facts in India that have been neglected until now.

For example, the elaborate hermeneutical system developed in the Pūrva-Mīmāṃsā for the complex sacrificial rites of the Vedic tradition has been appropriated almost everywhere in later scholastic traditions of India. Lawrence McCrea describes how Mīmāṃsā subserved Hindu law texts by providing the theological and philosophical foundations for law as well as technical rules for its interpretation, but he also shows how these two traditions had surprisingly few authors in common until the sixteenth century. More importantly, he nuances the changes in the textual formats for Dharmaśāstra (metrical rule-texts, commentaries, and digests) in relation to the sometimes fierce debates over Mīmāṃsā's construction of textual authority.

Timothy Lubin's chapter is an experiment in comparative jurisprudence, asking how Indic legal traditions conceived of what in the West is called "authority." The materials examined range from scholastic definitions (such as the śāstric notion of Vedic authority elaborated by McCrea) to formulations more closely attuned to the practice of the law. He finds that two influential Indic concepts – *pramāṇa* and *adhikāra* – largely cover the same ground as "epistemic authority" and "practical authority" in Euro-American jurisprudence, although in practice *pramāṇa* can do double duty, that is, as "proof" and as "authorization."

Ananya Vajpeyi investigates the still difficult question of caste in India through a study of seventeenth-century texts that focused in a newly intensive way on the usually despised figure of the low-caste Śūdra. She provides a careful study of the philological, historical, and philosophical reasons behind the emergence of this new thematization of the Śūdra as an important subject of *dharma* and law. The timing of this emergence, as well as its substance, challenges conventional social histories by showing caste in a contested and dynamic discourse, not a simple, hegemonic, and static theory that had no relation to social reality.

In what may be the first serious law and literature study of premodern law in India, Whitney Cox extends recent work on the politically constitutive role of Sanskrit literature (*kāvya*) in classical and medieval India by relating it to the constitutive work performed by Hindu law texts. In the end, he suggests that these two textual forms both served important political functions that differed from, but also related to, one another. His concluding suggestion – taken from the Kashmiri author Kalhaṇa – that, in some cases, the linguistic expression of the judge should be the moral model for the poet inverts the usual law and literature presuppositions about the possible ethical influence of literature on law.

Revisiting some of the most enigmatic portions of Dharmaśāstra, Robert Yelle examines the semiotic functions of poetic devices in Hindu law, such as hyperalliteration, folk etymology, and chiasmus. In so doing, he reveals the rationality underlying the at first incongruous performative elements of these texts. By interpreting these parts of the texts in terms of or in the imagined context of performance, Yelle makes sense of the nonsensical and, in the process, offers performance studies as yet another underexplored approach to law in India.

Part III

The final part focuses on the intersection of Hindu practice, legal ordering, and political cleavages during the colonial and post-Independence periods. These issues, tied to social, political, economic, and administrative pressures, have determined the subsequent development of Hindu law in the attenuated and novel form in which it persists today. The chapters in this part also address matters of Hindu religious practice within the modern secular legal system. It is inevitable that, due to the vast contrast between the sources available for premodern periods and those available for developments since 1750, Part III focuses considerably more on legal practice than is possible in Part II. Nevertheless, these two sections are unified by their thematic approach and their concern with the interrelations between law, religion, and other factors in Indian life.

Richard Davis begins Part III by providing a taut summary of the long history of recognizing the deities of Hindu temples as legal persons in a restricted sense. Addressing the classical sources, colonial views, and a celebrated modern case, Davis describes the continuous view – noted contrary opinions notwithstanding – that Hindu deities had "juristic personalities," enabling them legally to own temple property and perform other restricted legal actions. The ingenuity of Hindu jurisprudence on this issue speaks both to the Hindu understanding of the divine in legal terms and to the social manifestations of the divine through the earthly mechanism of the law.

Aditya Malik follows Davis's chapter with an ethnographic case study of one of the main temples of Goludev, the "god of justice" in the remote region of Kumaon, in the foothills of the Himalayas. There, pilgrims and devotees bring to the god their troubles of all kinds, submitting formal petitions, often written on the official "stamp paper" used for legal documents in India today. The petitions, which are posted around the temple, appeal for blessings of all kinds, but in particular for the god's intervention in legal and personal disputes, or in securing posts and positions. In return, the petitioners, many from metropolises like Delhi, vow to make material or sacrificial offerings. This tradition thus represents the importance of plural legal frameworks in India, and bears witness to the continuing salience of traditional religious conceptions of justice as divine will, and of the temple as a sort of court of last resort.

The focus then shifts to the overlapping spheres of constitutional law, politics, and public policy. Laura Jenkins, a longtime researcher on affirmative-action patterns in India, assesses where the debate over this policy currently stands both in government and within Indian society. Her focus in this chapter is threefold: to identify the present controversies surrounding caste and affirmative action in India; to highlight how within recent years there has been growing activism among international rights groups toward eradicating caste discrimination in India; and to show how affirmative action in India has moved beyond seeking to protect only disadvantaged caste-based groups. Her discussion, which includes a thoughtful constitutional component as well, serves as an important reminder of how studying caste and affirmative action in this context can often be complicated, highly political, and an empirically daunting challenge.

Smita Narula's chapter looks at how law, politics, and religion intersect. Narula's approach is to examine, jurisprudentially, how the Supreme Court of India has tackled a series of cases that involve Hindu nationalist movements. In addition, her chapter surveys the various historical strands of this form of nationalism, and evaluates how these developments have fit within India's constitutionally democratic framework. In particular, Narula's chapter uncovers a deep struggle (found in the Court's rulings and within the polity overall) between those who seek to preserve and promote India as a strongly secular state, and those who have a competing vision of wanting the country affirmatively to embrace what they see as its distinct Hindu character.

The final chapter of the volume, by Jayanth K. Krishnan, investigates the manner in which, and extent to which, Hindu identity has manifested itself outside of India, within what some observers refer to as the "Hindu diaspora." Drawing on the important contributions of Werner Menski, Steven Vertovec, and others, Krishnan traces where Hindus have migrated over time – including to places such as Southeast Asia, Africa, Fiji, Europe, North America, and Australia. His chapter describes the different reasons for these migrations, and in his discussion he comparatively assesses the legal and political problems Hindu communities have faced in their adopted homelands. He concludes by sketching the various layered identities Hindu immigrants have taken on as they have sought to adapt to their new environments.

A NEW DEPARTURE

In planning this volume, we began with a desire to redress the general lack of scholarly knowledge and reflection about the connections between Hinduism and law. The first step was to make accessible to a broader audience a legal tradition that remains neglected in studies of law and religion. Beyond that, we wanted to foster methodological innovation by including some provocative interdisciplinary and comparative studies.

Moreover, it is commonplace for newsworthy developments in India to be explained, in both journalistic and academic publications, by glibly invoking religion. A better understanding of the role of Hinduism in legal contexts, and of Hindus qua Hindus under Indian and foreign law, is imperative in an ever more culturally plural world. On the other hand, we are also concerned with a religious tradition, the unity and extent of which is hard to define clearly, that is invoked as a category in the Constitution and other laws of independent India and, yet, at the same time, a religion that has been divested, at least in most public discourse, of any connection with or interest in the law. The disjunction between the heightened religious and political valence of Hinduism and its diminished legal valence in public discourse is balanced by a persistence of legal intrusions into the now separate sphere of Hindu religion. In this sense, we are interested in both the political discourse surrounding law and Hinduism and what might be called the law-and-society issues that emerge in both courtroom litigation and informal legal processes.

The resulting volume offers, we hope, a substantially new orientation to its complex subject: an up-to-date, nuanced account of the crystallization, development, and modern reconfiguration of "Hindu law," complemented by an ambitious remapping of the relations between Hinduism and law before, during, and since its colonial encounter with Europe. We bring together contributions from disparate disciplines – classical philology, the study of religion, political history, ethnology, literature, and legal studies – in a forum in which they can speak to each other, and bring the Hindu experience to bear on comparative studies of religion and law.

PART I

Hindu law

CHAPTER I

A historical overview of Hindu law

Donald R. Davis, Jr.

Hindu law has always existed within a broader pluralism of legal systems in India that to a greater or lesser extent overlapped with one another in both form and substance. Distinguishing the specifically Hindu element in the larger history of law in India is difficult because of the notoriously poor record of premodern legal practice. Still, the history of Hindu law is part of the history of law in India and by describing the latter we necessarily comment upon the former as well. I define classical Hindu law as "a variegated grouping of local legal systems that had different rules and procedures of law but that were united by a common jurisprudence or legal theory represented by Dharmaśāstra" (D. R. Davis 2008: 225). Thus, while I consider Dharmaśāstra, Sanskrit texts dealing with religious and legal duties, to be the distinctively Hindu element in Hindu law throughout its history, I am not concerned in this overview with its jurisprudence.[1] Rather, I want to provide a skeletal history of legal practice in India that heuristically avoids Dharmaśāstra by limiting, somewhat artificially, references to the scholastic tradition to instances of the texts pointing beyond themselves.[2] The major factors I want to consider instead are broader historical trends and how these impacted the practice of law in India and, thus, also among Hindu communities. Because of the nature of the evidence, the history I give is more a hypothesis than a documented synthesis.

The principal legal actors or institutions that recur in the historical record of law in early India are corporate groups, rulers, and, later, temples. The

[1] For this, see the chapters by Olivelle, McCrea, and Lubin in this volume.

[2] A more specific analysis of the history of Hindu law would thus require a detailed correlation of evidence of developments within the Dharmaśāstra tradition with the broader historical trends examined here. The systematizing and scholastic nature of Dharmaśāstra, however, tends to thwart such analysis, especially in the absence of critical editions and chronological details for most texts. For standard accounts of the history of Hindu law written through the lens of the Dharmaśāstra texts, see Derrett (1968), Lingat (1973), and Kane (1968–75). Sarkar (1958) is certainly the best attempt to write a periodized history of Hindu law, but it too substitutes the history of the texts for the history of legal practice.

practice of law revolved around these three social agents. To place these agents in historical context, however, necessitates choosing a datable point from which to begin a description of the legal history of Hindu law. Several recent works have focused on the "between the empires" (Olivelle 2006a) period between the second century BCE and the second century CE as the formative era during which significant innovations in the social and political life of India occurred, including the political and financial solidification of the Buddhist monastic community; the early epigraphical and archeological evidence of maritime trade; the composition of culturally foundational Indic texts such as the *Rāmāyaṇa* and *Mahābhārata* epics, and the *Laws of Manu*, and, perhaps most importantly, the creation of a nonliturgical, literary use of Sanskrit and its close connection to the articulation of a cosmopolitan rulership (S. Pollock 2006).

In selecting a starting point, therefore, I will follow Pollock's argument that the Junāgaṛh inscription of Rudradāman *c.* 150 CE inaugurated a new era of political discourse and self-presentation in India (S. Pollock 2006: 67–9). Pollock makes the sweeping thesis that a new literary use of Sanskrit, signaled by an explosion both of secular poetry and drama and of epigraphical panegyric, was intertwined with a uniquely Indic mode of rulership. Sanskritic literary and political culture eschewed administrative centralization in favor of a replication of mytho-political genealogy that allowed local languages, politics, and laws to coexist within a cosmopolitan discourse of rulership. We may thus affirm that in the early Indic world, "no uniform code of law was ever enforced anywhere" (S. Pollock 2006: 277). The poetic and rhetorical construction of cosmopolitan political power hindered attempts to promulgate a centralized law and legal system in practice, and effectively obviated the need to do so. But the lack of a uniform code at the level of practice did not inhibit the presentation of a grandiose, cosmopolitan legal system in the idealized texts of Hindu jurisprudence.

In this way, the cosmopolitan expression of political imagination in new, specifically literary, genres of Sanskrit must be supplemented by a contemporaneous and related innovation in the imagination of law and the state in Hindu jurisprudence. Especially after the composition of the *Laws of Manu* in the second century CE, Dharmaśāstra presents a divided image of *dharma* in which the localized, household-oriented *dharma*s described in detail for Brahmins are juxtaposed to the image of rulers as the protectors of law and promulgators of a state characterized by great political and administrative aspiration. The legal cosmology of Dharmaśāstra thus parallels the replicative cosmopolitanism of literary discourse. *Dharma* as law was in practice to be negotiated and articulated locally under the control of a ruler, but its theological and political authority was part of the same cosmopolitan ethos – nonliturgical, replicable, and defined by an aspirational political theology rather than forcible practical implementation. In the Sanskrit cosmopolis, rulers protected and enabled the *dharma*s of the orders of life and caste; they did not forcibly legislate or promulgate that law.[3]

For the next thousand years, Sanskrit dominated the political discourse of South and Southeast Asia and with that domination went at least the rhetorical appropriation of the secular elements of *dharma*, namely, legal procedure, ideals of political administration, titles of law – i.e., *rājadharma*, the *dharma* of a ruler. The future course of Hindu law in practice was put in place by the linking of literary and dharmic discourses. Specifically, Hindu law was to remain until 1772 a resolutely local affair in the practical administration of legal norms, but also projected a capacious image of rulership that subtended the Sanskrit cosmopolitan style. Much like language and rulership, Hindu law superposed a cosmopolitan jurisprudence on separate and conceptually distinguished local legal practices. As with Sanskrit literary forms, or *kāvya*, this cosmopolitan jurisprudence played an important role in the development of vernacular legal thought in later centuries. In fact, the cosmopolitan political imagination was partially articulated by means of Hindu jurisprudence and not merely by literary texts and epigraphs. The circumscribed legislative and administrative power of the ruler in practice, the value placed on local, especially corporate, substantive laws, and the restriction of jurisprudential reflection to a Sanskritic idiom were characteristics of Hindu law that persisted as part of the cosmopolitan ethos and the subsequent emergence of vernacular literatures and laws.

It is also during the period between the Mauryas and Guptas that the first sustained information on corporate groups and their impact on law emerges in the historical record. Among these groups, the best documented and perhaps most influential was the Buddhist monastic community known as the Saṅgha. The practical administration of classical Hindu law occurred primarily at this level of society. Corporate groups including merchants, traders, guilds, soldiers, religious renunciants, Brahmins, pastoralists, farmers, castes, and family lineages possessed a body of substantive laws that they generally administered to their own members (see D. R. Davis 2005). While most corporate groups were nonreligious in their orientation and structure,

[3] Pollock makes a regular distinction between the "voluntaristic" cosmopolitanism of Sanskrit in South Asia and the "coercive" cosmopolitanism of Latin in Europe.

a few had a more specific connection with Hindu religious and social structure, namely groups of Brahmins settled through land grants by political elites (*brahmadeya*), Hindu monasteries (*maṭha*), and caste organizations (*jātisamūha*). Though certainly not a total innovation in early medieval India, the increasing historical presence of corporate groups at this time did put in place patterns in the practice of law that would persist until beyond the colonial period.

In particular, the epigraphical record of medieval India presents legal matters as primarily connected to and under the jurisdiction of various corporate associations. Individuals and smaller groups must have been part of several such corporate bodies simultaneously, such that (1) a guild-weaver might have both (2) a caste and (3) a village affiliation and live on land controlled by (4) a temple or *brahmadeya* – each of these imposing its own legal limitations and possibilities. Corporate groups might levy taxes or demand tithes; they might restrict business practices or fix rules for inheritance; or they might require certain forms of dress and religious observance. The substance of such laws emerged from within the groups themselves, probably from their own leadership, though Hindu jurisprudence both recognized the validity of those laws and sometimes influenced both the procedural and substantive legal practices of corporate associations. Rulers or appointed judges in turn sometimes adjudicated disputes that arose between corporate groups or those that for some other reason exceeded the jurisdiction of the group itself. On rarer occasions, rulers imposed their own decrees on a community or region.[4]

No firm date for this process of the formation of corporate groups can be given because references to various corporate groups extend deep into the textual history of India. Rather, the increasing presence and importance of regional corporate groups in classical and medieval India must be linked with larger, but geographically uneven, historical processes of urbanization, peasantization, and the expansion of regional polities. The cosmopolitan deployment of Sanskrit did not inhibit the "increasing scale of local state formation" between the third and fourth century CE and, in a different way, between the sixth and ninth century (Chattopadhyaya 1994a: 17, 34–5). Rather, the replicative cosmopolitanism of Sanskrit encouraged and abetted the proliferation of regional polities and inhibited the formation of a forced, incorporative cosmopolitanism of the Roman type.

Among the corporate entities that developed in early medieval India (*c.* 700–900), the most significant for the future of Hinduism was the

[4] See Michaels's chapter in this volume.

temple. Although Hindu temples have long been of interest to scholars for their role in political integration and legitimation, economic redistribution, and new modes of religious life,[5] their role in India's legal history has not been as fully discussed in such terms. In one sense, temples resemble other corporate bodies because they have powers of political and economic transaction and they impose restrictions on their "members," albeit through the important legal fiction that it is the deity itself that acts. In another sense, however, temples are distinctive, both because they were probably the most significant social institutions in medieval India and because they have a clear connection with Hinduism.

Several aspects of the impact of temples on law may be traced to the early medieval period. Temples, first of all, provided a permanent physical space in which the various social roles of law were centralized (Inden 2006: 95). This consolidation of power and authority in a definite location started the process of linking political, religious, economic, and legal interests together in a way that rulers' courts of earlier periods never accomplished. In fact, the distinctions between political and religious functions blurred as monumental temple-building and refashioned Hindu rites became central to the imperial aspirations of regional kingdoms such as the Pratihāras, the Rāṣṭrakūṭas, and the Pallavas (Inden 2006: 96). Through temples, therefore, rulers acquired a small measure of indirect control over their legal and administrative interests in taxation, commerce, and social stability.

Other influences of temples on law are more difficult to date historically, and the evidence is more abundant for the period after 1000 CE. Temples served as an additional structure for the adjudication of disputes between parties under their direct purview (priests, servants, landholders, etc.), but also served occasionally as a meta-structure for judging disputes that exceeded the control or jurisdiction of corporate groups.[6] The temple also became a site of promotion and propaganda for theological and jurisprudential views associated with sectarian traditions of Hinduism. Finally, the

[5] For excellent studies of the historical salience of Hindu temples, see Kulke (1978), Heitzman (1997: 82–142), and Talbot (2001: 87–125). But see also the criticism of the historical distortions introduced by focusing too much on temples alone in Narayana Rao, Shulman, and Subrahmanyam (1992: 31). While sympathetic to this criticism, I am skeptical about the claim that "over much of this period temples seem to have been far less significant mediators of royal power than they were to become in Coḷa-era Tamil Nadu or Gajapati-era Orissa, the two cases that are often illegitimately generalized to all of premodern South Asia" (Pollock 2006: 252–3). Inden's work on temple-building and Rāṣṭrakūṭa kingship (1990), Talbot's on the Kākaṭīyas of Andhra (2001), Kölver and Śākya's on Nepal (1985), and my own on Kerala (Davis 2004a) all suggest that the important political and economic role of temples was widespread.

[6] See Michaels's chapter in this volume.

historical evidence of temple inscriptions itself indicates an innovative function of temples with respect to the law, namely record-keeping. Stone and copper-plate inscriptions, and later palm-leaf records, pertaining to the temple's property holdings are essential sources for understanding history in India, especially its chronology. Since most inscriptions are records of gifts, almost every inscription records a legal act of donation, in addition to other information. Other records describe legal arrangements for the maintenance of the temple staff and buildings and for various capital outlays, mortgages, and so on. Overall, Hindu temples introduced several new legal possibilities into medieval India by providing a centralizing physical space critical for imperial actions, increased adjudication, religious and legal propaganda, and record-keeping.

The proliferation of Hindu temples as perhaps the primary public loci of Hindu religious practice continued during the military incursions of Turkic Muslims from Central Asia beginning in 1000 CE, but consolidated politically only in 1206 in the form of the Delhi Sultanate. Turkic military practice, Persian forms of governance, and Islam itself had a major impact on Indian society, especially on its displaced elites.[7] Muslim rulers of the regional sultanates introduced a variety of administrative legal terms, offices, and institutions that for the first time forged a closer link between state and law in India. This link emanates more from the traditions of rulership associated with Central Asia and Persia than from Islamic political theory, which insists on a rather clear separation of state and law, despite acknowledging and theorizing practical needs to the contrary. Thus, Islamic law in the sense of *fiqh* was never at the center of governance in the regional sultanates or in the Mughal Empire.

Nevertheless, the model of arrogating old administrative and taxation practices to the state and creating new ones in the regional sultanates set in motion a continuation of the process by other Indian states, including Vijayanagara and the Marathas, not to mention the Mughals. Indeed, most of the later British administrative vocabulary was adopted from the Persian terminology used in the sultanates and later in Mughal domains. What is not yet appreciated is the more encompassing process at work in the transformation of the language of administration by the "language of political Islam," namely the centralization of key aspects of law by the state. Put differently, both the Delhi Sultanate and the Mughal Empire

[7] For studies of the influence of Islam and Islamicate ideas and institutions on India, see, recently, Asher and Talbot (2006). Eaton (1993: 28–50) and Subrahmanyam (2005: 45–79) describe the development of "Perso-Islamic civilization" in Bengal.

promoted the use of a new language, Persian, that served both documentary and expressive purposes (Alam 2004: 115–40). In relation to law, what occurs strikingly in the flourishing of Persian in India is a novel adoption of a documentary language of administrative law, the law that describes and governs the relationship of the state to the people.[8] Sanskrit and Indian vernaculars possessed a great deal of administrative vocabulary, but a centralizing use of any language by a state for administrative documentation and dissemination occurred only after the introduction of Persian by the sultanates. In fact, the use of Persian for government documentation appears to have created the conditions under which the first truly centralized state in Indian history could emerge. The formalization of Persian as the language of administration occurred later in the sixteenth century during the reign of Akbar, but the spread of Persian and the realization of its political and legal utility long preceded the Mughals.

By this time, however, practices of legal documentation transcended geographic boundaries and, throughout the Eurasian world of commerce, cultural exchange, and migration, new forms of law and new legal institutions were rapidly shared across large expanses of Asia and Europe.[9] In other words, the move to increased documentation of the law cannot be attributed solely to the precedents of the Delhi Sultanates and their use of Persian. They must also be explained in part with reference to new intercontinental forms of cultural exchange, especially over time those associated with European colonialism to be discussed shortly.

Contemporaneous with the expansion of Islamic political power in India, and not entirely independent of it, was the development of new linguistic valences for vernaculars in the subcontinent and beyond.[10] The governmental documentary model of Persian set a precedent that was subsequently followed by every major polity in India, in many cases by adopting the Persian terminology itself. An early example of the increased use of vernaculars for legal documentation in connection with a state is the *Lekhapaddhati*, a

[8] Recent scholarship neglects the fact that documentary uses of language are as constructed and non-natural as literary uses. Documentary uses of language are generally taken for granted as part of the obvious communicative function of language. However, administrative language existed in Sanskrit and Indian vernaculars without the formation of systematic government documentation for any administration.

[9] I offer this as a tentative supplement to the forms of "connected history" identified by Subrahmanyam (1997) for early modern Eurasia. When read in relation to Benton's analysis (2002) of the connections between colonial legal regimes in the same period, the plausibility increases that legal documentation in particular constituted an important material vector of the early modern "world system."

[10] The best examples of this process outside India are the Dhammasattha texts of Burma and the Thammasat texts of Thailand. See Lingat (1973: 266–72) for a basic discussion.

collection of exemplars for executing various kinds of legal documents used perhaps in Caulukya and Vāghela states in Gujarat. The multiplication of legal documents occurred in many "princely states" as well, such as the Travancore kingdom, not to mention the massive Peshwa Daftar of the Marathas. In Nepal, Persian terminology of land revenue and taxation was incorporated into the practical law of the area, which also made use of laws emanating from Hindu jurisprudence.[11]

As a result, it is really in the period between 1500 and 1750 that extensive legal documentation became the norm for Indian states. The concomitant shift to vernacular political discourse of an expressive variety bolstered this expansion of documentary uses of vernaculars for political and legal purposes. There is almost no value for the label "Hindu" to describe any distinctive aspect of this massive transformation of legal practice in India, and yet the impact of the change on practical Hindu law was unavoidable – law gradually moved away from the domain of corporate groups and temples into the purview of political states, none of which made religious law central to their political identity or power. Perhaps the most we can say for the moment is that some ideas of Dharmaśāstra were, probably for the first time, consciously adopted by state-based institutions, on the model of the adoption of Persianate for other, different kinds of law. Prominent here was family law, including most of what would later be called "personal law," i.e., marriage, inheritance, adoption, and so on.[12]

A related phenomenon of this period, and one directly linked with Hindu law as a tradition, was the creation of a limited vernacular jurisprudence, i.e., Dharmaśāstra not in Sanskrit. Translations and original works of Dharmaśāstra began to appear at least in South Indian languages as early as the thirteenth century.[13] Persian translations are known from the seventeenth century.[14] Sanskritic jurisprudence, too, became both more regionally conscious and influenced by regional legal terminology and practices. The idea that legal reflection could be written in a language other than Sanskrit was completely new and signals at least some diminution of the hegemony of Sanskrit in academic discourse, on the one hand, but also an

[11] See the chapter by Michaels in this volume. [12] On this, see Sturman's chapter in this volume.

[13] Ketana's thirteenth-century Telugu translation of Vijñāneśvara's *Mitākṣarā* is found in Vasundhara (1989); Aḻakiṉ Perumāḷ's fifteenth-century Tamil rendering of the same was published by Rajagopalan (1960).

[14] Supriya Gandhi kindly made me aware of several Persian manuscript translations of the *Mitākṣarā*, e.g., Lal Bihari Bhojpuri, *Aḥkām-i avāmir va navāhī-yi maẓhab-i hunūd* (1658 CE), Aligarh Muslim University, Univ. 144 Rel. and Sufism.

increased valence for Dharmaśāstra rules and ideas in the practical legal systems of newly formed states.

The next major historical change to the Hindu law tradition came, of course, through the European colonies established in India beginning in the sixteenth century. Prior to 1772, the impact of colonialism was less direct in the area of law because of the more limited political role played by the various "trading companies" of Portugal, Holland, France, and England. Still, transformations associated more generally with "early modern" Eurasia resulted in changes in legal practices in India as well. Notably, as just suggested, the long-distance commerce characteristic of the period neccesitated the creation of expanded documentation to keep investors apprised and assured of the security of their investments. Legal documents thus became an important tangible material of colonialism, perhaps its most important artifact or by-product.

The direct impact of colonialism on Hindu law may be dated to 1772, the year in which Governor-General Warren Hastings announced his Judicial Plan. The relevant decree in the Plan declared that Dharmaśāstra would be the sole basis for Hindu law as administered by the British. At the time, none of the British knew Sanskrit. By 1776, however, Hastings had commissioned a digest of Hindu law that appeared as the *Code of Gentoo Laws*, a curious work that consisted of Nathaniel Halhed's English translation of a Persian rendering from an oral Bengali paraphrase of a Sanskrit original compiled by twelve pandits employed by Hastings. The Calcutta-based Orientalists, especially Jones and Colebrooke, who guided the early development of what came to be called Anglo-Hindu law relied exclusively on Dharmaśāstra as the source for practical Hindu law in British courts, essentially meaning that the translations provided by the Orientalists became a uniform basis for positive law among Hindus throughout the British-dominated regions of India. With this appropriation, Dharmaśāstra became completely enmeshed within the colonial state and its traditional standing in the realm of civil society was translated into British legal discourse and ossified through it.[15]

However, the British did not accept every aspect of Dharmaśāstra into the colonial legal system. Rather, primarily matters of religious relevance, meaning laws that attached to personal identity rather than civil identity, were placed under British jurisdiction. This is the foundation of the personal-law system in India today in which certain areas of law, namely marriage, divorce, adoption, inheritance, and maintenance are differentially

[15] Rosane Rocher's chapter in this volume treats this subject.

defined according to religious affiliation.[16] Hindu jurisprudential views of contract, crime, tort, procedure, and property were wholly ignored by the British. The adjudication of Hindu law in British courts was facilitated with the help of pandits appointed to the court to assist judges in determining the relevant law. The system was cumbersome and the order to consult Dharmaśāstra as positive law was frustrating both for the British judges who had no direct access to the law they were applying and for the Hindu court pandits who had to cope with this novel use of Dharmaśāstra in the context of a power dynamic that placed them in an inferior and structurally suspect position.

The year 1864 is the next notable date in the history of Hindu law because it was the year in which both Hindu pandits and Muslim maulvis were dismissed from their official service to the British courts in cases of Anglo-Hindu and Anglo-Muhammadan law respectively. With this dismissal, the last vestige of Hindu jurisprudence, its traditional living source, was disconnected from any formal legal recognition in British India. From then on, Anglo-Hindu law was determined and adjudicated on the basis of existing case law and textbooks that systematized it. It is also in this decade – under the influential views of Henry Sumner Maine – that the British formally assumed a new attitude to the proper source of Hindu law, shifting its primary source away from Dharmaśāstra to customary law. Especially in recently acquired areas of British India such as the Punjab, massive government collections of customary law were undertaken in order to ascertain the law in practice, including relevant aspects of Anglo-Hindu law.

Efforts to modify and/or codify some or all of the Anglo-Hindu law began as early as 1850,[17] but the culmination of those efforts did not come to pass until after Indian Independence in 1947. In the 1950s, as part of the constitutionally mandated efforts to work for a uniform civil code and after heated debates, a series of bills was passed by the Indian Parliament that partially codified what is now known as modern Hindu law.[18] In this way, continuities with the colonial personal law system prevail in the post-Independence system. Since this partial codification, Hindu law has generated little legal interest because of a perception that, for better or worse, it

[16] See the chapter by Williams in this volume.

[17] See Derrett (1963: 617–31) for the text of ten legislative acts passed by the British to amend Anglo-Hindu law as it was being applied in the courts. Only two were put in place in the nineteenth century, namely the Caste Disabilities Removal Act (1850) and the Hindu Widows Remarriage Act (1856). The remaining legislation began from 1928 onwards and is more indicative of the codification sentiment that resulted in the Hindu Code Bills of the 1950s.

[18] See the chapter by Williams in this volume.

is largely a settled matter. The one recurring area of legal and political debate in which Hindu law is still considered is the question of Indian secularism. A complex understanding of secularism, as constitutionally mandated, has emerged that accommodates the existence of the personal law system, though not without criticism. Recent political movements associated with Hindu nationalism have reignited the debate over secularism but so far with little impact on the practice of Hindu law itself. For the moment, it appears that Hindu law's primary public valence will be to act as one charged example in a political struggle over the proper direction for Indian secularism. In this context, however, we should not expect any serious engagement with the details of modern Hindu law or any aspect of its long history.

This historical overview of Hindu law has been necessarily cursory; some may even think it to be premature. Fortunately, several of the periods examined here are dealt with in greater detail in subsequent chapters. My attempt here has been primarily to describe the history of Hindu law in practice in such a way that one can begin to see how changes from one "period" to another also entailed the preservation of existing legal practices. Over the long timespan considered, however, classical Hindu law and modern Hindu law appear very different (though hardly more different than Roman law from modern civil laws). The starkness of the difference derives from a failure to seek out a history of law in between the timeless and synchronic jurisprudence of Dharmaśāstra and the radically different construction of Hindu law during and after the colonial period. The overview given here will hopefully make a first step toward better historical descriptions of the transformations and trajectories of Hindu law and the broader legal pluralism in which it has always existed.

CHAPTER 2

Dharmaśāstra: a textual history

Patrick Olivelle

With an unbroken history of over two millennia, the literary production in the field of Dharmaśāstra is undoubtedly the longest in Indian history. When, at the invitation of their colonial rulers, Brahmin pandits produced a *śāstra*, a treatise aimed at codifying the scattered rules of Dharmaśāstra,[1] they were following in the footsteps of their ancestors who, either at the behest of rulers or in the pursuit of scholarship, produced *śāstras* that presented anew and with hermeneutical acumen the inherited norms of conduct.

The beginnings of this literary tradition are lost in the fog of early Indian history, but by at least the third century BCE a genre of literature focusing on the central notion of *dharma* came into existence. Composed first in an aphoristic style (*sūtra*) and then, beginning around the turn of the millennium, in simple verse (*śloka*), this vibrant textual production continued probably until about the ninth century CE. It was around this time that another textual form took over. In place of independent compositions, experts in *dharma* began writing commentaries (*bhāṣya*) on the ancient *dharmaśāstras*, as well as thematically arranged digests (*nibandha*) with copious citations from the *dharmaśāstras*. Although these three stages of textual production broadly follow a chronological sequence, there is much overlap, with *sūtra* texts being produced as late as the seventh century CE and original *dharmaśāstras* being produced well into the Middle Ages.

There are many histories of the textual production in the Dharmaśāstric tradition, most notably the encyclopedic survey of P. V. Kane (1968–75) and the more concise work of Lingat (1973). It will be unproductive in this brief chapter to simply summarize their detailed studies. Instead, taking "history" in the title of this chapter seriously, I will present a narrative – tentative and hypothetical though it necessarily will be – that attempts to understand the intertextual relationships and the sociopolitical contexts of Dharmaśāstra texts.

[1] See Rosane Rocher's chapter in this volume.

BACK TO THE BEGINNINGS

In attempting to understand the beginning of this genre of literature, two issues present themselves, issues that have received little attention in histories of Dharmaśāstra. First is the very term "*śāstra*," which refers to a broad category of knowledge systems and related literary products; and the second is *dharma*, the specific topic that is the focus of this literature.

The absence of the term "*śāstra*" in the Vedic texts, including the later strata, the *brāhmaṇa*s and the *upaniṣad*s,[2] and the relative frequency of its use in the subsequent literature raise a set of questions relating to the emergence of the *śāstra* genre in the fourth and fifth centuries BCE. My focus here is on a single subgenre within *śāstra*, namely the Dharmaśāstra. Why did a class of technical literature (*śāstra*) devoted to *dharma* arise in the second half of the first millennium BCE? What were the social, political, and religious contexts within which this genre of literature was created? Was its creation simply a natural development of Brahmanical scholasticism, or was it a response to external challenges? And, finally, how did the expert tradition created by this genre respond to the new challenges and changing circumstances during the first six or seven centuries of its existence, centuries that saw the rise and demise of two empires, the Maurya and the Gupta, and the rise of foreign dynasties including the Greek-Bactrian, the Śaka, and the Kuśāna?

DHARMAŚĀSTRA AND THE SEMANTICS OF *ŚĀSTRA*

The term "*śāstra*" is found for the first time in Yāska's *Nirukta* (1.2, 14), where the reference is probably to the science or a text of etymology (*nirukta*). Likewise, the *Ṛg Veda Prātiśākhya* (11.36; 14.30) uses the term to refer to the *prātiśākya* tradition. The grammarians Kātyāyana and Patañjali use it with reference to Pāṇini's grammar, the *Aṣṭādhyāyī*.[3] Likewise, the *Vedāṅgajyotiṣa* uses the term to refer to astronomical treatises.[4] Significantly, however, the latter text uses the expression "*vedāṅgaśāstrāṇām*," indicating that the term "*śāstra*" may have been used as a generic term covering treatises dealing with the Vedāṅgas. Yet it is notable that "*śāstra*" is never used with reference specifically to ritual manuals, the *śrautasūtra*s and the *gṛhyasūtra*s. The term occurs only in the *Kātyāyana Śrautasūtra* (1.6.21), and there it appears to refer

[2] The term occurs only in a single passage of the *Ṛg Veda* (8.33.16), where its meaning is far from clear. For studies of the term "*śāstra*" see Pollock (1989a) and Olivelle (2005a: 62–6). Some parts of this chapter are taken from my earlier study (Olivelle 2006b).

[3] See especially Kātyāyana on Pāṇini 1.1.1 (1: 8); 1.1.1 (10); 1.1.62 (1); 2.1.1 (16); 6.1.84 (4).

[4] The Ṛgvedic recension, 25, 36.

to the Veda. We find "*śāstra*" used with reference to the literature on *dharma*, however, as early as the grammarian Kātyāyana, who uses the term "*dharmaśāstra*."[5] This brief sketch indicates that the word "*śāstra*" (derived from the verb "*śās-*," "instruct") may have referred to manuals of instruction that were useful in understanding the Veda and practicing the Vedic rituals, but significantly not with reference to specifically ritual texts.

Even though the tradition considers the earliest texts of *dharma*, the *dharmasūtra*s, to form part of the *kalpasūtra*s (ritual codes) that included also the *śrautasūtra*s (codes of the priestly "high cult") and the *gṛhyasūtra*s (codes of domestic ritual), it was only the texts dealing with *dharma* to which the label "*śāstra*" came to be attached. This may indicate that in reality the tradition considered texts on *dharma* to constitute a special category and that its connection to the other two categories of ritual *sūtra*s was not original.[6] I suggest that Dharmaśāstra did not develop as an integral part of the ritual literature produced within the Vedic *śākhā*s; it developed instead as an autonomous genre. How and why did this genre of literature come into being? This question, which has not been raised in any of the extant "histories" of Dharmaśāstra, needs at least a tentative answer if we are to understand the early history of this śāstric literature.[7]

DHARMAŚĀSTRA AND THE SEMANTICS OF *DHARMA*

One possible reason for the neglect to examine the origin of the Dharmaśāstra genre is the assumption by most scholars that the term and concept of *dharma* have always been central to the Brahmanical understanding of religion, society, and the cosmos, and that scholarly discourse on this topic must have been an ongoing activity among Brahmanical schools constituting the Vedic branches (*śākhā*).[8] Another reason may have been the conviction that *dharma* had a primarily ritual dimension and was ultimately based on the Veda, and exegetical and interpretive works dealing

[5] "*dharmaśāstraṃ ca tathā*." Kātyāyana on Pāṇini 1.2.3, *Vārttika* 39 (1: 242).

[6] This does not mean that Vedic *śākhā*s did not produce literature on *dharma*. They evidently did, as seen in the works ascribed to Āpastamba, Hiraṇyakeśin, and Baudhāyana. My point is that the expert tradition on *dharma* probably did not arise as an integral part of the ritual tradition of scholarship.

[7] A notable exception is Wezler (2004), who raises significant points regarding the origin and codification of the early Dharmasūtras.

[8] Kane (1968–75, vol. 1: 19) says: "It seems that originally many, though not all, of the Dharmasūtras formed part of the Kalpasūtras and were studied in distinct *sūtracaraṇas*," and views *dharmasūtras* as "closely connected with *gṛhyasūtras* in subjects and topics" (vol. 1: 20). Lingat (1973: 18) concurs: "Originally, it seems, most of these *dharma-sūtras*, if not all of them, belonged to a collection of *kalpa-sūtras* and were attached to a particular Vedic school."

with the Veda, therefore, must necessarily involve discussions of *dharma*.[9] Both these assumptions, I believe, are wrong.

The term "*dharma*" was probably a neologism invented by the poets of the Ṛgvedic hymns; it has no cognates in other Indo-European languages, including Avestan.[10] Although the term occurs sixty-seven times in the *Ṛg Veda*, the frequency drops dramatically in the middle and late Vedic literature. As I have shown elsewhere,[11] *dharma* is a marginal concept in the theology expressed in the *brāhmaṇa*s and the early *upaniṣad*s; it is used there principally within the royal rather than the strictly ritual vocabulary.[12] The likely reason for its rise to prominence within the religious discourse of India between the fourth and fifth century BCE is its assumption, along with other terms and symbols of royalty, by the newly emergent ascetic religions, especially Buddhism, and its use for an imperial theology by Aśoka in the middle of the third century BCE. Given the marginality of "*dharma*" in the Vedic vocabulary, it is unlikely that the term would have been the subject of intense scholarly or exegetical inquiry during the late Vedic period. To claim that during the Vedic period "*dharma* was *par excellence* the sacrificial act which maintains and even conditions the cosmic order" (Lingat 1973: 3) simply ignores the facts and projects later Mīmāṃsā views onto the Vedic discourse. The fact is that the major scholastic works on the ritual, the *śrautasūtra*s and *gṛhyasūtra*s, hardly ever use the term "*dharma*" either with reference to ritual activity or with reference to the ritual and other duties of a Brahmin. Why then do we see the proliferation of *dharmasūtra*s during the last three or four centuries BCE?

The hypothesis I want to propose is that once *dharma* had become a central concept in the religious discourse of Buddhism and once it had penetrated the general vocabulary of ethics especially through its adoption by the Maurya emperors, certainly by Aśoka and possibly also by his predecessors, in developing an imperial theology, Brahmanical theologians had little choice but to define their own religion, ethics, and way of life in terms of *dharma*. Indeed,

9 Lingat (1973: 3), for example, asserts: "During the Vedic period the fundamental laws of the universe were identified with the laws of the sacrifice. Consequently *dharma* was *par excellence* the sacrificial act which maintains and even conditions the cosmic order."

10 For detailed studies of the early history of the term "*dharma*," see Brereton (2004) and Horsch (2004).

11 For a longer discussion, see Olivelle (2005b).

12 The most frequent occurrence of the term is in connection with the royal consecration (*rājasūya*), but even though the consecration is a ritual act the term is used principally to point out the functions of the king. Here I disagree both with Horsch (2004) and with my friend and mentor Albrecht Wezler (2004: 633), who asserts: "I assume that the Mīmāṃsā was stimulated to apply this term [*dharma*] to the content of the Vedic prescriptions only by the Dharmaśāstra even though it has already been a well-known term in the sacrificial context, there denoting the cosmos-sustaining and life-preserving power." My studies of the Vedic vocabulary have shown that at best *dharma* is a marginal concept in the vocabulary of the middle and later Vedic texts.

the scrutiny of the early meaning of *dharma* within its Dharmaśāstric use suggests that it was not the Veda but the "community standards" prevalent in different regions and communities that were taken to constitute *dharma*. The early texts on *dharma* speak of *deśadharma*, *jātidharma*, *kuladharma* – the *dharma* of regions, castes, and families/lineages. Clearly, these texts regard *dharma* as multiple and varied; each of these kinds of *dharma* can hardly be expected to be based on the Veda.

The dharma *of the Dharmaśāstra*s

The tradition of Vedic exegesis and hermeneutics known as Mīmāṃsā exerted a strong influence on the Dharmaśāstric tradition, and gradually that influence led to the dominance of the Veda as the principal if not the single source of *dharma* within the theological understanding of the term. As we will see, "community standards" came to be restricted to the standards of a Brahmanical elite, the *śiṣṭa*s, living within a theologically defined sacred geography known as the *āryāvarta*. In spite of this theologizing, *dharma* of the *dharmaśāstra*s remained rooted in the normative practices of the various communities. Wezler (2004: 648) remarks that religiosity based on *dharma*, in contradistinction to the elitist sacrifice, led to "a democratization regarding the access to salvation." I think this is noteworthy and important, because, if we place the origin of Dharmaśāstra within the context of a Brahmanical response to the "democratic" ethics and religion preached by Buddhism and the new ascetic religions, we can better appreciate both the sociological context of the rise of this genre of literature and the significant role it played in the new Brahmanical religiosity and soteriology.[13]

Lariviere (1997) and Wezler (2004) have argued, convincingly I believe, that the historical source of *dharma* in the *dharmaśāstra*s is not the Veda but "custom" (*ācāra*), that is, the normative behavior and practices of various and varied historical communities. In seeing the Veda or some transcendent tradition as the source of *dharma*, historians of Dharmaśāstra have bought into the theological position enunciated in most of the *dharmaśāstra*s themselves as to the provenance of the *dharma* that they are teaching, thus confusing history with theology.[14]

[13] A similar hypothesis regarding the composition of the great epic, *Mahābhārata*, has been proposed by Hiltebeitel (2001) and by Fitzgerald (2004).

[14] Even the later Brahmanical tradition is not unanimous in seeing the Veda as theologically the single source of *dharma*. Medhātithi, the author of the earliest extant commentary on the *Mānava Dharmaśāstra*, in the context of the duties of the king states explicitly that not all of *dharma* is based on the Veda: "*pramāṇāntaramūlā hy atra dharmā ucyante na sarve vedamūlāḥ*" (on *MDh* 7.1).

All extant texts on *dharma* begin with a discussion on the means of knowing (*pramāṇa*) *dharma* or the sources of *dharma*. Although there are some differences in the texts, by and large, they point to three sources: Veda (or *śruti*), *smṛti*, and normative custom (*ācāra*). Gautama (*GDhS* 1.1–2) provides the most explicit statement: "The source [or root] of *dharma* is the Veda, as well as the tradition and practice of those who know it [the Veda]." The category of *smṛti* is somewhat unclear; it may refer to the living memory of the Brahmanical community or to written sources of such immemorial customs. Clearly by the time of Manu "*smṛti*" meant texts, because he equates the term with Dharmaśāstra (*MDh* 2.10). The Mīmāṃsā tradition of Vedic exegesis, which exerted a strong influence on the Dharmaśāstric tradition from its very inception, began to interpret the multiple sources of *dharma* as having their origin in a single source, the Veda. This is stated explicitly by Manu (*MDh* 2.7): "Whatever *dharma* Manu has proclaimed with respect to anyone, all that has been taught in the Veda, for it contains all knowledge." Veda contains all knowledge and thus, a priori, should contain all *dharma*. This position is already hinted at in the above statement of Gautama when he specifies that only the tradition and practice "of those who know the Veda" are authoritative. The authority of tradition and practice are here implicitly connected with the Veda.[15] Āpastamba (*ĀpDhS* 1.12.10–12) provides the earliest evidence of the hermeneutical argument for the position when he claims that all rules were originally found in the *brāhmaṇas*; but some sections of these were lost over time, and they can be recovered by observing actual practice: "All rules are described in the *brāhmaṇas*. The lost *brāhmaṇa* passages relating to some of them are inferred from usage." Here we have the Mīmāṃsā concept of *anumitaśruti*, that is, Vedic passages that are inferred to have existed on the basis of either *smṛti* or practice.[16] The "lost Veda" argument will be used by later authors to underpin the authority of other sources of *dharma* within the theological fiction that the Veda is the sole source of *dharma*. The Mīmāṃsā view of *dharma*, then, is that the Veda is the sole means of knowing it; when a specific Vedic text is wanting with regard to a particular aspect of ritual or behavior, one can then use supplementary sources, such as *smṛti* and normative conduct, on the basis of which one can infer the existence of a Vedic text.

[15] See the chapter by Lubin in this volume.

[16] This doctrine was known to Āpastamba (*ĀpDhS* 1.12.10–121.4.8), who says that "a Vedic text has greater force than a practice from which the existence of a corresponding Vedic text has to be inferred" ("*śrutir hi balīyasy ānumānikād ācārāt*").

This theological claim camouflages the historical sources of *dharma*. Indeed, as S. Pollock (1985, 1990) has shown, the reason for the "idiom of eternality and timelessness" is precisely the theological imperative that to be based on the Veda means to transcend time and historical context and change.

The historical reality is very different from this theological position. The *dharma* taught in the *dharmaśāstra*s has little to do with the Veda but reflects the actual practices of local groups; the *dharmaśāstra*s themselves are nothing but the textualization of such practice, along with a theoretical reflection on it that can be called jurisprudence. Evidence from texts belonging roughly to the last three centuries before the common era indicates that this is not merely a historical conclusion of modern scholarship; it appears to have been the view of at least three major authors belonging to the early period of Dharmaśāstric textual production: the grammarians Kātyāyana and Patañjali, and Āpastamba, the author of both a *gṛhyasūtra* and a *dharmasūtra*.

Kātyāyana, in his *Vārttika*s on Pāṇini's *Aṣṭādhyāyī*, makes a distinction between what is found in the Veda (*vede* and *vaidika*) and what is prevalent in the world (*loke* and *laukika*). The major use of these two categories is for grammatical purposes, giving examples from the Vedic texts and common speech, the two areas of language encompassed by the early Sanskrit grammars.[17] At least in Patañjali's understanding of Kātyāyana, the category of *laukika* (worldly) does not apply simply to what ordinary people say and do but to norms of behavior encoded in textualized form that are certainly Dharmaśāstric injunctions. The clearest example of such injunctions is found in Patañjali's commentary on Kātyāyana's *Vārttika* 5 (on Pāṇini 6.1.84; III: 57–8), which contains the expression "*yathā laukikavaidikeṣu.*" Here the examples given by Patañjali support the view that in teaching *dharma* (*dharmopadeśa*) the injunctions refer not to individuals (*avayava*) but to categories or classes (*anavayava*).[18] As *laukika* examples, Patañjali gives: "*brāhmaṇo na hantavyaḥ*" ("A Brahmin should not be killed"), "*surā na peyā*" ("Liquor should not be drunk"), and "*pūrvavayā brāhmaṇaḥ pratyuttheyaḥ*" ("An older Brahmin should be [greeted by] standing up"). If these injunctions are taken as referring to an individual rather than to a class, then someone could fulfill the obligations by not killing a particular

[17] See Kātyāyana's *Vārttika* 2 on Pāṇini 1.2.45 (I: 217); 15 on 6.1.1 (III: 3); 5 on 6.1.83 (III: 55); 2 on 6.2.36 (III: 125).

[18] The terms used here are "*avayava*" and "*anavayava*," literally "part" and "non-part." The terms are somewhat obscure, but they appear to refer to individuals (*dravya* or *vyakti*) and classes (*jāti* or *ākṛti*).

individual Brahmin, by not drinking liquor once, and by rising up to greet a single older Brahmin on a single occasion, after which time he is free to kill Brahmins, to drink liquor, and not to rise up to greet older Brahmins. This is obviously erroneous; so we must assume that the injunctions refer to classes rather than to individuals. The Vedic example given in this context is: "*vasante brāhmaṇo 'gniṣṭomādibhiḥ kratubhir yajeta*" ("In the spring a Brahmin should offer sacrifices such as the Agniṣṭoma"). Here also the obligation is a continuous one and cannot be fulfilled by doing this act once. In support of the *laukika* injunction that a younger person should rise when approached by an older person, Patañjali cites a verse, which is found also in Manu (*MDh* 2.120): "For when an older person comes near, the life breaths of a younger person rise up, and as he rises up and greets him, he retrieves them." Other *laukika* examples also show that they are actually Dharmaśāstric in nature. Thus on Pāṇini 1.1.1 (I: 5, 8) Patañjali repeats the following maxims twice: "*abhakṣyo grāmyakukkuṭo 'bhakṣyo grāmyaśūkaraḥ*" ("It is forbidden to eat a village fowl; it is forbidden to eat a village pig"),[19] injunctions that are common in the *dharmaśāstras*. He also gives the well-known maxim (on Pāṇini 1.1.1 [I: 5]) "*pañca pañcanakhā bhakṣyāḥ*" ("The five five-nailed [animals] may be eaten").

What is significant here is that for grammarians both the Veda and the *loka* are *pramāṇa*, authoritative with respect to correct speech. This authoritative nature of *loka* is carried over into the Dharmaśāstric framework when Patañjali cites injunctions. Clearly, not everything that is said or done in the world is so authoritative. Thus *loka* for Patañjali and most likely also for Kātyāyana referred to Dharmaśāstra. We have confirmation of this conclusion. The two examples cited above that Patañjali refers to *loka* at Pāṇini 6.1.84 (III: 57–8) – namely, not killing Brahmins and not drinking liquor – are cited by him again in his comments on Kātyāyana's *Vārttika* 39 on Pāṇini 1.2.64. The *Vārttika* reads "*dharmaśāstraṃ ca tathā*" ("And so also Dharmaśāstra"), and as an example of "Dharmaśāstra (tradition)" Patañjali gives: "*brāhmaṇo na hantavyaḥ surā na peyā*" ("Brahmin should not be killed; liquor should not be drunk"). Clearly, for Patañjali "*loka*" and "*dharmaśāstra*" are, if not synonyms, at least equivalents with respect to authoritative injunctions.

The question that still remains is whether "*dharmaśāstra*" as used by Patañjali refers to texts as treatises such as the extant *dharmasūtras* or to the individual maxims that he cites. Clearly "*dharmaśāstra*" in Patañjali may well refer to such individual legal or moral pronouncements. I think,

[19] Also repeated on Pāṇini 7.3.14 (III: 320).

however, that evidence points to the fact that Patañjali views the rules he cites as derived from "texts" in the sense of a complete treatise or *śāstra*. Patañjali uses the term "*dharmaśāstra*" with reference to such texts and cites individual norms from such treatises. The general pattern of use of the term *śāstra* during and prior to this period shows that it was used with reference to treatises, such as the Veda or the *Aṣṭādhyāyī*, rather than to single pronouncements. In his comments on Pāṇini 1.1.47 (I: 115),[20] Patañjali's statement: "*naiveśvara ājñāpayati nāpi dharmasūtrakārāḥ paṭhanty apavādair utsargā bādhyantām iti*" ("Neither does the Lord command nor do the authors of *dharmasūtra*s declare: 'General rules should be set aside by special rules'") also points in this direction. Not only does this show that Patañjali was familiar with the genre of literature called *dharmasūtra* that had authors, it also shows that in his mind the authors of *dharmasūtra*s paralleled *īśvara*. Now, it is unclear what or whom Patañjali refers to by this term. The term "*īśvara*" ("Lord") here, in the understanding of the later commentator Nāgojibhaṭṭa, refers to the Veda. According to this interpretation, for Patañjali the *dharmasūtra*s were as much texts as the Veda. It is more probable, however, that "*īśvara*" refers to the king,[21] in which case the authors of *dharmasūtra*s parallel the king in authority to pronounce on matters of public importance. It is extremely unlikely that singular injunctions are referred to here by "*dharmasūtra*," and that the authors are merely stating individual injunctions. In the early literature, furthermore, the titles *dharmaśāstra* and *dharmasūtra* were synonyms, the former referring to their substance and the latter to their linguistic form. Even in classical texts we do not find the distinction that modern scholars make between *dharmasūtra*s and *dharmaśāstra*s, the latter referring to texts composed in verse.

No other *śāstra* of the early period saw the need to explicitly address the question of how one comes to know (*pramāṇa*) its subject matter. The issue of sources is passed over in silence.[22] Why did the authors of the earliest texts on *dharma* feel the need to address this issue explicitly?

[20] The identical wording "*naiveśvara ājñāpayati nāpi dharmasūtrakārāḥ paṭhanti*" is also found in Patañjali's comments on Pāṇini 5.1.119 (II: 365).

[21] This is confirmed by Patañjali's statement on Pāṇini 6.1.2 (Kātyāyana's *Vārttika* 9; III: 7): "*loka īśvara ājñāpayati*," where the command of the Lord refers to worldly (*laukika*) matters and not Vedic. Here, clearly, the *īśvara* is the king and not the Veda or god. Further, in his comments on Pāṇini 1.1.38 (I: 177), Patañjali clearly states that "*īśvara*" is a synonym (*paryāya*) of "*rājan*" (king). See also his comments on Pāṇini 2.3.9 (I: 447). I thank Madhav Deshpande for his help in resolving the meaning of "*īśvara*" in Patañjali.

[22] Later texts, such as the *Nāṭyaśāstra* and the medical *śāstra*s, do deal with their provenance, not in terms of authoritative sources but in terms of their mythical origin from the creator god.

I want to propose the hypothesis that these authors were working both within the model provided by the Buddhist texts and in response to the Buddhist appropriation of *dharma*. The Buddhist theory of *dharma-pramāṇa*, that is, the way one knows whether a particular oral text is authoritative, is articulated in the doctrine of *buddha-vacana* ("Buddha's word"). Either proximately or ultimately all pronouncements on *dharma* must go back to the words of the Buddha himself for those pronouncements to have any authority or validity. This conviction is encapsulated in the opening words of every Buddhist text: "*evaṃ mayā śrutam*" (Pāli: "*evam me sutam*"): "Thus have I heard." It is probable that the Brahmanical scholars writing on *dharma*, a term that we have noted did not have a central role within the previous Brahmanical discourse, were consciously responding to this Buddhist theory by proposing a different *pramāṇa*, a different authoritative source of *dharma*. This source they found at first not in the Veda, which has little to say on the topic, but in the customary norms and practices (*ācāra*) of living communities, among which, we must suppose, the practices of the Brahmanical community were considered the model and yardstick. The conclusions of Wezler (2004) and the use of the term "*sāmayācārika*" (conduct that is normative and accepted by a community) by Āpastamba (*ĀpDhS* 1.1.1) as the first source of *dharma* support such a hypothesis. We also saw that for Patañjali Dharmaśāstric prescriptions were located principally in *loka*, that is, the actual practices, behavior patterns, and pronouncements of living communities rather than in the Veda.

The problem for the authors of the *śāstra*s was how to limit and control the enormous diversity with respect to norms of conduct prevalent in the different regions, castes, and communities across that vast land. The early history of the *dharmaśāstra*s testifies to the continuing efforts to define and limit the universally authoritative practices to those prevalent in Brahmanical communities, and even there to draw boundaries, both geographical and ideological, around especially authoritative Brahmins.

THE EARLY HISTORY: *DHARMASŪTRAS*

When the earliest *dharmasūtra*s were written (or orally composed and transmitted) has been a matter of scholarly conjecture. If my argument for the history of the term "*dharma*" and its incorporation into an expert tradition within Brahmanism is accepted, however, then the earliest writings on *dharma* cannot be earlier than the second half of the fourth century BCE. As we have seen, the earliest reference to "*dharmasūtra*" is by Patañjali, generally assigned to the middle of the second century BCE. The term "*dharmaśāstra*" is used by his predecessor Kātyāyana, who may be assigned to a period after the Maurya reforms (M. Deshpande 2006). If the Maurya reforms were an impetus for the rise of this genre of literature, then a date of the first half of the third century appears reasonable.

There are four extant Dharmaśāstric texts written in the *sūtra* mode and ascribed to Āpastamba, Gautama, Baudhāyana, and Vasiṣṭha.[23] It is evident, however, that a much larger body of literature on *dharma* preexisted the four documents that have survived, which cite or refer to opinions of seventeen authorities.[24] Although it is unclear whether the statements ascribed to them are single memorable quotes or derived from larger compositions authored by or ascribed to those individuals, it is probable that at least some of these authors did write *dharmasūtras* that have not survived.

This is clearly the case with Hārīta, who is cited eight times by Āpastamba, and once each by Baudhāyana and Vasiṣṭha. Hārīta's positions were conservative, clearly to the right of what Āpastamba considered the mainstream. Both Āpastamba and Baudhāyana cite him as saying simply and imperiously "That is false" ("*mithyā etat*") with reference to opinions of others: in Baudhāyana (*BDhS* 2.2.21) against those who say that the children of those excommunicated from caste do not become outcastes themselves; and in Āpastamba (*ĀpDhS* 1.28.16) against suicide as a penance for those who commit incest. At another point Hārīta claims that a person who for any reason takes another's property is a thief, an opinion shared by three other authors, Kaṇva, Kautsa, and Puṣkarasādi, whereas Vārṣyāyaṇi thinks that there are exceptions, such as fodder for an ox. Hārīta, however, is unconvinced and asserts that in all cases the owner's permission must be obtained (*ĀpDhS* 1.28.1–5). All the citations of ancient authors in the extant *dharmasūtras* are in the context of diverse opinions and controversies on various points of proper conduct and ritual procedure. Clearly we have here a vibrant scholarly debate on a variety of issues, very different from the later

[23] For the dating of these texts, see Olivelle (2000: 4–10). I take Āpastamba to be the oldest, followed by Gautama, Baudhāyana, and Vasiṣṭha. Wezler (2004: 650, n. 11) calls Kangle's argument for placing Gautama late "not entirely convincing." Besides the arguments I have spelled out in the above work, it is very clear that Gautama represents a much more advanced stage in the development of thinking regarding judicial procedure (*vyavahāra*), as can be seen by comparing the four Dharmasūtras on this subject in Olivelle (2005c).

[24] Aupajaṅghani (*BDhS* 2.3.33); Bhāllavins (*BDhS* 1.2.11; *VDhS* 1.14); Eka (*ĀpDhS* 1.19.7); Hārīta (*ĀpDhS* 1.13.11; 1.18.2; 1.19.12; 1.28.1, 5, 16; 1.29.12, 16; *BDhS* 2.2.21; *VDhS* 2.6); Kaṇva (*ĀpDhS* 1.19.3; 1.28.1); Kāṇva (*ĀpDhS* 1.19.2, 7); Kapila (*BDhS* 2.11.28); Kaśyapa (*BDhS* 1.21.2); Kātya (*BDhS* 1.3.46); Kautsa (*ĀpDhS* 1.19.4; 1.28.1); Kuṇika (*ĀpDhS* 1.19.7); Kutsa (*ĀpDhS* 1.19.7); Mahājajñu (*BDhS* 3.9.21); Manu (*ĀpDhS* 2.14.11; 2.16.1; *GDhS* 21.7; 23.28; *BDhS* 2.3.2; 4.1.13; 4.2.15; *VDhS* 1.17; 3.2; 11.23; 12.16; 13.16; 19.37; 23.43); Maudgalya (*BDhS* 2.4.8); Puṣkarasādi (*ĀpDhS* 1.19.7; 1.28.1); Vārṣyāyaṇi (*ĀpDhS* 1.19.5, 8; 1.28.1).

tradition which sought to present a singular point of view, eliminating or interpreting away divergent voices.

The structure of the *dharmasūtras* as evidenced in Āpastamba is simple. After an introduction regarding the means of knowing *dharma*, the text deals with the duties of the Vedic student and the Brahmanical householder, with parenthetical discussions of the rite of initiation, the duties of the "bath-graduate" (that is, a person who has completed his Vedic studies), the orders of life (*āśramas*), and the duties of a king, with cursory comments on judicial procedure. As opposed to Manu and later *dharmaśāstras*, the *dharmasūtras* present themselves as nothing more than scholarly works. There is no literary introduction; the author gets right down to business. He presents his material in a straightforward manner, and on points of controversy and debate he presents opposing viewpoints.

Āpastamba is also unique in acknowledging that a person can learn from the traditional knowledge found among women and Śūdras because this knowledge is also part of *dharma*. He strongly supports monogamy and has no discussion of mixed castes. He also acknowledges the legitimacy of the ascetic modes of life, accepting the system of four *āśramas*, albeit in an early form, as non-sequential alternatives (Olivelle 1993). These may represent both chronological and geographic differences, or even the individual opinions of Āpastamba. The absence of the term "*dvija*" (twice-born) to identify Brahmins or the three upper *varṇas*, a term in frequent use in later works, however, is another indication that we have in Āpastamba one of the earliest attempts at writing a treatise on *dharma*.

Gautama, on the other hand, along with Baudhāyana, rejects outright the system of *āśramas*, recognizing the validity of only the householder. Gautama, however, is silent about polygamy. He has a separate section devoted to a long discussion on penance, which becomes standard in later texts. Gautama's discussion of law and legal procedure is also the most developed among the authors of *dharmasūtras*. He is also a significant source for later works, especially for Manu (Olivelle 2007). The text is composed entirely in prose *sūtras*, without any cited verses. Some have taken this as a sign of its early composition; but the evidence points to the fact that the author used this technique to artificially approximate the notion of a proper *sūtra* text, such as that of Pāṇini. Indeed, many of his *sūtras* scan, thus indicating verses as their sources.

Baudhāyana's text has undergone significant modifications, and it is difficult to discern what the original structure of the text might have been

(Olivelle 2000: 191). Both he and Vasiṣṭha, however, introduce into the Dharmaśāstric discourse the concept of a sacred geography, a region called Āryāvarta in which exemplary Brahmin communities live;[25] the practices of these communities become normative for all.

Vasiṣṭha's text also has been badly transmitted and appears to have undergone repeated redactions. It is clearly the latest of the early *dharmasūtras*, composed at a time not too distant from Manu. The way topics are arranged is haphazard, the only noteworthy point being that the section on penance is placed last, a practice followed by later writers. Vasiṣṭha is a transitional figure also in terms of style; he uses more verses in his work than any other early author, 28 percent of the text being composed in verse.

A final issue in the early history of Dharmaśāstra concerns the eponymous authors to whom the texts are ascribed. Looking at the four authors of *dharmasūtras*, we see that Āpastamba and Baudhāyana are founders of ritual traditions to whom their major ritual texts are ascribed; this is consistent with the fact that their *dharmasūtras* form part of the respective *kalpasūtras*. Gautama and Vasiṣṭha, on the other hand, represent a growing tradition of ascribing texts to significant figures from the remote past. This is especially true with regard to independent texts that are not integral parts of *kalpasūtras*. When we look at the names of authorities cited in these texts, some, such as Aupajaṅghani, Hārīta, and Puṣkarasādi, appear to be names of individual scholars, while others, such as Kaṇva and Manu, are associated with Vedic schools, and still others, such as Kapila, are simply well-known seers of the past. The tendency in the later tradition, however, is to select seers or divinities to lend greater authority to the respective texts.

THE *DHARMAŚĀSTRA* OF MANU

The treatise ascribed to Manu opened a new chapter in the history of Dharmaśāstric literature. It was a watershed not only because it departed so radically both in style and in substance from the previous literature but also because all the subsequent texts of Dharmaśāstra work within the frame provided by Manu; indeed, they can be seen as extended commentaries on and updates of Manu, taking him in new directions.

I have argued elsewhere (Olivelle 2005a) that the treatise of Manu was composed by a single author. One argument for this is the deeply embedded

[25] This concept was already introduced by the grammarian Patañjali in his comments on Pāṇini 2.4.10 and 6.3.109.

structure of the treatise that I uncovered, a structure that lay latent within the later division into twelve chapters imposed on the text and that is marked by what I have called transitional verses marking the passage from one topic to another. This author also instituted other significant changes.

With regard to style, Manu composed his work entirely in verse (*śloka*), thus departing from the previous tradition of prose *sūtras*. The reason for this change is not altogether clear, but other texts belonging roughly to the same period were also being composed in verse, including the two epics (the *Mahābhārata* and the *Rāmāyaṇa*) and Buddhist epic stories such as Aśvaghoṣa's *Buddhacarita*. S. Pollock (2006) has drawn attention to the "Sanskrit cosmopolis" beginning around this time where court literature composed primarily in verse becomes a carrier of authority and prestige. Further, even in earlier literature, such as the *upaniṣads* and *dharmasūtras*, verses are cited as authorities in support of positions presented in prose. With a couple of exceptions, all later authors of *dharmaśāstras* will compose their works in verse.

The author also presents his text not as a scholarly work in the tradition of the *dharmasūtras* but as the authoritative statement on *dharma* by Manu himself, the son of the creator, using his pupil Bhṛgu as his intermediary. The frame story, another innovation of Manu, presents the real author of this text as the creator god himself. Within this literary setting, the *dharma* is promulgated authoritatively; there cannot be any debate, dissension, or scholarly give and take, which are the hallmarks of the earlier *dharmasūtras*.

Manu represents a watershed in the history of Dharmaśāstra also because of his integration of the Arthaśāstric tradition bearing on king, state, and judicial procedure. The most obvious borrowing is Manu's adoption of the eighteen *vyavahārapadas*, or Grounds for Litigation (often called Titles of Law). These continue to be the core of discourses on legal procedure in later *dharma* literature. Some of these grounds for bringing a lawsuit are given in the earlier literature, but never in such a systematic manner; neither are they called by the technical term *vyavahārapada*. According to Manu, a plaintiff when bringing a case before a tribunal has to indicate the exact *vyavahārapada* under which he is filing the suit. The significance of this topic for Manu is indicated by the fact that he devotes 745 verses or 27.8 percent of his entire book to it, and it covers two entire chapters (8 and 9) of the twelve-chapter work. Indeed, if we add up all the verses bearing on king, state, and law, they amount to over one fifth of the entire book.

Another new feature of Manu is the introduction of themes relating to liberation (*mokṣa*). The early *dharmasūtras* have nothing to say on the matter, the very term "*mokṣa*" in the sense of personal liberation being absent in them. Vasiṣṭha is the first to introduce this theme in several verses

(*VDhS* 10.20, 23; 20.20), but he does not have a systematic discussion of it. Manu, on the other hand, calls the life of a wandering mendicant by the technical term "*mokṣa*" (*MDh* 1.114; 6.35–7). Further, he devotes almost the entirety of Chapter 12 to the discussion of the way humans are kept bound to the cycle of rebirth and how they can liberate themselves from it. The topic of *mokṣa* will become an integral part of later Dharmaśāstric discourse.

We do not possess any external evidence for determining the date of Manu. Internal evidence is not always convincing and can be interpreted in many different ways. Given the developments of law and society detectable in this work, nevertheless, I think it is appropriate to assign it to the second century CE (Olivelle 2005a). This date also agrees with the date of the earliest gold coins in circulation in the north-central regions of India during the Kushana period. Manu is the first author within either the Dharmaśāstric or the Arthaśāstric tradition to prescribe fines in gold coins.

If we at least assume that this text was composed during the first couple of centuries CE – and I think this is a plausible assumption – then we may be able to speculate about the social and political environment of the author and perhaps the motivations for its composition. Recently similar questions have been raised with reference to the *Mahābhārata*. I think the sociopolitical environment that prompted the composition of the great epic was not too different from that of Manu. The time frame and the geography are more or less the same, and the authors of both works probably came from the class of educated and somewhat conservative Brahmins intent on protecting the rights and privileges of their class.

We can isolate at least three sociopolitical elements that provide the background to the composition of Manu's text. The major element is certainly the historical reality and especially the historical memory, of two or three centuries later, of the Maurya state and especially of the Aśokan political, social, and religious reforms. Aśoka was certainly a Buddhist; whether he was anti-Brahmanical is debatable. One thing that his reforms did was to displace the Brahmin from his privileged position within the social structure. The special relationship between the political power (*kṣatra*) and the religious establishment (*brahma*) was broken. The Sanskrit compound "*śramaṇa-brāhmaṇa*" used frequently by Aśoka in his inscriptions indicates that his social philosophy envisaged a dual class of religious people worthy of respect and support: the newly formed ascetic communities and the old Brahmin class. His prohibition of animal sacrifices,[26] furthermore,

[26] See Rock Edict 1: "*hidā nā kichi jive ālabhitu pajohitaviye*"; Sanskrit "*iha na kaścit jīva ālabhya prahotavyaḥ*." The term "*prahotavya*" has clear reference to Brahmanical sacrifice.

undercut the very raison d'être of Brahmanical privilege: the Brahmin's ability to perform sacrifices for the well-being of society and for the furtherance of royal power symbolized principally in the royal horse sacrifice.

To add insult to injury, the Mauryas, as well as the Nandas who preceded them, were considered at least within Brahmanical historical memory as Śūdras. The usurpation of Kṣatriya royal privileges by Śūdras and the ensuing suppression of Brahmins are presented as the sure signals of the corrupt times of the Kali age. Such a political situation creates the mixture of *varṇas* (*varṇasaṅkara*), the most serious social and moral corruption within Brahmanical ideology.

Finally, there was the contemporary political reality of the Kushana Empire. There were foreign invasions first in the border regions of the northwest and then within the heartland that established foreign rule. The Kushanas ruled a wide swath of northern India, and they favored Buddhism. If we are correct in thinking that the *Mānava Dharmaśāstra* was written during the Kushana period, then Manu was faced with what amounted nearly to another Maurya regime with the added dimension that these were also foreigners, Mlecchas.

Reading Manu, one cannot fail to see and to feel the intensity and urgency with which the author defends Brahmanical privilege. A major aim of Manu was to reestablish the old alliance between *brahma* and *kṣatra*, an alliance that in his view would benefit both the king and the Brahmin, thereby reestablishing the Brahmin in his unique and privileged position within society. We hear repeated emphasis on the inviolability of the Brahmin in his person and in his property. He has immunity from the death penalty, from taxes, and from the confiscation of his property. The king is advised repeatedly that a Brahmin's property is poison. Stealing a Brahmin's gold is one of the five grievous sins, and the death penalty is imposed on the perpetrator. Devotion to Brahmins is a cardinal virtue of kings: "Refusal to turn back in battle, protecting the subjects, and obedient service to Brahmins – for kings, these are the best means of securing happiness" (*MDh* 7.88). The reason why foreign ruling classes, such as the Greeks, Śakas, Persians, and Chinese, have fallen to the level of Śūdras, once again, is their lack of devotion to Brahmins (*MDh* 10.43).

POST-MANU COMPOSITION OF *DHARMAŚĀSTRAS*

Manu was a pioneer; he set the standard for the literary activities of his successors in style and in substance. Both Yājñavalkya and Viṣṇu follow

Manu in the introductory frames of their works. Like Manu, Viṣṇu begins with the story of creation. It is the Earth personified as a woman who requests the creator, Viṣṇu, to teach her *dharma* (*VDh* 1.48). Yājñavalkya's frame is brief. The sages approach Yājñavalkya in Mithilā and ask him to teach them *dharma* (*YSm* 1.1). In all these we hear the echo of the early verses of Manu. After Manu, *śāstras* are presented no longer simply as scholarly productions in the manner of the *dharmasūtras* but as teachings imparted by a god or some other exalted being.

The influence of Manu on the later literature, however, runs deeper. One tradition speaks of several redactions (*saṃhitā*) of the original composition of Manu, that of Bhṛgu being only one. The text of Nārada is explicitly viewed by the tradition as just such a redaction. Yājñavalkya (*YSm* 1.4–5) places Manu at the head of his list of the authors of *dharmaśāstras*, the first such list in existence, even though I express below reservations about the authenticity of these verses.

Bṛhaspati follows Manu so closely that it appears likely that he had a copy of Manu's work before him while he composed his text. Several verses of Bṛhaspati are actually commentaries on passages of Manu. Indeed, a later tradition recorded in the *Skanda Purāṇa* (Jolly 1889: 274) takes Bṛhaspati as one of the redactors of Manu. Bṛhaspati (Saṃskārakāṇḍa 13) pays the ultimate tribute to the authority of Manu, dismissing any other text that is opposed to Manu, whom he takes as the ultimate authority in matters of *dharma*.

Dharmaśāstra *of Yājñavalkya*

Among the post-Manu *dharmaśāstras*, the one ascribed to Yājñavalkya is certainly the most significant. Yājñavalkya also represents a clear advance over Manu, especially with respect to statecraft and jurisprudence, both in sophistication and in vocabulary. He is concise to the point that many of his verses appear to be metrical *sūtras*. The best assessment of his work is given by Lingat (1973: 98): "[Yājñavalkya's] fame is explained by the intrinsic qualities of the work. Of all the *smṛtis* which have come down to us that of Yājñavalkya is assuredly the best composed and appears to be the most homogeneous ... We are struck ... by the sober tone, the concise style, and the strictness with which the topics are arranged."

In spite of the clear advance over Manu, Yājñavalkya leans heavily on his predecessor; many of his verses are condensations of several verses of Manu (Kane 1968–75, vol. 1: 430; Olivelle 2005a: 67–8). Yet the advances are equally obvious. First, there is the clear division of the work into three parts of roughly equal size dealing with proper conduct (*ācāra*), legal procedure (*vyavahāra*), and penance (*prāyaścitta*). This division will become standard in later Dharmaśāstric discourse. Within this tripartite division, he provides further subdivisions according to topic (*prakaraṇa*). Although it is unclear whether both kinds of divisions are original, they are found uniformly in both the manuscript and the commentarial tradition.

Second, we detect advances in legal procedure. With respect to evidence, Yājñavalkya lists documents, witnesses, and ordeals, in that order. Previous writers, including Manu, had paid little or no attention to documents, pointing to a more oral culture. Yājñavalkya devotes eleven verses to documents, describing the marks of a valid legal document. He also appears to assume (*YSm* 2.84) that every transaction or contract should be accompanied by a proper legal document with the signatures of witnesses. Indeed, Yājñavalkya is the first to use the technical term "*lekhya*" for a document; the term is absent in the vocabulary of earlier texts, including Kauṭilya's *Arthaśāstra*. He also requires the court to prepare a written document in the presence of the plaintiff and defendant at the start of any trial, a document containing the plaint, the defendant's plea, and the kinds of evidence both parties will present during the trial. He also tells debtors and creditors to write down the amounts owed and paid on the original contract. All this points to a time when writing was common and at least a good percentage of people entering into monetary transactions and legal proceedings were literate.

The third means of proof in a trial is the ordeal. This practice antedates Yājñavalkya but is paid little or no attention in the earlier literature. There is not even a technical term for it. Manu uses the term "*śapatha*" for both oath and ordeal, and does not make a sharp distinction between the two. Yājñavalkya is the first to use the technical term "*divya*" for ordeal and the first to devote considerable space to describing five kinds of ordeal.

Another innovation pertains to courts. Yājñavalkya is the first to indicate a hierarchy of courts, consisting of courts appointed by the king himself and those appointed by other bodies, such as guilds and communities (*YSm* 2.30). He also implies that there was a system of appeal to higher courts against judgments rendered by lower ones.

The third innovation is not directly related to law; it is the way Yājñavalkya presents the ascetic orders of the forest hermit and world renouncer. Previous writers had placed these institutions in various positions within their literary structures; Manu gives them at the conclusion of his treatment of the Brahmin. Yājñavalkya, departing from previous practice, places these within his discussion of penance (*prāyaścitta*), thus presenting them not as modes of life opposed to the householder but as special ways in which people can lead penitential lives in their old age. The connection of these ascetical institutions with penance and vows (*vrata*) will continue in the later Dharmaśāstric tradition.

The treatment of *mokṣa* introduced by Manu is taken to a new level by Yājñavalkya. He has a long section on meditation, especially on the fleeting nature of the human body, including the long anatomical description borrowed from a medical treatise, a description that is reproduced by Viṣṇu.

Even if we discount arguments from his knowledge of Greek astronomy and the use of the term "*nāṇaka*," given the prominence he gives to writing and documents and the advances in judicial procedure and law, a considerable span of time must have intervened between Manu and Yājñavalkya. A time during the height of the Gupta dynasty appears reasonable, probably between the end of the fourth and the first half of the fifth century CE.

Almost its entire second chapter on *vyavahāra* is given in the *Agni Purāṇa* (253–8), and the *Garuḍa Purāṇa* (93–106) gives large sections of the first and third chapters. It was the subject of a commentary of Viśvarūpa in the ninth century CE. This indicates that Yājñavalkya's work had become prominent by the last few centuries of the first millennium CE.

Dharmaśāstra *of Viṣṇu*

Among the extant *dharmaśāstras*, the one ascribed to Viṣṇu is the last to deal with all the subject matter falling under *dharma*. As I have demonstrated elsewhere (Olivelle 2009), this text was composed in Kashmir around the seventh century CE. The author belonged to the Kāṭhaka branch of the Veda and was a fervent devotee of Viṣṇu, probably connected with the Pāñcarātra form of Vaiṣṇavism.

The text is divided into one hundred sections and is written in a mixture of prose and verse, several chapters being composed entirely in verse. Although it may have undergone redactions after its composition, the thesis put forward by Jolly (1880) that it was a Vaiṣṇava recast of a *Kāṭhaka Dharmasūtra* is without basis. Viṣṇu, nevertheless, borrows heavily from his predecessors, especially Manu and Yājñavalkya.

Viṣṇu's work, however, contains significant innovations. It is the only *dharmaśāstra* that does not deal with the means of knowing *dharma*. Given that Viṣṇu is the author of the text, one can argue that any other source of *dharma* would have been superfluous and counterproductive. Viṣṇu is also the first to mention a widow following her husband onto the funeral pyre: At 20.39 it is referred to in language that suggests *anugamana*, and at 25.14 it is called "*anvārohaṇa*." These are the only places that widow burning is recorded in any of the early *dharmaśāstras*; this custom should be seen as a somewhat late introduction into the Dharmaśāstric tradition.

Another obvious feature of this work not shared by any other *dharmaśāstra* is its strong *bhakti* orientation. Ritual worship (*pūjā*) of Viṣṇu is recommended as a daily practice, and there are descriptions of Vaiṣṇava iconography originating in Kashmir (Olivelle 2009).

Dharmaśāstra *of Nārada*

After Yājñavalkya, there appears to have been a focus within the expert tradition of Dharmaśāstra on law and legal procedure. This seems to have been the beginning of specialization in Dharmaśāstric literature, a feature we encounter especially in the medieval period with monographic texts focusing on individual topics of *dharma*. The text of Nārada is the earliest representative of the tradition specializing in jurisprudence.

Tradition presents Nārada as one of the many recensions of Manu (Lariviere 1989a, vol. II: xxiii), establishing its direct connection to that authoritative text. In the text of Nārada, however, there is nothing that marks it as the communication of a god or exalted being; it has the hallmark of a scholarly treatise.

Nārada takes the discussion of legal procedure to a new level both in its precision and its analysis of court procedure, and in the clarity of its presentation. Lingat (1973: 102) cites A. Barth's assessment of the scholarly merit of Nārada's treatise: "If we except the monuments of Roman legislation, antiquity has not perhaps left us anything which is so strictly juridical." Nārada (*mātṛkā* 1), however, has a penchant for classification, as when he says there are two kinds of evidence (documents and witnesses), two types of legal procedure with four feet, four means, four beneficiaries, eight limbs, and eighteen titles, and extending to four and producing four.

The date of Nārada cannot be determined with any degree of certainty, and it is also unclear whether he is earlier or later than Yājñavalkya. Arguments have been presented for both positions (Lariviere 1989a, vol. II: xxii). If, however, the specialized branch of law and jurisprudence is a later development, we may be permitted to assign to it a date somewhat later than Yājñavalkya. A date between the fifth and sixth century CE may be reasonable.

Dharmaśāstra *of Parāśara*

The hypothesis of specialization within the Dharmaśāstra tradition is supported by the text ascribed to Parāśara. It has survived probably because it was the subject of the extensive commentary by Mādhava in the fourteenth century CE. The text is small, containing only 592 verses, and deals only with the two broad areas demarcated by Yājñavalkya: proper conduct (*ācāra*) and penance (*prāyaścitta*). The field of law and jurisprudence (*vyavahāra*) is left out.

Parāśara mentions both Manu and Yājñavalkya and presents itself as the *dharmaśāstra* most appropriate for the present Kali age, assigning Manu for Kṛta, Gautama for Tretā, and Śaṅkha-Likhita for Dvāpara. Throughout the text, further, there are references to the opinions of Manu. This kind of textual stratification, as well as the eulogy of the immolation of widows (*satī*), indicate a rather late date for Parāśara. The citation of a large number of verses from Parāśara in the *Garuḍa Purāṇa* (Chapter 107), which has been dated to the tenth century CE, and by Viśvarūpa (ninth century CE) provide a *terminus ante quem*. We may not be far off the mark in assigning it to a period between the seventh and eighth century CE.

Dharmasūtra *of the Vaikhānasas*

This text has received little attention since its edition and translation by Caland (1927, 1929). The section on *dharma* is embedded within the *Smārtasūtra*, which also contains the *Vaikhānasa Gṛhyasūtra*. Like the *Viṣṇu Dharmaśāstra*, this text was composed within a Vaiṣṇava community, here the Vaikhānasas. It has the hallmarks of a late composition. Caland placed it after the fourth century CE and drew attention to its dependence on Manu.

The Vaikhānasa has a strong ascetic bias. It gives classifications of forest hermits and wandering ascetics that are reminiscent of similar classifications in the Saṃnyāsa Upaniṣads (Olivelle 1992). It does not deal with many of the topics common to other *dharmaśāstras*, such as the duties of the king, law, judicial procedure, and penance, while giving prominence to the duties of the four *āśramas*. Its probable date can only be an educated guess, but placing it between the seventh and eighth century CE is reasonable.

EXTINCTION OF DHARMAŚĀSTRIC TEXTS

It is a fair assessment that in all likelihood close to 90 percent of all the literary products of the Dharmaśāstric tradition between the third century BCE and tenth century CE has been lost. Kane (1968–75, vol. I: 304) estimates that approximately one hundred *dharmaśāstras* are cited in the medieval commentaries and digests. Of these, we have only ten texts that we can be fairly certain have survived more or less in their original form. Large numbers of *smṛtis* exist in manuscripts coming from the medieval period; some of these have been printed in collections published in India. These, however, have the marks of very late collections of verses ascribed to various eponymous authors.

The reasons for this large-scale extinction of texts are unclear. As many scholars have noted, a text lacking an ancient commentary did not survive long. This is only a partial reason, because the extant *dharmasūtras* survived for well over a millennium without the benefit of commentaries, and we have numerous manuscripts of extant *dharmaśāstras* that have only the texts and not the commentaries. The voluminous commentaries and digests of the medieval period that presented topically arranged citations from the ancient texts may themselves have made experts less dependent on the original texts. We know that, given the climate of tropical India, manuscripts deteriorate fast, and if a text is not transcribed within a century or two it is likely to fall victim to decay and insects.

One may also question whether all the authors cited in medieval texts actually composed *dharmaśāstras*. There is a likelihood that at least some of the verses cited may have been floating in the collective memory of the expert tradition and not directly derived from manuscripts containing entire works on *dharma*. Nevertheless, much of what they cite comes from complete texts, for when we can check large quotations, such as those from the *dharmasūtras* and Viṣṇu, we see that they correspond exactly to the extant text.

Attempts have been made to reconstruct some of these lost *dharmaśāstras* by collecting the fragments found in medieval texts. The most successful of these have been the reconstructions of the texts ascribed to Bṛhaspati and Kātyāyana. Nevertheless, the arrangement of the fragments in these collections is done according to structures imposed by the editors. We are unable, therefore, to assess the way the original authors structured their discourses. It is also unclear whether what we have in these collections is the entirety of the original works, or even whether individual verses originally belonged to these texts or were misidentified by medieval authors who cited them.

Dharmaśāstra *of Bṛhaspati*

Jolly (1889) published a collection of 711 Bṛhaspati fragments pertaining to law and legal procedure.[27] He has demonstrated the close dependence of

[27] Rangaswami Aiyangar (1941a) prepared a new and larger collection of roughly 2,400 verses of Bṛhaspati dealing not only with law but also with other aspects of *dharma*.

Bṛhaspati on Manu; Bṛhaspati affirms that Manu's work is the most authoritative of all *dharmaśāstras*. Indeed, later tradition presents the work of Bṛhaspati as one more version of Manu.[28]

Although there are fragments of Bṛhaspati in medieval texts dealing with areas of *dharma* other than law and legal procedure, I share Jolly's (1889: 276) view that the text of Bṛhaspati, as those of Nārada and Kātyāyana, belonged to the specialized tradition focusing on *vyavahāra*, and that the original text probably contained only the *vyavahāra* section.

Whether Bṛhaspati is earlier or later than Nārada has been a matter of dispute. We may not be far wrong in assigning him a date not too distant from that of Nārada, that is, approximately between the fifth and sixth century CE.

Dharmaśāstra *of Kātyāyana*

Fragments of Kātyāyana's work on *vyavahāra* containing 973 verses were collected by Kane (1933), to which Rangaswami Aiyangar (1941b) added 121. Kātyāyana, like Nārada and Bṛhaspati, probably is a representative of the Dharmaśāstra tradition specializing in *vyavahāra*. He clearly depends on Manu and Yājñavalkya and, according to Kane (1968–75, vol. I: 501), presupposes both Nārada and Bṛhaspati. Viśvarūpa (ninth century CE) cites verses from Kātyāyana. Therefore, it is reasonable to date him to between the seventh and eighth century CE.

Kātyāyana presents a stage of development in the scholarly discourse on law and the legal process beyond that of Nārada and Bṛhaspati. Kane (1968–75, vol. I: 501) notes several new technical terms given by Kātyāyana. He devotes fifteen verses to corporate law and has a more extensive discussion (twenty-seven verses) of the property of women than any other Dharmaśāstric writer.

THE CANON OF *DHARMAŚĀSTRAS*

As I have already noted, the tradition was self-reflective about the genre of literature that is Dharmaśāstra. We have seen that early grammarians Kātyāyana and Patañjali, as well as Manu himself (*MDh* 2.10), refer to "*dharmaśāstra*" as a class of literature. The authors of *dharmasūtras* cite the opinions of other experts in *dharma*. The earliest canon of such texts,

[28] Jolly (1889: 274) gives the tradition recorded in the *Skanda Purāṇa* that there are four versions of Manu's *dharmaśāstra*: those of Bhṛgu, Nārada, Bṛhaspati, and Aṅgiras.

however, is found in Yājñavalkya (*YSm* 1.4–5) where a list of twenty authors of *dharmaśāstras* is given headed by Manu: Manu, Atri, Viṣṇu, Hārīta, Yājñavalkya, Uśanas, Aṅgiras, Yama, Āpastamba, Saṃvarta, Kātyāyana, Bṛhaspati, Parāśara, Vyāsa, Śaṅkha, Likhita, Dakṣa, Gautama, Śātātapa, and Vasiṣṭha.

Attention has been drawn to the anomaly of Yājñavalkya listing himself as one of the authors and to the anachronism in listing some, such as Parāśara and Kātyāyana, who are definitely later than Yājñavalkya. Many ingenious solutions have been offered; but the most straightforward one is to see these two verses as interpolations that have crept into the text from a commentary. It omits important early writers such as Baudhāyana and Nārada. Doubt regarding its authenticity comes also from an authoritative source; Medhātithi in his commentary on Manu (*MDh* 2.6) says that this list has no real authority. Even though he does not state it explicitly, it appears that he did not believe these verses to be the authentic words of Yājñavalkya.[29] Nevertheless, these verses must have entered the text at a very early date, because versions of these are recorded both by Viśvarūpa and in the *Garuḍa Purāṇa* (93.4–6).

Several other lists that attempt to produce a canon of *dharmaśāstras* are given in medieval texts. The *Aparārka* (on *YSm* 1.4–5) gives a list of thirty-six authors of *dharmaśāstras* ascribed to Gautama. The *Pādma Purāṇa* (Uttarakhaṇḍa 263.86–9) gives an interesting threefold classification of eighteen *smṛtis* into Sāttvika that leads to liberation, Rājasika that leads to heaven, and Tāmasika that leads to hell. The first group of six consists of Vasiṣṭha, Hārīta, Vyāsa, Parāśara, Bharadvāja, and Kaśyapa. The second: Yājñavalkya, Atri, Tittiri, Dakṣa, Kātyāyana, and Viṣṇu. The third: Gautama, Bṛhaspati, Saṃvarta, Yama, Śaṅkha, and Uśanas. Significantly, Manu, Āpastamba, Baudhāyana, and Kātyāyana are absent in this list.

With these reflections on the canon of Dharmaśāstra we enter the period of commentaries and digests, probably around the eighth or ninth century CE. Lingat (1973: 107) suggests that, given the supra-human character ascribed to the *dharmaśāstras* authored by ancient seers, "it seems more probable that a long interval elapsed between the publication of the last works appertaining to the *smṛti* category and the appearance of the first

[29] Medhātithi says: "*ata eva smartṛparigaṇanā manur viṣṇur yamo 'ṅgirā iti nirmūlā*" ("For the same reason, the list of *smṛti* authors 'Manu, Viṣṇu Yama, Aṅgiras . . . ' is unfounded." He refers to the fact that several acknowledged writers of *dharmaśāstras* such as Paiṭhīnasi, Baudhāyana, and Pracetas are not mentioned in Yājñavalkya's list. Although the beginning of the list cited by Medhātithi is different from the reading in the vulgate version of Yājñavalkya, Medhātithi's version is the one recorded in the *Garuḍa Purāṇa* 93.4–6 and Viśvarūpa's commentary.

commentaries." This is too idealistic a view regarding the motivations of authors. We know, for example, that *upaniṣads*, which as Vedic texts (*śruti*) had an even greater sanctity and transcendence than the *dharmaśāstras*, continued to be composed well into the late medieval period. *Dharmaśāstras* such as that of Devala, moreover, indicate a time well after the coming of Islam into India. It appears more probable that at least for several centuries commentaries, digests, and *dharmaśāstras* all continued to be composed by various individuals for a variety of purposes.

THE AGE OF COMMENTARIES AND DIGESTS

Most of the Sanskrit śāstric texts produced after the middle of the first millennium CE are in the form of commentaries. Even when they are not strictly speaking commentaries, like the Dharmaśāstric digests (*nibandhas*), they are set in the commentarial genre, citing and explaining authoritative texts. "Works of commentary," as Tubb has noted, "pervade the history of Sanskrit thought to a degree that is unparalleled in the writings of most other traditions" (Tubb and Boose 2007: 1).

There are four major commentators whose works have at least partially survived from the period between the eighth and tenth century CE: Asahāya, Bhāruci, Viśvarūpa, and Medhātithi. Fragments of Asahāya's commentary on Nārada have survived (Lariviere 1989a); and he is cited by both Viśvarūpa and Medhātithi. Bhāruci's commentary on Manu, only Chapters 6–12 of which survive, appears to have been used extensively by Medhātithi (Derrett 1967). There is no certainty or consensus about the dates of these two authors; we would not be far wrong, however, in assigning them to the eighth century CE.[30] Viśvarūpa's is the oldest surviving commentary on Yājñavalkya. His identity has been subject to some dispute, Kane (1968–75, vol. 1: 564) identifying him with the Advaita theologian Sureśvara, a pupil of Śaṅkara. This, however, is far from certain, although a date of early ninth century CE for Viśvarūpa appears reasonable. Medhātithi's is the most extensive and detailed commentary on Manu that has survived. He was probably from Kashmir and drew on earlier commentaries in composing his work, referring to several of his predecessors including Bhāruci, Bhartṛyajña, and Asahāya.

From the citations in the extant commentaries from the period, it is clear that many other commentaries and digests were composed between the

[30] Derrett's (1975, vol. 1: 10) date of 600–650 CE for Bhāruci is not completely borne out by the evidence he produces.

eighth and twelfth century.[31] The next major author whose work has survived, however, is Vijñāneśvara (early twelfth century). His scholarly and detailed commentary on Yājñavalkya called *Ṛjumitākṣarā*, or *Mitākṣarā* for short, became an authoritative text on law in medieval and modern India.[32] The other much less detailed commentary on Yājñavalkya is the *Aparārka* composed by or under the patronage of Aparāditya, a ruler from Konkan. He probably knew Vijñāneśvara's work and can be assigned to the twelfth century. Yājñavalkya was the focus of several other commentaries:[33] by Śūlapāṇi (*Dīpālikā*) in the fifteenth century and by Mitra Miśra in the seventeenth. Sub-commentaries on the *Mitākṣarā* were written until the nineteenth century when the *Bālambhaṭṭī* was written by Bālakṛṣṇa Pāyaguṇḍa, who worked for the British administrator Colebrooke.

Besides Bhāruci and Medhātithi, there are seven other extant commentaries on Manu written in the medieval period: Govindarāja (twelfth century), Sarvajña-Nārāyaṇa (twelfth–fourteenth century), Kullūka (fourteenth century), Rāghavānanda (fifteenth–sixteenth century), Nandana, Rāmacandra, and Maṇirāma (the last three rather late writers of uncertain date). Besides that of Asahāya, there is another commentary on Nārada written by Bhavasvāmin.[34] Commentaries were also written on the early *dharmasūtras*: by Haradatta (twelfth–fourteenth century) on Āpastamba and Gautama, by Maskarin on Gautama,[35] and by Govindasvāmin (date unclear) on Baudhāyana. Only Vasiṣṭha appears not to have attracted a commentary until the nineteenth century, when the Banaras pandit Kṛṣṇapaṇḍita wrote his commentary. The text of Viṣṇu also did not attract an early commentary; the commentary on it by Nandapaṇḍita was written in 1679 CE.

The text that presents itself as a commentary but has many of the characteristics of a legal digest is Mādhava's (fourteenth-century) commentary on Parāśara called *Pārāśaramādhavīya*, a voluminous work that contains large sections, principally on law and legal procedure, that are independent compositions.

The most common genre in which works on *dharma* were composed during the medieval period was not the commentary but the digest

[31] Kane (1968–75, vol. II) gives six such authors or works: Dhareśvara, Devasvāmin, Jitendriya, Bālaka, Bālarūpa, and Yogloka.

[32] This was facilitated for the colonial period by the adoption by the British authorities of the *Mitākṣarā* as authoritative for all of India in matters of inheritance, except in Bengal where Jīmūtavāhana's *Dāyabhāga* was considered authoritative.

[33] Kane (1968–75, vol. I: 1092) lists five other commentaries.

[34] Dated 750–1000 CE by Kane. Derrett (1975, vol. I: 14–16) thinks that he is even older than Bhāruci, based mostly on style.

[35] Maskarin's date is uncertain, although Derrett (1975, vol. I: 16) places him close to Bhāruci.

(*nibandha*), even though the commentaries themselves often digress from their root text and operate very much in the digest mode. The digest writers arrange their works according to topics and give copious citations from the *dharmaśāstras*, as well as from the *Mahābhārata* and the *purāṇas*, bearing on the topic, often with glosses and comments. The intent was to bring together authoritative sources bearing on a particular issue so as to present scriptural authorities in support of the author's views and interpretations. Indeed, there appears to have been a literary precedent for the digests; there were texts composed prior to the twelfth century that were probably anthologies of Dharmaśāstric pronouncements such as the frequently cited *Smṛtisaṃgraha* and the *Ṣaṭtriṃśanmata*.[36]

The earliest, largest, and best-known of the digests is Lakṣmīdhara's *Kṛtyakalpataru*, an encyclopedic work in fourteen parts, each devoted to a single topic of *dharma*, composed in the twelfth century. Similar encyclopedic works were composed by Devaṇṇabhaṭṭa (*Smṛticandrikā*, twelfth–thirteenth century), Hemādri (*Caturvargacintāmaṇi*, 1260–70), Caṇḍeśvara (*Smṛtiratnākara*, 1314–24), Nīlakaṇṭha (*Bhagavantabhāskara*, 1610–45), and others such as the *Madanaratna* (fifteenth century).

Other authors adopted a different strategy, writing monographic compositions on individual topics of *dharma*, such as purification, punishment, pilgrimage, legal procedure, funerals, ancestral offerings, gift giving, asceticism, and Vedic initiation. Examples of this genre are Mādhava's *Kālanirṇaya*, Varadarāja's *Vyavahāranirṇaya* (fifteenth century), Vācaspatimiśra's *Vivādacintāmaṇi* (fifteenth century), and Vardhamāna's *Daṇḍaviveka* (fifteenth century). The *Dāyabhāga*, the treatise on inheritance by Jīmūtavāhana (beginning of the twelfth century), occupies a special place in this genre because it was adopted by the British colonial courts as authoritative for Bengal.

Some of these digests, such as the *Smṛticandrikā*, are well-argued compositions, while others are simply compilations of citations. The total number of digests produced between the ninth century and modern time dealing with some aspect of *dharma* is immense. Kane (1968–75, vol. 1: 989–1,158) lists close to 5,000 texts that either exist in manuscript or are mentioned in existing texts.[37] Only a tiny fraction of this corpus has been edited or published.

[36] See Kane (1968–75, vol. 1: 535–41). Derrett (1975, vol. 1: 9) refers to a *Smṛtisārasamuccaya* ascribed to Bhāruci.

[37] I counted 4,847 separate entries, not counting the classical *dharmaśāstras* or the ritual texts such as the *gṛhyasūtras* (and their commentaries) that Kane lists. Even if we discount 10 percent of the entries as duplicates or spurious, still the entire corpus is immense, especially if we take into account the fact that Kane's list does not contain all the texts produced during this period, many of which may have perished without leaving any trace.

THE SOCIOLOGY OF TEXTUAL PRODUCTION

Why does someone spend time and energy to write a book? There is no simple or single answer to this; different reasons, including personal satisfaction and prestige, may have motivated different authors. Nevertheless, it seems likely that at least the more extensive digests may have had royal patrons and served political ends.

As opposed to commentaries, which follow a millennium-old tradition, the legal digests (*nibandha*) constitute a new genre of literature. The first and most prominent of the digests was composed by Lakṣmīdhara, who calls himself the "minister of war and peace" of King Govindacandra, ruler of Kanoj and Kāśī during the early part of the twelfth century. The introductory verses to this work make it clear that it was done under royal patronage; Lakṣmīdhara was probably the editor who supervised the work of pandits working under him on this gigantic literary project. He mentions his victory over an Islamic ruler named Hammīra, indicating that Islamic power was at least part of the political context of the time.

Likewise, Hemādri, who wrote the voluminous *Caturvargacintāmaṇi*, was in charge of the royal records of the Yādava king Mahādeva (1260–71). Mādhava was associated with the early Vijayanagara rulers. Indeed, many of the digest writers of medieval India were closely associated with rulers and probably worked under their patronage.

Taking Lakṣmīdhara as exemplary, S. Pollock (1993: 106) has presented the attractive hypothesis that it was written in the context of the Turkish invasion, "at the moment when the total form of the society was for the first time believed . . . to be threatened." Pollock also notes that the production of legal digests "almost perfectly follows the path of the advance of the Sultanate from the Doab to Devagiri to the Deccan (Lakṣmīdhara, Hemādri, Mādhava)." The presence of a threatening "other" or the need to consolidate power that is under threat is often the impetus to textual creation, especially the creation of authoritative or scriptural texts.

Another factor we would have to consider is the impact Islamic Sharia law may have had on the production of legal digests. Long before the British colonial courts sought to enforce "native laws on the natives," Islamic courts in areas under their jurisdiction used Hindu law when trying cases brought by Hindu litigants.[38] It is also clear that Sharia law was textualized in India at least by the thirteenth century and may have been used in court proceedings. What impact all this had on the Hindu rulers and their desire to

[38] See Eaton (1993, 2005: 145–50).

produce digests of Hindu law is a question that requires further research into court practices and textual production during the period of interaction between Islamic and Hindu states.

POSTSCRIPT: ON DATING THE *DHARMAŚĀSTRAS*

Kane's (1968–75) monumental encyclopedia has been the main source for scholars in dating the *dharmaśāstras*. Yet his methodology is subject to question. Lingat (1973: 123) shows a deep skepticism about the possibility of dating these texts: "In my own view almost insurmountable obstacles stand in the way of any solution being given to the chronological problem." He points out the pitfalls inherent in the methodologies used by scholars, such as the use of isolated words and advances of thought, practices, and procedures.

Nevertheless, if we are to use these texts, which provide a mine of information about society and social mores for historical purposes, it is imperative that they be dated at least hypothetically and provisionally within reasonable bounds. To date a text to a 400- or 500-year period serves no purpose.

First, we must grant that Lingat is correct in rejecting the criterion for dating based on the use of a single isolated term, such as *dīnāra* and *yavana*. Given the uncertainty of textual transmission, such criteria stand on flimsy foundations. The most reasonable method is to base dating on a cluster of factors that support each other. We must also recognize that the authors of these texts worked not in isolation but within an expert tradition; they show remarkable knowledge of the works of previous scholarship. It is, therefore, likely that once a major concept or legal development enters into that tradition, it is never ignored by later writers. Thus, for example, the notion of a sacred region ("Āryāvarta") whose language and mores are authoritative, a notion that arose in the second century BCE in the writings of the grammarian Patañjali and is reflected in Baudhāyana and Vasiṣṭha, could not be ignored by later writers. Its absence in Āpastamba and Gautama indicates that they were writing at a time prior to the invention of this concept, or at the least in a region where the concept was not yet current.

Likewise, the use of gold coins for transactions, including fines, indicates a time when gold coins were in circulation, probably in or after the second century CE. The prominence given to written documents over live witnesses also indicates a time frame later than texts which disregard documents in legal proceedings. In my new critical edition of the *Vaiṣṇava Dharmaśāstra* (Olivelle 2009) I have used its description of iconography to date and geographically locate this document (to seventh-century Kashmir).

If we are able to bring several of these and similar criteria to bear on a document, I think we can arrive at a plausible date, however provisional and tentative it may have to be. Hence, I give below hypothetical dates of the major *dharmaśāstras* based on the methodology outlined above:

Āpastamba	third century BCE
Gautama	early second century BCE
Baudhāyana[39]	mid to late second century BCE
Vasiṣṭha	first century BCE
Manu	second century CE
Yājñavalkya	fourth to fifth century
Nārada	fifth to sixth century
Bṛhaspati	fifth to sixth century
Viṣṇu	seventh century
Kātyāyana	seventh to eighth century
Parāśara	seventh to eighth century
Vaikhānasa	seventh to eighth century

[39] Here I refer only to what I have called Proto-Baudhāyana, namely the early part consisting of the first and most of the second books; see Olivelle (2000: 191).

CHAPTER 3

The practice of classical Hindu law

Axel Michaels

INTRODUCTION

To what extent has Hindu law been applied in the premodern juridical and legal procedure of South Asia? To what extent was the Dharmaśāstra an applied source of jurisdiction? These questions have puzzled and troubled many scholars of classical Hindu law.[1] Some scholars opine that the Dharmaśāstra is concerned with law cases decided by concerned bodies (corporate groups, administrative institutions of rulers, temple authorities): "There can be no doubt that the smriti rules were concerned with the practical administration of law" (John D. Mayne as quoted by L. Rocher 1978: 1,299). Other scholars believe that the Dharmaśāstra is purely or mostly concerned with moral and religious norms which have some but not a very close relationship to legal practice, or that the *smṛtis* did not embody the law of the land but were entirely scholarly texts or commentaries on ancient authoritative texts. It was also argued that Hindu law was administered on the basis of unwritten maxims, floating verses of rules preserved by memorization and partly written down into Sanskrit law books, most of them applicable to specific social groups and castes only, so that it should be understood as a record of regional customs but not just as legal codes or Brahmanical moral fantasies.

No doubt, with the exception of Warren Hastings's Judicial Plan of 1772, when Brahmin pandits were attached to Anglo-Indian courts and the Dharmaśāstra literature partly gained the status of legislation, classical Hindu law was never codified law *sensu stricto*. Although it is debated to what extent custom has influenced or even shaped classical Hindu law, it is now generally accepted that until 1772 Hindu law by and large was a local and regional affair, despite its cosmopolitan claims (see Chapter 1), and local

[1] See L. Rocher (1978: 1,299, and 1993), Lingat (1973), Lariviere (1997), and D. R. Davis (1999) for a summary of the discussion.

customs and regional laws have profoundly influenced the Brahmanical norms of the Dharmaśāstra. The Dharmaśāstra itself acknowledges that various laws are specific to country, family, lineage, castes, women, or even animals (*deśa-*, *kula-*, *jāti-*, *strī-*, or *paśudharma*) – the latter rather being a form of non-*dharma* (*MDh* 9.66). (Pre-modern) Hindu law therefore also incorporates many non-Brahmanical sources and is thus more than Dharmaśāstra. The word "*dharma*" does not even appear in a number of legal sources (D. R. Davis 2004a: 18).

The notion that Hindu law recognizes the laws of regions (*deśadharma*) is reaffirmed by Devaṇṇabhaṭṭa in his *Smṛticandrikā* (first half of the twelfth century):

> And Bṛhaspati [says]: By the twice-born of the South, the daughter of the maternal uncle is taken in marriage. In the Middle Country they work as laborers and artisans, and are beef-eaters; in the East men are fish-eaters, and the women addicted to adultery. In the North, women drink liquor [and] menstruating women can be touched by men. Uterine brothers take to wife the brother's wife when without a husband. He states the authoritativeness (*prāmāṇya*) of these [regional *dharmas*] by local ordinance (*deśa-vyavasthā*). And those dharmas propounded by country, caste, and families should be protected as such, lest the people be disturbed.
>
> And Devala [says]: The gods in whatever countries, the twice-born in whatever countries, the water in whatever countries, and the earth there too, whatever the [standard of] purity in such places, and whatever the practice (*ācāra*) of *dharma* – one should not despise those things, for such is *dharma* in those places. In whichever country, city, village, assembly of learned Brahmins (*traividya*), or town, whatever *dharma* has been ordained there, one should not abrogate.[2]

Thus, the *dharmaśāstrins*, the indigenous scholars of classical Hindu law, never wanted to record and codify all law applicable for all times. They accepted various sources and authorities, for instance the "four feet" of legal procedure (compare *NSm* 1.11–12, probably based on *ArthaŚ* 3.1.39–40): *dharma*, legal procedure (*vyavahāra*), custom (*caritra*), and the king's decree (*rājaśāsana*).[3] The king was obliged to respect the customary laws (*MDh* 8.3, 41, 46); if he would decide according to his personal predilection even though a (codified) norm or text exists, it would distract him from heaven (Kātyāyana 5.44).

[2] For older definitions of "*deśadharma*": *ĀpDhS* 1.7.20.6–7 (compare Lariviere 1989a, vol. 1: 5–6), *BDhS* 1.1.2.3 ff., *GDhS* 11.20, and *YSm* 2.1. See Wezler (1985) for further references.

[3] For a more profound discussion of this principle, see Lingat (1962), L. Rocher (1979), Lariviere (in *NSm* 1.5–6), and Lubin (2007: 98–100).

The concepts of custom (*ācāra, caritra*), moral "boundaries" (*maryādā*) or conventions (*samaya*), and other terms referring to local law have therefore become crucial for understanding Hindu law.[4] Some scholars even go so far as to say that custom was the only real law India had ever known, that the *dharmaśāstras* had nothing to do with law at all (Lingat 1973: 139 referring to H. Nelson), or that "the whole of the *dharma* corpus can be viewed as a record of custom" (Lariviere 1997: 98).

However, Donald R. Davis (2004a: 12–18 and Chapter 5) has aptly shown that all *ācāra* is *dharma* (even for the *dharmaśāstrins*), and that nothing has confused the discussion on Hindu law more than the vague conception of custom, and the lack of differentiation between custom, norm, standard, behavior, and customary law. I would not go so far as Davis and say that "Dharmaśāstra represents the theoretical jurisprudence of classical Hindu law, while ācāra, local law, is the basis for practical jurisprudence" (D. R. Davis 2004a: 13, n. 24), because the Dharmaśāstra, too, concerns practical jurisprudence even if this is not preserved in the texts themselves, and other sources prove that the Dharmaśāstra has been enforced by juridical, political, or religious authorities.[5] By way of being written down, published or publicized, standardized, and loaded with priestly or royal authority the rules of the Dharmaśāstra were often also transformed into local norms and customs. Both *ācāra* and *dharma* are acting within a given normative system and in an imagined moral society on the basis of more or less codified, written or oral, maxims for the conduct of social and religious life.

The agency for the decision between good and bad, acceptable and unacceptable, allowed and forbidden was often with respected and pure people, mostly with the Brahmins or representatives of the dominant castes (Cohn 1959). *Ācāra* was principally the custom of the good and learned (*sadācāra* or *śiṣṭācāra*). However, the elite's resolution of moral or legal problems and conflicts did not only depend on the Dharmaśāstra texts. Hindu law was not only "black-letter law" (Lariviere 1997: 101), in other words, written and printed texts, but also *lex non scripta*, orally transmitted law based on floating versified maxims and unwritten local norms (L. Rocher 1993). In fact, Hindu legal practice was often independent of the Sanskrit scriptures, as Mountstuart Elphinstone observed among

[4] For extensive elaborations on the relation between *dharma* and *ācāra* see G. Jha (1930: 33–7), Lingat (1973: 176–206), Derrett (1979: 25–50), D. R. Davis (2004a: 13 and 18). For a short survey of epigraphical invocations of *ācāra* as a basis for law, see Sircar (1984).

[5] See the chapter by Lubin in this volume.

the Marathas: "The Hindoo Law was quite disused, probably owing to its absurdity; and, although every man is tolerably acquainted with its rules in civil cases, I do not believe that anyone but the very learned has the least notion of its criminal enactments" (Elphinstone 1821: 53).

Given these facts, the history of legal practice of classical Hindu law must include other sources and material than the Sanskrit texts of the Dharmaśāstra. It must refer to evidences of legal or juridical conflicts, cases that had to be decided, and to legal procedure as practiced in the regions. The following is an attempt to gather such material from various sources and regions. Due to the lack of research in this field, it cannot be more than an assembly of fragments. I will focus on only a few regions (Nepal, Kerala, Maharasthra, and Tamil Nadu) and concentrate on law cases, in other words moral or legal conflicts (*vivāda*) which had to be decided by authoritative persons or bodies, leaving mostly aside norms that chiefly (though by no means exclusively) concern the individual, namely norms regarding impurity (*aśauca*), life-cycle stages (*āśrama*) and rituals (*saṃskāra*), festivals (*utsava*), pilgrimages (*tīrthayātrā*), sacrifices, asceticism, vows (*vrata*), and so on – institutions that all form a part of the Dharmaśāstra.

SOURCE MATERIAL

Owing to the paucity of historical material regarding the application of Hindu law and legal practice in general it is easier said than done to write the history of legal practice in South Asia: "Next to nothing is known about actual legal practice in ancient India" (L. Rocher 1978: 1,302). Legal cases were hardly ever recorded and, if they were, the minutes or written decisions have not survived due to the fugacity of the material. The same holds true for judgments (*jayapattra*) in earlier times.[6] On the other hand, it is mentioned in an inscription of the fifth century CE (EI 31: 6) that grants were written on "leaves of the Palmyra tree" (*tālapattra*). There are also references to court files written on cloth or palm leaves:[7] "the evidence (*pramāṇa*) (of a land donation) should be furnished with (the king's) own seal, written (*likhita*) on a piece of cloth (*paṭī*) or on a copper plate (*tāmrapaṭṭa*)" (*VDh* 3.81–83).[8] However, almost all this material has decayed.

[6] Kane (1968–75, vol. III: 381); for comparatively early *jayapattras* (dated 829 CE), see Jayaswal (1920); for a later document of this type, see Lariviere (1984).

[7] See Sircar (1965: 61 f.), Sharma (1966: 104), Njammasch (1984: 108).

[8] Compare *YSm* 1.317–19, *BSm* 3.12–17; see the next section.

The early written material that did not perish reflects the legal practice of Hindu law somewhat asymmetrically. It is dominated by royal material and deals mostly with cases of land sales, mortgages, the law of obligations (contracts, pledges, donations, and treaties), and diplomatic documents. Documents pertaining to criminal law as well as private, personal, or family law are missing or comparatively late. The fragile paper documents are supplemented by a number of inscriptions and early colonial, missionary, or anthropological reports.

Inscriptions

Until today no systematic study of the legal practice as reflected in the rich inscriptional material of South Asia has been produced.[9] As it seems, in some cases the epigraphical records supplement legal problems that are dealt with in the normative texts of the Dharmaśāstra.

The majority of such inscriptions relates to land donations mentioning the lands and property rights conferred, the donor, and the recipient. Occasionally, however, one also encounters resolutions of disputes over land tenure (e.g., SII 20, nos. 24 and 232).

The second largest number of inscriptions probably concerns royal edicts (e.g., Derrett 1968: 169, 188–95; Sircar 1966), which are linked to various public or administrational affairs but rarely imply aspects of criminal law. However, in some cases such as the Lāhaḍapura inscription (Sircar 1974: 82–7), criminal law was enforced by recording a *saṃvid* (decree), declaring the penalties imposed on thieves by a council of Brahmins (EI 32: 305–9). Similarly, such a decree has enforced the "gift of the daughter" (*kanyādāna*) form of marriage (SII 1, no. 56; Lubin in press and p. 151 below), and recorded punishments by corporate groups (D. R. Davis 2005: 107 ff.).

Although inscriptions seldom cite Dharmaśāstra texts verbatim – as, for instance, the Nellore inscription (SII 5, no. 496) does the *Mānava Dharmaśāstra* (D. R. Davis 2005: 107) – they do have a direct bearing on śāstric vocabulary and conceptions. More often inscriptions mention local customs (*ācāra*) – the most prominent inscription being perhaps the charter of Viṣṇuṣena with a list of seventy-two customs (*ācāra*) current in western India in the sixth century (EI 30: 163–81; and Lubin's chapter in this volume).

[9] Cursory reviews can be found in Sircar (1974), Derrett (1968: 162, 168, 188–91, and 1979: 47 ff. and 76 ff.), Njammasch (1984), Salomon (1998: 251), D. R. Davis (2005: 102–11), and Mathur (2007).

Another important aspect of inscriptions concerns temple affairs and regulations. They mostly have to do with gifts and donations to religious institutions. Thus, in an inscription from the Sangli District in Maharashtra, dated 1143/4 CE (EI 19.4B), one finds, for instance, a conventional decree (*śāsanamaryādā*) regarding the collection of wealth for a temple. Numerous inscriptions have to do with temple renovations, organizing festivals or rituals and other acts of religious virtue (*dharmakārya*). Such epigraphic documents testify and contribute to the political integration and legitimating of a given ruler or social group, especially by pilgrimages that are organized for and around the temples.

Documents and formularies

From early on, written documents were considered to provide more evidence than oral testimonials: "It is said everywhere that only documents (*lekhya*) are stronger (evidence) than words of witnesses" (*SmC* 3.1, p. 151).[10] Such documents in legal procedure of Hindu law were accepted on the basis of the theory of the threefold evidence (*trividha-pramāṇa*) as given in the *nibandhas* and developed in the section on the settlement of debts (*ṛṇadāna*): written document (*lekhya*), witness (*sākṣin*), and possession (*bhukti*). Legal procedure therefore is based on the law of obligation. However, the early *dharmasūtras* do not acknowledge written documents in legal procedure.[11] This also holds true for the *Mānava Dharmaśāstra* and the *Arthaśāstra* of Kauṭilya, although writing is known to them. *MDh* 9.232, for instance, mentions forgery of documents, and the *Arthaśāstra* (*ArthaŚ* 2.20) dedicates a whole chapter to certificates or royal edicts (*śāsana*) without mentioning written documents in civil or personal law.[12] The *Yājñavalkya Smṛti* (*YSm* 2.84–94 and 1.318–20), *Nārada Smṛti* (*NSm* 1.115–26), and *Viṣṇu Smṛti* (*VDh* 7.1–13) mention written documents in public or private law. The Dharmaśāstra texts, especially the *Bṛhaspati Smṛti* (*BSm* 1.6.4–5), *Vyāsa Smṛti* (as quoted in *DhK* 374–777), and *Vasiṣṭha Dharmaśūtra* (*VDhS* 16.10–15; compare attributed passages in *DhK* 348), contain elaborate references to documents.

10 See Strauch (2002: 19–52) for an excellent excursus on the development of legal documents in medieval India. The following is basically a summary of his findings.

11 Strauch (2002: 51) proves the only exception (*VDhS* 16.10) to be an interpolation. On the *dharmasūtras* see Olivelle's chapter in this volume.

12 According to Strauch (2002: 32–5), neither *deśa* nor *karaṇa* can be understood as written evidence (*lekha*).

Legal documents can therefore be found in large numbers in various public, private, and temple collections.[13] The early period is primarily preserved on copper and gold plates (*tāmra-* and *suvarṇapatra*). Since the close of the eighteenth century, more and more paper documents (*lekha*, in Nepal mostly native rice paper) have replaced stone inscriptions and copper or gold plates. Early documents, especially land deeds with clay seals, are often preserved on palm leaves.

The great variety of legal and administrative documents[14] covers royal orders or edicts which often bear the seal of the king (*rājadeśa*, *rājaśāsana*, Nep. *lālmohor*); orders or notifications (*vijñaptikā*, Hindi *sanad*, Nep. *rukkā*, Arab. *ruq'a*) from the Prime Minister or other officials which often bear another symbol such as a sword symbol (Nep. *khaḍganisāna*); land grants or sales (*bhūmidānapatra*, *bhūmikrayapatra*, and *vikrayapatra*); deeds of donation and beneficiary deeds (*śāsana*, *dānapatra*); pawn obligations (*valitapatra*, *bhogabandha*); debt obligations (*vyavahārapatra*, Nep. *bharpāi*); tax assessments (*paṭṭaka*); writs and orders (*ājñālekha*); documents relating to ordeals (*dharmacīrikā*, *divya*, *kriyā*); applications laid before a judge (*patra*, Arab. *maḥzar*); judgments or decisions (*jayapatra*, *nyāyavāda*, Mar. *nivāḍapatra*); letters of appointment (*nīrūpaṇā*); balance sheets, lists (*vyaya*, *sucīpatra*, *ṭippaṇa*, *upagatā*, Nep. *bahi*); contracts and receipts (Urdu, Nep. *tamsuk*); travel documents and permits (*deśottāra*, *gacchampatra*, *bahirpatra*); letters and petitions (*pattra* / *patra* / *pātra*, *bintipatra*); or (voluntary) declarations of sins (*doṣapatra*, *chitrapātra*) and letters of rehabilitation (Nep. *purji*).

The vast majority of these documents has not yet been published, let alone sufficiently studied, though it seems that some regions are better dealt with than others. In Nepal,[15] for instance, only a few documents of the Malla and Śāha periods, dealing mainly with documents on certain Buddhist monasteries (Rudravarṇa Mahāvihāra), Hindu temples (Paśupatinātha), or certain regions (Mustang, Tharu), have been published and analyzed. Other documents such as royal orders (*lālmohor*) (Dangol 1991–2) or official letters (*ciṭhṭhī*) (Śarmā 2000) have been edited, but not adequately explored. A systematic catalogue of approximately one thousand Malla documents (1299–1774) is to be published by Mahes Raj Pant. The thousands of Śāha documents (1768 to the present day) have so far not been recorded systematically.

[13] For bibliographies see Sen and Mishra (1951) and Strauch (2002).

[14] The *Lekhapaddhati* mentions in its introduction forty-six public and private forms of documents and adds seventeen further categories. See the glossaries of Gune (1953: xxii–xxvii) and Strauch (2002: 486) for more indigenous document terms. See also Thakur (1927–8).

[15] See, for instance, Kölver and Śākya (1985), Michaels (1994: 328–80), Pant (2002), Regmi (1965–6).

In Kerala over a million documents are preserved, dating back to the fourteenth century. But only some collections containing the records and chronicles from various temples have been brought to the public (see D. R. Davis 2004a: 30–2): *Vanjeri Grandhavari* (M. Narayanan 1987), *Koodali Granthavari* (Kurup 1995), *Chronicles of the Trivandrum Pagoda* (Maheshwaran Nair n.d.), and *Peruvanaṃ Kṣetra Granthavari* (Krishna Varier 1979). Similar documents have been published in modern historical works: Logan (1887), *The Travancore State Manual* (Velu Pillai 1940, vol. II), and Krishna Ayyar (1938). A valuable source is also the collection of letters and records by the German missionary Hermann Gundert, *Talaśśēri Rēkhakaḷ* (Skariah 1996). The Vanjeri records are mostly mortgages, contracts of loans or land tenures, statements of accounts, or other civil transactions between two parties. The Tellicherry documents contain a great deal of information on criminal law. Texts like the *Laghudharmaprakāśikā*, alias *Śāṅkara Smṛti* (seventeenth century), contain Kerala-specific customs and sixty-four "wrong practices" (*anācāras*) of Kerala Nambudiri Brahmins that deviate from the normal Dharmaśāstra rules (D. R. Davis 1999: 164).

In Maharashtra, only the judicial institutions of the Marathas have been studied, especially by Mountstuart Elphinstone (1821) and Vithal Trimbak Gune (1953, see below). Gune provides the analysis of 616 judicial *maḥzars* (public attestations or statements laid before a judge) and deeds or other documents (*nivāḍapatra*, *watanpatra*), 260 orders pertaining to crimes and punishments of criminal cases, and 46 documents pertaining to sins and expiations. Chronologically the subject is focused on the periods between Shivaji and his successors (1550–1750) and the rule of the Peshwas (1750–1818), when the Maratha power came to an end. Gune's study deals with historical development, constitution, and functioning of the royal institutions of justice as well as the indigenous or popular legal structures, processes for the prevention of crime and apprehension of the criminals, and punishments and expiations. The book also contains information on land revenue and the administrative institutions. It is shown how far the judicial institutions in the seventeenth and eighteenth centuries in Maharashtra had maintained continuity with the ancient Hindu traditions and to what extent they were influenced by the Muslim institutions of the immediate past. Further editorial and analytical work on such documents remains a desideratum (see also O'Hanlon 2009).

Broadly speaking, these legal texts distinguish between public or royal (*rājakīya*) and private (*jānapada*, *laukika*) law (Pant 1997: 183). Gune (1953: xv) differentiates between judicial and administrative documents. However, it seems more adequate not to make such separations because many documents refer to public and private, judicial and administrative contexts.

Standards of written documents and records often resemble Dharmaśāstra norms. Such accordance has been shown for land sales (D. R. Davis 1999: 184, 2004a: 58–62; Kölver and Śākya 1985), usufruct mortgages vis-à-vis *bhogyādhi* mortgage (D. R. Davis 1999: 168–70, 2004a: 62–8), slavery (Jayaswal 1920; Pant 1997), or diplomatic documents.[16] Many documents are based on forms and styles compiled in Sanskrit texts such as the *Lekhapaddhati*, Vararuci's *Patrakaumudī*, Dalapatirāya's *Praśastiratnākara*, Bālakṛṣṇa Tripāṭhin's *Praśastikāśikā*, or Vidyāpati's *Likhanāvalī* (see I. Jha 1969).

Similar to medieval documents in Europe, Indian documents are mostly divided into three parts following formal elements, which, however, need not appear all together or in the sequence given here.[17]

The introductory part could cover *invocatio*: an invocation of a favored deity (e.g., *śrī*); *apprecatio*: an initial auspicious word or symbol (e.g., *oṃ*, *śrī*, *śubham*); *benedictio*: a benediction or sign of auspiciousness (*maṅgala*: e.g., *siddhiḥ* or *svasti*); *intitulatio*: name and title of the sender (*uddeśaka*), often together with his father's name and title or even genealogies – in land-sale documents of medieval Kerala, the parties' younger brothers also had to be mentioned (D. R. Davis 2004a: 60 f.); where the king or his representatives issue the document, the *intitulatio* is expressed by the *praśasti* or *prakīrti*, eulogist formulas that are often in Sanskrit and follow a certain scheme known from inscriptions (Horstmann 1998); *inscriptio*: name and title of the addressee (*uddeśya*), often together with his father's name and title; *salutatio*: expressions for the addressee's well-being (*kuśalalekhana*); in letters the addressee often precedes the sender. Between *invocatio* or *benedictio* and the main text, a stamp or seal of the issuing body was sometimes used.

The main part (*textus* or *contextus*) could contain the content of the document, i.e., *narratio*: narratives of the offence and information on what the document is about, sometimes with references to the history of the case, names of the parties and others involved, amount of the loan and interest; *dispositio*: decision of the case and mention of the punishment ordered; *sanctio*: threat of punishment, penalties, or force in case the *dispositio* is not followed; *corroboratio*: names of the witnesses (*sākṣin*) and consenting neighbors in case of documents written by another person (*anyakṛta*); documents written by one's own hand (*svahastakṛta*) did not have to be witnessed. For most documents three witnesses were required.[18]

[16] See the special issue of *The Indian Historical Review Journal*, vol. xxv (1998).

[17] Compare Gune (1953: 135–6) for judicial documents (*maḥzars*), as well as D. R. Davis for land sales (1999: 173 and 2004a: 53), and Kölver and Śākya (1985: 31 ff.) and D. R. Davis (2004a: 66) for mortgages.

[18] On witnesses see also Kane (1968–75, vol. III: 330–60) and Kölver and Śākya (1985: 48–51).

The final part (*eschatocol*) could include *subscriptio*: signatures (*mata*) of the parties or stamps, sometimes the name of the scribe is also mentioned; *apprecatio*: blessings (e.g., *śrīḥ*, *śubham*, "hail"), authoritative confirmations (e.g., *pramāṇa*) or liability clauses in order to avoid any obstacles; *eschatocol*: date and place where the document was issued, sometimes together with astronomical details; these data are often also mentioned in the beginning of a document; *particularia* (Arab. *tafṣīl*, Nep. *tapasil*): particulars and details about the fines and fees, or the location, size, and delimitation of plots (in land deeds and mortgages).

Colonial, missionary, and anthropological reports

Further valuable sources on the history of legal practice are pre- or para-colonial or missionary reports of travelers, missionaries, and officials, or the highly underestimated field of legal anthropology. Malinowski (1926) was the first to point out that there is law in so-called primitive societies, and Lawrence Rosen's study of Islamic law (1989) is a model of what one would wish to have for India. However, most anthropologists have not focused on such themes, which would build a counterpoint against the dominance of legislation and written law texts. This is also due to the fact that research on Hindu law was for a long time dominated by the textually based works of J. Jolly, P. V. Kane, and J. D. M. Derrett, which, however admirable in their own right, left little space for an anthropological approach.

The most valuable sources for the study of such material are the early gazetteers and reports of colonial officials. An important source is, for instance, Elphinstone's report on the legal practice at the Marathas between 1798 and 1818, in which he describes the revenue system as well as the police, and the criminal and civil justice systems (Elphinstone 1821). Among missionaries, one could mention as more or less reliable witnesses of the legal practice Hermann Gundert (D. R. Davis 2004a: 31), whose collection of letters and reports have been mentioned above; Father Jean Venant Bouchet (early eighteenth century), who pointed out early on that custom takes precedence over legal manuals in Hindu law (L. Rocher 1984a and 1993: 261; Clooney 2005); or the Abbé Dubois (1765–1848), who gave a fair account of the administration of civil and criminal justice in the Madras Presidency (Dubois 1897: Chapter 8).

Among the more recent anthropologists Bernard S. Cohn should be especially mentioned, who in the mid-twentieth century published seminal articles based on fieldwork observations in North India (Cohn 1952–54, 1959), which most likely reflect many legal practices of older times.

LATE MEDIEVAL AND EARLY MODERN HINDU LAW IN PRACTICE: AN OVERVIEW

Given the scarcity of edited and analyzed material, it is still impossible to write a reliable history of legal practice of Hindu law. The following can therefore be no more than a rough sketch, concentrating on the sixteenth to mid-nineteenth centuries. More detailed accounts can be found in studies on some regions and periods, such as in Maharashtra, Nepal, or Kerala (see below). These regional systems – "Mahārāṣṭra-," "Nepāla-," or "Kerala-dharma," i.e., *dharma*s specific to the particular regions (see S. Guha 1995: 103) – should not be taken as representative for the whole of South Asia.

If one speaks of Hindu legal practice, one has to differentiate between the political, religious, and social aspects of law and its bodies. It then becomes evident that the political and social realms are also religious and, to a more limited extent, vice versa. The individual was a citizen or member of a state, religious community, village or neighborhood, caste, kin group, lineage, or family. Conflicts were resolved within the concerned bodies and corporate guilds,[19] such as the royal institutions (*rājasabhā*, *dharmasabhā*), district institutions of the rulers (*gotasabhā*), temple authorities or religious institutions (e.g., *brahmasabhā*, *saṅgha*, *maṭha*), village councils (e.g., *pañcāyat*), caste or clan organizations (*jātisabhā*, Nep. *guṭhī*), kin groups, military units, and neighborhoods, or they were decided by clan or family elders. In many cases it was the whole village with an arbitrator that ended a conflict, and the village members accepted the resolution. The weight of the arbitrator was higher the more learned he was, especially if he could claim Vedic authority, so that in many cases the *śāstra* became local law (D. R. Davis 1999: 194).

The ruler had to execute or supervise what was often decided in bodies that were not directly under his jurisdiction. The king, however, did not accuse himself. There were no offences for which proceedings were brought directly by the royal or public prosecutor's department. Individuals made complaints to various institutions and then action was taken. According to the Dharmaśāstra, a king should never initiate lawsuits (*MDh* 8.43). In most cases, he had to respect, endorse, or add his imprimatur to the resolutions and decisions of diverse courts and councils. Normally his authority and

19 Indigenous terms: "*saṅgha*" (*ArthaŚ* 3.7), "*samūha*" (*YSm* 2.192), "*naigama*" (*YSm* 2.192), "*samaya*" (Subrahmanya Aiyar 1954–5); for an extensive discussion of the importance of corporate groups such as merchants, traders, religious specialists, soldiers, etc., for the creation and administration of law, see Majumdar (1969) and D. R. Davis (2005).

power was not even invoked in religious or caste matters, but he could interfere with the decisions if he wanted. He was more a symbol of supremacy and command than a legislator. Moreover, royal legal practice often was independent of the written law. It sometimes was arbitrary and subject to power interests.

The territorial power of the supra-regional ruler was mainly guaranteed through the loyalty of more or less dependent regional and local rulers and their little kingdoms, as well as through feudal land tenures given to individuals. Brahmins and high-caste officials in the districts (Pers. *paragaṇā*, Arab. *tarf*, Nep. *adālat*, Mal. *nāṭu* and *deśaṃ*) and villages were commonly entrusted with such privileges, which often also entailed executive rights. Frequently such positions were hereditary.

The (royal) courts and councils – *pariṣad*, (*rāja-*, *dharma-*)*sabhā*, *svarūpa*, Mal. *yogaṃ*, Arab. *majlis* – had jurisdiction over legal, judicial, administrative, religious, and social problems. The composition of a district court[20] could involve the head of the district or governor (Mar. *deśamukha*, *deśapāṇḍe*, Mal. *deśakoyma*), Hindu or Muslim law officers (*dharmādhikārin*, *smārta*, *maulavī*, *qāzī*), the presiding priest (*purohita*), other district officers (Mal. *nāṭu-* or *dēśvalī*) or representatives of the king (*rājapratinidhi*), the investigators (*mīmāṃsaka*), the village headman (*grāmapati*, *pāṭil*), the village record keeper (*kulakarṇi*, *kāyastha*), land holders and liege lords (*jāgirdār*), elders, and common people. These functionaries were the judges (*prāḍvivāka*, *adhyakṣa*, *sabhāpati*, *dharmādhikārin*); individual (or even independent) judges were exceptional.

In most regions, temples with tutelary deities or special links to the palace functioned as courts. It was the place where Brahmins ruled and where the deities could be included as witnesses. However, the execution mostly did not take place in the temple but in the palace or at the king's offices. "Courts ... were not institutions, they were events" (D. R. Davis 2004a: 82). Most medieval states did not have a standardized court system and special law-court buildings. However, in the old Madras Archives there is repeated mention of the "Justices of the Choultry." A building of this kind, a resting place for travelers and public forum, served also as a venue for courts of law. Otherwise, cases were resolved in the king's palace, the temple, the governor's office, or simply on the central village places, depending on the matter and severity.

Hindu kings, as the upholders of the *dharma*, and the royal and district courts ruled with the help of a number of religious advisers. The sacramental

[20] See, for instance, *LDhP* 8.1, Lubin (2007: 112–15), Gune (1953: 123).

bond between the king and his priest is best seen in the jurisdiction. It was mostly the learned Brahmin who advised the king on matters of Hindu law and the interpretation or application of the Dharmaśāstra. However, the status of the Brahmin as a legal adviser was claimed and contested by at least three religious functionaries: the royal chaplain or *paṇḍita* preceptor (*rājapurohita*), the *paṇḍita* minister, and the *paṇḍita* judge (*dharmādhikārin*) (Michaels 2001, 2005). Among the criteria most mentioned for such advisers are Brahminhood, good conduct (*sadācāra*, *śīla*), and learning (*śiṣṭa*, *paṇḍita*), the latter basically characterized by the knowledge of the Veda and the Dharmaśāstra. In many kingdoms, the Brahmin priest of the royal family (*purohita*, *rājaguru*), the main adviser for the king in religious matters, was more and more supplanted by the *paṇḍita* who did not necessarily occupy a hereditary post, but acquired the status of a minister or high officer. Both *purohita* and *paṇḍita* were considered supporters of the kingdom, but the *purohita* was basically a priest, spiritual preceptor, and teacher (*guru*) to the king, while the *paṇḍita* was a minister or judicial functionary, sometimes even a judge (*sabhya*: *MDh* 8.9; *YSm* 2.2–4). To be sure, the *purohita* had a number of political and administrative duties such as adjudication in cases where penances had to be prescribed, or supporting the king and his soldiers in the war by, for instance, consecrating the weapons, elephants, and horses in the state army. One sometimes therefore finds the *purohita* listed among the ministers (*amātya*, *mantrin*), but "according to most authorities he played a role that was pre-eminently religious" (Kane 1968–75, vol. III: 119).

At the village level, depending on the severity of the case, it was the local officer who set the judicial machinery in motion and saw that the concerned court or council tried cases properly. In some regions, the village and often caste-based *pañcāyat* functioned as the most important council. It consisted of three to fifteen members headed by a headman (*mukhya*, Arab./Nep. *ḥākim*), nominated by the king, governor, or village elders, or agreed upon by the conflicting parties.

In disputes relating to property (Derrett 1962a), resolution of conflicts mostly took place in councils consisting of members of the same caste, but not in lower castes because mortgage and sales of land were elite transactions. Apparently many guilds and other corporate groups had their own arbitral courts (D. R. Davis 2005).

In religious and moral matters – in cases of violation of personal law or religious norms – it was often a kind of religious court (*brahmasabhā*, *pariṣad*: Lingat 1973: 14–16) of more or less learned Brahmins (*brahmasabhā*) which administered and decided on penances (Lubin 2007; Michaels 2005; O'Hanlon 2009). A chief judge occasionally called "*dharmādhikārin*" headed it. The *brahmasabhā* and also caste councils (*jātisabhā*) could expel individuals from their caste on grounds of impurity or impose fees and other sanctions.

Little is known about the court or council procedures. One can assume that it was a peculiar combination of customary law and the requirements of practical life. During the course of the trial, more importance was given to the satisfaction of the aggrieved party than to the rules of the procedure and law. Judgments were not based on a mere application of written law books or standardized moral maxims. They were tailored to the circumstances of the case, taking the special persons, facts, and power relations into consideration. Any case, thus, "was a unique event and not a rote application of a penal code" (D. R. Davis 2004a: 88). This was in accordance with the Dharmaśāstra, for the king also had to consider the ability of the criminals and the severity of the crime (*MDh* 8.126). The course of a case followed the usual scheme of complaint or apprehension, trial, judgment (*parihāra*), and punishment (*daṇḍa*). There was no such institution as defense lawyers.

A trial for adultery that might give a fairly true picture of the procedure in court cases in late medieval Kerala is described in the *Laghudharmaprakāśikā* (8.1, see Lubin 2007: 109–12): The plaintiff brings the case directly before the king asking him to preserve the *dharma*. The king then sends a Brahmin representative, a Brahmin adviser (*smārta*), and four investigators. The trial itself takes place in the house of the plaintiff. The investigators (*mīmāṃsaka*), the *smārta*, and the royal representative (*rājapratinidhi*) enter the house in order to question the accused woman. They remain hidden behind a wall, and the royal representative keeps his head covered by a veil throughout the procedure unless an inappropriate or impertinent question is asked. After the investigation the *smārta* informs the royal representative of his conclusion and reports to the king while the royal representative monitors the accuracy of the report but mostly keeps silent. Only if he dissents does he interfere with a gesture of disapproval, for instance by dropping his veil. By this procedure and by involving the Brahmin adviser as a de facto judge, the king fulfills his duties as protector of the *dharma*.

Evidence in a trial was provided by written or oral testimonies, and a system of ordeals. Especially important were witnesses (*sākṣin*) whose statements were examined and often taken down in writing. Torture was sometimes employed to make the culprit confess and compel the disclosure of accomplices (Elphinstone 1921: 51).

As it seems, the right to inflict punishment was often exercised by influential people or members of the dominant castes. In severe cases, however, punishment (*daṇḍa*) was a matter for the king. It was up to him to execute capital and corporal punishments (*YSm* 1.359), to arrest, to collect fines and fees, but it was more the responsibility of the temple or caste authorities to excommunicate individuals from caste and to impose penances (D. R. Davis 2004a: 90–4; S. Guha 1995). The account of the *Śukranīti* (B. K. Sarkar 1923: 130) on forms of punishment is probably close to reality: "The various species of methods of punishment are the policies of censure, insult, starvation, imprisonment, oppression, destruction of goods, expulsion from the city, marking the body, shaving of half portions of the body, carrying the persons over ignoble animals (e.g., asses), mutilation, execution as well as warfare." In general, punishments were a mixture of power demonstration, compensation and moral or social rehabilitation (*prāyaścitta*). Except for certain fees, there were hardly any standardized forms of punishments. Thus, social ranking and standing or wealth influenced the form and severity of punishment. Fees were levied according to the capacity of the party before the execution of the decision and if the party was unable to pay them orders were issued to the local officers concerned, to execute the decision and recover the dues later by installments. Parties were not required to pay any court fees at the time of filing a suit or during the trial. Many fees, especially for penances, went to temples rather than the palace (D. R. Davis 2004a: 119; Michaels 2005: 43–50).

After going through the punishment ordered by the government, the offender was often required additionally to purge himself of his sin by performing penances. Only then could he rejoin his family.

In reality, an appeal against a judgment was almost impossible notwithstanding other rules in the Dharmaśāstra.[21] However, there were different courts with differing responsibilities. The final decision remained with the king. In some regions it happened that individuals protested against a resolution or punishment by public fasting ritual (Hindi *dharnā*, Mal. *paṭṭini*), or by petitioning to submit to an ordeal.

REGIONAL LEGAL SYSTEMS

The Marathas

Rarely has a regional judicial system been better studied than the system of the Marathas, which is particularly interesting because it replaced the administrative and legal practices of the Mughal rulers and the sultans

[21] *BSm* 1.29–30, *Mitākṣarā* on *YSm* 2.30; Jolly (1896: 136).

by Sanskrit traditions in law and politics (S. Guha 1995; Gune 1953; Lubin 2007: 112–13). This is mainly due to Vithal Trimbak Gune's masterful study, *The Judicial System of the Marathas* (1953), a book that is extremely valuable for the history of Hindu jurisprudence during the medieval period.

Hindu law was mainly (re)established by Śivājī who enthroned himself in 1764 with Vedic rituals but reconstructed the judicial system of the Islamic Bahmani Sultanate, which basically remained unchanged until the end of the Maratha kingdom. Śivājī's juridical system entailed a number of political, social, and religious institutions. The king was the executive authority, and a symbol of power and the *dharma*. He followed the advice of his various courts or assemblies (*sabhā*, Mar. *majlis*) distributed over several territorial communities (Mar. *gotā*): *rājamaṇḍala* or *dharmasabhā*, an administrative and judiciary body replacing the old *rakhtākhānā*, the central government and court of the Sultanate, which was convoked in major cases and sometimes presided over by Śivājī himself; the *dharmasabhā*, locally better known by its old name *huzūr hāzir majlis*, an assembly of up to 238 members from the *rājamaṇḍala* and the *gotā* that heard suits; the *brahmāsabhā*, an assembly composed of learned Brahmins and presided over by a chief (religious) judge or public censor (*dharmādhikārī*) responsible for personal, social, and religious law cases and administering penances (*prāyaścitta*); and the *jātisabhā*, an assembly that had jurisdiction over matters pertaining to castes and community.

The legal process during the rule of the Peshwas in Maharasthra has been summarized thus (Gune 1953: 128):

> The government officer summoned the members of the *Panchayat*. The final award of the members of the *Panchayat* was known as "Saramsa" (summary of the decision). The *Saramsa* was then approved by the public officer concerned and the *Nivadpatra* was issued, in favour of the successful party from the secretariat, after receiving the government fees for the same. The names of the Panchas were never recorded in the *Nivadpatra* nor was their attestation necessary. The *Nivadpatra* was thus purely a royal document, whereas the *Mahzar* as seen above was rather a popular document and the sanction of the people was behind it. Thus it seems that the concentration of justice took place into the hands of the royal officers and the members of the Gota gradually lost their customary rights of dispensing justice during the Peshwa period.

Given this administrative and juridical structure the king's jurisdiction was limited in caste and religious matters. Similar to the system laid down in the Nepalese *Mulukī Ain* (see below), a culprit was therefore often disciplined by a combination of state-administered punishment, ritual penances, and social disabilities.

Nepal

As in other regions of South Asia the premodern law in Nepal consists of written laws as well as customary laws of the various castes and ethnic groups.[22] In the pre-Rāṇā period – that is, before 1846, when Jaṅga Bahādur Rāṇā became Prime Minister and de facto ruler of the country – the evidence of legal practice basically consists of royal decrees as manifested in inscriptions and documents. In the Rāṇā period (1846–1951) various laws were codified in the *Mulukī Ain* of 1854 (see below); after this period, constitutional law based on the Panchayat system (1963–90) or multiparty system (since 1990) ruled the country. Except for some edicts, inscriptions, and paper documents, legal texts in Nepal until the mid-nineteenth century were dominated by works of Dharmaśāstra, which comprise one of the principal classes of manuscripts filmed by the long-term and large-scale Nepal–German Manuscript Preservation Project. Even the extant Newari *Nyāyavikāsinī* (fourteenth century) is more a translation of a Sanskrit commentary on the *Nārada Smṛti* than an original work.

In the pre-Rāṇā period, the king was the supreme authority in legal matters since important cases were decided or affirmed by him. He was supported by the *rājagurus* (royal priests and preceptors) who kept the highest position in the legal administration of the palace. From the eighteenth century they were supplemented by the chief (religious) judge (*dharmādhikāri[n]*) who decided according to the customary law(s) of the country to sometimes apply Hindu law principles of penance and religious behavior. He could grant expiation (Skt. *prāyaścitta*) and rehabilitation (Nep. *patiyā*) when somebody was afflicted by impurity, especially when he or she had been polluted by sexual or bodily contacts with impure persons, including spouses and other family members. In such cases he could grant partial or full readmission to his or her caste. For this purpose, the *dharmādhikārin* had to issue a writ of rehabilitation, a kind of letter of indulgence. The ordeal was a common method of collecting evidence. Modes of punishment included beheading, imprisonment, facial branding, confiscation of property, and degradation of caste status.

In the Rāṇā period, the Prime Minister had supreme and absolute power, but most legal cases were decided neither by him nor by the king, but by various courts of justice (Nep. *adālat*, *amāli*, *bhārādāri kausal*, *aḍḍā*, *kacāhari*). In some cases, where the Prime Minister interfered in court decisions during his audiences and in major decisions, such as degradation

[22] The following is based on Michaels (2005 and 2009).

or capital punishment, the courts of justice were supposed to consult the Court Council (*bhārādāri kausal*). The council consisted of 230 noblemen and included all the senior Rāṇās, royal priests (*rājguru*), royal collaterals (*chautariyas*), and many civil and military officers.

Although some Śāha rulers issued some rules and royal decrees (Nep. *thitibandej*) of behavior for their subjects, law was not fully systematized. Only with the *Mulukī Ain* (*MA*) was law codified. The *Ain* (as it was called until 1927 or 1952) was the legal code of Nepal, prepared at the initiative of Prime Minister Jaṅga Bahādura Rāṇā (in office from 1846 to 1857) and promulgated on January 5 or 6, 1854 (7 Puṣa, VS 1910), during the reign of King Surendra Vikrama Śāha (who reigned from 1847 to 1881). The Persian name of this code – "*ā'in*," "code," together with the later addition of "*mulukī*," "royal" – itself reveals the influence of Mughal institutions. The sources of the text, however, are not only Islamic precepts and maxims of the Mughal administration, but also the *dharmaśāstras* and many customary laws.

Within a month after his return from a trip to London and Paris, Jaṅga Bahādur Rāṇā appointed a Law Council (*ain kausal*) to bring the various already existing legal documents (*sanad*, *rukkā*, *savāl*, etc.) into a standard form. His goal was to establish a national caste hierarchy for the multiplicity of Nepal's ethno-cultural units, to bring about a homogeneous legislation as well as a uniform system of administration, and, through such legal control over remote areas and separate ethnic groups, to strengthen Rāṇā rule, to reinforce Hindu law in contrast to the British influence in India, and to point out that Nepal is "the only Hindu kingdom left in the Kali age" where cows, women, and Brahmins are especially protected.

The *Mulukī Ain* of 1854, comprising 163 chapters and nearly 1,400 pages, is a kind of constitution, a code of civil and penal regulations dealing with land ownership, revenue administration, hereditary matters, marriage regulations and purity rules (particularly regarding commensality), murder and killing (not only of humans but also of cows), theft, witchcraft, slavery, and so on. Such odd acts as farting and spitting in public, or throwing chili into people's eyes or onto their genitals, are also regulated in separate paragraphs. The *Ain* of 1854 was repeatedly amended and supplemented and is still in use today, although its present form differs totally from the first version.

Kerala

The documentary material of Kerala is especially interesting because it represents Hindu law with very little or no Islamic influence. Donald

R. Davis (1999, 2004a, 2004b) has worked on several sets of records, mostly palm-leaf manuscripts, from Kerala temples dated between the fourteenth and eighteenth century. The majority are contracts pertaining to temple lands, movable property, and expenditures, but also to criminal and administrative affairs. They come primarily from three widely literate high-caste groups in medieval Kerala: Nambudiri Brahmins, Nambyārs, and Sāmantas ("royals"). Councils (*sabhā*, *yogaṃ*, *kalakaṃ*, *saṅketaṃ*, *svarūpaṃ*) managed the administration of law in the temples.

The material challenges conventional notions about the dominance of Brahmins and temple-centered villages (*grāma*), inverting the classic Brahmin–king relation. Brahmins and temples controlled considerable land and material resources, and temples became the source for prestige, power, and wealth. The king had only a more or less token role in ritual events.

Tamil Nadu

In the Madras Presidency, the East India Company had the right to punish offenders from December 1600 onwards. When in 1640 Fort St. George was established by the Company, a court known as the "choultry court" was founded, presided over by the "Adigar" or governor of the town. The choultry courts tried minor cases; important cases – those in which English subjects were involved – were remitted to England. From 1678, when the first Court of Judicature was established in Madras, cases were decided according to the laws of England.

As in Nepal, the local laws of French-administered Pondicherry were given official recognition. The French, unlike the British, attempted to administer indigenous law without a formal codification of principles, but by a regulation of October 1766 it was decided to keep the decisions of the tribunals in the choultries. About one tenth of the vast body of records of those decisions has been compiled by Jean-Claude Bonnan (1999).[23] It shows that the law of these courts was far less śāstra-based than that of the Anglo-Indian courts. The law mainly concerned the representatives of local groups, villages, and castes. It was thus much more grounded in custom than in the Dharmaśāstra. In a way, the choultry court was a customary legal institution refereed by foreign judges. The manner of presentation of the cases was probably quite conventional, but the reasoning behind the decisions followed the French magistrates' own sense of justice.

[23] See also the analysis of Annoussamy (2005: 197–266).

CONCLUSION

Given the medieval and regional sources that are not dependent (or only indirectly dependent) on the Dharmaśāstra, the practice of premodern Hindu law appears as a complex and dynamic mode of mediating social, economic, and religious disputes. It shows several specific characteristics:

State and religion are rarely sharply distinct. The king had religious power since penalties ordered by him could have expiatory, purifying results. The individual is not separated from his social group. This holds especially true for offences entailing pollution. Moreover, Hindu law is not a natural right but the law of castes and regions. It does not sharply differentiate between positive law and morality. Judicial, administrative, social, or even psychological forms of pressure may be mingled together. Finally, subjectivity or the motive of criminal actions is given less weight than in Roman or modern Western law. Punishment in Hindu law is less a question of feeling guilty than of the objective consequences of an action. Therefore, several important legal issues such as intent, guilt, criminal responsibility, innocence (due to senility, for instance), mitigation, and complicity are organized differently in Hindu law.

Insofar as Hindu law claims to be rooted in the unchanging Veda, it sees itself as timeless, yet in fact it incorporates or at least recognizes the validity of a great deal of customary law. On the one hand, it proves to be neither positive nor conventional law, legislated by human beings to realize a social ideal. Neither does it appear to be natural law based on universal principles, independent of human codifications and valid beyond historical communities and states. Rather, it is (as all law, perhaps) relational law (*svadharma*), that is law relative to specific groups, times, or places, to castes and life stages (*varṇāśramadharma*), dependent on the dynamics of power and authority of various elites, especially the king and the Brahmin, as well as on a wide range of customs. In this complexity, Hindu law does not aim at pure neutrality or consistency. It is located between public law and private law, temple and palace, penance and penalty. To a certain extent, it depends on the Dharmaśāstra but even more so on circumstantial, local, and non-Brahmanical forms of law and custom. It is this fluidity that makes it a rewarding challenge for any further study of law.

CHAPTER 4

The creation of Anglo-Hindu law

Rosane Rocher

Anglo-Hindu law was born in Calcutta on August 21, 1772, when the Bengal government adopted "A Plan for the Administration of Justice in Bengal" (usually referred to as the Judicial Plan) framed by Orientalist Governor (later Governor-General) Warren Hastings. Seven years after the Mughal emperor had granted the East India Company the *diwani* (revenue collection) of the provinces of Bengal, Bihar, and Orissa, Hastings was bringing to an end an initial "dual system" of government, and assuming full British control. Hastings was particularly concerned at the chaotic state of the court system and of the administration of law. In addition to setting up a pyramid of British courts, the Judicial Plan laid out principles on which judgments were to be rendered. These were the foundation of Anglo-Hindu law, which was to evolve to meet further concerns of the colonial administration.

QUEST FOR LEGITIMACY

The first question the newly empowered British administration faced was which laws should be applied in their new courts. Military officer and leading historian Alexander Dow opined in "An Inquiry into the State of Bengal," prefixed to the third volume of his *History of Hindostan*, that by reason of conquest and since Indians were divided into religious communities that would not submit to the laws of one another, it was "absolutely necessary for the peace and prosperity of the country" that the laws of England should prevail (Dow 1770–2, vol. III: cxliii). Hastings and fellow Orientalist administrators were, to the contrary, of the opinion that imposing foreign, English law on Indians was unwarrantably coercive, and potentially dangerous. At a time when the English East India Company had a still tenuous hold on limited coastal territories, and when its civil servants did not yet entertain "the illusion of permanence" (title of Hutchins 1967), ruling in ways that would arouse as little dissatisfaction and unrest as possible was deemed prudent. Respecting the personal laws, or "prejudices," of the natives was a central element in their policy. Yet the British were as ignorant of the laws by which Indians abided as Indians were of English law. Hastings's plan put the burden on the British to be the learners.

With the limited information at their disposal, the question was where to find the laws applicable to India. The questions of whether dividing law along religious lines, Hindu and Muslim, was part of a conscious policy of "divide and rule," and whether reaching for canonical sources rather than applying customary laws was fundamentally sound, have been the object of much discussion among later scholars and politicians. These issues were not debated at the time. In what was a harbinger of things to come, the grounds on which a decision was made accommodated prejudices in the imperial metropolis of London rather than in the Indian metropolis of Calcutta.

Hastings's Judicial Plan laid out that "in all suits regarding inheritance, marriage, caste, and other religious usages, or institutions, the laws of the Koran with respect to Mahometans and those of the *Shaster* [*śāstra*] with respect to Gentoos [Hindus] shall be invariably adhered to." British administrators did not know then the extent or the content of the *śāstra* (canonical literature), nor were they familiar with Sanskrit, the language in which it was written. Pandits were attached as "law officers" to the British courts, not only to advise them by issuing *vyavasthā*s (determinations written in Sanskrit and translated into Persian, which remained the administrative language until 1830), but also to legitimize the courts' judgments in the eyes of Hindus.

In addition to warding off potential contestation in India, Hastings needed to convince the home administration of the Company and legal authorities in Britain of the intellectual and juridical legitimacy of Hindu law, to stave off a feared imposition of English law on Indians. To this end, and at a time when religion was legitimized in the West by being "of the book," it was important to demonstrate that Indians – Hindus in this instance – had a body of written laws, not just a set of traditional rules and practices. In March 1773, less than a year after issuing his Judicial Plan, Hastings and his colleagues in Calcutta commissioned a committee of pandits to consolidate the rules of Dharmaśāstra into a code, which became the first in a series of Sanskrit texts produced at the instance of "the British as patrons of the śāstra" (Derrett 1968: title of Chapter 8). Hastings also obtained that the East India Company sponsor the publication in London of an English version, *A Code of Gentoo Laws*, by Nathaniel Brassey Halhed (Halhed 1776).

Notwithstanding an (unacknowledged) disfiguring string of translation from a Sanskrit compendium to the published English version, via a Persian abstract of an oral rendering in Bengali, the *Code of Gentoo Laws* fulfilled Hastings's purpose of convincing authorities in London that there was a body of written Hindu law that had reached an acceptable level of sophistication (R. Rocher 1983: Chapter 4). It aroused enough interest in Europe to be translated, two years after its publication, into French by J. B. R. Robinet, and into German by R. E. Raspe. In India, it was received with reserve. It was occasionally quoted in the courts, but Sir William Jones, who knew the Sanskrit original text and the Persian version, soon discredited the *Code* as being unreliable: "whatever be the merit of the original, the translation of it has no authority . . . properly speaking, indeed, we cannot call it a translation" (letter to Governor-General Cornwallis, March 19, 1788, in Cannon 1970: 797). Pandit assistants to the British courts were happy to include the *Vivādārṇavasetu*, "a bridge across the sea of litigations," the Sanskrit text from which the *Code of Gentoo Laws* was drawn, among sources for their *vyavasthā*s, but it carried no more weight with them than any other of the many *nibandha*s (compendia) of Hindu law that had been composed over centuries.

QUEST FOR AUTHENTICITY

The fact that, however creative, the Hindu tradition rhetorically presented itself as derivative from the pronouncements of hallowed sages reinforced widely shared, Western, eighteenth-century notions, that a once glorious Hindu Indian civilization had decayed, and that its essence had to be retrieved from foundational texts. For a critical moment, a British jurist, who, in England, would of course have sought to enforce the latest legislation, did not appear to find it odd to vest the authenticity of Hindu law in its most ancient recoverable sources. Sir William Jones, who was not a servant of the East India Company, but who, as a judge of the Supreme Court of Bengal appointed by the Crown, also had occasion to apply Hindu law, sought a manuscript of what he believed to be the most ancient *dharmaśāstra*, and resolved to learn Sanskrit to gain unmediated access to it. Jones, who dated the *Mānava Dharmaśāstra* to 1580 BCE, about a millennium and a half earlier than the period that is now commonly accepted, rated it a "system of duties, religious and civil, and of law in all its branches, which the *Hindus* firmly believe to have been promulgated in the beginning of time by MENU; . . . a system so comprehensive and so minutely exact, that it may be considered as the *Institutes of Hindu Law*" (Jones 1794: iv). His translation made of what became most commonly referred to as "The Laws of Manu" the embodiment of Hindu law and social practices, alternately most revered and most reviled, in later times, for its endorsement of caste-based discrimination and the subjugation of women. It inaugurated a pattern that showcased and privileged texts that had been translated.

Jones's Institutes of Hindu Law long remained the only translation of any text of the *smṛti* tier, be it *dharmasūtra* or *dharmaśāstra*. The next translation of an ancient *smṛti* text, the *Yājñavalkya Smṛti*, would come sixty years later, no longer at the hands of a British jurist, but into German by a philologist (Stenzler 1849). Indeed, British judges in India soon learned that the more complete and coherent solutions to legal problems were to be found in the commentaries on, and in the compendia compiled from, the ancient *smṛti* texts.[1]

QUEST FOR CONTROL

When applying Hindu law, British judges were at the mercy of the pandits who served as law officers of their courts, and who quoted diverse authorities for their *vyavasthā*s according to their lights and to occasionally contradictory results. Going from frustration to suspicion was an easy step. Jones, for one, doubted the integrity of court pandits, declaring "I could not with an easy conscience concur in a decision, merely on the written opinion of native lawyers, in any cause in which they could have the remotest interest in misleading the court." He sought to rein them in by producing a new digest of Hindu law, to be translated into "perspicuous English," for the benefit of the vast body of judges who did not know Sanskrit. Differently from the *Code of Gentoo Laws* which Hastings had commissioned in 1773, the *Digest* for which he obtained Governor-General Cornwallis's support in 1788 was to be composed under his personal superintendence, and he was to translate it directly from Sanskrit (Jones to Cornwallis, March 19, 1788, in Cannon 1970: 794–803). Jones died before the project was completed, but the translation of *A Digest of Hindu Law on Contracts and Successions*, by Henry Thomas Colebrooke, appeared in 1798 in four volumes issued by the Honourable Company's Press in Calcutta (Colebrooke 1798).

The fear of the government of Bengal that they might not find a person capable of translating the *Digest* after Jones's premature death brought home to them the importance of Sanskrit for the administration of justice for Hindus. In 1801, when Governor-General Wellesley founded the College of Fort William for the education of the East India Company's

[1] See Olivelle's chapter in this volume.

civil servants, Colebrooke was appointed professor of Sanskrit and Hindu law. Sanskrit and Hindu law were twinned at the College, not only in the title of the professor, but in the examinations for the few, elite learners of Sanskrit, which consistently focused on texts of Hindu law (Roebuck 1819). There was no attempt to coax large numbers of civil servants to learn a language that was notoriously difficult and of lesser utility for everyday communication with the general population. The colonial government banked instead on providing English-language sources to serve as a check for the vast body of judges on the *vyavasthā*s of the pandits who assisted their courts, and they relied on a few experts in Sanskrit and Hindu law at the top. For the thirteen years, from 1802 to 1814, when Colebrooke served as a judge of the Superior Court in Calcutta, not only was he the person who attested to the competence and character of court pandits throughout Bengal, but the *vyavasthā*s of the pandits of the Superior Court – and even of the Supreme Court, with which he had no official position – were entered into the record only after Colebrooke had certified them as conformable to Hindu law. This new procedure represented an upending of the original plan to have pandits' determinations serve as the basis on which British judges rendered judgment (R. Rocher 2007).

QUEST FOR CONSISTENCY

Concerns for the legitimacy of judgments rendered, for the authenticity of the law applied, and for control over the dispensation of justice remained constant in the development of Anglo-Hindu law. They paled, however, in comparison with a quest for consistency in judicial decisions, which led the government of Bengal to sponsor advanced native education in Sanskrit as a necessary basis for the administration of Hindu law. One of the primary goals of the Sanskrit College which Orientalist Resident Jonathan Duncan founded in Banaras in 1791 was to become "a nursery of the future doctors and expounders [of Hindu law] to assist European judges in the due, regular and *uniform* administration of its genuine letter and spirit to the body of the people" (Nicholls 1907: 2, emphasis added). Better than trusting the recruitment of pandits as assistants to the courts to their local reputation for learning, training them at a common institution and on a common curriculum offered the prospect of producing cohorts of like-minded law officers. In 1794, when the Bengal government proceeded to a systematic review of the credentials and performance of the native officers attached to district and city courts, they sought a ranked list of graduates from Banaras Sanskrit College, from which they proceeded to make appointments

(Nicholls 1907: 5). This effort fizzled when Indian pandits proved to be less inclined than British civil servants to accept posting in remote locations with which they had no ties.

A desire for consistency at the appellate level prompted the Bengal government to sack, also in 1794, the pandits who had assisted the Superior Court, and to replace them with the two pandits who had been the principal coadjutors for Jones's *Digest*. The stated aim of this change in personnel was that the two new appointees were expected "to render the Digest the book of authority for determining legal questions and consequently to attain the desirable object of introducing uniformity in the decisions of the courts" (R. Rocher 1989: 632). Colebrooke proposed to go a step further, and to have manuscript copies made, in Banaras, of the *Vivādabhaṅgārṇava*, "a sea of waves of litigations," the Sanskrit text from which the *Digest* was translated, for distribution to the pandits of all district and city courts. The government chose instead to explore the possibility of having the Sanskrit text printed in Calcutta (Rocher and Rocher 2010: Chapter 3). Nothing came of it. The *Vivādabhaṅgārṇava* remains unpublished to this day. Uniformity in court decisions would be achieved on the basis of texts in English, at the hands of British judges. Pandits would continue to serve as assistants to the courts and to buttress their legitimacy, but they would labor under conditions of increasing dependence and marginality, until Act XI of 1864 did away with them altogether.

QUEST FOR PARTICULARITY

The Bengal government had originally decided that canonical Dharmaśāstra, not customary law, was to be the source and foundation for judicial decisions. Yet, as the East India Company expanded its territorial possessions, regional differences became a growing concern. It became all the more tempting to interpret differences between the several commentaries and compendia as reflections of regional traditions, since some of them were clearly better known in some areas than in others. The law of inheritance was the concern in which most significant differences occurred, and also the one in which the state had the greatest stake, since ownership determined from whom to collect property taxes. Jones had shown great interest in exploring the current state of the traditional panditic establishments of Mithila in Tirhut, Bihar, and of Nadiya in Bengal. He had taken care to hire two pandits, the Bihari Sarvoru Trivedi, and the Bengali Rādhākānta Tarkavāgīśa under the mantle of his celebrated teacher, Jagannātha Tarkapañcānana, as principal coadjutors for his *Digest* (R. Rocher 1989: 631). But it was Colebrooke who ushered in the concept of different "schools of Hindu law" with his translation, published in Calcutta in 1810, of *Two Treatises on the Hindu Law of Inheritance* (L. Rocher 1972a). Jīmūtavāhana's compendium on inheritance, the *Dāyabhāga*, and the section on inheritance in the second chapter of Vijñāneśvara's *Mitākṣarā*, a commentary on the *Yājñavalkya Smṛti*, were constituted into the schools of Bengal and of Banaras, the latter deemed to extend, with other texts, "to the southern extremity of the peninsula of India" (Colebrooke 1810: preface).

The division of Hindu law into two schools, with four sub-schools for the *Mitākṣarā*, stands out as the most transforming innovation in the substance of Anglo-Hindu law. Her Majesty's Most Honourable Privy Council in London, which was the final court of appeal for Indian cases, was to affirm in 1868 that "[t]he duty of an European judge who is under the obligation to administer Hindoo law, is not so much to enquire whether a disputed doctrine is fairly deducible from the earliest authorities, as to ascertain whether it has been received by the particular School which governs the District with which he has to deal" (*Collector of Madura* v. *Moottoo Ramalinga* [1868], 12 MIA 397, 436).

Colebrooke's conceptualization of regionally differentiated schools of law met with direct challenges, particularly from Madras, where, in matters whether political, linguistic, or legal, British administrators often chafed at being thrust in the position of playing second fiddle to the Calcutta metropolis. These challenges were slow to develop. Chief Justice of Madras Sir Thomas Strange frequently sought Colebrooke's advice given in letters from Calcutta in 1813, which Strange included in notes to his *Elements of Hindu Law*, published after both had returned to Britain (Strange 1825). Francis Whyte Ellis, author of "the Dravidian proof" in matters linguistic (Trautmann 2006: Chapter 5), nonetheless followed Colebrooke's lead in the distribution of regionally dominant law treatises (Ellis 1827, posthumous). Not so James Henry Nelson fifty years later. Nelson might have been less opposed to the use of the *Mitākṣarā*, which he took to stem from the northern school of Mithila, had he known that its author hailed from Kalyana near Hyderabad (Kane 1968–75, vol. 1: 607). Yet, in the south of India, where Brahmanical authority was more fraught than in the north, Nelson argued above all for the application of local and group-specific customs (Nelson 1877, 1881, 1887). Both in a war of pamphlets and from the bench, Lewis C. Innes, the Senior Puisne Judge of the Madras High Court, objected, however, that Nelson's recommendations would result in a balkanization of Hindu law and chaos in the courts (Innes 1882; Nelson 1882). Nelson became "a forgotten administrator-historian of India"

(Derrett 1976–8, vol. II: 404–23). The regional differentiation that Colebrooke had established remained paramount.

Yet customary law did become increasingly recognized. It was commonly assumed that differences between commentaries on, and compendia of, *smṛti* texts largely reflected local customs. Thus, making these texts primary sources for legal decisions was deemed to be a step toward administering Hindu law along customary lines. This assumption and the fact that *smṛti* texts, commentaries, and compendia all recognized the customs of families, castes, guilds, and corporations as valid sources of law fed a growing acceptance of customs, even unwritten, in the courts. The Bombay Presidency led the way under Governor Mountstuart Elphinstone, with Section 26 of Regulation IV of 1827, which stated that "cases should be decided according to the custom of the caste, and established usage." In the same year, and as a part of the same effort, Arthur Steele published a survey of caste customs on which cases could be so decided (Steele 1827). There were to be extensive discussions over the years about the criteria by which customs could be assessed as valid, but the general rule that the Privy Council set in the case just cited was that "under the Hindu law, clear proof of usage will outweigh the written text of the law" (*Collector of Madura* v. *Moottoo Ramalinga* [1868], 12 MIA 397, 436). In a reversal of what Hastings had set out to do in 1772, customary law was to become increasingly applied as it became better known.

QUEST FOR REPLICABILITY

As shown above, consistency in legal decisions was a longstanding, primary object of the colonial administration. Channeling pandits into a common curriculum, and British judges into a set of recognized authoritative texts in English translation, was a first step, yet an ultimately inefficient way to achieve this goal. The quest for consistency morphed into a quest for replicability, shifting from as faithful an application of original textual and customary sources as seemed feasible, to foregrounding precedents. A system of case law came about, a conception of law that was a hallmark of British common law, but which was alien to Hindu law. From 1816 on, a spate of volumes appeared, which collected exemplary cases and disserted on legal principles and precedents. First came Sir Thomas Strange's three volumes of *Notes of Cases in the Court of the Recorder and in the Supreme Court of Judicature at Madras*, followed by his two-volume *Elements of Hindu Law; Referable to British Judicature in India* (Strange 1816, 1825). Cases from the Superior Court of Bombay soon kicked in (Borradaile 1825).

William Hay Macnaghten, who had started his studies at the College of Fort William just as Colebrooke prepared to retire from East India Company service, dealt with Calcutta in four volumes of *Reports of Cases Determined in the Court of Sudder Dewanny Adawlut* (1827–35) and two volumes of *Principles and Precedents of Hindu Law* (1828–9), after producing like volumes on Muslim law and on criminal cases. These collections of cases were the antecedents of the *Indian Law Reports*, which would begin to be published on a comprehensive and regular basis in 1876. The *Law Reports* and their precursors had the effect of fostering regional specificity of a new kind. As Calcutta's position of leadership eroded, and since the high courts of Calcutta, Madras, Bombay, Allahabad, and more, were independent from one another, subject only to final review by the Privy Council in London, provincial courts of appeal severally set standards for their lower courts to observe. Yet no firewall was erected between provincial courts. Ancient texts, whether perceived as pan-Indian or regional, continued to be quoted, but less and less afresh, and increasingly through prior cases. From 1911 to 1916, T. A. Venkasawmy Row would edit seventeen retrospective volumes of *Indian Decisions (Old Series)* for the use of judges and lawyers, a majority of whom, by that time, were no longer British, but Indian (Venkasawmy Row 1911–16). Less effort was applied to providing pandits with collections of prior *vyavasthās*, even though Rāmajaya Tarkālaṅkāra, pandit of the Supreme Court in Calcutta and former instructor at Fort William College, published a short *Vyavasthāsaṅgraha* at the same time as W. H. Macnaghten issued his collections of cases (Rāmajaya Tarkālaṅkāra 1827).

Prior dispositions of cases were, of course, not always found to have been right, but precedents they tended to remain, due to principles that were tellingly expressed in Latin, not in Sanskrit. There were no provisions in Hindu law that were equivalent to the maxims of "*stare decisis*" ("stand by prior decisions") and "*communis error facit ius*" ("a common error makes law"). In such cases, Anglo-Hindu law amounted to an Anglo disposition of Hindu law.

QUEST FOR ACCEPTABILITY

As the British expanded and consolidated their control over large territories in India, their fear of causing offense to native populations waned. Supported by Indian reformist movements, the government felt increasingly empowered to abrogate practices that, even if countenanced by the *śāstras*, were judged unacceptable in enlightened times. The fact that the *śāstra*s did not mandate the burning of widows (*satī*), though some allowed it, was marshaled for its abolition and criminalization by Regulation XVII of 1829. The courts became an increasingly self-referencing, professional enterprise, prepared not only to apply Hindu law, but to shape it. As early as 1824, Francis Workman Macnaghten, William Hay's father, prefaced his *Considerations on the Hindoo Law, as It Is Current in Bengal* with the unambiguous statement, "It is our duty to select such parts of the code, as may be most beneficial to the people . . . we may hope, in time, to cleanse the system of its exaggerated corruptions, and to defecate the impurity of the ages" (F. W. Macnaghten 1824: vi). When an occasion arose, such as when Hindu law did not spell out "a specific law or usage" on which to make a judgment, Section 26 of Regulation IV of 1827, in Bombay, already cited, gave judges license to apply principles of "justice, equity and good conscience," criteria that were apparently viewed as universal, and not culturally bound.

Another, and most significant, way in which Anglo-Hindu law lost much of its Hindu identity resulted from British judges' resolve to draw a distinction between what was religious and what was legal. Although the Judicial Plan of 1772, which had been the charter for Anglo-Hindu law, specifically stated as its purview "all suits regarding inheritance, marriage, caste, and other *religious usages, or institutions*" (emphasis added), British judges sought increasingly to focus on the legal, to the exclusion of religious rules, with which they were less comfortable. In matters of marriage and of adoption, in particular, it was deemed that the rites the *śāstra*s prescribed were not absolutely required to make a marriage or adoption valid. In such and other cases, another Latin maxim, "*quod fieri non debuit factum valet*" ("what ought not to have been done is valid, once done"), was brought forth (Derrett 1976–8, vol. III: 1–24). An isolated statement in the *Dāyabhāga* (2.30), to the effect that "even a hundred texts cannot cancel a done deal," made with regard to the validity of gifts and sales, was secondarily marshaled to buttress this Latin maxim (L. Rocher 1995).

Separating the religious from the legal domain was a long process. From the start, British interest in the Dharmaśāstra had been prompted by the needs of judicial administration. While it was true that Hindu law was grounded in the Dharmaśāstra, representing Dharmaśāstra as "the laws of" Manu and others, or a "code," was profoundly mistaken and misleading. *Dharmaśāstra*s were canonical texts (*śāstra*s) on *dharma*, which is best translated as "righteousness" or "duty" in an encompassing religious and social spectrum. Severing the religious from the legal did violence both to the Sanskrit texts and to Hastings's decision to administer law along religiously defined lines. Ironically, in a reverse process, modern Indian languages were at the same time adopting and adapting the term "*dharma*" to translate "religion."

LEGACY

The Judicial Plan of 1772 had been hatched in profound ignorance of the complexity of the *śāstra*s on which the administration of justice to Hindus was ordained to be based. As difficulties of access, translation, interpretation, and application mounted, British judges resorted to their own lights, while becoming increasingly dissatisfied. J. H. Nelson's opinion may have been curter than most, but it was by no means isolated, when he branded Anglo-Hindu law "a phantom of the brain, imagined by Sanskritists without law, and lawyers without Sanskrit" (1877: 2). Yet a hybrid Anglo-Hindu law found wide acceptance among Indians. A host of disputes evidently continued to be adjudicated by private arbitration, either by pandits on the basis of the *śāstra*s or by local authorities according to regional, caste, guild, or other customs. Yet, for certain, Hindus resorted to the official, British, courts in droves, when they had the means to do so. The crushing volume of cases was often blamed on an allegedly inveterate propensity to litigiousness among Indians, but the operative reason was clearly the prospect of effective enforcement of judicial decisions for the winning side (L. Rocher 1972b).

Court proceedings underwent no significant changes when Indian judges and lawyers began steadily to outnumber British judges and attorneys. By the mid-nineteenth century, however, the government became increasingly of a mind to cut through difficulties by legislation. This process led to a series of acts, already in the waning years of the Company Raj, picking up steam during the British Raj, and further, on a wider scale, under the government of India. Although aspects of Hindu law which were not covered by the acts were to continue, by default, to be governed by Anglo-Hindu law, these acts and later legal activism had the effect of largely abrogating the authority of rules from the *śāstra*, causing Derrett to pen an "epitaph for the Rishis" (subtitle of Derrett 1978a). What still survives of Hastings's Judicial Plan, under recurrent pressure from demands for a uniform civil code, is the separation of family law along religious divides.

CHAPTER 5

Marriage and family in colonial Hindu law

Rachel Sturman

The title of this chapter suggests a particular approach to the study of law, in which legal systems are examined for their treatment of a given subject, for example, race in American law, lunacy in medieval French law, or, in this case, marriage and the family in colonial Hindu law. While I will certainly provide such an analysis, I propose to do so through a somewhat different exploration: of marriage and family *as* colonial Hindu law. Marriage and family formed the core of colonial Hindu law both within contemporary legal scholarship and in the actual adjudication of the courts. Attending to this centrality of the family enables a more serious reflection both on the system of colonial Hindu law as a component of the modern colonial state, and on its implications for those who were subject to its jurisdiction. Ultimately, the colonial state's construal of Hindu law (as well as Muslim law) as primarily law of the family formed part of broader eighteenth- and nineteenth-century Western reformulations of the family and of religion as distinct from – and as objects of – state power. In the colonial context, religious law integrated aspects of Indian nomos,[1] but it treated those elements as fundamentally external to the overarching values, principles, and beliefs of the state. This disjuncture led to the apotheosis of a paradoxical conceptualization of "Hindu law" as at once a narrow domain of "private" indigenous concerns inessential to matters of state interest, and as a morally and politically volatile arena that demanded state protection, attention and at times intervention.

If colonial religious law (also called "personal" law) was defined as essentially family law, however, this law primarily concerned the property rights and entitlements that the relations of family entailed. This centrality of property within colonial personal law linked it to the broader foundational connections that prevailed in British legal and political thought

[1] Defined in the *Oxford English Dictionary* as "the law; the principles governing human conduct, esp. as defined by culture or custom" (*OED* online, accessed September 12, 2007).

between property and legal capacity. Accordingly, the foundational assumptions of liberal thought came to pervade personal law, with the capacity to hold property and equal rights to property coming to signify autonomy, equality, and full legal subjecthood. In this context, because colonial personal law construed Hindus and Muslims, men and women, as different kinds of legal subjects with divergent rights and statuses enforced by the state, the rights of property and personhood within personal law became a critical idiom for new political claims.

This chapter begins by questioning *why* colonial Hindu law was defined as essentially family law, and by considering the nature of colonial Hindu law as a system of religious law operating within the overarching civil law of the colonial state. It then turns to the actual treatment of marriage and the family within colonial Hindu law. Finally, it addresses the politics and politicization of colonial Hindu law, especially the intertwined politics of gender and of religious community, which have had significant legacies up to the present.

COLONIAL HINDU LAW AS STRUCTURE AND SYSTEM

Colonial Hindu law was a system of civil law that applied to persons from the Indian subcontinent who were not Muslim, Christian, Jewish, or Parsi. Thus, in addition to those denominated "Hindu," Hindu law applied also to Sikhs, Jains, and Buddhists. Hindu and Muslim law were the two systems of "personal" law (so called because it was based on personal, or ascriptive, status regardless of territorial location) recognized by the British.[2] In addition to personal law, secular civil as well as criminal law applied to all matters outside the cognizance of personal law and to all those subject to the territorial jurisdiction of British India. As Rosane Rocher describes in this volume, this system was originally formulated by Warren Hastings, in his 1772 "Plan for the Administration of Justice," which provided the foundation for the judicial system he put in place as first governor-general of India. In Hastings's renowned words, "in all suits regarding inheritance, marriage, caste, and other religious usages, or institutions, the laws of the Koran with respect to Mahomedans, and those of the Shaster with respect to Gentoos [Hindus], shall be invariably adhered to" (Ilbert 1915: 278). Hastings's formulation established the colonial legal system as a plural legal regime, in the sense that it involved the coexistence of multiple domains or legal orders exerting regulatory power through practices of adjudication and

[2] Parsi family law was also codified in 1865.

sanction (e.g., the overlapping jurisdictions of secular and personal civil law within the colonial state), but this entailed a quite limited form of legal pluralism (Griffiths 1986; Merry 1988; Moore 1973; Teubner 1992). Although the colonial state recognized the operation of what it considered Indian religious laws in certain matters, it took over the role of applying those laws. In this sense, as Lauren Benton has described (2002: 28, 127–52), this colonial form of legal pluralism involved an abridgment of earlier forms of legal pluralism that had previously prevailed both in Europe and in the now-colonized regions, and their replacement by a state-centered legal order. In this sense, it marked a fundamental shift in the treatment of preexisting nomothetic sensibilities and practices. Although the colonial claim that it preserved and applied Indian religious (and eventually also customary) law was critical to British claims to legitimacy in India,[3] one of the central operations of colonial personal law was to distinguish what constituted "law" and would be enforceable by the state from what would be subject merely to social, religious, or moral sanction. If, as legal scholars argue, the distinction between law and morality forms a feature of all legal systems, nonetheless, under British rule, law became tied to state power in fundamentally new ways. This was a long and uneven process, in which the establishment of particular normative dictates, conventions, and regulatory practices as integral to the state system of personal law, and the separation of others from the state, constituted a critical facet of the colonial legal formation.

Indeed, as many scholars have recognized, despite the originary principle articulated by Hastings that the colonial power would preserve Indian religious laws and hence refrain from intervening in matters relating to religion, caste, and the family, in fact, the colonial state both intentionally and unintentionally regularly intervened in such matters (Carroll 1983; Chakravarti 1998; Cohn 1996c; Derrett 1976–8, vols. II and III; Galanter 1989). This intervention was in some sense inevitable in a system where matters of personal law were adjudicated by the state. Had the colonial state defined the jurisdiction of its courts to exclude matters of personal law altogether, in a form of legal pluralism that left such matters to the adjudication of caste, village, or other corporate bodies, the vicissitudes of colonial personal law would have taken a different shape (although, as the example of indirect rule in Africa suggests, one no less colonial). What colonial personal law in fact entailed was a system in which (as we will see, specific elite versions of) societal nomos were incorporated into regular state

[3] See Rosane Rocher's chapter in this volume.

practice, but in a separate legal domain. Another way of conceptualizing this is that the colonial legal arena configured personal law as a separate legal domain *within* the overarching jurisdiction of the state.

Returning to the question of why the family formed the most insistent and nearly exclusive focus of colonial personal law, scholars who have addressed this issue have pointed to a number of factors. J. D. M. Derrett's work has shown how topics such as adoption, partition, and inheritance had gained in importance in the late medieval Sanskrit textual corpus, pointing to a precolonial centrality of these issues (Derrett 1962a: 36). He also noted that the colonial formulation of personal law was based on the model of ecclesiastical courts in England, which had jurisdiction over probate and matrimonial disputes (Derrett 1968: 233). From another perspective, David Washbrook (1981) has suggested that the interests of a capitalist economy structured the colonial treatment of property, while, somewhat covertly and paradoxically, in the arena of personal law, the colonial state bolstered premodern forms of social power, including those of family and community. These various explanations provide important elements toward understanding the curious content of colonial Hindu law. Yet a crucial – if long unquestioned – part of this story also involves the early modern and modern British formulation of religion as potentially distinct from and subordinate to the state, and of the family as object of, rather than model for, sovereign power (Foucault 1991). These shifts may be understood as part of the crucial reformulation of the classical Western distinction between public and private, in all its complexity, during this era (McKeon 2005; Weintraub 1997). In this sense, the colonial formation of Hindu law as the law of marriage and family involved a conceptual doubling of the Western categorization (itself ever-incomplete) of religion as private with the powerful fiction of marriage and family as quintessential areas of private life. Such a conceptualization of religion as a category in itself and as separate from the primary functions of the state was a relatively recent formulation in the West and had never formed part of South Asian thought. Yet these Western formulations were also fictions and incomplete because, despite their positive power, in fact the British state both at home and in the empire always presumed (Christian) religious principles (indeed, Anglicanism remained the Church of England) and always regulated and intervened in relations of marriage and family.

In denominating marriage and family as the primary subjects of religious law, the colonial power both claimed to be attending to the affective significance of these matters for Indians, and also subjected them to state scrutiny and jurisdiction. This involved a fundamental reformulation of politics in South Asia. According to Chatterjee (2004: 3–45), the family in India only emerged as such with the depoliticization of the power and capital generated by elite households, which had earlier formed the quintessential site of politics. Yet this colonial treatment of the family as external to primary matters of political power and interest did not involve the removal of marriage and family from state oversight, but rather, a determination that such oversight would occur through the lens of personal law. In the end, however, precisely because personal law was considered divergent from the foundational principles of the colonial state, that lens was itself never applied consistently. As we will see, throughout the nineteenth century, both criminal law and secular civil law injected new terms of legality into colonial Hindu law.

Hastings's original formulation did not conceive of Hindu law as appropriate for the regulation of areas of social life beyond religion, caste, and the family, such as property or trade, despite the fact that both textual and customary traditions associated with Hinduism included dictates concerning all manner of social relations.[4] And it was in the arena of property regulation that British law came to operate most powerfully in colonial India: British laws of contract, tort, insolvency, transfer of property, and the like came to shape property relations outside the family, especially following the establishment of Crown Rule in 1858. Yet colonial Hindu law also conceptualized the family as a property-holding unit and relations of family as jural relations of property and entitlement. It was a commonplace of colonial governance that property in India was primarily held by families or other corporate groups, and thus inherently involved personal law. Indeed, the several areas marked out by Hastings as subject to personal law were in fact treated differently: Matters relating to marriage and inheritance were subject to the jurisdiction of colonial personal law, whereas matters relating to caste status and religious prescription were largely excluded from the jurisdiction of the colonial courts, *except* insofar as they could be construed as relating to property (Derrett 1968: 290–1).[5] Property thus occupied a place of central, if paradoxical, significance within both secular and religious civil law. Ultimately, the regulation of property and the enforcement of differential property rights under both personal and secular law produced differential legal subjecthood within the colonial state. This multivalence of property across personal and secular civil law would ultimately have profound effects on actual adjudication within colonial Hindu law.

[4] See Donald Davis's chapter in this volume.

[5] The question of colonial jurisdiction over disputes involving caste honors and perquisites was decided somewhat differently in the courts of the different presidencies. See Mulla (1901).

THE JURISPRUDENCE OF MARRIAGE AND FAMILY IN COLONIAL HINDU LAW

Colonial Hindu law in practice

Postcolonial scholarship on colonial Hindu law, although reflecting several divergent disciplinary perspectives and concerns, has coalesced to form a coherent, if complex, narrative concerning the formation, operation, and effects of colonial Hindu law. As Rocher describes in this volume, in the late eighteenth century, the early colonial legal system tended to privilege the dictates of the Sanskrit textual tradition as the primary source of law. Although it employed Brahmin pandits to interpret these texts and to provide opinions (*vyavasthās*) as part of the formal adjudication of court cases, in so doing, it transformed both the nature of such pandits' authority and their interpretive practice long before they were "superseded" by the courts in 1864 (Cohn 1996c; Lariviere 1989b; Mani 1998). Moreover, starting in the early nineteenth century, and particularly in the Madras and Bombay presidencies and areas of later conquest, a new generation of officials began to challenge the primacy of ancient texts. As they reassessed the chasm between ancient textual prescription and contemporary practice, they valorized the latter as the real source of law. Yet this shift in official emphasis from authoritative texts to custom as the primary source of law involved its own ironies. Most prominently, the emphasis on custom ultimately itself involved a process of textualization, both through the production of authoritative compendia on caste and regional customs for use in the courts, and through the formation of a body of case law that served as legal precedents in cases involving custom. This process of rigidification or fixing of custom was in fact recognized even at the time. Ironically, Henry Maine, whose *Ancient Law* (Maine 1861) has been identified as highly influential in shifting the legal emphasis from textual authorities to customary practice, himself ultimately argued to this effect: "Usage, once recorded upon evidence given, immediately becomes written and fixed law. Nor is it any longer obeyed as usage. It is henceforth obeyed as the law administered by a British Court, and has thus really become a command of the sovereign" (Maine 1871: 72). In other words, Maine argued that the very process of attempting to grant custom the force of law in fact transformed custom into positive law. This recognition fundamentally altered his opinions, and in his *Village Communities of the East and West*, written after his experience in India as law member of the governor-general's Council, he abandoned his prior emphasis on custom and called for codification of Indian law, "formed for the most part upon the best European models" (Maine 1871: 76).

Moreover, this process of rigidification of custom was accompanied by an eventual expansion of reliance on textual authorities and homogenization of legally recognized practice. This was because in the actual practice of the courts, proving local or community custom was notoriously difficult, not least because disputing parties would set up opposing claims as to which customs prevailed in their community (Maine 1871). In this context, the courts tended to continue to expand the authority of textual dictates over customary practice, even when they had the opposite mandate.[6]

Further, because the textual tradition established elite caste practice as the preferred form (for example relating to marriage), practices that had historically been the exclusive privilege of the high castes were in the colonial courts interpreted as normative and extended to lower castes as well. This historical shift was in fact embraced by many reformist judges and lawyers at the time, both Indian and British, who viewed it as bringing the lower castes up to the standards of morality, and hence respectability, of the higher castes, and as enabling the lower castes to partake of the privileged forms previously reserved for the higher castes.[7] Thus, legal scholars and practitioners at the time were broadly aware of some of the most significant processes of transformation that were occurring through the operation of colonial Hindu law, but they often viewed those changes as inevitable or as salutary.

Marriage: gender and caste[8]

As this process of legal change suggests, the colonial law and jurisprudence of Hindu marriage highlighted the mutual constitution of gender and caste. Caste, as a hereditary form of differentiation, depended upon endogamy, and the regulation of women's sexuality thus occupied a critical place in its reproduction. In this sense, as postcolonial feminist scholars have argued, the colonial reconstruction of patriarchy and of caste were intertwined processes (Chakravarti 1998; Rao 2003). One of the defining features of these processes was the expansion of patriarchal practices regarding

6 *Jugmohandas Mangaldas* v. *Sir Mangaldas Nathubhoy* (1886), ILR 10 Bom 528.

7 *Reg.* v. *Sambhu Raghu* (1876), ILR 1 Bom 347; *Mathura Naikin* v. *Esu Naikin* (1880), ILR 4 Bom 545; *Tara* v. *Krishna* (1907), ILR 31 Bom 495; *Jagannath Raghunath* v. *Narayan Shethe* (1910), ILR 34 Bom 553.

8 Evidence for the discussion in this and the next subsection is drawn primarily from research on the Bombay Presidency.

marriage, divorce, widowhood, and the like to lower-caste communities that had never previously practiced them (Carroll 1983; Chakravarti 1998: 123–38). Non-elite marriage forms that historically recognized the contribution of daughters and wives to their natal and marital households through the institution of bride-wealth (in which a preponderance of gifts moved from the husband's family to the bride's family) were increasingly replaced by dowry marriage, which placed the bride's family in a denigrated position, burdened by the daughter who needed to be married. Likewise, the focus on regulating women's sexuality as a critical component in ensuring caste purity and elite caste status was associated with practices of child marriage and enforced widowhood. Although the colonial state viewed these elite customs as barbaric and oppressive to women, it also criminalized lower-caste customs that recognized the validity of divorce and remarriage (the 1861 Indian Penal Code defined such practices as bigamy or adultery), and it subjected widow remarriage, which was regularly practiced within these communities, to the less progressive constraints of new legislation designed to address high-caste Hindu widows (Hindu Widows Remarriage Act, Act XV of 1856). Such legislation thus actually worsened the legal position of lower-caste widows (Carroll 1983). Judicial decisions on these issues as they came before the courts further enforced this marginalization of non-elite practices (Agnes 1999; Carroll 1983; Chakravarti 1998; Sturman 2006). A similar process occurred with the matrilineal and polyandrous family form (*Marumakkathayam*) among the Nayars on the Malabar coast (Arunima 2003). Notably, however, alongside elite reformist legal personnel (both British and Indian) who advocated these changes, many caste groups also actively participated in this process, adopting a variety of new patriarchal practices to facilitate claims to higher status or respectability (Arunima 2003; Chakravarti 1998: 92, 151–9). Thus, although colonial officials regularly denigrated elite Hindu marriage forms as oppressive to women, both legislation and jurisprudence treated such forms as normative, expanding their application and prohibiting non-elite forms. Finally, an important point that emerges from this history is the interpenetration of diverse legal instruments and jurisdictions in the regulation of Hindu marriage: Hindu law was ultimately defined by colonial legislation, including both criminal and civil statutes, and by judicial precedent, as much as by textual authorities and custom.

Inheritance: defining the joint Hindu family form

Colonial Hindu law early developed and largely maintained a number of basic premises and legal assumptions that shaped adjudication in the courts.

Of these, the most important was that the normative Hindu family form was what became known as the "joint" or "undivided" Hindu family, defined in British legal language as a coparcenary, in which multiple generations of lineal males lived and ate together in the same household, and held in common any family property. In the language of the courts, the legal assumption was that all Hindu families were joint, and all property was joint family property. According to this model, wives, unmarried daughters, widows, and disabled or otherwise dependent males had a right to maintenance, but they were not members of the coparcenary. In areas of India outside of Bengal and Assam, Vijñāneśvara's *Mitākṣarā*, a late eleventh-century commentary on the *Yājñavalkya Smṛti*, was considered the primary textual authority, while in Bengal, Jīmūtavāhana's early twelfth-century *Dāyabhāga* was treated as primary.[9] In areas governed by the *Mitākṣarā*, every lineal male held by birth a claim to an equal share of the family property, but the individual shares of men and boys living in a joint family were never calculated, except on the break-up or partition of the family itself (and the formation of new joint families), usually after the death of the patriarch. In Bengal and Assam, a son could claim his share of family property only after the death of his father, and, unlike in the *Mitākṣarā*, the father was accorded full power during his lifetime over both ancestral moveable and immoveable property, as well as over separate property. Under the *Mitākṣarā*, such power existed only as an exception in times of necessity.

These characterizations were treated as settled matters of law. Nonetheless, the actual practice of the courts worked to shift the meaning and implications of the colonial definition of joint family as early as the 1860s, and, by the 1930s, quite different assumptions had come into play (I. Chatterjee 1999; Derrett 1968: 400–36; Sturman 2005). Most notably, despite the attention – both colonial and postcolonial – devoted to the condition of high-caste Hindu women, it was in the juridical treatment of high-caste Hindu men that the most profound shift occurred (Sreenivas 2004; Sturman 2005).

Until the 1860s, the colonial courts in regions governed by *Mitākṣarā* treated the coparcenary as a single, indivisible property-holding unit, meaning that individual men within the family could not ordinarily mortgage, sell, or otherwise transact with their share of the property. According to legal rulings in the 1830s and 1840s, the mere calculation of a son's share was tantamount to partition of the family and family property, amounting to

[9] On this, see Rosane Rocher's chapter in this volume.

the dissolution of the existing coparcenary and the founding of new coparcenaries. Indeed a son's right to call for partition from his father during the latter's lifetime and against his will was a subject of considerable dispute, and in general the courts confirmed the rights of the father against those of the son. Moreover, the courts confirmed that any economic support from the joint family property provided for a boy's education rendered any property he later acquired as a result of that education joint family property. Thus, property that could be classified "self-acquired," separate from joint family property and under the individual's control, remained an extremely narrow category during this period. This weighty union of interest was also expressed in the colonial enforcement of the inheritance of debts, a stipulation also drawn from the Sanskrit textual authorities, that rendered sons liable for the debts of their fathers even if they did not inherit any property from them (Derrett 1968; Sturman 2005).

Starting in the 1860s, however, all of these terms began to change. The high courts began to treat coparcenary property as conceptually divisible into shares, with each male family member entitled to mortgage or sell his share, while still remaining joint with the family. In Bombay, the Bombay Hindu Heirs Relief Act of 1866 limited a son's liability for his father's debts to the amount of any property inherited from him. And within a few decades, it became an accepted legal principle that a son had the right to call for partition and claim his share of both moveable and immoveable property even against the wishes of his father.[10] In 1930, the Hindu Gains of Learning Act rendered property a man acquired as a result of his education (for example, in the new colonial professions), free from the claims of the joint family, thereby dramatically expanding the category and mobility of "self-acquired" property. And perhaps most strikingly, a ruling by the courts later in that decade reversed the underlying legal assumption that had prevailed throughout the operation of colonial Hindu law: that property held by a joint Hindu family was presumed to be joint family property.[11] These historical shifts in the jural meaning of the joint Hindu family in some sense represented an emancipation of sons from the burdens of family. While sons nonetheless remained subject to colonial Hindu law, court judgments on the application of Hindu law to able-bodied caste Hindu men increasingly came to treat those men as autonomous subjects of the state, and personal law increasingly came to be associated with the particular disabilities of women.

[10] *Jugmohandas Mangaldas* v. *Sir Mangaldas Nathubhoy* (1886), ILR 10 Bom 528.
[11] *Babubhai Girdharlal* v. *Girdharlal Hargovandas* (1937), 61 Bom 708.

The legal treatment of women (and of non-coparcener dependent subjects more generally) as property holders was uneven. While women were excluded from the coparcenary, the Sanskrit corpus included a concept of "women's wealth," or *strīdhana*, which had been defined differently by different *smṛti* writers and commentators. Although primarily consisting of gifts given to a girl on her marriage, some commentators also included "gifts from affection" from her husband, property inherited from her mother or her father, and even property acquired through purchase, finding, or her own labor. Yet the kinds of property it included and the nature of ownership it entailed remained highly contested. As the legal scholars Raymond West and Georg Bühler cited one commentator in their work on the legal opinions of *śāstrīs* in the Bombay Presidency (1878: 64): "The question, what constitutes Stridhana, the separate property of a married female, as well as its descent, are topics regarding which, as Kamalakara in the Vivadatandava despairingly exclaims, 'the lawyers fight tooth and nail,' (yatra yuddham kachakachi). It is impossible to reconcile with each other even the views of those lawyers whose works are the authorities in this Presidency." Fundamentally, even beyond the disputes among Sanskrit authorities, British conceptions that linked property and autonomy made it difficult to square the meaning of *strīdhana* with their notions of property rights, particularly given the notoriety of the passage of the *Mānava Dharmaśāstra* that rendered females subject to perpetual tutelage. Although the Bombay courts were widely viewed as granting daughters and sisters a more favorable position in the order of succession and stronger powers of ownership than in other presidencies,[12] these were to some extent weakened from the turn of the twentieth century, bringing Bombay in line with the more restrictive treatment of *strīdhana* in the other presidencies (Sturman 2005).

In a separate category altogether, never treated as part of *strīdhana*, was the property a widow inherited from her husband. Indeed, the unevenness in the legal treatment of women perhaps emerges most conspicuously in the case of caste Hindu widows, whom colonial officials frequently considered the most abject subjects. On the one hand, the courts treated them as exceptional and incomplete owners, importing the British legal concept of the "widow's estate," in which the widow was conceptualized as a placeholder, a tenant-for-life, until the property "reverted" to her husband's heirs upon her death. Likewise, the courts formulated widows and deserted wives'

[12] For two important cases defining the rights of daughters and of widows, see *Pranjivandas Tulsidas* v. *Devkuvarbai* (1859), 1 Bom HCR 130; *Bhagirthibai* v. *Kahnujirav* (1886), ILR 11 Bom 285.

right to maintenance as based in their non-autonomy and permanent legal dependence (Agnes 1999; Kapur and Cossman 1996). And yet the same notions of liberal property rights and of the rights-bearing subject that came to shape the legal treatment of Hindu men in the late nineteenth century also came to pervade legal practice relating to women. Most strikingly, the Hindu widow inheriting from her husband gradually came to be defined as a "full owner" bearing all the rights of ownership, with the sole limitation that her alienation of immoveable property made without legal necessity was voidable at law. Ironically, this legal position was essentially congruent with the treatment of Hindu men under early colonial Hindu law (Sturman 2005). As caste Hindu men were increasingly treated as autonomous property holders, this expansion of Hindu widows' rights under colonial Hindu law took on an asymptotic quality: with the widow ever approaching but never quite attaining the legal position of Hindu men. Such an asymptotic expansion of rights was, and is, characteristic of modern liberal states, as claims to equality inherently reinforce the difference they aim to eradicate (U. Mehta 1999; Povinelli 2002; Scott 1996).

What is most significant about this historical process, then, is that it occurred within the domain of personal law. In other words, colonial Hindu law was pervaded by the logics (and the contradictions) of liberalism and its concepts of property, of rights, and of the rights-bearing subject. Indeed, by the early twentieth century, topics of Hindu law that the courts had earlier treated as fundamentally matters of spiritual concern, such as adoption (to provide a lineal male heir when a man had none), came to be treated as essentially secular acts in which ritual counted little and the conveyance of property was of equal if not greater concern.[13] In this sense, a transformation occurred within the content and practice of colonial Hindu law, bringing Hindu law increasingly into line with the secular civil law of the colonial state.

THE POLITICS AND POLITICIZATION OF COLONIAL HINDU LAW

The dual structuring features of colonial personal law – as delimited to issues involving the family, and as a separate legal domain, free from colonial intervention (even as it formed an integral part of the colonial legal regime) – also help explain the politics and politicization of Hindu law that occurred

[13] *Lakshmibai* v. *Ramchandra* (1896), ILR 22 Bom 590; *Anandi Pai* v. *Hari Suba Pai* (1909), ILR 33 Bom 404.

in the nineteenth and twentieth centuries. The textual traditions and practices that came to be classified as "Hinduism" had always been intertwined with forms of worldly power, but Hindu law became a particular kind of politicized site in the context of the modern colonial state, and indeed operated as a critical locus in the formation of modern Hinduism as a unified corpus of beliefs, texts, and practices. In this context, the politicization of Hindu law needs to be understood as an artifact of the paradoxical form of recognition of Hindu nomos within colonial law.

Colonial Hindu law involved the legal recognition of (a version of) Hindu societal values and practices, but the colonial power equally sought to bolster its legitimacy through a critique of Hindu law and society, carving out a role for itself as humanitarian savior of oppressed Hindu women (Mani 1998; Spivak 1988). As an aside, it is thus all the more ironic that the new social norms regarding marriage that the colonial state enforced under the rubric of Hindu law typically failed to have the envisioned liberating effect. But more importantly, the ethical claims of colonial Hindu law sat uneasily with the morality of the state. Gayatri Spivak's famous characterization of colonial state ideology regarding the 1829 abolition of *satī* as "saving brown women from brown men" (1988) could thus be revised and extended in the more general context of colonial Hindu law in the following ventriloquism: "We will rule you by your own laws, but the debased nature of your own laws is precisely why we must rule you." In other words, officials and institutions of the colonial state at once decried the immorality and oppression inherent in Hindu law, treated it as a primary reason for colonial governance, and insisted on enforcing it, as the law appropriate to this debased people.

Given its primacy in colonial ideology, it is not surprising that the "status of women" in Hindu society and the nature of Hindu marriage in particular came to form the core of a variety of efforts by Hindu elites to reclaim for themselves a moral terrain as the basis for political – and ultimately nationalist – claims. Yet it is crucial to recognize that this was so in large part because colonial formulations regarding the status of women meshed in important ways with powerful precolonial Indian ideologies in which women's comportment signaled community status. Within both premodern and colonial Indian contexts, women's comportment was key to differentiating Hindu from non-Hindu, elite Hindu from non-elite Hindu, as well as status within a given community (Chakravarti 1998; T. Sarkar 2001); to these, the colonial context added an emphasis on gender itself, construing "woman" as a universal category in relationship to that of men, rather than as a signifier of a variety of social distinctions. These related British and Indian significations gave the image of women a complex symbolic weight within public debates. In this context, Hindu reformers and eventually reformist nationalists sought to transform the treatment of women within Hindu society as the means to national liberation, pushing the colonial state to enact measures such as ending elite prohibitions on widow remarriage, eradicating female infanticide, and raising the age of consent. (The colonial state enacted legislation on each of these issues in 1856, 1871, and 1891 respectively.) In contrast, Hindu conservatives and conservative nationalists sought to preserve the ethical claims of customary practices that revolved around women's modesty and chastity, demanding exclusive control over the putatively private domains of religion and family as the original terrain of national sovereignty. Partha Chatterjee's influential treatment of this history, aiming to explain the depoliticization of the "woman question" at the turn of the twentieth century, points to a process of "nationalist resolution," in which reformist and conservative nationalists converged in construing the inner domain of the family as their own sovereign territory, not to be encroached by the colonial state (Chatterjee 1990). Bal Gangadhar Tilak's albeit highly contentious public campaign against the 1891 Age of Consent Bill (which raised the age of consent for girls from ten to twelve years of age) forms a signal example of this. Yet in fact all the parties to these debates sought state enforcement of (their vision of) Hindu law. They did not seek a state withdrawal from governance of marriage and the family. Moreover, as Mrinalini Sinha has argued, during the twentieth-century interwar era, anticolonial nationalists and Indian feminists shifted the earlier nationalist treatment of the "women's question," even as they also reconceptualized the prevailing colonial ideology that India's maltreatment of women mandated its political subordination. Instead, they argued that Indian women's subjection was a *product* of India's political abjection, making the social liberation of Indian women (as a universal category) conditional on the political liberation of the Indian nation (Sinha 2006). Although this argument lost force in the context of communal politics in the early 1940s, it posited what would become an ongoing critical legacy in the postcolonial era: As enshrined in the Indian Constitution, women are legally conceptualized as a universal category, and at the same time they are legally differentiated as subjects with divergent rights according to gender and religion under the jurisdiction of personal law.

By claiming to recognize Hindu and Muslim religious forms and values, construing them as determinative of Indians' legal identities, and yet also demarcating them as separate and divergent from the secular, liberal, and authoritarian principles of the colonial state, the system of personal law underscored the contradictory relationship of Indian nomos to the colonial state. As such, it also brought into relief the way that the colonial state inevitably embodied the ethics of the ruling society, rather than the "laws" and values of the society it ruled. In some sense, this failure merely amplified the paradox that pertains throughout the modern normative context of rule of law: that the social values, principles, practices, and beliefs that take shape in law are always inherently selective and the product of social struggles and forms of domination. But as a product of colonial power, and of colonial histories of rigidification, marginalization, and homogenization of social practice, this legal formation both embodied and produced these struggles in a highly distorted form. In particular, the "Hindu" quality of colonial Hindu law took on a heightened symbolic valence in the terrain of nationalist politics, even as its content – the laws regulating marriage and the family – was increasingly brought into line with secular laws and theories of property.

By the 1930s, colonial Hindu law entailed a modern religious law. At the level of form, Hindu law had become subject to new modes of bureaucratic rationality, as seen in the development of case law, legal reporting, citational practices, and the like. Although efforts at codification in the early 1940s foundered, these efforts themselves bespeak the extent to which Hindu law formed an integral part of modern state practice.[14] More significantly, because personal law rendered Hindu and Muslim identities the terms of recognition by the state – that is, people came before the state as Hindu or Muslim legal subjects – it became a critical site of politicization.[15] In this context, Hindu law was defined by the colonial state and tied to state power, while the actual beliefs that were meaningful to those denominated Hindu remained largely irrelevant to the state.

Like all legal systems, colonial Hindu law operated not merely as a system of adjudication, but also as symbolic of broader moral claims, in this case coming to stand for the status and strength variously of the community, nation, or civilization in relationship to the colonial state. Colonial Hindu law singled out the family, and ultimately women, as the symbolic terrain of Indian nomos. It posited gender (rather than caste or sect) as the primary distinction among persons subject to Hindu law, and it utilized the gendered nature of legal subjecthood and rights *within* Hindu and Muslim personal law to distinguish these religious communities. Ironically,

[14] See the chapter by Williams in this volume.
[15] See the chapters by Narula and Jenkins in this volume.

although by the late colonial era the changes that had occurred in the jurisprudence of Hindu property and families had in fact begun to undermine the characterization of Hindu law as representing a separate domain of Hindu social life, by the early decades of the twentieth century the symbolic significance of Hindu law as the domain of the nation and civilization had become amplified within public debate. Colonial British and Indian treatment of marriage and family as the essence of Hindu law thus rendered this putatively private domain a primary terrain of politics.

CHAPTER 6

Hindu law as personal law: state and identity in the Hindu Code Bills debates, 1952–1956

Rina Verma Williams

INTRODUCTION

As India negotiated the transition from the colonial era to Independence, issues of religion and law came to the forefront of the political agenda. One of the first major legislative accomplishments of India's newly elected Parliament was the passage of the Hindu Code Bills (HCB) between 1952 and 1956.[1] This series of four bills sought to codify and reform Hindu personal law – a project begun but ultimately abandoned by the British colonial government. A source of significant social and political controversy, this legislation outlined and prefigured the shape that Hindu law as personal law would take in independent India. The politicization of the personal laws reached its apogee in the years after Independence, as Hindu personal law came to be entangled in issues of community, identity, and politics.[2] Two key transformations begun in the colonial era came to fruition in this critical period: Gender became the site *on which* modern Hindu law (as personal law) has been constructed; and the modern state became the institution *through which* modern Hindu law (as personal law) must be negotiated. Examining the debates over, and surrounding, these bills – both within and outside the institutions of government – demonstrates these key transitions in Hindu personal law post Independence.

These two processes worked ultimately to disengage the legal category of "Hindu law" from its traditional roots in Dharmaśāstra: Rather than religious texts being the guiding force in defining Hindu law, Hindu personal law came to be embedded instead in the discourses and contradictions of modern identity and state power. The first site of transformation was gender: Religious and national identities were constructed in gendered terms during the debates. Secular nationalists supported the bills as a way to

[1] Hindu Marriage and Divorce Act (1955); Hindu Succession Act (1956); Hindu Minority and Guardianship Act (1956); Hindu Adoptions and Maintenance Act (1956).
[2] See Sturman's chapter in this volume.

achieve national unity and progress by enhancing and modernizing Hindu women's legal rights and social status. Religiously oriented opponents of the bills sought to preserve a socioreligious conception of Hindu social customs and traditions by immobilizing any perceived change to them, and thus to women's legal and other rights and status.

Second, because these gendered identities were embedded in a *legal* system – of Hindu personal law – they perforce had to be negotiated through the state. This has been true since then Governor-General Warren Hastings's institutionalization of the system of personal laws in 1772.[3] As India transitioned to independence, the postcolonial Indian state inherited the mantle of its colonial predecessor as the institution through which changes to Hindu personal law had to be negotiated. The influence of government and political institutions was evident in the debates over the HCB, and pointed up the contradictions inhering in the tripartite relationships between religion, law, and state.

This chapter draws on Parliamentary debates; legislative and government reports; correspondence of political leaders; public opinion surveys; and the activities of social organizations in the 1950s to trace these two processes that shaped the development and evolution of Hindu law as personal law in postcolonial India. The first section will briefly outline the historical background of the HCB. The second and third sections will examine, in turn, gender as the site *on which* Hindu personal law was constructed, and the role of state as the institution *through which* Hindu personal law was negotiated. In a brief final section I will touch on some implications of the analysis.

HISTORICAL BACKGROUND: HINDU LAW TO PERSONAL LAWS

India's personal laws represent a key part of the persistent legal legacy of the British colonial era (Dhavan 2001; Williams 2006). After their institutionalization in India in 1772, India's personal laws served as a template for British colonies in Africa and elsewhere. When these colonies attained independence, many of them retained the personal laws. Most personal laws today are an amalgam of three types of laws: (1) customary laws, originally unwritten but codified over time, based on the traditions and practices of different regions or communities; (2) imported Western laws and accumulated case law; and (3) religious laws, associated with the religions that evolved their own self-contained, self-regulating social

[3] See Donald Davis's chapter in this volume.

systems, including a legal system. The last category includes Islamic, Hindu, and Judeo-Christian laws. In South Asia and parts of the Muslim world, personal laws are applied primarily on the basis of religion. In other parts of Asia, Africa, and the Caribbean, they are applied on the basis of tribe, custom, and ethnicity as well as religion (Hooker 1975; Menski 2006).

The HCB represented the culmination of more than a century of debate about the relative virtues and vices of codifying Indian laws (Hussain 2003). Following Derrett (1957), "codification" refers to the creation of a comprehensive code of laws with minimal room for interpretation and applicable to all members of the community for which it is meant. "Reform" is widely construed to mean substantive modernization of the laws, often with the goal of securing greater equality on the basis of gender. Reform and codification may or may not necessarily occur together. Both have implications for the śāstric sources of Hindu law. Reform, by definition, means a break with the substantive content of original sources. Codification is more subtle: Though it purports to be about form and not content, several studies have shown how the processes of compiling, collating, and documenting worked to rigidify and solidify customs and traditions which had been lived and experienced flexibly and contextually. The net effect was to flatten into two dimensions what had been multi-dimensional lived realities – more often than not to the particular disadvantage of women (Oldenburg 2002). In British India, proponents of codification carried the day, except with respect to personal laws. In the middle of the nineteenth century, three Indian Law Commissions produced the Code of Civil Procedure (1859); the Indian Penal Code (1860); and the Code of Criminal Procedure (1861). The idea of codifying the personal laws seems to have arisen around this time as well, but the government was disinclined to make such an effort. The reasons are not entirely certain, but there was hesitation to interfere in what were seen as "native religious affairs," combined with the conviction that codifying religious personal laws would be an exceedingly complicated and controversial task (Williams 2006: 74–5).

Until the 1920s, neither the British colonial government nor Hindu community leaders seemed inclined to consider either the reform or codification of Hindu personal law. However, this did not mean that extensive social reform legislation was not pursued throughout this era. British colonial authorities reformed aspects of Hindu social tradition in a piecemeal fashion throughout the latter half of the nineteenth century and into the early twentieth century; by one count, over twenty legislative acts that affected Hindu social and religious tradition were passed between 1865 and 1939 (Mitra and Fischer 2002). Examples of such legislation included the abolition of *satī* (1829); the Caste Disabilities Removal Act (1850); the Hindu Widows Remarriage Act (1856); and the Age of Consent Act (1891). Many of these acts were meant ostensibly to improve the status of "native" Indian women – in Gayatri Spivak's now (in)famous terms, such legislation represented "white men ... saving brown women from brown men" (1988: 296). These reforms were often carried out with the support of, and even at the behest of, Indian reformers such as Raja Rammohan Roy – though with minimal involvement of women themselves. The literature on this social-reform legislation is extensive and will not be covered here (Carroll 1983; P. Chatterjee 1996: Chapter 6; Mani 1998; Sinha 1995). Rather, the important point for this analysis is, on one hand, the sharp disjuncture between a rhetoric of noninterference with respect to Hindu personal law and, on the other hand, an extensive interference with Hindu social customs in a piecemeal fashion. A comprehensive analysis of the causes and consequences of this fairly striking contradiction is much needed and would fill an important gap in our understanding of the development of Hindu law as personal law.

After the late nineteenth century, some discussion of codifying Hindu personal law arose again in the 1920s. In 1921, resolutions were introduced into the Council of State and the Legislative Assembly (the upper and lower houses, respectively, of the Viceroy's Legislative Council), by Indian members of the Council. These resolutions called on the government of India to form a committee to study the possibility of drafting a Hindu Code. In this early stage, concerns about the strength and integrity of links between Hindu personal law and its śāstric bases were evident on both sides of the debate. Proponents of codification expressed their concern that the original, religious textual sources of Hindu personal law were being eroded by piecemeal legislation. They saw codification as the best means to preserve the original religious sources and substantive content of the laws, and protect Hindu law from the ravages of modernization and piecemeal legislation. Opponents of codification, on the other hand, viewed codification as the "enemy" of classical Hindu law. They feared it would create rigidity in the laws and stamp out local customs, and destroy the flexibility and interpretive aspects of the original laws. Either way, both sides framed their arguments for or against codification in terms of its anticipated effects on religious textual laws. In the end, the government succeeded in convincing the movers to withdraw their resolutions. Thus they managed to avoid a vote and evade the issue (Levy 1973).

The impetus to take on the reform and codification of Hindu personal law emerged finally in the 1940s. The 1937 Hindu Women's Right to

Property Act (also known as the "Deshmukh Act") introduced substantial changes in how Hindu joint family property devolved, creating significant difficulties of interpretation and application. To sort the situation out, the government formed the first Hindu Law Committee (under the chairmanship of Sir B. N. Rau). The Committee recommended in 1941 that key aspects of Hindu personal law should be reformed and codified, beginning with the laws of succession and marriage. Subsequently, a second Rau Committee was appointed; in 1944, they reiterated their recommendation to codify and reform Hindu personal law, and presented the government with a draft Hindu Code. These proposals generated enormous controversy (including heated support as well as opposition), but ultimately gained government favor.

A significant question yet to be fully analyzed in the literature is how and why this change in British colonial government policy came about – from opposing or avoiding the issue to supporting codification and even reform of Hindu personal law. By the 1940s, it was evident that a transfer of power to Indian hands was coming. The debates of the 1940s prefigured, in many ways, the post-Independence debates on the HCB that were to come. They captured the transition to postcolonial modes of thinking about Hindu personal law, in which the connection to classical Hindu law recedes as a concern, to be replaced instead by modern concerns of identity and state power. During the 1940s, discourses of modernization, progress, religious and national identity, and women's rights emerged in ways they had not in prior decades. Supporters argued the need for Hindu society to modernize itself, and held that reform and codification would build unity within the community. Opponents, on the other hand, held that reform and codification would lead ultimately to the destruction of Hindu society itself, and that without public support and popular demand, such changes would constitute government interference in religious affairs. Here a concern for conformity with religious textual sources, or the preservation of links to them, was virtually absent from the debates. It was at best represented by a concern for the foundations of Hindu *society*: Religion and society were transposed in such a way that Hindu social customs and traditions were more at issue than Hindu law *per se*.

This transition away from the Dharmaśāstric bases of Hindu law, and to modern discourses of identity, was virtually cemented after Independence. India's first Prime Minister, Jawaharlal Nehru, made reforming and codifying Hindu personal law a top priority of his government. He revived the second Rau Committee's draft code and placed it under the stewardship of B. R. Ambedkar, a prominent Dalit leader and India's first minister of law.

Ambedkar's omnibus Hindu Code Bill consisted of eight major parts. Part I defined who was a Hindu: It stated that the Hindu Code would apply to any Indian who was not a Muslim, Parsi, Christian, or Jew, and established one personal law applicable to all Hindus. Part II of the Code dealt with marriage; Part III dealt with adoption; Part IV dealt with guardianship; and Part V, perhaps the most controversial part, with joint family property. Part VI of the Code concerned women's property; and Parts VII and VIII dealt with succession and maintenance, respectively. The Code departed from classical Hindu law in four main ways. First, it provided for separation or dissolution of a Hindu marriage, previously unknown in Hindu law (although lower castes had long practiced divorce and remarriage by custom). Second, it abolished the *Mitākṣarā* joint family system and established the *Dayābhāga* for all Hindus.[4] Third, it gave a share of inheritance to daughters in intestate succession; and, finally, it gave widows absolute rather than restricted (or limited) property rights (Gajendragadkar 1951).

Debate on the HCB began in the Constituent Assembly in February 1949. It encountered stiff opposition from conservative Assembly members from the start, and its progress was sporadic. As the debates drew to a close, it became clear that major compromises would have to be made if there was to be any hope of passing the bill. Yet repeated concessions seemed only to revitalize the opposition rather than pacify them, and to discourage further the supporters of the HCB. In October 1951, Nehru formally announced that the government would delay consideration of the HCB until after the first general elections. Just days later, Ambedkar resigned as law minister, citing Nehru's abandonment of the HCB as primary among his reasons for doing so.

Despite these setbacks, Nehru made the HCB a central theme of the election campaign. The election results certainly seemed to give Nehru the necessary mandate to pursue the HCB in the newly elected Parliament. The Congress Party swept the Lok Sabha, winning 364 out of 489 seats and 45 percent of the vote. In the Rajya Sabha, they controlled 146 out of 216 seats. The HCB was split into the four constituent bills that were introduced, debated, and passed by Parliament between 1952 and 1956. In the debates over these bills, gender and state became critical sites of transformation as Hindu personal law became progressively enmeshed in modern, gendered constructions of religious and national identity.

[4] On this, see the chapters by Rocher and Sturman in this volume.

MODERN IDENTITY IN HINDU PERSONAL LAW: GENDER, RELIGION, NATION

As concern for the integrity of the śāstric bases of Hindu personal law declined, the importance of gender, religious, and national identity became a central focus of concern in debates over the HCB. While religion was an important feature of the debates, the Hinduism in these debates represented more a set of social and economic customs and traditions, than classical textual religion. Neither proponents nor opponents of the HCB made significant reference to the Dharmaśāstric sources of Hindu personal law; rather, both sides framed their arguments in terms of modern, gendered identities.

Proponents of the HCB came from a wide range of groups. Within the Parliament as well as outside, they included both men and women representing a range of political parties – the Congress Party, of course, included many supporters, as did the parties of the left. Women Parliamentarians were overall staunch supporters of the HCB. The first Lok Sabha included twenty-three women. The majority (fifteen) belonged to the Congress Party. One belonged to the Communist Party and another to the Hindu Mahasabha. (The rest were independent or did not have a party affiliation specified.) The picture in the Rajya Sabha was quite similar: Of twenty women, at least seventeen were members of the Congress Party (another was nominated and two were listed as belonging to "other" parties).[5]

Virtually all those who spoke against the bills within Parliament were men. Only a handful were from the opposition parties of the Hindu nationalist right. These parties vigorously opposed the bills, but they won minimal representation in India's first Parliament: The Hindu Mahasabha and the Jan Sangh together held a mere six seats. Instead, much of the conservative opposition came from within the Congress Party itself. Even Dr. Rajendra Prasad, India's first president and a leading member of the Congress Party, butted heads with Nehru over the HCB.[6] No women spoke against the bills in Parliament, although several conservative Hindu women's organizations (composed largely of upper-caste and upper-class Hindu women) formed to oppose the legislation.

[5] See http://parliamentofindia.nic.in and http://rajyasabha.nic.in, accessed May 3, 2010.

[6] Prasad hinted that, as president, he might consider the option of not approving the bills if they passed Parliament. Nehru's response was that such an action on Prasad's part would precipitate a constitutional crisis that India's fledgling democracy probably could not withstand. Their correspondence on the issue can be found in R. Prasad (1984–95).

Throughout the debates on the HCB, gendered arguments waxed as concern for classical religious law waned. Both opponents and supporters referenced religion in their arguments, but in very different ways. Opponents of the HCB used the language of religion, religious tradition, and even Hindu religious texts to argue against the HCB. They did make scattered references to the śāstric (and even Vedic) roots of Hindu personal law – as when Jaswant Singh asserted that the HCB went "against the tenets of our Shastras and against our Vedas."[7] But such remarks were few and far between, made not by religious scholars but by lawyers and politicians. The Hinduism they sought to protect was more a socioreligious tradition than a return to, or a resurrection of, classical or textual Hindu law.

Religion also played an important role in supporters' arguments for the HCB, but in the reverse way. HCB supporters flatly denied that the personal laws were exclusively or even primarily matters of religion. Rather, they maintained that modern personal laws were largely a British colonial creation: "Today we are following Mayne's codification of Hindu law; we are not following Manu or any other law giver. We are following the law as interpreted and accepted for practice in the British courts of law."[8] Supporters noted that classical Hindu lawgivers never hesitated to innovate custom and law and adapt them to local circumstances and the needs of the day. So HCB supporters saw Hindu personal law as already being one step removed from its classical, religious textual roots.

Despite the critical role of religion in the arguments of both supporters and opponents of the HCB, the Hinduism at issue was increasingly unmoored from its roots in Dharmaśāstra – as concern for classical Hindu law receded, discourses of gender, religion, and nationalism took center stage. The conservative conception of Hindu religion was not tied to classical or textual law, but was based on social and family structures and economic concerns. The Hindu socioreligious traditions they sought to preserve turned critically on the differential roles of women and men within the context of traditional Hindu society. Opponents began with the premise that men and women were different, and had different roles to play in society. Because men and women had different responsibilities in society, they had different rights. Based on this view, granting women greater (or even just different) legal and social rights would upset the entire balance

[7] Jaswant Singh, *Council of States Debates* (hereafter *CSD*) (May 15, 1956), p. 2,207. See also: Devaprasad Ghosh, *Lok Sabha Debates* (hereafter *LSD*) (December 20, 1952), p. 2,666; Dr. Radha Kumud Mookerji, *CSD* (December 9, 1954), p. 1,346.

[8] Dr. Jaisoorya, *LSD* (May 12, 1954), p. 7,223.

of Hindu society.[9] Opponents held that the women demanding equality and greater legal rights represented a minority, only one small class of Hindu women: overeducated, Westernized, and unrepresentative of Indian women at large. If such women insisted on demanding equality, the very foundations of the Hindu social and religious order would be shaken.

Opponents' concerns were also economic, as their detractors were quick to point out. A prime example was their objections to granting a share of inheritance in intestate succession to daughters. Opponents feared that this provision, if passed, would accelerate land fragmentation in the countryside and generally "upset the whole economy of the country."[10] Yet they rarely expressed their objections in these terms. Discursively, their opposition was expressed in terms of the expected effect on Hindu socioreligious tradition, the Hindu joint family, and the stability and harmony of family relations. HCB supporters charged that opponents were not genuinely concerned with religion, society, or tradition, but with property.[11] They held that the main opposition to reforms came from those who simply wanted to protect their existing position of privilege in society. As Dr. Seeta Parmanand put it, the "opposition to this Bill comes" not from the truly or genuinely religious, but "from those who wish to mislead the Indian masses *in the name of* religion."[12]

Proponents supported the HCB as a way of enhancing Hindu women's legal rights and social status. Women were the most likely of all supporters to construct their arguments in these terms. But ultimately supporters believed that raising the status of women was critical not for its own sake, but because national progress depended on it. They reiterated the maxim (originally attributed to James Mill) that "the state of a civilization is judged by the status of the women in it."[13] Most supporters emphasized that the correct basis on which to judge the bills was whether they would benefit society as a whole, not just women in particular.[14]

Nivedita Menon has argued convincingly that, in this period, the struggle for gender equity in India "was never consciously articulated as distinct

[9] See B. K. Mukerjee, *CSD* (March 11, 1954), p. 2,539–40; H. C. Mathur, *CSD* (March 11, 1954), p. 2,865; Dr. R. K. Mookerji, *CSD* (March 23, 1955), p. 2,943; Jaswant Singh, *CSD* (November 27, 1956), p. 810; R. C. Gupta, *CSD* (March 23, 1955), p. 2,925.

[10] B. B. Sharma, *CSD* (November 23, 1955), p. 378.

[11] S. N. Mazumdar, *CSD* (November 30, 1955), p. 1,028.

[12] Dr. Smt. Seeta Parmanand, *CSD* (March 11, 1954). English translation of Hindi speech. Appendix, vol. VII, Annex no. 140, p. 345. Emphasis added.

[13] Bhupesh Gupta, *CSD* (March 10, 1954), p. 2,314–15.

[14] H. V. Pataskar (minister of law), *CSD* (March 22, 1955), p. 2,732; Seeta Parmanand, *CSD* (December 7, 1954), p. 1,085.

from the mainstream discourse of national integration. The two aims of gender justice and national integration seemed to be part of the same project" (2000: 82–3). Thus the relationship between nation building, modernization, and women's rights was one of virtual identity for these groups. I would argue that this assumed identity did not fully break until the 1974 publication of *Towards Equality*, the path-breaking report prepared by the Commission on the Status of Women, appointed by Prime Minister Indira Gandhi in preparation for the United Nations Decade for Women (1975–85). The report concluded that, in many ways, women's status in India had actually worsened after Independence – implying that, in some ways, Indian women might have been better off under British colonial rule! This finding was entirely unexpected, more than shocking, and provided the impetus for the growth of the modern Indian women's movement (Kumar 1999).

It also revealed the critical disjuncture between nationalist and feminist goals and agendas. In the HCB debates, some other, "larger" purposes were sought in the reform and modernization of Hindu personal law – progress, unification, and the revitalization of Indian (or at least Hindu) society. HCB supporters saw the emancipation of women as necessary *in order for* national unity and social progress to be achieved – not the reverse. This made national unity and social progress the end, and giving women more legal rights became a means to that end. So reforms meant at one level to benefit women became a site for the construction of Indian national unity and identity (Williams 2005). In this way, women came to represent modernization and progress (for HCB supporters) as much as they represented tradition and custom (for HCB opponents). So gender became central to both supporters and opponents' arguments while the classical, textual roots of religious law diminished in significance. The way the interaction between discourses of gender, religion, and nation played out was, in turn, shaped by political factors and the role of the state.

THE STATE AND HINDU PERSONAL LAW

The state has been critical in shaping the evolution of Hindu law as personal law ever since Hastings's declaration of 1772. Previous chapters in this volume, in addition to this chapter, posit clearly that Hindu personal law is *par excellence* a colonial legal system. This contradiction itself suggests the unique status of the postcolonial state as a form of the modern state. The Indian postcolonial state is clearly not a simple or mere continuation of its colonial predecessor. But it has not necessarily fully broken from its colonial legacies either. As a colonial Indian state became a postcolonial state, the impact of government and political leaders was central to shaping the outcomes of the debates and the final form of the HCB.

The HCB were indelibly marked by the institutions of modern government, including political leadership, institutions, and processes. Foremost among these were Nehru's unwavering commitment to a secular Indian nationalism and a particular conception of democratic process. Nehru wanted the HCB passed, but he preferred the bills pass democratically – which meant, to him, by free voting. Thus, despite the overwhelming majority the Congress Party held in Parliament, he refused to issue a party whip, which would have required Congress MPs to be present and to vote for the legislation. Practically, this meant major concessions had to be made to a strong and vocal opposition – much of which, as we have seen, resided within his own party. These concessions accumulated over the life of the HCB, and included both procedural and substantive concessions.

The government did place importance on enhancing legal rights for Hindu women: The HCB gave women greater rights, at least on paper, than they had previously possessed. But ultimately Nehru and his Congress government, like other supporters, believed that women's rights had to be enhanced in order to advance the progress of the nation as a whole. Nehru believed, like other supporters, that a civilization could be judged by the condition of women: "I have long been convinced that a nation's progress is intimately connected with the status of its women" (Nehru 1990: 384, May 10, 1956). Thus the procedural and substantive concessions that Nehru and the Congress Party government made to the bills were overwhelmingly those that compromised women's rights, watering down the actual content of the reforms and curtailing legal and social rights Hindu women might otherwise have won. These included the following changes:

(1) The original HCB abolished the *Mitākṣarā* joint family system and replaced it with the *Dayābhāga* joint family system (which was widely seen as more progressive) for all Hindus (Kishwar and Vanita 1990). Progressives even argued that the joint family system should have been abolished altogether. The final version reestablished the *Mitākṣarā* system.
(2) The original HCB provided for separation or dissolution of a Hindu marriage. The final version included a restriction allowing divorce only after three years of marriage.
(3) The original HCB abolished custom altogether; the final version included the reestablishment of customary law.

(4) The rights of women to adopt children were severely restricted, as was the option of adopting girls rather than boys.
(5) The original HCB had given daughters a full share equal to the share of sons in intestate succession. This was already a very limited property right, since by definition it excluded agricultural land and joint family property, and included only self-acquired property and, of course, property that had not been otherwise willed away. The final version of the bill reduced this to half a share. In addition, an amendment was added that allowed sons to buy out a daughter's share of inheritance with her "consent."

When all was said and done, the vast majority of those who supported the HCB felt its substantive reforms were actually quite limited.[15] Women MPs in particular expressed their sense that the HCB in its final form did not equal even the most progressive of local Hindu customary practices.[16] Government leaders acknowledged that reformers and progressives were dissatisfied with the limited extent of the reforms. And subsequent studies have shown that the HCB had, and has had, minimal impact on most women's lives (Agarwal 1994; Basu 2001; Luschinsky 1963).

But where concerns of gender equity were compromised, those of nation-building were not. This can be seen most clearly in the HCB's definition of whom it would apply to – that is, who counted as a Hindu. By defining a Hindu as anyone who was *not* a Muslim, Parsi, Christian, or Jew, the HCB sought to erase distinctions of caste, sect, and region within Hinduism, and even reached to include other religious traditions. The HCB elided religious distinctions among Hindus, refusing – or at least failing – to acknowledge the vast regional divergence of customs or divisions of caste and *jāti* among and between Hindus. It did not even define Sikhism, Jainism, or Buddhism as separate religious traditions. All three of these religions had originated as reform movements within Hinduism, but certainly by the 1940s were widely accepted as separate religious traditions by the Indian government itself. Indeed, the Census Bureau of India continued to collect data by the following religious categories: Hindu, Muslim, Christian, Sikh, Buddhist, Jain, and "Other" (defined to include "all other religions and persuasions").[17]

[15] See Krishnamurthy Rao, *CSD* (March 24, 1955), p. 3,035; Seeta Parmanand, *CSD* (December 20, 1952), p. 2,685.
[16] Seeta Parmanand, *CSD* (November 28 and 29, 1956); Smt. Pushpalata Das, *CSD* (March 23, 1955); Smt. Bedavati Buragohain, *CSD* (March 24, 1955); Smt. Lakshmi Menon, *CSD* (March 23, 1955).
[17] Census of India 1991, Part vB(ii)–Religion. Table C-9, www.censusindia.net/, accessed May 3, 2010.

But the nationalist conception of 1950s progressives served precisely to minimize or erase distinctions within the Hindu community and create Hindu social unity through legal uniformity – the actual reality of the multiplicity of ways of being Hindu notwithstanding (Agnes 1996). Thus, like most forms of group social identity, the HCB's definition of "Hindu" worked to elide difference *within* the "community" (which it was itself defining), while simultaneously instantiating difference *between* Hindus and "other" communities – most notably and especially, Indian Muslims. This is not to say that the HCB were *successful* in erasing distinctions within the Hindu community; even a cursory overview of modern Indian politics would belie such an inference.

Rather, the institutionalization of a modernizing, nationalist vision of Hindu personal law has served over time (and in conjunction with the state's approach to Muslim personal law) to entrench a conception of Hindu personal law as progressive and "reformed" – standing in purported contrast to Muslim personal law and (whether intentionally or not) providing grist for Hindu nationalist communal politics in subsequent decades. But this nationalist reformism came at the expense of genuinely substantive improvements in Hindu women's legal rights. The myth was thereby perpetuated that significant reform of Hindu personal law had been accomplished, when in fact by many standards (and certainly by standards of women's rights and gender equity), the HCB fell far short of achieving large-scale change – even if meaningful implementation had been possible or practiced.

The system of Hindu personal law throws into relief the complexity inhering in the tripartite relations between religion, law, and state. Throughout this volume, contributors explore the extent to which, and with what consequences, law and Hinduism have been constitutive of each other over the course of Indian history. Since Hastings's 1772 declaration, religion has come to be represented in law, while religious law has come to represent religion and religious community identity. As religion and law came to be mutually constitutive of each other from the colonial to the postcolonial era, religion as law became progressively engaged with the state at the same time that law became progressively disengaged from religion.

The eminent sociologist Max Weber identified, nearly a century ago, the mutually constitutive, perhaps even tautological, relation between law and the state. The modern state is the sole enforcer of law(s); at the same time, law serves as the basis of legitimacy of state authority. Weber identified law – rule of, and by, law – as the defining characteristic of modern state power. It was what set the modern state apart, indeed marked it as modern, from the despotic and otherwise personalistic rule of its predecessors (Cotterrell 1983). Legal scholars have extensively addressed the extent to which – and with what implications – law can, should, or must be viewed as uniquely connected to and enforceable by the state (Tamanaha 2001).

Unlike most systems of personal law established in Britain's later colonies (primarily in Africa), which had dual court systems to implement dual legal systems, India's court system remains singular, and secular. That is, one court system has adjudicated the religious personal laws as well as civil and criminal laws. Indeed, the passage of the HCB, along with subsequent developments in both Hindu and Muslim personal law, has firmly established the institutions of the state – particularly Parliament and the courts – as the only valid arena in which changes or modifications to personal law can and must be made. Far from a secularism that raises illusory "walls" between religion and state, then, religious personal laws deeply and directly implicate religion in the state, and the state in religion – or, at least, in the incarnation of religion that personal laws represent.

Weber argued that religious law(s) could not provide the basis for legitimacy of a modern state, because such a situation might split the loyalties of the people – between their loyalty to the state, and to the religion that was the source of the laws. He also saw the presence of religion in politics as increasing the possibility that greater coercion would have to be used by state elites (Weber 1946a).[18] It is certainly the case that religious personal laws have been an ongoing dilemma for the Indian state, for political parties, and for political leaders from Independence on. This has been true even as Hindu law has become disengaged from its roots in Dharmaśāstra. Indeed, a central premise of this chapter has been that the exigencies, institutions, and modalities of modern state power have themselves played a significant role in that very process of disengagement.

CONCLUSION

This chapter has identified two critical shifts that marked the transformation of Hindu law as personal law in India's early postcolonial years. In one critical shift, gender emerged as the key site *on which* Hindu law as personal law came to be constructed. While discourses of gender equity and women's rights became a central part of the debates over reforming and codifying Hindu personal law in this period (in a way they had only begun to be central under British colonial rule), this is not to argue that the debates or

[18] I am grateful to Jayanth K. Krishnan for bringing this point to my attention.

legislation were aimed solely or even primarily at securing gender justice. Rather, discourses of religious and national identity shaped the central concerns of the opponents and the proponents, respectively, of the bills. Examining their arguments showed that while religion was central to the debates, concern for a return to the classical or Dharmaśāstric roots of Hinduism or Hindu law receded, replaced instead by modern conceptions of both religious and national identity constructed in gendered terms.

The second critical shift was to the (modern, postcolonial) state as the key institution *through which* Hindu law as personal law had perforce to be negotiated. The state became the venue for the personal laws to be debated, modified, or otherwise considered in any meaningful capacity. The influence of the state was apparent in very specific ways in the development and outcomes of the HCB. Nehru and the Congress Party government, strong proponents of the HCB, prioritized nation-building concerns over those of gender equity.

Neither gender nor the state as critical sites of transformation was exclusive to postcolonial or post-Independence India. Both of these shifts were begun in the colonial era itself, as prior chapters have amply documented. Yet a fundamental shift in meaning came with the transition from colonial to independent rule that had broader implications for the tripartite relations between religion, law, and the state. The legacies of the HCB and the 1950s continue to manifest in the politics surrounding the personal laws in India in multiple ways, many of which will be examined in subsequent chapters in this volume. These include the rise to national political prominence of Hindu nationalism in the 1990s, a rise built to a significant extent on the further politicization of the personal laws through the 1980s, and the indictment of the Congress Party's purported appeasement of minorities and "pseudo"-secularism.[19] Gender continues to be the critical site on which constructions of the personal laws are built – indeed more recent debates have been framed almost exclusively in terms of women's rights. And the implications of religion as identity, manifested in religious law, now reverberate globally, well beyond the subcontinent.[20] The roots of these developments can all be traced in an important sense to the evolution of Hindu law as personal law in the early years after Independence.

[19] See Narula's chapter in this volume. [20] See Krishnan's chapter in this volume.

PART II

Law in ancient and medieval Hindu traditions

CHAPTER 7

Hindu jurisprudence and scriptural hermeneutics

Lawrence McCrea

In classical Hindu India the discipline of legal theory or jurisprudence (Dharmaśāstra) always bore close conceptual links with that of scriptural hermeneutics (Mīmāṃsā). Mīmāṃsā provided what came to be the dominant account of the nature and origin of legal texts and the rules they encoded, and the most widely accepted justification for their validity and trustworthiness as codes governing human conduct. The practitioners of Mīmāṃsā (or Mīmāṃsakas) became what one might call the primary ideologists of Dharmaśāstra, taking it upon themselves to construct airtight arguments for its authority,[1] and defending it against any legal/moral textual traditions which sought to rival it (most notably Buddhism and Jainism, but not limited to these, as we shall see). Yet despite this close linkage at the level of theory, for much of their history the practitioners of Mīmāṃsā and Dharmaśāstra show some surprising divergences in their interests, preoccupations, and textual practices. There was very little professional overlap between the two fields: Up until the sixteenth century, there were only a handful of people who wrote in both areas. More notably, though, most writers on Dharmaśāstra seem to have had little or no interest in the epistemic justification of the authority of Dharmaśāstra in general, or of the specific texts they were concerned with. They seem prepared to take this authority for granted, and devote themselves instead to the specifics of interpretation: trying to determine exactly what actions the *dharmaśāstras* prescribe, rather than explain just why it is that we should believe them. In

[1] "Authority" here should be understood purely in an epistemic sense (see Lubin's chapter in this volume). The Mīmāṃsakas are concerned with why we should regard Dharmaśāstric texts in general as a reliable authority for the guiding of human conduct, and (as we shall see) with *which* of such texts we should so regard, but they are wholly unconcerned with legal authority or with the *enforcement* of any of the rules contained in Dharmaśāstric texts. Their operative assumption (which treats Dharmaśāstric rules as basically similar to ritual performances) is that any rational person will ordinarily *want* to perform those acts that constitute *dharma* without the need for any social or legal coercion, since such actions are (by definition) conducive to his or her ultimate welfare (since their performance will generate good karma, while violating them will lead one to incur karmic penalties).

doing so, as we shall see, they show extensive familiarity with, and make extensive use of, hermeneutic principles developed by the Mīmāṃsakas, but they tend to avoid or downplay any potential questions about the authenticity or authority of the basic texts of Dharmaśāstra – questions which, as we shall see, were of major concern to the Mīmāṃsakas in their own discussions of Dharmaśāstra.

In what follows, I will present in brief the Mīmāṃsā arguments for the epistemic authority of Dharmaśāstra, followed by an overview of some of the ways Dharmaśāstra authors between the mid-first and mid-second millennium do and do not engage with these arguments in their own works. I will conclude with some remarks on the changes that took place in and after the sixteenth century, when the professional divergence between Mīmāṃsā and Dharmaśāstra seems largely to have broken down, and consider the impact this had on the later Dharmaśāstra literature.

THE MĪMĀṂSĀ ACCOUNT: "HEARING" AND "MEMORY"

The central concern of the Mīmāṃsakas, from the beginning, was to develop principles for the correct understanding and interpretation of the Vedas (the principal scriptures of early Hinduism). These they understood chiefly as manuals for the performance of sacrifices, which were understood to produce, by transcendent means, certain specific benefits for their performers, either in this life or in future ones. Their interest in the justification of Dharmaśāstra, and their understanding of its nature and its importance, is an adjunct to their understanding of the Vedas, and can only be understood against this background.[2]

The Mīmāṃsakas take the Vedas to be the prototypical, and indeed ultimately the only, source for our knowledge of *dharma*, which they define as "a good indicated by Vedic command."[3] *Dharma* is for them, stipulatively, something we can learn of only from a scriptural source. A key element in the Mīmāṃsā defense of Vedic authority is the absolute denial of any human capacity for direct awareness of the truths the Veda is taken to convey. There is no way we, or any other person, could know by our own

[2] For our knowledge of early (pre-seventh-century) Mīmāṃsā we are dependent almost entirely on the brief and sometimes cryptic *Mīmāṃsāsūtra* of Jaimini (*c.* 200 BCE) and the oldest surviving commentary on it, the *Mīmāṃsābhāṣya* of Śabara (*c.* fifth century CE). In both texts we find brief references to other authorities with sometimes divergent views but in any case Śabara's commentary provides the baseline understanding of Mīmāṃsā positions for all later authors within the tradition, and is the primary basis for the account of their position given here.

[3] "*codanālakṣaṇo 'rtho dharmaḥ*" (*MīmS* 1.1.2; Abhyankar and Joshi 1970–7: 1.13).

experience that, for example, the offering of certain substances into a sacrificial fire, accompanied by the recitation of certain ritual formulas, will produce for us a result such as rebirth in heaven. Such things are beyond the realm of human perception, and any person, now or in the past, who claims to know such a thing from experience cannot be trusted. Yet the Vedas do tell us such things. And they can be relied upon precisely because (it is argued) they are not produced by any person at all. The Mīmāṃsakas take the Vedas to be eternal and authorless, and therefore not subject to doubt on the grounds of their authors' incapacity.[4] The Vedas speak of things of which no human knower can have any knowledge, and hence their claims necessarily stand uncontradicted by any countervailing authority which could place their truth in doubt. It is precisely because no person can have knowledge of such things that we must, perforce, take the Veda's claims to be valid.

Yet, in defending the validity of the basic texts of the Dharmaśāstric tradition, the Mīmāṃsakas are forced to unsay, or at least to significantly qualify, much of what they have said before regarding textual authority. For the foundational texts of the Dharmaśāstra tradition present themselves as, and are taken by the tradition to be, the products of human authors – ancient sages such as Manu and Yājñavalkya. Hence, if they are to defend the validity of these texts, and of the social practices founded upon them, they must explain – without compromising their own basic position on Vedic authority – why these, and only these, human-authored texts should be taken as authoritative on matters of *dharma*. This constitutes the basic problematic for the Mīmāṃsakas in dealing with the authority of Dharmaśāstra, and of "tradition" and social custom more generally: How can one establish criteria that allow certain human claims and practices regarding *dharma* to be taken as authoritative, without creating a free-for-all, such that anyone and everyone can claim similar authority for their own texts and practices? They must open up the canon of sources of *dharma* to include some texts apart from the Vedas themselves, while still limiting and maintaining control over that canon.

[4] The cornerstone of the epistemology that underlies this claim is the Mīmāṃsakas' theory of "intrinsic validity" (*svataḥ prāmāṇya*), which holds that all cognitions whatsoever must be accepted as valid, unless and until some grounds are found for taking them to be false. Claims to supernatural knowledge made in the texts of Buddhists or Jains (the Mīmāṃsakas' principal sectarian rivals), can be falsified because we know them to proceed from human authors – the Buddha and the Jina, the founding figures of these two faiths. Our knowledge that humans are unable to directly cognize the supernatural gives us grounds for concluding that the claims of the Buddha and the Jina are unreliable, but no such grounds can be found in the case of the Vedas, as they have no author. Their claims stand unfalsified and hence, on the theory of "intrinsic validity," must be taken as true. For further discussion of this, see Bhatt (1962) and Taber (1992).

The basic response to this dilemma is a simple one.[5] The Mīmāṃsakas continue to maintain that it is really the Vedas and the Vedas alone from which reliable knowledge of *dharma* can arise. But the entire corpus of Vedic texts is not accessible to us. There are four main divisions of the Veda (*Ṛg*, *Yajur*, *Sāma*, and *Atharva*), and each of these exists in many different recensions or "branches" (*śākhā*). No one person can know them all, and, as these recensions may be geographically dispersed, it is always possible that there are any number of actually existing Vedic commands which are unknown to us. When Dharmaśāstra texts make claims about *dharma* that cannot be substantiated, we may, under certain conditions, infer that these claims are based on other Vedic texts to which their authors had access but we do not.[6] Thus, the *dharmaśāstras* are taken to represent the contents of Vedic texts of which the actual recited and memorized words are no longer accessible (to us, at least). For this reason, the Mīmāṃsakas refer to extant Vedic literature by the term "*śruti*" – "that which is heard" – and to Dharmaśāstra and other literature presumed to embody the content of lost Vedic texts as "*smṛti*" – "that which is remembered" (Brick 2006; S. Pollock 1990: 323 ff.). These terms were adopted as standard by many, including those within the field of Dharmaśāstra itself, for whom "*smṛti*" comes to be the standard term for the basic texts in their own tradition. So, even when we learn about *dharma* from a text of human authorship such as the *Mānava Dharmaśāstra*, it is really not on the basis of Manu's personal authority that we judge his claims to be valid, but rather on that of their (inferred or "remembered") Vedic source. It is always and only the Veda from which knowledge of *dharma* ultimately derives, even though this knowledge sometimes reaches us through a human intermediary.[7]

How then is one to know if a purported *smṛti* really does derive from Vedic sources? The basic criterion, as set forth by Jaimini, is "sameness of agents."[8] Because *smṛti* authors such as Manu were also scholars,

[5] The Mīmāṃsā position on the authority of the *dharmaśāstras*, and on other textual, cultural, and linguistic practices not specifically authorized by known Vedic texts, is given in section 1.3 of the *Mīmāṃsāsūtra* and its commentaries.

[6] The question of whether such inaccessible Vedic texts have actually ceased to exist, continue to exist somewhere outside the range of our experience, or have never existed as anything other than inferred bases for a beginningless chain of *dharmaśāstras* was much debated in the later tradition, chiefly by Śabara's rival commentators Kumārila and Prabhākara (both seventh century) and their respective followers, though others, such as the Nyāya logicians, sometimes contributed to the debate as well.

[7] This basic view was widely accepted, and is reflected in some of the *smṛtis* themselves, e.g., *MDh* 1.7, which declares "Whatever *dharma* Manu declares for any person, it is all stated in the Veda, since that consists of all knowledge" (G. Jha 1920–9, vol. 1: 69).

[8] "Or rather, the authority is inference [of an unperceived Vedic text], because of sameness of agents" ("*api vā kartṛsāmānyāt pramāṇam anumānaṃ syāt*"): *MīmS* 1.3.2 (Abhyankar and Joshi 1970–7: 2.74).

performers, and defenders of such Vedic texts as are known to us, and of Vedic tradition in general, we can legitimately infer that whatever they tell us about *dharma* is based on some legitimate Vedic source text, even if that text is not currently available to us. This criterion at least provides sufficient grounds for ruling out the validity of Buddhist and Jain texts as authorities, as these often directly criticize the Vedas, and as their upholders would in any case not wish to claim that they are based on any lost Vedic texts.

But problems still remain. Having offered this general defense of the authority of *smṛti* in *Mīmāṃsāsūtra* 1.3.1–2, Jaimini (as interpreted by Śabara) goes on to set forth two significant qualifications: *smṛti* texts are not to be taken as authoritative if they directly contradict *śruti* (*MīmS* 1.3.3), or if they appear to be prompted by a self-interested motive (*MīmS* 1.3.4). In the former case, according to Śabara, we must accept that the *smṛti* passage in question is a "confusion" (*vyāmoha*), and is not based on any Vedic source (Abhyankar and Joshi 1970–7: 2.87 ff.). In the latter case, for example when it is claimed that sacrificial priests should receive gifts above and beyond those specified in the relevant Vedic texts, Śabara observes as follows (Abhyankar and Joshi 1970–7 : 2.104–15): "[Such a] *smṛti* is not authoritative. Here there is another basis [apart from a lost Vedic text]. Certain people have done this out of greed, and the *smṛti* is based on this. And this is more reasonable than postulating a Vedic statement [as the source]." From this we see that, at least up until Śabara's time, the Mīmāṃsakas, while defending the authority of *smṛti* in general, were explicitly concerned with the problem of corruption, in both senses of that term: the possibility that innocent errors and confusions could creep into otherwise authoritative *smṛti* texts, and also that unscrupulous people could introduce spurious rules into *smṛti* to serve their own selfish interests.[9]

In commenting on Śabara's discussion of these issues, Kumārila takes quite a different line, radically minimizing the permissible grounds for questioning the authority of purported *smṛti*s. Kumārila, after offering a straightforward and sympathetic exegesis of Śabara's argument on *Mīmāṃsāsūtra* 1.3.3–4, turns around and attacks Śabara, offering a radically different interpretation of both *sūtra*s (Abhyankar and Joshi

[9] S. Pollock (1990: 328) is too quick to dismiss in particular the latter ground for questioning the authority of specific *smṛti* passages. Even from the brief discussion above it should be clear that it is an overstatement to say that "'interest' as such is never problematized" in the Mīmāṃsakas' treatment of *smṛti*. It is true that in the light of Kumārila's subsequent revision of Śabara's position, the question of deliberate and self-interested tampering with *smṛti* texts is largely marginalized, at least for Kumārila and his followers. But Śabara's concern with the issue is quite plain, and it is never forgotten, even by the later tradition.

1970–7: 2.104–15). Kumārila is deeply troubled by the implications of Śabara's position, which he sees as undermining the entire case for the authority of *smṛti*. One can only infer the existence of a lost *śruti* as the source of a *smṛti* if there is no other possible cause for it; once error (or greed) is admitted as a possible cause in one case, it will be impossible to categorically exclude it in any case whatsoever, and it will therefore be impossible to reliably infer that any of the particular commands contained in the *smṛti*s ultimately derive from a Vedic source. For this reason, he goes to great lengths to demonstrate that there simply are no cases in which a genuine *smṛti* truly contradicts an extant Vedic text.

Yet, even for Kumārila, the question remains: What, exactly, counts as a genuine *smṛti*, and how is one to know it when one sees it? Kumārila does not of course wish to allow the authority of *smṛti* to any work whatever that lays claim to it. The problem of screening remains. One needs a criterion that lets in the "right" *smṛti*s and keeps the others out. Having rejected Śabara's interpretation of *Mīmāṃsāsūtra* 1.3.3–4, Kumārila offers several possible alternative interpretations, one of which holds that the point of the two *sūtra*s is not to call into question the authority of individual commands in otherwise valid *smṛti*s, but rather to exclude entire texts from the realm of *smṛti* – texts which, while they may be "permeated with the scent of bits of meaning which agree with *śruti* and *smṛti*, such as nonviolence, truth-speaking, self-control, generosity, and compassion," are nevertheless "not accepted by knowers of the three Vedas" (Abhyankar and Joshi 1970–7 : 2.112). The list he offers of such spurious *smṛti*s is noteworthy: "compositions on *dharma* and *adharma* incorporated in Sāṃkhya, Yoga, Pāñcarātra, Pāśupata and Buddhist texts." Despite the inclusion of the Buddhists, most of the groups listed would generally be considered "Hindu," and their authors and adherents would presumably acknowledge at least nominally the scriptural authority of the Vedas. It is not simply a matter, then, of excluding the texts of those who, like the Buddhists, openly attack the Veda and disavow any association between it and their own "*smṛti*s." Even some of those who would consider themselves as belonging to the Vedic fold must be kept out. How then does one distinguish the good *smṛti*s from the bad ones? Kumārila is not as explicit about this as one might like, but he does address the issue briefly: "Only the statements of those authors of *dharma*-compilations . . . whose status as teachers is proclaimed by the Veda itself are authoritative, not those of anybody else – this is the conclusion" (*Tantravārttika* on *Mīmāṃsāsūtra* 1.3.7, in Abhyankar and Joshi 1970–7: 2.122).

Kumārila identifies a passage from the Veda that specifically mentions Manu as a worthy teacher, and hence the authority of his *smṛti* is attested to by the Veda itself.[10] Kumārila does not identify any other *smṛti* authors who are Vedically certified in this way, and it is not clear that this would resolve all doubts about the legitimacy of other putative *smṛti*s, but it at least secures the authority of the *Mānava Dharmaśāstra*, and provides a definite criterion by which at least some putative *smṛti*s could be ruled out. That at least some putative *smṛti*s may be corrupt or spurious remains a real threat which, while seldom addressed directly in the later commentarial literature, still looms in the background.

AUTHORITY AND AUTHENTICITY IN DHARMAŚĀSTRA COMMENTARIES

Somewhat surprisingly, most authors on Dharmaśāstra in the centuries following Śabara and Kumārila show little or no interest in the Mīmāṃsakas' arguments defending the authority of *smṛti*. Dharmaśāstra literature between the seventh century and the twelfth took the form mainly of commentaries on the existing *smṛti* compilations of Manu, Yājñavalkya, and others, and the authors of these commentaries seem to have seen themselves more as exegetes than as polemicists. They seem content for the most part to assume their audience will accept the texts they comment upon as authoritative without extensive argument. They cannot have been unfamiliar with the Mīmāṃsā arguments; most of them show a very detailed knowledge of Mīmāṃsā interpretive principles,[11] and, when they do refer in passing to the source of authority attaching to the *smṛti*, they generally do acknowledge that it is "rooted in the Veda."[12] A few of the more ambitious commentators do offer a fairly detailed overview of the general Mīmāṃsā theory of *smṛti* and its relation to *śruti*,[13] but even they steer clear

[10] "The verses of Manu are for kindling the sacrificial fire. Whatever Manu has said, that is medicine for healing" (*Tāṇḍyamahābrāhmaṇa* 23.16.6–7; Chinnaswami Sastri 1936: 526). There is a slight problem here, as the Mīmāṃsakas contend elsewhere (in *MīmS* 1.1.27–32), that the Veda, being eternal, cannot refer to particular historical occurrences or individuals. Kumārila gets around this by arguing that terms such as "Manu" are not simply the names of individual historical persons, but "eternal names" or recurring titles that are successively held by different individuals in different ages of the world. The Veda cannot refer to specific individuals, but can refer to recurring types, just as it can refer to "the Yajurvedic priest," even though every such priest is a historic individual (Abhyankar and Joshi 1970–7: 2.122–3).

[11] The specific Mīmāṃsā interpretive principles employed by a wide variety of Dharmaśāstra commentators and digest compilers have been catalogued in great detail by S. G. Moghe in a series of publications – see Moghe (1984, 1991, 1998).

[12] As is clear, for example, from the commentaries on *MDh* 2.7 printed in Mandalik (1886: 1.102–3).

[13] See especially Medhātithi's long commentary on *Mānava Dharmaśāstra* 2.6 (Mandalik 1886: 1.93–101), and Viśvarūpa's on *Yājñavalkya Smṛti* 1.7 (Ganapati Sastri 1921–2: 1.12–27).

of the discussions of corruption and inauthenticity touched on by Śabara and Kumārila.

When confronted by potential contradictions either within a particular *smṛti* text or between different *smṛti*s, these commentators, rather than attempting to assess the relative authoritativeness of the conflicting passages, usually attempt to resolve or explain away the conflict, often by a fairly sophisticated application of Mīmāṃsā hermeneutic principles. For example: *Yājñavalkya Smṛti* 1.49–50 states that: "A perpetual [*naiṣṭhika*] student should live with his teacher or, in his absence, with his son, or his wife, or his fire. Controlling his senses, taking his body to its end by this rule, he attains the world of Brahmā, and is not born here again" (Ganapati Sastri 1921–2: 1.56). In his discussion of this passage the eighth-century commentator Viśvarūpa confronts a potential objection:

> This *smṛti* enjoining perpetual studentship is in conflict with traditional texts. Why? There are perceptible traditional texts stating that "One should offer the Fire Offering as long as one lives", and "One should offer with the New and Full Moon Sacrifices as long as one lives." And this would be prevented if one is a perpetual student. And *smṛtis* which contradict these [traditional texts] are not authoritative. (Ganapati Sastri 1921–2: 1.57)

These lifelong sacrifices can be performed only by a married sacrificer, and hence cannot be performed by one who remains a student in his teacher's house and never becomes a married householder. Hence, a "perpetual student" would necessarily violate these Vedic commands, and the injunction to perpetual studentship must be dismissed as inauthentic. In reply to this objection, Viśvarūpa defends Yājñavalkya's rule, relying principally on the Mīmāṃsā-derived notion of "eligibility" (*adhikāra*) to limit the scope of the injunctions to lifelong sacrifice, and hence to remove the seeming contradiction (Ganapati Sastri 1921–2: 1.57–8). Injunctions to sacrifice apply only to those eligible to perform them. Persons may be disqualified from performance by various factors such as physical disability or improper caste status, and in such a case no penalty attaches to failure to perform sacrifices. Marriage too, Viśvarūpa argues, is a precondition for eligibility to sacrifice, but not a positive obligation. One may or may not choose to marry, and if one does not, then the sacrificial injunctions do not apply. But the taking of a wife is neither required nor implied by these injunctions; resorting to Mīmāṃsā terminology again, Viśvarūpa argues that marriage cannot be regarded as something "for the sake of the sacrifice" (*kratvartha*), such that the injunction to perform sacrifices would entail an injunction to marry as well. Rather, it is something a man may or may not undertake based on his own desire. Hence the rule regarding perpetual studentship is in no way contradicted by the commands to sacrifice, and both must be accepted as valid.

The commentators' resolution of apparent conflicts within or between *smṛti*s often hinges on a careful discrimination among the various sorts of injunctive rules (*vidhi*s) first analyzed by the Mīmāṃsakas. This can be seen, for example, in their treatment of the question of exactly when and how often a man should have sex with his wife. On this matter, the *Yājñavalkya Smṛti* declares that:

> Since the attainment of continuity in the world, and of heaven, depends on sons, grandsons, and great-grandsons, therefore women should be approached sexually, supported and well-protected.
>
> The fertile season of a woman is for sixteen days [after the onset of menstruation]. One should approach her, during that time, on even numbered days. One should avoid the "juncture" days[14] and the first four days, remaining celibate.
>
> Thus approaching one's wife, once, when she is willing and when the moon is well positioned, one should avoid [days when the moon is in the constellations of] Maghā and Mūla. [Thereby] a man may produce a son endowed with auspicious marks. (*YSm* 1.77–9; Ganapati Sastri 1921–2: 1.80–1)

Commenting on this passage, Viśvarūpa observes as follows:

> From the first verse, [which indicates that] "women should be approached sexually for the sake of sons", it is implied that one should approach a woman during her fertile season. Therefore these [latter] two verses, since their point is to restrict the "going" to only "once", should be seen to result in preventing one from going on other nights during the woman's fertile season. But the passage in Manu stating that "one should approach a woman sexually during her fertile season" (*Manusmṛti* 3.45) should be explained as being for the purpose of restriction [*niyama*], since [the term used for "approach" (*abhigāmin*)] ends in the suffix "*-in*", which [the grammarians] remember as signifying a vowed observance [*vrata*]. (Ganapati Sastri 1921–2: 1.82)

Viśvarūpa's position is that neither Yājñavalkya's command that "One should approach her, during that time," nor the parallel passage from the *Mānava Dharmaśāstra*, "One should approach a woman sexually during her fertile season," are positive commands which impose a definite obligation on a husband. Both are to be understood as "restrictive injunctions" (*niyama-vidhi*s), whose real purport is not to require the husband to approach his wife sexually, but rather to restrict the frequency and the possible days on which he may do so: He should approach her only once

[14] The new-moon and full-moon days, as well as the eighth and fourteenth days of each half-month.

during each menstrual cycle, and only on one of the specified days of the lunar month.

While later commentators on both *Yājñavalkya Smṛti* and *Mānava Dharmaśāstra* generally accept Viśvarūpa's conclusion that both of these should be seen as restrictive injunctions, several feel the need to indulge in quite elaborate discussions of injunctive typology to justify this conclusion and to rule out alternative interpretations. The Mīmāṃsakas divide injunctions broadly into three categories: "new injunctions" (*apūrva-vidhi*s), which enjoin actions not previously known such that in the absence of the injunction one would not know to perform them at all, "restrictive injunctions" (*niyama-vidhi*s), which limit the range of options one may follow in carrying out an act the need to perform which is known from some other source,[15] and "exclusionary injunctions" (*parisaṃkhyā-vidhi*s), which enjoin the performance of acts under certain conditions while simultaneously ruling out their performance under other conditions.[16] Medhātithi (ninth century), commenting on *Mānava Dharmaśāstra* 3.45 (the same passage quoted by Viśvarūpa above), seeking to defend the position that this is a restrictive injunction, enters into a quite thorough discussion of the three types of injunction, offering many examples for each type, both from the Vedic sacrificial commands cited in Mīmāṃsā texts and from *smṛti* sources (G. Jha 1920–9, vol. 1: 228–30). His main concern is to refute an alternative interpretation of *Mānava Dharmaśāstra* 3.45 which reads it as an exclusionary injunction. Vijñāneśvara (eleventh century, Karnataka), commenting on *Yājñavalkya Smṛti* 1.77 ff., takes a similar approach, supporting his reading of the injunction "One should approach her, during that time, on even numbered days"[17] with a comprehensive overview of the three categories of injunction which closely parallels, and seems to be directly modeled on, that given by Medhātithi on *Mānava Dharmaśāstra* 3.45. These commentators' efforts reflect not merely the occasional and offhand deployment of Mīmāṃsā concepts in the interpretation of *dharma* texts, but an increasingly systematic application of Mīmāṃsā interpretive techniques. So, while the *smṛti* commentators mostly steer clear of debate over the

[15] For example, given that wives are to be approached sexually for the purpose of procuring offspring, one would, in the absence of any specific rule to the contrary, be able to do so on any day during her fertile season. The injunctions discussed above, by proscribing certain days of the fertile season, restrict the range of days on which one may do so.

[16] If the injunction regarding permissible days for sexual intercourse were interpreted as exclusionary, it would both *require* (rather than merely allow) one to have intercourse on the permitted days and prohibit one from doing so on the days excluded.

[17] This is *Yājñavalkya Smṛti* 1.79 in Vijñāneśvara's version (Pandey 1967: 31), but equivalent to 1.78 in Viśvarūpa's text (Ganapati Sastri 1921–2: 1.80).

authenticity of either *smṛti* in general or specific *smṛti* texts along the lines pioneered by the Mīmāṃsakas, it should be clear from the foregoing examples that they typically bring to bear in their analyses a quite sophisticated knowledge of Mīmāṃsā hermeneutics, upon which they often rely heavily in attempting to extract a clear and consistent meaning from the texts they comment upon.

Despite their general dismissal or avoidance of the question of authenticity and inauthenticity of *smṛtis*, there is a divergence in the practice of these commentators that appears to tacitly presuppose the preeminent status of Manu's *smṛti*, as suggested by Kumārila's argument. While commentators on the other *smṛtis* (*Yājñavalkya*, *Parāśara*, etc.) very frequently cite parallel passages from other *smṛtis* in support of those they comment on, most often from the *Mānava Dharmaśāstra* itself, it is very unusual for commentators on Manu to cite other *smṛtis* in this way. However confidently commentators on other *smṛtis* proclaim the reliability of their own texts, they seem to feel that it is always best to find confirmation for their claims in Manu wherever possible.

The only *smṛti* commentator to directly address Kumārila's comments on authenticity and to apply his criterion for establishing it, as far as I can determine, is Mādhava (fourteenth century), in his commentary on the *Parāśara Smṛti*. Mādhava, probably not coincidentally, was one of the very few authors before the early modern period to write on both Mīmāṃsā and Dharmaśāstra.[18] Mādhava begins his text by presenting the view of an opponent who at first rejects the authority of *smṛti* as a whole (largely adopting the arguments of the opponent in Kumārila's *Tantravārttika*), after which he remarks as follows: "Or, let it be the case that somehow or other there is validity for the *Manusmṛti*. Nevertheless, what bearing would that have on the case in hand, the *Parāśarasmṛti*? For nowhere does the Veda declare the greatness of Parāśara, as it does of Manu. Hence, it cannot be determined that his *smṛti* is valid" (Tarkalankara 1893: 1.7–8). The opponent dismisses the authority of the *Parāśara Smṛti* by applying Kumārila's criterion, and Mādhava, in response, attempts to show that this text too can satisfy the criterion:

It is not the case that the greatness of Parāśara is not mentioned in *śruti*, since in this *śruti* passage – "Indeed, Vyāsa, the son of Parāśara, has said this"[19] – Vyāsa is praised in reliance on his being the son of Parāśara. If being the son of Parāśara is relied

[18] The only others of note are Bhavadeva (eleventh century, Orissa) and Halāyudha (twelfth century, Bengal).

[19] *Taittirīya Āraṇyaka* 1.9.2 (Mahadeva Sastri and Rangacarya 1985: 68).

upon to praise Vyāsa, the divider of the Vedas, whose greatness is acknowledged by all, then all the more so it must be said that Parāśara is great. (Tarkalankara 1893: 1.10)

Mādhava was the first person to comment on the *Parāśara Smṛti*, and this introductory discussion seems to suggest that he is somewhat uncomfortably aware of its marginality. It is perhaps for this reason that he felt the need to explicitly refer to and satisfy Kumārila's criterion when others pass over the issue in silence. In any case, his work stands out for the directness with which he addresses not only the general question of *smṛti*'s validity, but also that of the authenticity of the specific text he is commenting on.

SUMMARY AND CRITIQUE IN THE LATER *DHARMA* LITERATURE

Beginning around the twelfth century there is a marked shift in Dharmaśāstra literature, as commentary ceases to be the dominant mode of textual production and more and more *dharma* authors choose to write in the form of *nibandha*s or "digests" – topically organized compilations of quotations from various *smṛti*s (and, increasingly, from Purāṇic sources as well) (Lingat 1973: 115 ff.). The earlier works of this genre – Lakṣmīdhara's (twelfth century) *Kṛtyakalpataru* and Hemādri's (thirteenth century) *Caturvargacintāmaṇi* are noteworthy and typical examples – are, if anything, less concerned than the commentators were with Mīmāṃsā-derived debates over the authority of *smṛti*, or with demonstrating the authenticity of specific *smṛti* texts. Their method of composition is basically additive, simply assembling all the passages concerning a particular topic from as many putatively authoritative sources as possible, and seldom, if ever, pointing out potential conflicts between them or seeking to weigh their relative authority against one another.

In the sixteenth century, things seem to change rather markedly again, as a quite different sort of *dharma* compilation comes increasingly to the fore: one which casts an explicitly and programmatically critical eye on earlier works in the field. The production of this literature was centered mainly around Varanasi, which became an increasingly important site for the practice of Dharmaśāstra during this period. In marked contrast to earlier periods, most of the Dharmaśāstra authors of this time, particularly those based in Varanasi, wrote on Mīmāṃsā as well, and this growing professional convergence between the two fields is perhaps related to the shift toward more overtly critical methods in the Dharmaśāstra literature of the period.

Perhaps the starkest example of this new critical approach is Śaṅkarabhaṭṭa's (late sixteenth century) *Dharmadvaitanirṇaya*, "Dharmic Dilemmas Resolved" (edited in Gharpure 1943). As its title suggests, this text is organized entirely around dilemmas presented by the extant *dharma* literature: situations where several putatively authoritative texts are seen to point to different and contradictory conclusions about the proper rules governing a given practice. It does not simply deal with contradictions incidentally as they crop up in attempting to definitively establish a consistent set of rules. Rather, it makes the seeking out and arguing through of contradictions the fundamental method for analyzing *dharma*.[20] The main targets of criticism in this and similar works are the commentators and earlier digest-authors. Seldom if ever are actual verses from the *smṛti*s themselves attacked as incorrect or dismissed as spurious (though their proper interpretation and application are often disputed).

The most celebrated and heated controversy over the authenticity of purported *smṛti* texts in this period occurs not in the field of Dharmaśāstra itself, but in the field of theological metaphysics (Vedānta), which likewise draws heavily on Mīmāṃsā hermeneutics in its approach to textual interpretation and authorization. Vedānta authors rely heavily on both *śruti* and *smṛti* texts as the principal sources of their doctrines and arguments. Madhva (thirteenth century), founder of the dualist (Dvaita) school of Vedānta, cites a wide variety of obscure *smṛti* texts, many of them totally unknown apart from his references. This led some critics of Madhva's system, most notably the great sixteenth-century South Indian intellectual Appayyadīkṣita, to accuse Madhva of simply fabricating texts to support his views; a charge hotly denied, of course, by Madhva's own followers.[21]

There were no comparable charges of large-scale *smṛti* fabrication in the Dharmaśāstra literature of the late medieval and early modern periods. Nevertheless, despite the general absence of such open controversy over the authority of particular *smṛti* passages in the later Dharmaśāstra literature, there are indications that the issue was on the minds of at least some authors in the tradition. This can be seen, for example, from the manner in which they cite their sources. As already noted, as the digest form rose to prominence, it became more common for authors to cite passages from the Purāṇas as sources of dharmic rules. The Purāṇas, vast and diffuse encyclopedias of traditional learning, were generally regarded by the Mīmāṃsakas

[20] The rather more famous *Nirṇayasindhu* ("Ocean of Resolution") of Śaṅkarabhaṭṭa's nephew Kamalākarabhaṭṭa adopts basically the same method.

[21] The controversy is explored in detail in Mesquita (1997).

and those who adhered to their account of textual authority as a kind of *smṛti*, and hence indirectly partaking of Vedic authority in the same manner as the *Mānava Dharmaśāstra* and other such foundational Dharmaśāstra texts. Nevertheless, the texts of most of the major Purāṇas were highly fluid, and varied greatly from region to region and even from one manuscript to another, as was well known to writers on Dharmaśāstra. And, reflecting this, it becomes common among sixteenth- and seventeenth-century Dharmaśāstra authors, when quoting Purāṇa passages given in earlier digests, to specify the source from which they draw these passages. For example, in his *Nirṇayasindhu*, the great sixteenth-century juridical theorist Kamalākarabhaṭṭa routinely introduces quotations with labels such as "the *Bhaviṣyapurāṇa* [as quoted by] Hemādri"[22] ("*hemādrau bhaviṣye*") or "the Devīpurāṇa [as quoted] in the *Kṛtyakalpataru*"[23] ("*kṛtyakalpatarau devīpurāṇe*"). By identifying the passage as "the *Bhaviṣyapurāṇa* as quoted by Hemādri," rather than simply as "the *Bhaviṣyapurāṇa*," Kamalākarabhaṭṭa, without directly challenging the authority of the quoted passage, at the very least brackets the question of its authenticity – this is *what Hemādri says it says* in the *Bhaviṣyapurāṇa*. This is certainly nothing like the kind of outright attack on the authenticity of purported *smṛti*s found in Appayyadīkṣita, but it does at the very least suggest an awareness of the complexity of textual transmission and the attendant potential for textual corruption and this, coupled with the critical and argumentative methods championed by authors such as Śaṅkarabhaṭṭa and Kamalākarabhaṭṭa, makes the status of the truths and the commands for living found in the *dharma* literature come to seem ever more subject to contestation and to doubt.

So, despite the general suppression of overt disputes over the authenticity of purported *smṛti* texts in the later Dharmaśāstra literature, questions of authority and authenticity prove hard to avoid, and it comes to seem more and more difficult for authors in the field to arrive at anything approaching consensus over what, exactly, *dharma* is. This produces a decided change of tone in the Dharmaśāstra literature. What one gets from these texts comes to sound less and less like an unshakably authoritative and oracular voice of truth and more and more like an interminable, and ultimately irresolvable, argument.

22 The (thirteenth-century) author of the *Caturvargacintāmaṇi*, one of the best known and most influential of the early digests.

23 Another important early digest, composed by Lakṣmīdhara (twelfth century).

CHAPTER 8

Indic conceptions of authority

Timothy Lubin

INTRODUCTION

The term "authority" is used to denote a variety of related but distinct notions in studies of law. The Euro-American philosophy of law contrasts "theoretical authority" (the capacity to define what one should know) – which I prefer to call "epistemic" authority – with "practical authority" (the capacity to provide a sufficient reason for others to act) (e.g., Finnis 1980, 2007; Raz 1986, 1990). Practical authority may be further broken down into a capacity to enjoin (to create a duty) and a capacity to permit (endow with a right or privilege), which includes a capacity to delegate similar authority to others, in other words to "authorize." One should distinguish between the notions of de facto authority (which is backed only by the threat of force) (Thomas Hobbes, John Austin) and legitimate authority (which is recognized as morally obligatory by at least a significant portion of a society or an influential segment thereof) (Hart 1961). All forms of legitimate authority are delimited by jurisdiction: the geographic, political, bureaucratic, or situational range in which a given authority has force or is recognized.

This chapter identifies some of the main Indic concepts that are comparable to these notions, describing how they are presented in the available sources, and the religious and legal contexts in which they apply. Our primary Indian sources include early wisdom literature, ritual codes, compilations of precepts of *dharma* and the extensive medieval commentaries thereon,[1] and similar material included in other forms of literature. The ideas articulated in these sources may be compared with the assumptions that seem to underlie references to authority in such legal documents as have survived from before the colonial period. Such documents take the form of inscriptions on stone and copper plates, formulary anthologies, and

[1] On these, refer to Olivelle's chapter in this volume.

the few collections of documents on perishable materials that remain in archives.[2]

DHARMA AS JUSTICE BEYOND THE RULE OF MEN

A few early wisdom texts express something not far from the idea, promoted in the West by Aristotle (*Politics* III.15.1,286a–IV.4.1,292a), that the "rule of law" is preferable to the "rule of men" (e.g., the tyranny of a king or assembly). For example, the *Bṛhad Āraṇyaka Upaniṣad* proposes that *dharma*, which is identified with truth, is the highest creation of the Brahman (the prime source and essence of all things), and asserts that it is the basis of a king's power: "It is *dharma* that is the ruler's power to rule [*kṣatrasya kṣatram*] – nothing is higher than this *dharma*. And so it is that a powerless man makes demands upon a powerful man by means of *dharma*, just as he might by means of a king" (1.4.14). This concept is reaffirmed in the *Mānava Dharmaśāstra* (*MDh* 7.26–8) and elsewhere, where it is stated that an unjust or cruel king not only destroys his kingdom, but perishes and is afflicted with the taint of the sins of others. Although there is no one on earth with the authority to punish the king, he is still subject to *dharma*'s own inexorable cosmic law, of which he is merely the earthly instrument. In this sense, as a grand ideal, *dharma* may best be rendered as "Justice" or "the Right," although in other cases the term can denote "duty" or "moral precept," as well as individual "rules" or "pious acts."

TYPES OF AUTHORITY IN THE DHARMAŚĀSTRA

We may speak in terms of "authority," then, when it is a matter of identifying the means of knowing *dharma*, and the means of realizing it or applying it in *vyavahāra* (i.e., social interaction or legal procedure). These two general aspects of the problem are addressed directly for the first time in scholastic literature in Sanskrit. Scholastic works (called *sūtra*s and *śāstra*s, and the commentaries, digests, and treatises that take them as their basis) engage in a sort of jurisprudence in the sense of formulating and explaining a systematic body of precepts and hypothetical casuistry. The more discursive of these works appeal to philosophically developed concepts to provide a model of legal authority, while documentary sources provide examples of how authority is invoked in practice.

[2] The chapter by Michaels in this volume provides an overview.

The most extensive tradition of this jurisprudence from premodern India (apart from monastic codes) comes to be known collectively as the Dharmaśāstra (see Chapter 2). Its Sanskrit technical vocabulary allows us to recognize analogues of some of the different modes of authority that Western legal philosophers took pains to distinguish. The notion of "*pramāṇa*," and the related abstract noun "*prāmāṇya*" or "*pramāṇatva*," encompass much of the legal scope of epistemic authority. Built upon its fundamental, non-technical sense of "[standard of] measure," the term "*pramāṇa*" is applied in philosophical literature to mean "criterion" or "means of valid knowledge." In legal documents, the term acquires the specialized sense of "valid or authoritative legal instrument." It can also be used to describe a person whose judgment is decisive in some matter. By contrast, the idea of practical authority falls within the scope of "*adhikāra*," a term which has commonly been glossed, depending on context, as "legitimate power," "entitlement," "qualification," "right," "responsibility," or "[official or ritual] capacity."

There is of course the risk of distorting the Indic evidence in order to match it with facets of the non-Indic category of authority. At the same time, the exercise in comparison has the potential to help us see the Indic material from another angle – one that the indigenous scholastic tradition did not happen to adopt.

PRĀMĀṆYA

Every school of thought in India began by delimiting the sorts of *pramāṇa* (the "criteria of valid knowledge") that it accepts. The Dharmaśāstra adopts the list accepted by the Mīmāṃsā school of ritual exegesis (see Chapter 7): (1) *śabda* ("word," viz., of the Veda, which was deemed to be "not of human authorship" and thus eternally true); (2) *pratyakṣa* ("direct perception," that which can be apprehended by the senses); and (3) *anumāna* ("inference," or reason in general). The last of these, *anumāna*, becomes the basis for the śāstric argument that the customary practices of the learned and virtuous (*śiṣṭācāra* or *sadācāra*) represent a recollection of authentic Vedic revelations now lost (i.e., *smṛti*).

Beyond the abundantly recorded rules of Dharmaśāstra, there is a vast and mostly unchartable sea of other norms, rules, and customary standards that has variously been labeled "folk law," "customary law," "convention," or simply "custom."[3] It has long been debated how much of this constitutes

[3] The chapters by Donald Davis, Michaels, and Malik in this volume address aspects of such forms of law.

"law" (or in what sense it does, if it does). Observing Busoga legal proceedings in 1950s Uganda, Lloyd Fallers offered this aphorism: "customary law is folk law in the process of reception," that is, it is "a kind of legal situation which develops in imperial and quasi-imperial contexts, contexts in which dominant legal systems recognize and support the local law of politically subordinate communities" (Fallers 1969: 3). This definition grew out of his observations of traditional civil litigation as it was received in the colonial British courts, but it applies equally well to the reception of local and group-specific rules in Dharmaśāstra and in royal charters in premodern Indian states. (It leaves open the question of the nature and status of "folk law" before its reception.)

In spite of the fact that the Dharmaśāstra is intended to define the generally applicable rules of correct practice, one of those general rules directly confers authority on the standards of practice recognized as applying within particular social groups and organizations. Although such standards are commonly called varieties of *ācāra*, in some passages they are directly called *dharma* as well: "Whatever *dharma* is customary in a particular country, caste [*jāti*], association [*saṅgha*], or village, one should accordingly administer its law of inheritance [*dāya-dharma*]" (*ArthaŚ* 3.7.40), a rule Manu in turn extends to other matters (*MDh* 8.41).

This *lex non scripta*, comparable with other sorts of uncodified "common law," seems to have been the law most widely observed in India right up to the modern period (Holden 2003; Ishwaran 1964). In a long letter written in 1714, a French Jesuit missionary, Father Jean Venant Bouchet, gave a detailed account of contemporary legal practice around Pondicherry (Bouchet 1843; translated with commentary in L. Rocher 1984b). Bouchet observed that, rather than appealing to the Veda, Dharmaśāstra treatises such as that of Vijñāneśvara (the *Mitākṣarā*), or literary sources, the Tamils relied on fixed customs, many of which are crystallized in unwritten maxims and verses in the local tongue (see translated examples in L. Rocher 1984b: 38–48). "The equity of all their verdicts," Bouchet writes, "is entirely founded on a number of customs which they consider inviolable, and on certain usages which are handed down from father to son." The village head acted as the "natural judge in suits arising within his village," deliberating in consultation with "three or four of the most experienced villagers, who sit as assessors." A losing party can make an appeal to the district superintendent (*maṇiyakkāraṉ*), and a further appeal to the king's officers. In caste-related disputes, the heads of castes preside, and a religious preceptor can adjudicate disputes between his disciples. Brahmins might be consulted in regard to "particular" laws. Bouchet gave examples, too, of the admissibility in court of written documents (such as *muṟi*, a debt-bond), witnesses, and ordeals such as plunging an arm into a pot of boiling water or oil, or plucking a ring out of a pot containing a viper (L. Rocher 1984b: 18–37). Voltaire called Bouchet an "imbécile" for being impressed with such spectacles (1880: 443, n. 1), but all three of these categories of proof (*pramāṇa*) are recognized also in Dharmaśāstra (see Chapters 2 and 3, and below).

The authoritativeness of custom is such that, outside of śāstric literature, the relation between *ācāra* and Veda can be inverted. Thus Bhīma tells Hanumān in the *Mahābhārata* (3.149.28): "*Dharma* has its origin in custom; the Vedas are established from *dharma*; sacrifices are produced by the Vedas; the gods are established by the sacrifices." By contrast, in the Dharmaśāstra, customary laws are justified only by imputing to them, by inference, an origin in Vedic injunctions that have not themselves been preserved in the oral record. This "rootedness in Veda" (*vedamūlatva*) of *ācāra*, which becomes an article of dogma, is meant to protect the exclusive authority of the Vedic revelation, and of the Brahmin scholars whose patrimony it is.

Moreover, this notion provides broad scope for treating particular "experts" as authorities in themselves. Persons themselves were not commonly referred to as "*pramāṇas*," but there are notable exceptions. Kauṭilya speaks of the theoretical authority of experts in terms of *prāmāṇya* (*ArthaŚ* 1.5.6): "But discipline and restraint in the sciences individually [are derived] from the authority of the teacher." Learned (*vedavid* and *dharmajña*) Brahmins were presented as indispensable participants alongside the king in any legal process (*vyavahāra*). Brahmins appointed as *sabhya*s ("assessors") of the court could be said to have *prāmāṇya*. Later, an office of *dharmādhikārin* would be distinguished, but his *adhikāra* would be the duty to act with the king's sanction in prescribing penances and certifying compliance. The authority of the *sabhya*, on the other hand, is an epistemic authority, the authority of the expert.

But epistemic authority in the courtroom was not restricted to the *sabhya*s. *Nārada Smṛti* 3.1 preserves the royal prerogative by declaring that "one should never speak in a trial unless he has been appointed to do so [by the king]" ("*nāniyuktena vaktavyaṃ vyavahāre kathaṃcana*"). However, the commentator Asahāya cites a verse arguing just the opposite (in *NSm* 3.1): "Whether he has been appointed or not, one who knows the *śāstra* may speak. One who lives by the *śāstra* speaks divine words." A variation on this verse appears in *Bṛhaspati Smṛti* (1.1.108): "Whether he has been appointed or not, one who knows the *śāstra* may speak. Whatever he says in court is *dharma* – there is no doubt about this." It is not called *prāmāṇya* in either of these places, but the views of an expert in Dharmaśāstra are explicitly said to represent *dharma*. This gives him not just the right but the obligation, too, to proclaim what is right, quite independent of the king's otherwise absolute practical authority to appoint counselors and adjudicate cases.

Asahāya goes on to explain that such intervention might be called for in the event that the officers of the court, whether by reason of corruption or because of intemperance, "depart from the path of reasoning propounded in the *śāstra* and become inclined to give a judgment incompatible with the legal reasoning": "And if perchance some Brahmin happens to be present who knows legal method according to the system of the *smṛtis*, he should contradict the court officers, citing passages from statements made in the *śāstra*. Speaking thus and making them aware, he does not prevaricate." This is a defense of the notion that the truly learned Brahmin has more authority, by virtue of his learning in the sacred science, than any court official (*sabhya*) has by virtue merely of his having been appointed by the king. It is a practical application of the principle that, although the king presides over *vyavahāra*, the sphere of *vyavahāra* itself is valid only insofar as it remains in accord with the higher principle of *dharma*, which is embodied in holy writ.

Robert Lingat once opined that "the classical legal systems of India substitute the notion of *authority* for that of legality" (1973: 258). By this he meant that legal decisions were determined more by a relatively arbitrary exercise of informed discretion by authoritative persons than by a relatively systematic operation of impersonal legal mechanisms such as published statutes or recognized precedents. In fact, anthropologists of law have observed that such distinctions can be easily overdrawn: The judgments of "a kadi under a tree dispensing justice according to considerations of individual expediency" are not as arbitrary as they can seem to European and American jurists (Felix Frankfurter, quoted by Rosen 1989: 58), and conversely the decisions of European and American courts depend greatly on the vagaries of judicial discretion, not to mention extra-legal factors such as the prevailing sociopolitical climate and the interplay of group-specific rules and current customary standards.[4]

The Dharmaśāstra asserts that learned, virtuous Brahmins may properly be delegated practical authority as well. Thus, although adjudicating disputes is a king's proper duty, he may delegate it to others: "When he

[4] In place of instrumentalist conceptions of the effectiveness of legal rules, Griffiths has proposed a model of the "social working of law" that takes into account the inherent pluralism of law in practice (1991, 1995).

becomes tired of trying lawsuits filed by people, he should install on that seat a leading minister who knows the Law, is wise and self-disciplined, and comes from an illustrious family" (*MDh* 7.141).

The concluding section of the *Mānava Dharmaśāstra* (12.108, 113) asserts the absolute authority of the Brahmin: "If the question arises of how to proceed in cases where [particular] laws have not been handed down by tradition [*anāmnāteṣu dharmeṣu*], whatever learned Brahmins say is indubitably the *dharma*." This point is made even more forcefully a few lines on: "When even a single [Brahmin] who knows the Veda determines something as the Law, it should be recognized as the highest Law, and not something uttered by myriads of ignorant men."

The crucial training, which makes a Brahmin "learned" or "cultured" (*śiṣṭa*) is stated to comprise formal study of the Veda and its supplements, and the capacity to form a valid argument by appealing to textual (scriptural) warrant, direct perception, and logic (*śruti-pratyakṣa-hetu*) (*MDh* 12.109).

Seeming to belie all this high-minded insistence that the authority of Brahmins resides in their learning are other remarks defending Brahmin prerogative on a caste basis alone. *Mānava Dharmaśāstra* 8.20–2 enjoins that a king had better appoint a "Brahmin in name only" to interpret *dharma* (*dharma-vivecana*) than let a Śūdra do it; Manu warns that letting Śūdras decide law leads to disaster and the kingdom's downfall.

We can also find inscriptional evidence that Brahmins in general, and certain preeminent Brahmins in particular, were to be obeyed – that is, were supposed to be treated as practical authorities, not mere theoretical ones. Thus, a copper plate of Samudragupta recording his gift of two villages to a learned Brahmin addresses the inhabitants thus: "So you should listen to this Traividya [one who has studied three Vedas] and obey his commands" (ll. 7–8).

It is possible to hear a more jaundiced view of the authority of the sage, as in a later textual layer of the *Mahābhārata* (3.297.61–32.65–8): "Argumentation lacks a firm basis; revealed texts are diverse. There is not one sage whose opinion is a *pramāṇa*. The essence of *dharma* is hidden in a cave. Whatever way 'great men' go is the [right] path." But it is the king himself who, hearing a case, is the last authority in settling it. The *Bṛhaspati Smṛti* even declares him to constitute a *pramāṇa* when other proofs are absent (*BSm* 1.1.104–5): "Where there is no document [*lekhya*], nor witness [*sākṣin*], nor [evidences of] possession [*bhukti*], there are no probative criteria [*pramāṇa*]. In that case, the king is the sole criterion [*pramāṇa*].[5]

[5] In such a situation, *YSm* 2.22 prescribes an oath or ordeal.

Of those doubtful cases which may be impossible to decide, the king should be the criterion [*pramāṇa*], since he has power over all."[6] To call the king a *pramāṇa* here is something of a figure of speech, since his actual role is to render a decision, rather than to provide the basis for a decision – unless we say that he in effect does both simultaneously.

"Human" and "divine" pramāṇa *in the courtroom*

The *Arthaśāstra* explicitly gives priority to courtroom reasoning (*ArthaŚ* 3.1.45): "Should *śāstra* conflict with some reasoning [*nyāya*] about *dharma* the reasoning is the standard [*pramāṇa*], for in that situation a textual passage [*pāṭha*] loses its validity." The role of rational method appears also in Manu: "Just as the hunter follows the deer's track by the drops of blood, so too the king should follow the track of *dharma* by means of analogy [*anumānena*]" (*MDh* 8.44).

Nevertheless, Manu emphasizes that reason cannot override Veda; it can only serve to resolve ambiguities (12.106): "The man who scrutinizes the record of the seers and the teachings of the Law by means of reasoning [*tarka*] that is not inconsistent with the precepts of the Veda – he alone knows the Law and no one else." *Mānava Dharmaśāstra* 2.11 is even blunter on the limits of reason: "If a twice-born disparages these two [viz., Veda and *smṛti*] by relying on the science of logic [*hetu-śāstra*], he ought to be ostracized by good people as an infidel and a denigrator of the Veda."

Within the practical sphere of legal procedure, *pramāṇa* takes more tangible forms: written documentation, witnesses, possession (in the case of property disputes), and (as a distant fourth) "divine" proof (furnished primarily by oaths and ordeals). *Yājñavalkya Smṛti* (2.89) provides a clear warrant for treating documents as *pramāṇa*: "But any document written in the [party's] own hand is considered an authoritative document, even if unwitnessed, unless made by force or by fraud." Such documents (*lekha, lekhya*) include the *prajñāpana-lekha* ("confirmation" or "certification"), *ājñā-lekha* ("writ" or "order"), and *paridāna-lekha* ("surety bond"): "Where honor joined with real virtue is observed, whether in [offering] a pledge [*ādhi*] or a surety [*paridāna*], those two become [instruments of] conciliation" (*ArthaŚ* 2.10.42).[7] Apart from the few surviving individual examples of such documents (most in the form of inscriptions), there are a

[6] Also quoted in *Vīramitrodaya* 1.44 and *Mitākṣarā* 2.1.6.

[7] Understood by Kangle (1969) as "Awards" – "honors bestowed according to merit, or in distress or (general) giving."

few surviving compendia in which such examples are adapted to serve as models for such documents, an indication of a desire for a degree of standardization in the creation of written legal instruments. The chief example is preserved in multiple forms under the name *Lekhapaddhati* or *Lekhapañcāśikā* (*LP*).[8]

The standardization is particularly evident in the opening and closing sections of each model document, and their authoritativeness as legal instruments is reinforced by the inclusion of an authorizing signature (*mata*), with date, and sometimes other particulars such as a reference to the pertinent administrative department. One version of this compendium (contained in manuscript B, a sixteenth-century codex from Bombay that includes only legal documents [i.e., no models of private letters]) goes so far as to append the tag "this is authoritative" ("*pramāṇam iti*") to most documents, thereby signaling their "official" status explicitly.[9] In promulgating a royal order, this is strengthened by asserting a corresponding duty to comply (*LP* 2.1.2): "The messenger bears my august personal order; [its] authority must not be violated even in thought" ("*dū[yake] śrīsvayamādeśaḥ pramāṇaṃ manasāpi nollaṅghanīyaṃ*") (Strauch 2002: 115, 243). Moreover, authority is claimed not merely for the legal act or command, but for the written instrument itself, as in the case of a *bhūrjapattra* (official revenue-office order) which concludes "this is written authority" ("*iti likhitaṃ pramāṇam*") (*LP* 2.12.3), and many similar documents.

Authority is especially invoked to justify a court decision (*nyāya-vāda*): "Without authority, a penalty cannot be imposed" (B: "*pramāṇaṃ vinā daṇḍasādhyā na bhavati*"), although another manuscript (Bar1) concludes with "In this, the king's command is authoritative" ("*atra rājādeśaḥ pramāṇam iti*"). Moreover, special care is taken to establish the validity of such a document, even if it has been drafted carelessly: "This document ... is valid [*pramāṇa*] despite missing or extra letters" ("*patram idam ... hīnākṣaram adhikākṣaram vā pramāṇam iti*," 2.42.2). Likewise, a tax code for a village (*grāma-saṃsthā*) concludes "this is authoritative," adding a mention that the code is kept in the revenue office (*śrīkaraṇa*) (*LP* 2.17.2).

It is notable that barely any case has been found in which a specific scriptural warrant (i.e., from a *dharmaśāstra*) is cited in actual legal documents. One important exception is found in land-grant inscriptions that quote Sanskrit stanzas on the sanctity of gifts of land to Brahmins and the

8 Strauch (2002; edition with German translation); Prasad (2007) is an English translation, but it is less reliable.

9 This tag does appear occasionally in other versions.

karmic consequences of revoking or interfering with such grants. These stanzas were identified in the inscriptions as belonging to a text of "Dharma" or "Dharmaśāstra," sometimes specifying Vyāsa or Manu as the author. In fact, although the *Mahābhārata* contains a long section on the "gift of land" (*bhūmi-dāna*, 13.61), and although the *Mānava Dharmaśāstra* also contains similar material, most of these stanzas do not appear in either source. The names Vyāsa and Manu rather stand for Dharmaśāstra in general, and the stanzas seem to be drawn from a loose body of maxims transmitted orally (except insofar as they are reproduced in inscriptions). They vary in form and sequence from one epigraph to the next, even between those close in time or issued by the same donor.[10] Nevertheless, they are clearly intended to be accepted as a valid *śabda-pramāṇa* (authoritative sacred scripture).

To assess the last type of "courtroom *pramāṇa*" – the *divya* or "divine" proof – a special class of ordeal experts is alluded to both in Dharmaśāstra (*divya-viśārada*, *BSm* 8.15) and in inscriptions (*divyādhyakṣa-tulādhārin*; cited by Lariviere 1981a: 17). Although exceptions were sometimes made for a few grave crimes and for instances in which other, "human" forms of evidence (*mānuṣa-pramāṇa*) were inconclusive or open to challenge, recourse to "divine proof" (*daivika-pramāṇa*) was as a rule restricted to cases in which such evidence was unavailable. Such indications were elicited by a party to the suit making a solemn oath and/or submitting to an ordeal. The practice is quite ancient. In the *Chāndogya Upaniṣad* 6.16, a man accused of theft is made to take hold of a red-hot axe-head: If he is not burned, his innocence is proven. In other texts from the same Vedic tradition, trials by fire and water are used to prove Brahmin purity.[11] The first rulebooks to prescribe such methods are *Gautama Dharmasūtra* (13.12–13), which notes that "some" accept a *śapatha* ("vow" [or ordeal?]) as an "act of truth," and *Āpastamba Dharmasūtra* (2.5.11.3, 2.11.29.6) includes *daiva* ("divine means") as standard procedure alongside questioning and other ("human"?) evidence (*liṅga*).

Manu, however, provides the earliest full discussion. The assumption was that if one swore to a falsehood, some notable misfortune would strike the guilty party or his family within a short period (usually two weeks). Similarly, one undergoing an ordeal would remain unharmed if innocent. There are records of ordeals being used to appeal a wrong verdict, but also of

[10] Sircar (1965: 170–201 [Appendix II]) presents a compilation of these verses.

[11] *Pañcaviṃśa Brāhmaṇa* 14.6.6, *Jaiminīya Brāhmaṇa* 3.234 f; all of these texts belong to the *Sāma Veda*.

being rejected when other evidence has been deemed persuasive. The choice was left to the discretion of the judge.

A formal distinction between oath and ordeal is first identified by Vijñāneśvara (*Mitākṣarā* on *YSm* 2.96):

> Although the oath too is deemed a *divya* ["divine proof, ordeal"] according to the popular notion that whatever yields a decision in a case that cannot be decided on "human proofs" is a *divya*, nevertheless the fact that it yields a decision after a space of time points to its difference from ordeals such as the balance, which yield an immediate decision.

This distinction turns on the question of how a *divya* works (Bhāruci, *c.* 600): Its legal value depends upon the presumption that, if correctly performed, a divinity associated with the divinatory mechanism will necessarily manifest a judgment through the observable outcome: If the *śodhya* (the "party to be cleared") is innocent or speaks the truth, he or she will not suffer any harm, but the guilty will. Most ordeals provide immediate or nearly immediate indication of guilt or innocence; as Vijñāneśvara points out, some time, say, two weeks, must be allowed to pass before the consequences of an oath can be expected. Either way, however, the result is taken as valid evidence in court, amounting to a sort of divine witness. Thus, a stanza quoted in the *Lekhapaddhati*'s description of a *dharmacīrikā* (2.18) invokes Dharma personified: "Come, come, Lord Dharma! Enter into this *divya*, along with the hosts of Vasus, Ādityas, and Maruts, the World-Protectors! / Sun, Moon, Wind, Fire, Sky, Earth, Water, Heart, Yama [lord of the dead], Day, Night, Sunrise and Sunset, as well as Dharma, know what a man does." The intrinsic drama of the *divya* has made it a popular motif in literary depictions of disputes and judgments.[12] In the *Rāmāyaṇa*, when Sītā's fidelity was publicly challenged by her husband, Rāma king of Ayodhyā (and avatar of Viṣṇu), she committed herself to a burning pyre from which Agni, the god of fire, rescued her unscathed.

Whatever might be inferred about popular beliefs in the miraculous or the love of spectacle, it must be remembered that all other forms of evidence were generally deemed to have greater probative force; oaths and ordeals remained a gambit of last resort, or even a gesture of desperation when faced with an otherwise unwinnable case.

The *Lekhapaddhati* provides a model of a document recording the verdict in a trial settled by an oath. In it, a woman charged with adultery presents

[12] Hara (2009) reviews many examples, noting the range of deities invoked.

herself at the court of justice (*dharma-adhikaraṇa*) and indignantly vows before the learned Brahmin pandits that if she has deceived her husband "in thought, in word, or in deed," lusting for another man, "then only a blow to my family [will be] the proof" ("*tadā mama kula-praharam eva pramāṇaṃ*").[13] The court's verdict itself ratifies the validity of such a proof (2.15.2):

> Having heard the complaint and the reply, the pandits reached a decision: "The judgment [*nyāya*] is clear. [In light of the fact] that there is no eye-witness to the crime, and no one who heard it, then a divine means (viz., oath or ordeal) [is to be considered] as proof [*pramāṇa*]. Without proof, she cannot be subject to punishment. This is the verdict."

Another striking example of a direct appeal to divine authority in legal contexts is the *paḍthal*, a procedure commonly used in Maratha law to seek testimony from divinities to learn the identity of humans and ghosts (*bhūt*) involved in criminal acts.

Several accounts of such "divine hearings" are given in *nivāḍa-patra*s (settlement documents) preserved in the Peshwa Daftar. In three cases discussed by N. K. Wagle (1995, cases I–III), the divine testimony, conveyed through the mouth of a man understood to be possessed by the deity,[14] was used to confirm the accuracy of other evidence presented in court. The records use a legal formula to describe the value of such testimony: The gods confirmed the evidence (*pramāṇe*) already before the court.

To sum up, *pramāṇa* in the abstract is the standard or criterion of validity – both of legal principle and of valid evidence – hence, the epistemic basis for a decision. A person whose word can provide such a basis may be called a *pramāṇa*, as may a particular text, document, or demonstration in court.

ADHIKĀRA

General usage of adhikāra

The other main concept invoked in connection with legal matters is *adhikāra*. *Adhikāra* always entails an act. Outside of specifically ritual or legal contexts, *adhikāra* can be nothing more than an acknowledged competency in a particular activity: *vikrama-adhikāra* ("competency in valor")

[13] Thus manuscript B (sc. *-prahāram*); compare manuscript P: "*kula-prāhārakam*." Strauch (2002: 300) misunderstands this; Prasad's paraphrase (2007: 90) comes closer.

[14] Malik's chapter in this volume also discusses this phenomenon.

and *lakṣyalambha-adhikāra* ("competency in hitting a target") (*ArthaŚ* 7.17.23–4).

Ritual adhikāra

However, far from being merely descriptive, in most spheres of discourse, the term denotes a capacity or power with normative value. The concept of *adhikāra* was first theorized in a Vedic ritual code, the *Kātyāyana Śrauta Sūtra*, which takes it as a point of departure (1.1.1 ff.). The ritual or sacred character of *dharma*'s obligations is reinforced by the views of the school of thought known as (Karma-)Mīmāṃsā, "Investigation of Ritual Action," which defined the key terms in which Dharmaśāstra theorists came to conceive of their enterprise.[15] Jaimini's foundational work of that school begins with the proposition that "[any] objective identified [solely by a sacred] injunction is *dharma*" ("*codanā-lakṣaṇo 'rtho dharmaḥ*," *MīmS* 1.1.2; cf. McCrea's comments on this passage, pp. 124–5 above). The word "injunction" alludes to the use of verb forms with injunctive force in rules for performing particular acts (*karman*, *kriyā*). In Jaimini's work, these are primarily ritual acts forming part of the Vedic sacrificial liturgy, and Vedic ceremonial more broadly, but the precise scope of this model is restricted to a higher aim, the sublime Good disclosed exclusively by the Veda, rather than to any worldly matters about which we are informed by our senses.

In a short study of the concept of *adhikāra*, Richard Lariviere (1988) asserted that this term implies not just a "right," "qualification," or "eligibility" but also an "obligation" or "responsibility." This dual nature of the notion can be illustrated by a passage from Manu (*MDh* 2.16): "In this *śāstra* one should recognize the *adhikāra* of him for whom the [ritual] rule is prescribed [to be performed] with mantras, from insemination rite to funeral – and of no one else." This implies that full ceremonial preparation is a prerequisite for both legal rights and duties. Medhātithi understands *adhikāra* here more as a responsibility than an entitlement. "It is to be understood as 'I must perform this'" ("*adhikāro mayaitad anuṣṭheyam ity avagamaḥ*").

Legal adhikāra

In the legal sphere, *adhikāra* is authority vested in persons to perform various forms of legal work, such as ordaining or enforcing duties, rights,

[15] For a thorough discussion of this, see McCrea's chapter in this volume.

privileges, and punishments.[16] The status, or office, of persons so invested is itself often called "*adhikāra*,"[17] although many other terms for "appointment" or "delegation" also occur. Officers "appointed to protect" (*rakṣādhikṛta*) the people of a provincial district are liable to be punished for corruption or for shirking their responsibilities (*MDh* 7.123, 9.272; compare *YSm* 1.338).

With reference to a king, *adhikāra* relates to his royal duties. The *Vyavahāra Mayūkha* begins by asserting that "a king is someone [ritually] qualified[18] to protect his subjects, not just [any] Kṣatriya" (1.1). In other words, the ritual of royal consecration endows an otherwise suitable individual with the authority to govern. Thus consecrated, he may sit in judgment over criminal cases, and render decisions in civil cases (although he is not entitled to *initiate* a civil case). In theory, the king is the agent of all punishment; it should even be meted out by his hand. In practice, he is allowed to delegate the responsibility to try cases and to punish the guilty. Thus when he grows weary of hearing cases, the king may "place on the bench" ("*sthāpayed āsane tasmin*") "a prominent minister who knows *dharma*, wise and disciplined" (*MDh* 7.141).

The classical definition of a court of justice includes mention of such appointments (*MDh* 8.9–11):

> When the king does not try a case personally, however, he should appoint a learned Brahmin to do so.
>
> Entering the main court itself accompanied by three assessors, he should try the cases brought before the king, either seated or standing.
>
> The place where three Brahmins versed in the Vedas and a learned officer of the king sit, they call the court of Brahman.

Among the members of the court, we can distinguish the "assessors" (*sabhya*), who have primarily epistemic authority – that is, expert authority in *dharma* – from the king's officer (*adhikṛta*), who wields the king's practical authority to render a decision, to bind or to loose.

Beyond the court of justice, individual acts of a king having legal force are called "ruling" or "edict" (*śāsana*). *Arthaśāstra* 2.10 describes the types of ruling and the proper way of recording one in a written document (*lekha*).

[16] In reference to land law, *adhikāra* is "the right and responsibility to perform certain acts such as the sale of family property" (D. R. Davis 2004a: 70).

[17] Thus Kauṭilya speaks of "*mānādhikārābhyāṃ bhraṣṭaḥ*," "one fallen from honor or office" (*ArthaŚ* 1.14.2); and of honest and effective officials who should be endowed with "permanent office" ("*nityādhikāra*") (*ArthaŚ* 2.9.36).

[18] *Adhikṛta*, that is, qualified by virtue of his having been ritually consecrated as king, but implying also a personal capacity to execute the royal functions.

Among the types of records are "authorization" (*nisṛṣṭi*) and "exemption" (*parīhāra*) from certain taxes. Authorization consists in "delegating authority to speak [i.e., issue orders] or to act toward some purpose" (*ArthaŚ* 2.10.38, 43), while exemption is "a concession [*anugraha*], by order of the king, to a caste in particular towns, villages, or regions" (2.10.42).

Whatever the *Arthaśāstra* says, such powers were not limited to kings. In a Tamil inscription of 1426 from Tamil Nadu[19] we find a Brahmin council passing a statutory reform of marriage law that criminalizes the payment of bride-price (a customary practice in the region) and establishes the śāstric model of *kanyādāna* ("gift of a virgin") as the recognized mode of contracting a legitimate marriage. The law, applying to all Brahmins within the kingdom of Paḍaivīḍu, was passed in the form of a *dharma-sthāpana-samaya-patra*, a "record of an agreement establishing *dharma*" which was "made" in the presence of an image of the deity Krishna by the "Great Men learned in all subjects" ("*aśeṣavidyamahājanaṅ kaḷ*"), that is, the Brahmins of the council (ll. 5–12):

> the Great Men [i.e., Brahmins of the assembly] learned in all subjects, of the kingdom [*rājyam*] of Paḍaivīḍu, drew up, in the presence of [the god] Gopinātha [of] Arkapuṣkariṇī, the record of an agreement establishing *dharma*. According to [this document], if the Brāhmaṇas of this kingdom of Paḍaivīḍu, viz., Kaṉṉaḍigas, Tamiḻs, Teluṅgas, Ilāḷas, etc., of all *gotras*, sūtras and *śākhās* conclude a marriage, they shall, from this day forward, do it by *kanyādāna*. Those who do not adopt *kanyādāna*, i.e., both those who give a girl away after having received gold, and those who conclude a marriage after having given gold, shall be liable to punishment by the king and shall be excluded from the community of Brāhmaṇas. Thus the record of an agreement establishing *dharma*, written by the [undersigned] Great Men learned in all subjects.

Two penalties are prescribed for violation of this law: a punishment imposed by the state (*rājadaṇḍa*, "the king's punishment"), and a social disability imposed by the caste elders. The caste elders themselves have the customary authority to excommunicate the offender, but the Great Men have further invoked the temporal authority of the king to enforce both the law itself and the customary caste penalty.

On the other hand, there seems to be hardly any example of a king publishing a generally applicable law on his own authority, let alone promulgating an entire code. Rather, it seems to have been assumed that his central role was executive and judicial: to hear and adjudicate civil suits, to

[19] SII 1, no. 56 (Viriñcipuram Temple, front gopuram), pp. 82–4; adapted from Hultzsch's translation. Discussed also by D. R. Davis (2005: 103).

judge criminals, and to assign punishments for the guilty. The king could also be called upon to propose further penalties for the neglect of religious and social sanctions applied by other legal bodies (viz., a *dharmādhikārin* or Brahmin council, or a caste or guild council). This assumption finds justification in the Dharmaśāstra, which affirms that the king does not make *dharma*, but only enforces and protects it. All individual rules derive their authority in theory from their consonance with the laws enunciated in the Veda.

Nevertheless, the king's command has the force of law, and records of his occasional commands and enactments constitute legal documents. Moreover, kings were sometimes called upon to recognize formally in a charter (*pattra* / *patra* / *pātra*) the until-then unwritten customary laws (*ācāra* or *sthiti*) of a particular group. This type of document is called an "[*ācāra-*]*sthiti-pātra*" or "*sthiti-vyavasthā*" ("charter of statutes"). An early and extensive example is the Charter of Viṣṇuṣena of 592, issued by a petty ruler at the request of a merchant guild in his town, and subsequently endorsed by a local vassal.[20] The Sanskrit copper-plate inscription records seventy-two statutes which were to be recognized as law where members of this group are concerned, including their legal obligations to the state as regards taxes, fines, and other levies. In that case, however, it is really the conventional standard (*samaya-ācāra*) that is the underlying *pramāṇa*; the king then endorses it and puts the force of the state behind it.

In sum, then, *adhikāra* in its most general application is "legal competence." The prescriptions of Vedic ritual, for instance, simply do not apply to anyone else. This implication is made explicit (*MDh* 10.126): "For the Śūdra, there is no mortal sin, nor does he merit sanctification. He has neither competence [*adhikāra*] in *dharma*, nor prohibition on account of *dharma*." From this declaration, it would seem that the Śūdra is outside the moral universe of *dharma*. That does not mean that Śūdras have no standards among themselves, or even that they can do no wrong according to a rule of *dharma*, but they are not measured on the scale of the twice-born. But Śūdras are promised worldly and otherworldly rewards for imitating the practices of their betters: "Obedient service to Brahmin householders is their highest dharma" (MDh 9.334).

Śūdras constitute a problematic, ambiguous place in the Dharmaśāstra. Although the rules are meant to cover it, this class, which has no access to the Veda or to Brahmin priestly services, is not for that reason put beyond the pale of *dharma*. Those rules that include variations according to class

[20] Sircar (1953–4 [= EI 30: 166], 1974: 172–96); D. R. Davis (2005: 106).

generally include the Śūdra. Mitramiśra in his *Vīramitrodaya* (*c.* 1600) (Śarmā, Bhāṇḍārī, and Upadhyāya Bhaṭṭa 1916: 9) goes so far as to say that at *Mānava Dharmaśāstra* 2.6 ("the conduct of good men"), Manu meant to imply that "the practice [*ācāra*] of faultless men, even if they do not know the Veda, is authoritative [*pramāṇa*]. So too the practice of good Śūdras becomes authoritative for their sons and other (Śūdras)."

CONCLUSION

In a couple of passages in the *Mahābhārata*, the divine Kṛṣṇa is described as constituting the *pramāṇa*, that is, the grounds or justification, for all obligatory acts or responsibilities (*adhikaraṇa* or *kārya*).[21] However, aside from expressions of such exalted sentiments, *prāmāṇya* and *adhikāra* are not discussed together as part of a broader notion of authority. Nevertheless, it should be clear that India's legal traditions – in the *śāstra*s and in legal practice – have developed sophisticated notions of both epistemic and practical authority. Although these complementary notions largely correspond to the notions expressed by the terms "*pramāṇa*" and "*adhikāra*," the former in some contexts partakes of the character of practical authority, most notably when it is applied to persons.

[21] *Mahābhārata* 1.111.37: "*pramāṇabhūto lokasya sarvādhikaraṇeṣu ca*"; similarly: *Mahābhārata* 2.14.6:167.8 "*tvaṁ me pramāṇabhūto 'si sarvakāryeṣu keśava.*"

CHAPTER 9

Śūdradharma *and legal treatments of caste*

Ananya Vajpeyi

INTRODUCTION

Śūdradharma, literally, *dharma* for the Śūdra, is an old topic in the Dharmaśāstra, part of the standard list of topics in *dharma* texts from the earliest period. From 1350 to 1700 CE we find a number of texts in the genre of the *dharma-nibandha* (digest on *dharma*), devoted wholly and solely to the topic of *śūdradharma*. We are able to locate several of these texts, especially those produced between 1550 and 1680 CE, a period conventionally designated as late medieval, though it is increasingly referred to as early modern. I call this corpus the "Śūdra archive" (Vajpeyi 2004). The *dharma-nibandha* was a genre of text produced profusely, with much royal patronage, all across Deccan India from the early twelfth to the late sixteenth century (Table 1). As the name of the genre indicates, these texts were compendia of earlier materials on various topics in *dharma*. The *śūdradharma-nibandha* is a subgenre within this larger category of text.

The Śūdra archive is interesting for many reasons. It is produced in a limited period of time, and that, too, relatively late in the history of the Sanskrit literature on *dharma* (Table 2). Unlike most of the early works on *dharma*, for this corpus we are able to find historical authors, and to tell where the texts were written. This level of historicity is simply not available for the bulk of the Dharmaśāstra. Second, we see here one of a long list of topics gain salience and become the subject of book-length treatments. Questions arise: Why *śūdradharma*? Why did this topic suddenly become so important as to merit entire digests, and why at this time and not earlier or later? What do the choice of subject matter, and the choice of textual genre in which to process it, tell us about the Śūdra archive? Why were late medieval Brahmins (and Brahmins alone) writing legal digests about the Śūdra?

A third reason that makes the Śūdra archive intriguing, besides its unprecedented historicity and its novelty, is one of its authors, and possibly

Table 1 Dharma-nibandha *and* smṛti-bhāṣya *texts in the Deccan: early twelfth to late sixteenth century. These digest texts treat a variety of topics within the broad rubric of* dharma *(from Ranbaore 1974).*

Text	Author	Title	Court / dynasty	Place	Time (century)
Mitākṣarā	Vijñāneśvara	–	Cāḷukya	Kalyāṇī	1st qtr 12th
Bhāṣya on the *Yājñavalkya Smṛti*	Aparāditya	King	Śilāhāra	Kokaṇa	1st qtr 13th
Smṛticandrikā	Devaṇṇabhaṭṭa	–	–	–	13th
Caturvargacintāmaṇi	Hemādri	Minister	Yādava	Devagiri	late 13th
Sarasvatīvilāsa	Pratāparudradeva	King	Kākaṭīya / Gajapati	Warangal	early 14th
Pārāśaramādhavīya	Mādhavācārya	–	Vijayanagara	Vijayanagara	late 14th
Nṛsiṃhaprasāda	Dalapati	Minister	Nizām Shāhī	Ahmadnagar	16th
Ujjvalā	Haradaṭṭa	–	–	–	late 16th

its last great exponent, Gāgābhaṭṭa. This man not only wrote in the genre of the *śūdradharma-nibandha*, he also wrote about *rājadharma*, the *dharma* of the king, *kāyasthadharma*, the *dharma* of the Kāyasthas (a caste of scribes and accountants), and about *jātinirṇaya*, the adjudication of matters pertaining to *jāti* (caste). He performed the *rājyābhiṣeka* or the royal consecration of the first Maratha ruler, Shivaji (1630–80 CE), in 1674 CE. Shivaji was a Śūdra warlord who had to be made into a Kṣatriya king, and it was Gāgā who improvised the rituals and composed the justificatory texts necessary for this transformation (Vajpeyi 2005).

In addition, since his scholarly and ritual work made him an authority on *dharma* as it was to be determined and apportioned according to *varṇa* and *jāti*, throughout his life Gāgā presided over legal disputes between members of different castes. The personality and activity of Gāgābhaṭṭa, no doubt one of the most important intellectuals of the Sanskrit world at the end of the medieval period, enlivens the history of the Śūdra archive. Singling out this arcane topic from the plenitude of Sanskrit textuality, Gāgā brings it to our notice more than three centuries later. If the eighteenth century brings us to the death of Sanskrit, as S. Pollock (2001b) describes it, then the work of Gāgābhaṭṭa is surely one of the dying breaths of this knowledge tradition.

Table 2 Śūdradharma-nibandha *texts in northern India: mid-twelfth to seventeenth century. These texts take the Śūdra as their organizing topic (from Vajpeyi 2004).*

Text	Author	Author's place of origin	Place of composition	Date / century	Author's patrons
Ācāracandrikā[a]	Srīnāthācāryacūḍāmaṇī	–	–	–	–
Śūdradharmabodhinī or *Smṛtikaumudī*	Viśveśvarabhaṭṭa	South India	Delhi environs / Banaras	1360–90	Madanapāla of Kāṭha, vassal of Delhi sultan
Śrīdharapaddhati or *Śūdrīpaddhati*	Kṛṣṇatanaya Gopāla "Udāsa"	–	–	1442	–
Śūdrācāracintāmaṇi	Vācaspatimiśra	Mithilā	Mithilā	1450–80	Kāmeśvara kings: Harinārāyaṇa, Rūpanārāyaṇa
Śūdrakṛtyavicāraṇatattva	Raghunandana Bhaṭṭācārya	Vandhyaghāṭī, Bengal	Bengal	1510–65	–
Śūdrācāraśiromaṇi	Śeṣakṛṣṇa	Maharashtra Deccan	Banaras	1520–90 / late 16th to early 17th	Pilāji, Kalyāṇa of Antarvedi, Narottama of Tāṇḍava
Śūdrakamalākara or *Śūdradharmatattva (prakāśa)*	Kamalākarabhaṭṭa	Paiṭhan, Maharashtra	Banaras	1610–40	–
Smṛtikaumudī / *Śūdradharmotpaladyotinī*[b]	Rāyamadanapāla	–	Aurangabad, Maharashtra	1681	–
Śūdradharmoddyota	Dinakarabhaṭṭa and his son Gāgābhaṭṭa	Paiṭhan, Maharashtra	Banaras	1640–1700 / 1620–85	Shivaji

[a] No details are available; note that "śūdra" does not appear in the title.

[b] This text is noted in the Anup Sanskrit Library Catalogue. I suspect it is just a late copy of Viśveśvarabhaṭṭa's text of the same name that was in fact produced in the mid-fourteenth century under the patronage of King Madanapāla (see the second entry in Table 2). Calling someone "Rāyamadanapāla" is just the same as saying "King (= Rāya) Madanapāla," and I would hazard that the original author and original patron have been conflated in the later copy.

PHILOLOGY

The *śūdradharma-nibandha* texts, especially the longer and more elaborate ones, by Kṛṣṇaśeṣa, Kamalākarabhaṭṭa, Dinakarabhaṭṭa, and Gāgābhaṭṭa, tend to follow a certain pattern in terms of topics covered. Since "*śūdradharma*" means "*dharma* pertaining to the Śūdra," the broadest questions to be addressed in these texts and providing their organizational logic are: (1) Who is a Śūdra? (2) What is his *dharma*? Answering (1) means asking:

(i) What is *varṇa* and who has it?
(ii) What is *śūdra-varṇa* and who has it?

To answer these questions, the texts generate long lists of types of persons who do *not* have *varṇa*: these are the *antyaja* category (last-born or outcaste), some of whom count as equivalent to Śūdra (*śūdra-samāna*), while others are inferior. Women, notably, are *śūdra-samāna* across the board, on account of the a priori parity between the woman and the Śūdra (*strī-śūdra-samānatā*). Proposing definite answers to (i) and (ii) above entails a discussion of what *varṇa* is (*varṇatva*), and of the essence of the four *varṇa* categories – *brāhmaṇatva*, *kṣatriyatva*, *vaiśyatva*, and *śūdratva*.

Rules governing marriage (*vivāha*), endogamy (*savarṇa-vivāha*), hyper- and hypogamy (*anuloma / pratiloma*), miscegenation (*saṃkara / varṇasaṃkara / jātisaṃkara*), sexuality, and the status of women, as the constitutive elements of a patriarchal caste system, must then be thoroughly explicated and debated. Taxonomies of mixed castes, together with their male and female parentage, their alternative names, their proper as well as optional professions, and any other typical characteristics are set out, usually in the very beginning of the *śūdradharma* text. The taxonomies of miscegenation have a generative aspect (*utpatti*) as well as a determinative or classificatory aspect (*nirṇaya*). The mechanical mixture of mixed castes produces an almost uncontrollable proliferation of subgroups (*saṃkīrṇasaṃkara*). Like women, those of mixed caste also have either parity or inferiority with respect to the Śūdra, and are designated *śūdra-samāna*, *ati-śūdra*, *antyaja*, *sat-śūdra / asat-śūdra*, and other micro-classifications.

Most *sūdradharma* digests are devoted to question (2) above: What is the *dharma* of the Śūdra? The answer lies in numerous dos and don'ts associated with the rituals a Śūdra must perform. In this sense, "*dharma*" becomes synonymous with "*saṃskāra*," and the minutiae of the various daily, monthly, annual, periodic, and life-cycle rituals prescribed for the Śūdra extend into pages and pages of text. These portions of the Śūdra archive are curiously static. On the one hand, we cannot tell if we are looking into the seventh or the seventeenth century, so suspended is this discourse in the timeless ether of Brahmin normativity. On the other hand, it is marked historically, because modern Indians know immediately that what they are looking at is the past, not the present. Apart from a few rites associated with major life events – birth, naming, marriage, and death – few Indians of almost any caste inhabit any longer a living, coherent social world wherein these rituals make sense.

To attempt to write the history of *dharma* in the narrow sense of life-cycle rites (*saṃskāra*) is premised on the apprehension of a lapse in cultural memory that is disquieting. Some epistemological break has occurred in our history to inhibit us, indeed debar us, from entering in our imagination the universe where it might have mattered to someone whether or not he had the capacity to perform a certain ritual of *śūdradharma* in a certain way. Of course, one may question whether the discourse of Dharmaśāstra ever, at any point in time, had a strong and demonstrable relationship to how people lived, thought, and acted. But suffice it to say that, from the vantage of the present, the sections of our texts dealing with *śūdra-saṃskāra* appear archaic, if not altogether fantastic. Sarma's recent quasi-fictional autobiography, *The Last Brahmin* (2007), explores the aporia that characterizes our relationship to this once vibrant world of Brahmanical rituals.

In an exhaustive treatment of the Śūdra archive, I focus on the place of language in these texts, in order to elucidate what I call their "poetics of contempt." Language is key in two ways: First, the Śūdra is defined as a person who stands at a particular, exactly measured, and strictly enforced distance from Sanskrit; and second, the language used to describe, police, revile, punish, and exclude the Śūdra from realms of upper-caste privilege is startling in its force. It should be noted that both these uses of language in the hierarchical world of *varṇāśramadharma* (the *dharma* of caste and life-stage) – as a measure of lowliness and as a weapon of humiliation – are as old as all of the phenomena under study: the category of the Śūdra itself, the Sanskrit language, and the system of Dharmaśāstra. There is no respite to be had from the contempt characteristically associated with the Śūdra when the new digests are written between the fourteenth and the seventeenth century. Rather, they become reiterations of very ancient, sedimented forms of social inequality that are inscribed into the language itself.

One may investigate the language through which *dharma* is differentially apportioned to the twice-born and to the Śūdra in a variety of genres. However, the relationship of the Śūdra to Sanskrit and thence to entire realms of social prestige and political power, is most clearly and metonymically figured in the relationship of the Śūdra to the Veda. If we diagram a paradigmatic speech situation, the Śūdra appears as a silent listener and indirect addressee, never as a speaker or a direct addressee: a perfect image of the Śūdra's exclusion from or marginal status with respect to caste society as a whole. In the social world that we can project from the speech situation sketched in Sanskrit texts, the Śūdra, mostly shut out altogether, is, at best, the designated eavesdropper. The historical depth of this contempt for the Śūdra in the long life of Sanskrit is revealed in the sources cited by the digest authors, primarily a small set of stories from the *upaniṣads* and interpretations of these stories in major Vedānta commentaries (see Vajpeyi in press). It turns out that the figure of the Śūdra haunts the Brahmanical literature from some of its earliest phases, and always at the heart of the othering of the Śūdra lies a set of maneuvers whose locus is language.

In the context of current scholarship on India, the topic of the Śūdra and, more specifically, of the relationship between the Śūdra and language, immediately calls to mind the school of Indian historiography we know as subaltern studies. Historians of this school have worked almost exclusively on colonial India, particularly on peasant groups and their politics from the late eighteenth to the early twentieth century. While *śūdradharma* as a subject of Sanskrit systematic thought is strictly speaking a precolonial phenomenon, the Śūdra should be thought of as a kind of subaltern. The question to ask of the Śūdra archive is: "Can the subaltern speak?" in or through these texts (Spivak 1988). The answer, for the seventeenth century as for the twentieth, appears to be the same – "No." The *śūdradharma* digests do not reveal anything about either the Śūdra as a historical agent or the constitution of any given Śūdra collectivity as a class in a feudal society, nor do they entextualize what Guha would describe as "subaltern mentality" (R. Guha 1998). Rather, because Brahmins, even when they write about the Śūdra, appear to write exclusively for other Brahmins, the *śūdradharma* digests they compose embody and convey "elite mentality" par excellence.

Śūdradharma-śāstra as an elite discourse successfully represses all traces of the subaltern it takes as its principal object. We may read and re-read the Śūdra archive to try and find in it the historical conditions to which it responds; it remains almost completely unyielding. There is a complex story behind why and how Sanskrit discourses, especially those in the *śāstra* mode, achieved this near-perfect repression of subalternity or indeed alterity of any kind – in other words, what the linguistic, epistemological, and ideological features of Sanskrit discursivity are that make it so perfectly an idiom of domination. Suffice it to say that the elision of *historicity* from Sanskrit discourse is related to its repression of *subalternity* – the two reinforce one another to produce the total absence of subaltern speech, even in our texts that are entirely about the Śūdra.

In the study of precolonial India, the trace of subaltern subjectivity has traditionally been sought in *bhakti* poetry and other sorts of radical texts, usually in the vernaculars rather than in Sanskrit for obvious reasons. But records of legal disputes too, when these disputes were between subalterns and elites – here, Śūdra groups and twice-born groups – ought to provide some insight into Śūdra mentality. A dispute, no matter how skewed its historical record, must necessarily capture two (or more) sides in a given disagreement. Unfortunately, to the extent that the modality of legal dispute resolution (i.e., law) in cases involving *jātinirṇaya*, *jātidharma*, and *varṇāśramadharma* was tied to legal disputation, precolonial caste disputes too show a tendency to assimilate to the Brahmanical repression of Śūdra speech that characterizes the theory and practice of all *śāstra*. In this sense, the moment the Śūdra comes into the purview of *dharma*, whether in *śāstra* texts (disputation) or in Marathi *grāmaṇya* records (disputes), the answer to the question "Can the subaltern speak?" goes into the negative.

The evidence preserved in the documents recording the judgments given (*vyavasthā-patra*) indicates only that the Śūdra disputants wanted to be recognized as not really being Śūdra at all, but instead as being Brahmin, Kṣatriya, Vaiśya, or Kāyastha. This is perhaps the most successful elision of Śūdra subjectivity: supposedly at the hands of the Śūdra agents themselves, as it were. It would appear from the legal record that all the Śūdra ever wants is not to be one. The dispute then becomes a contest between the presence and absence, or the assertion versus the denial, of Śūdra subjectivity, not a contest between Śūdra subjectivity and twice-born subjectivity over a set of rights and privileges. Even worse, the positive assertion – "This group here consists of Śūdra individuals" – comes from the Brahmin side, while the denial – "We are not Śūdras" – comes from the Śūdra litigants themselves. Thus even the body of legal disputes we can recover in a fragmentary fashion from sixteenth- and seventeenth-century Varanasi and in a more complete fashion from eighteenth- and nineteenth-century Maharashtra does not assist us in moving from the philology of oppression to the practice of subaltern history.[1]

[1] Chapter 5 of Vajpeyi (2004) deals with the history of caste disputes in detail, building on N. K. Wagle. Madhav Deshpande, Christopher Minkowski, Rosalind O'Hanlon, and Lawrence McCrea have been incrementally extending the work on caste disputes.

HISTORY

Even as the Śūdra fails to speak through or in the *dharma-nibandha* archive, the elephant in the room, as it were, is caste. It does not matter whether we translate "*varṇa*" as "caste," or "*jāti*" as "caste," or both, or if the meaning of "caste" alternates between these two indigenous terms. The question of how to translate "caste" in this context is beside the point. The fact is that within the sphere of Sanskrit intellectual production in the sixteenth and seventeenth centuries, prior to the colonial period, Gāgābhaṭṭa and others like him were reflecting very deeply on the meanings of the category of the Śūdra, and a variety of related categories that had to do with the place as well as the relative ranking of individuals and groups in a social structure. This structure – with its axes of ritual status, occupation, endogamy, power, and so on – cannot be understood except as caste society. Reflection on the subject of the Śūdra, fittingly, was going on within the discourse of *dharma*, and that too within the ambit of legal and juridical literature, the Dharmaśāstra.[2]

In reframing the large and variegated body of the Dharmaśāstra within the relatively narrow genre of the *dharma-nibandha*, and in taking the Śūdra as the overarching topic of discussion, jurists and scholars from 1550 to 1680 CE were engaging, precisely, in legal treatments of caste. Gāgābhaṭṭa himself presided over and conducted caste-related rituals, for royals as well as laypersons; further, he adjudicated caste disputes between Brahmins and non-Brahmins. We could say that he was active in the theory, practice, and politics of caste, in his capacity as both a scholarly expert on and a respected practitioner of the law. Gāgā was, undoubtedly, a precolonial figure, and as such he dramatizes the centrality of caste to precolonial intellectual life, legal practice, polity, and statecraft. He was not alone in his interest in both caste and the law (via the disciplines of Dharmaśāstra and Mīmāṃsā) – he came from a family of scholars and jurists, the Bhaṭṭas of Banaras. His father Dinakarabhaṭṭa began writing a text titled *Śūdradharmodyota* ("Elucidation of the *Dharma* of the Śūdra") that Gāgā himself completed. His uncle Kamalākarabhaṭṭa wrote possibly the most important *nibandha* about the

[2] Dharmaśāstra is traditionally only one of many loci for the entextualization of *dharma* in Sanskrit knowledge systems, but it became the preferred locus at this time. In remoter phases of premodernity, the discourse of *dharma* and, specifically, of *śūdradharma*, was not confined to the Dharmaśāstra. I have followed the discussion on *śūdradharma* in a number of genres of text: Veda, Mīmāṃsā, Vedānta, Itihāsa, etc., at least insofar as those discussions are referred to in the Śūdra archive (Vajpeyi 2004). From the Puruṣa Sūkta ("Hymn to the Cosmic Man") in the *Ṛg Veda* (10.90), to stories in the *upaniṣad* texts, to the treatises of Śaṅkara and Rāmānuja, to episodes in the *Mahābhārata*, the problem of the Śūdra is a very old one in the Sanskrit discourse on *dharma* (Vajpeyi in press).

Śūdra, titled *Śūdrakamalākara* ("Kamalākara's Digest on the Śūdra") sometime between 1610 and 1640 CE, a text still taught in Sanskrit pedagogical environments today.

The Bhaṭṭas had moved to Banaras from Paithan, in Maharashtra, in the fifteenth century. Paithan used to be a center of Brahmin learning during Yādava rule, but upon the fall of the Yādava capital of Devagiri between 1295/6 and 1325 CE, its intellectuals began to migrate north to Banaras. By Gāgā's lifetime, Banaras had entirely replaced Paithan as the headquarters, in northern India, of Brahmin intellectualism, much of it diasporic. Besides his own family, the Śeṣas of Banaras, another family of migrants from Paithan, were also famous as legal scholars. Gāgā's uncle Kamalākara's older contemporary Śeṣakṛṣṇa wrote yet another significant digest on the Śūdra, titled *Śūdrācāraśiromaṇi* ("Crest Jewel of Śūdra Conduct") sometime in the late sixteenth or early seventeenth century (Benke 2010).

Gāgābhaṭṭa participated in the institution of the *brahmasabhā*, a council of Brahmins called to adjudicate various sorts of disputes, including caste disputes. Both late medieval Banaras and, before that, early medieval Paithan knew this institution, and it appears that local rulers, whether Hindu or Muslim, would often direct disputing parties to these learned assemblies in order to have their issues settled according to the rules of the Dharmaśāstra.[3] On matters of *dharma*, including *varṇa* and *jāti*, non-specialist administrative and legal functionaries of regional courts, lacking in Sanskrit knowledge, deferred to specialist Brahmins living in places like Paithan and later Banaras. Dalmia describes Banaras as a "supra-regionally recognized" locus of juridical authority (Dalmia 1996: 322–3). The *brahmasabhā* would issue a decision, recorded in a document called a *vyavasthā-patra* ("document [*patra*] bearing the decision [*vyavasthā*]") or *vijaya-patra* ("document spelling out the victory [*vijaya*] of the authoritative claim [*siddhānta*]").[4] The disputants would carry out the injunctions of this document, and their local political authority would not object.

Gāgābhaṭṭa's ancestor Rāmeśvara migrated from Paithan to Banaras in the early sixteenth century. S. Pollock records the names of several

[3] Telang (1900: 278–9 [126–7 in the 1961 edition]) has an account of how, when a group of disputing CKPs and Brahmins from coastal Maharashtra went before the Muslim law officer of Bijapur for redress, he referred them to the Banaras pandits, saying he was ignorant of the *dharma* texts and therefore not competent to judge this particular case, but he promised to enforce the pandits' judgment.

[4] We find reference to two *vyavasthā-patra* documents, of 1583 and 1658 CE, signed by councils of scholars resident in Banaras but originating from different parts of the subcontinent: Maharashtra, the Deccan, the South, Gujarat, etc. The second of these documents is a judgment about the actual caste status of a *jāti* called the Devarṣi, who were, in their own estimation, Brahmin (S. Pollock 2001b: 21 and 21n).

prominent Marathi scholars resident in seventeenth-century Banaras (2001a and 2001b). Gāgā lived in Banaras but, nonetheless, probably because he spoke Marathi and had family ties with his ancestral homeland, he became involved in a number of cases surrounding the ritual status of a caste belonging to coastal Maharashtra, the Cāndrasenīya Kāyastha Prabhu (CKP).[5] This caste, today referred to in Maharashtra's caste politics as "CKP," was traditionally a highly literate group associated with scribal and accountancy work, and connected, therefore, with royal courts and their administrative divisions. One of Shivaji's closest ministers, Bālājī Citnis, was a CKP.

The CKP is one of a group generically referred to in the *dharma* literature as Kāyastha, a caste, as already mentioned, of scribes and accountants. Like Brahmins, historically Kāyastha communities can be found in many parts of the subcontinent, and in different places they have distinct *jāti* names, as well as localized stories about their origins, their proper work, their true status, their position relative to other local castes, and so on. In Shivaji's reign the CKP were politically powerful, and Gāgā was enlisted to establish, textually as well as through his judgments on particular cases, that the CKP shared characteristics with the Brahmin as well as the Kṣatriya, both high castes, but not with the lowly Śūdra. Sometime between 1669 and 1672 CE he presided over a case involving the CKP (Bendrey 1960). Probably in this same period, Gāgā wrote *Kāyasthadharmadīpa* ("Elucidation of the *Dharma* of the Kāyastha"), which is a *nibandha* text about *kāyasthadharma*. It closely resembles, in purpose as well as form, the digests about *śūdradharma* written by Gāgā and other authors.

While Gāgā was clearly a caste expert, living in Banaras (then a late medieval university town), and regularly traveling to his hereditary place of origin, Maharashtra, to pronounce on legal matters there, the biggest case of his long and illustrious career, surely, was that of Shivaji. To crown Shivaji king was quite a complicated legal problem, and one that Gāgā was given very little time – though rather a lot of money! – to solve to his patron's satisfaction. In a scarce few days in the summer of 1674 CE, he had to make one argument from genealogy, another one from ritual, and yet another one from textual authority, to be able to transform Shivaji, a Maratha chieftain of the Bhosaḷe clan, heretofore deemed a Śūdra, into Chatrapati Shivaji Maharaj, a Kṣatriya king (Vajpeyi 2005). In June 1674 CE Gāgā hastily

[5] In 1663 Gāgā adjudicated a dispute about the ritual status of one of the Brahmin communities of this same region, coastal Maharashtra, called the Sārasvata (Bayly 1999; Wagle 1970).

composed a Sanskrit text titled *Śrīśivarājābhiṣekaprayoga* ("Manual for the Royal Consecration of Shivaji").

Gāgā's interest and expertise in *jātinirṇaya* (the adjudication of caste) notwithstanding, *rājadharma*, *dharma* for kings, and *rājyābhiṣekapaddhati*, technique for royal consecration, were nonetheless areas that he knew relatively less about, and perhaps never expected to have to know for any practical purpose. Banaras at the time fell within the vast sweep of Aurangzeb's Mughal Empire, and most of what is today Maharashtra was portioned out to the various Deccan Sultanates. Only when Shivaji presented the actual historical possibility of establishing in Maratha country a kingdom that is today retrospectively characterised as "Hindu" did the need arise for Gāgā to research the precedents for Kṣatriya kingship in the *dharma* texts of the Brahmin traditions. In order to write *Śrīśivarājābhiṣekaprayoga* he had to hurriedly consult his friend and fellow Maharashtrian scholar Anantadevabhaṭṭa, who directed Gāgā's attention to the *Viṣṇudharmottarapurāṇa* ("Viṣṇu's Lore on the Higher *Dharma*"), the *locus classicus* of discourse about royal *dharma*, as well as to his own work on the same subject, *Rājadharmakaustubha* ("Crest Jewel of Royal *Dharma*").[6] There is evidence to suggest that Anantadeva joined Gāgā in presiding over the caste disputes involving Kāyastha and Brahmin groups in coastal Maharashtra.

The legacy of men like Gāgā and Anantadeva carried on through the unstable years of Maratha rule following Shivaji's death in 1680 CE, and continued well into the Peshwa period in the eighteenth century, when caste disputes and their settlement became routine affairs in Maharashtra. Examining the Peshwa archives, collectively called the Daftar, N. K. Wagle (1970, 1980, 1982, 1987, 1998, 2005) has documented these disputes about the ritual status of a variety of groups (a monumental task that is ongoing even today). These include Brahmin, non-Brahmin, and Kāyastha litigants. In 1827 CE the CKP cited an old Banaras *vyavasthā-patra* to bolster their claims to high-caste ritual privileges, specifically, the permission to recite Vedic mantras during certain ceremonies, a privilege called "*vedokta*" (literally: "the enunciation of Vedic syllables"). Ultimately, by 1830 CE,

[6] Anantadeva, who was a great-great-grandson of the Marathi saint-poet Eknāth, lived in Banaras but was patronized by the Cānd king of Almora, Bāj Bahādur. Ananta's great-grandfather Haripaṇḍita migrated to Banaras from Paithan. Gāgā also had a kinsman – Kamalākarabhaṭṭa's son and Gāgā's first cousin – Anantabhaṭṭa, who may have assisted Gāgā in his scholarly and legal work. We find traces of both men with the name "Ananta" in connection with Gāgā in the historical sources of the period. Lawrence McCrea has suggested to me that the best way to distinguish them is to think of one as Anantadeva (Eknāth's descendant) and the other as Anantabhaṭṭa (Gāgā's relative).

even the descendant and heir of Shivaji, the Chatrapati Bhosaḷe of Satara, Pratāpasiṃha, was having to (re)claim and (re)establish his Kṣatriya credentials in the face of opposition that sought to demote him and his family back to the very Śūdra status that Shivaji had hired Gāgābhaṭṭa to consign to the past a good 150 years earlier.

Right from the first texts of the Śūdra archive, as early as 1350 CE, through to the difficulties of the Satara Chatrapati in 1830 CE, for 500 years before the establishment of the rule of the British Crown in India in 1857 CE, both before and after the arrival of the colonial powers on the subcontinent, caste, especially *śūdradharma*, was the subject of intense intellectual, legal, and political activity. I have traced this history of the legal treatment of caste, along with related intellectual and political developments, only in Banaras and in Maharashtra, through the figure of Gāgābhaṭṭa who lived in both places and traveled constantly between them in connection with his work. But similar histories can be discovered for medieval and late medieval Mithilā, Bengal, and large parts of the peninsular south, all of which had long-running traditions of Dharmaśāstra scholarship, plenty of Sanskrit intellectuals, a range of high, low, and middling castes in fluctuating relationships with structures of political power, and historical memories if not continuing experiences of "Hindu" rule of one sort or another.

True, it is difficult to find a monarch as charismatic as Shivaji in any part of the subcontinent during or immediately after the high era of Mughal rule (ending with Aurangzeb's death in 1707 CE), or during Britain's slow ascendancy, first through the Company in the eighteenth century, and then through the Crown in the nineteenth century. But Shivaji, as pointed out earlier, was an exception, even for his personal pandit, Gāgābhaṭṭa. Apart from the individual and exceptional case of Shivaji, the larger trend that I have tried to sketch here, of treating caste as a matter of law, can and must be generalized over many parts of the subcontinent, throughout the medieval, late medieval, and early colonial periods. I say "must be generalized" by historians because there is every reason to believe that the Śūdra archive, which was generated along the full swath of the Gangetic Plain – from areas close to Delhi in the west, to Almora in the Himalayan foothills, via Banaras and Mithila, to Bengal in the east – both reflected pan-regional concerns about the place of *jātidharma* in intellectual discourse, and fed back into legal practice as well as political activity on the ground.[7]

[7] D. Davis's work on *deśamaryādā* or locally valid customs and conventions that were made authoritative (which means "prescribed," though still not "enforceable," unlike modern laws) by translating

Whether or not Śūdra warlords had to be made into Kṣatriya potentates, the status claims of a plethora of powerful or aspirant groups – entrenched Brahmin elites as well as on-the-make Kāyastha, Śūdra, and other castes – had to be adjudicated. When canonical Dharmaśāstra texts did not provide specific enough indications, specialist *nibandha* texts were written to address problems concerning the absolute and relative ritual status, marriage, inheritance, property, occupations, nomenclature, diet, dress, worship, punishments, expiations, duties, and so on of the Śūdra, as well as other castes. It is noteworthy that these *śūdradharma-nibandha* texts were produced entirely *before* the Orientalizing and essentializing gaze of the European colonists encountered India with its numerous cultures, and set out to comprehend caste society through the multiple operations of Indology, linguistics, and the ethnographic state. The legal treatment of caste was by no means the outcome exclusively of India's long engagement with the colonizing Other.

them into the idiom of Dharmaśāstra (Davis 2002) indicates that more empirical work is necessary to see whether the *śūdradharma* texts of the late medieval period were intended to authorize local practices connected to the Śūdra (D. R. Davis 1999). What would be the relevant *deśa* or locality, if the new precepts were conceived as an instance of *deśamaryādā*? What independent evidence can we garner of local customs with regard to the Śūdra – in, say, Banaras, Mithilā, Bengal, or Maharashtra, where our texts were produced and circulated – which we could then argue were fixed into the *śāstra* idiom via these texts?

CHAPTER 10

Law, literature, and the problem of politics in medieval India

Whitney M. Cox

PROLOGUE: KALYĀṆA, DECEMBER 25, 1087 CE

It was a great occasion, with all the appropriate fanfare. The capital city stood in the center of a windswept plain. The air must yet have borne a chill that day, but one that foretold the return of warmth and life to the kingdom and its subjects. For this particular holding of court marked a special moment, when the sun reached the end of its northward journey, and began its return to the south: It was the shortest day of the year, and the promise of new life that it held called for a celebration. At its center, shaded by a parasol and flanked by fan bearers, stood the king. The appropriateness of the occasion was probably lost on no one who was present, for was not the king called Vikramāditya, Sun of Valor? It was a name held by generations of his ancestors, with a pedigree stretching back even further, to the greatest king of the old legends.

The notables of the kingdom flocked all around Vikramāditya: his queens and their children, members of his family both near and distant, his generals and guards, the lords of the realm. Perhaps there was a deputation of the Five Hundred Masters, the far-wandering merchant syndicate from the dynasty's ancient homeland, complete with their ceremonial peddler's bags and daggers; and perhaps there were embassies there from the courts of the king's relations, allies, and enemies. Certainly there were Brahmins; an important event like this needed to be celebrated with food offered and gifts given to them. Among them, there are two we may single out. The first was a renunciant, a man who had voluntarily extinguished his ritual fires, and so proclaimed his death to worldly life. Accompanied perhaps by other members of his order, his body bearing the signs of the conch and discus of Viṣṇu, he would have carried a beggar's bowl in his right hand and a staff of three reeds lashed together in his left, a staff – we may be certain – not a finger's breadth higher than the top of his head. His presence at court surely merited curious and respectful attention, for he was not merely some *sannyāsin* come for a free meal, but a man renowned for his astounding learning in the moral sciences, who lived up to his sobriquet Vijñāneśvara, the Lord of Discernment.

The second of our two Brahmins was himself also an outsider, though a very different man from the otherworldly renouncer. In his dress, his speech and manner, he stood out as a foreigner, a man from Kashmir, a world away in the far north. But there was more: Even in the presence of the king he was trailed by a parasol bearer, and he may have arrived at court that day in style, on the back of a caparisoned elephant. He was called Bilhaṇa, and he was the king's *vidyāpati*, the master of learning, a member of the court's glittering inner circle.

INTRODUCTION

This scene is an imagined one, but in its details it is quite plausible. King Vikramāditya, the sixth of that name to rule in the imperial Cālukya family, did in fact hold court in his royal capital on what several thousand miles to the west was celebrated as Christmas Day of the year 1087. We know this because a lord owing him allegiance, one Palatapāṇḍya, formally entreated the king on the auspicious occasion of the winter solstice to endow a village to a group of Brahmins, and an official record of that grant was incised onto copper plates that have survived to the present.[1] Almost certainly Bilhaṇa was then resident in the imperial capital at Kalyāṇa, for it was around that time that he was completing his long verse eulogy on his royal patron's rise to power, *The Deeds of King Vikramāṅka* (*Vikramāṅkadevacarita*, hereafter *VDC*). It is somewhat less certain, but very likely, that Vijñāneśvara was also present at this time and place. His *magnum opus* was an extensive digest on *dharma* in the form of a commentary on the *smṛti* text attributed to the sage Yājñavalkya, called rather ironically *The Concise Gloss (Mitākṣarā-vivṛti*, hereafter *Mitākṣarā*). This long work ends with verses in praise of the city and its ruler, and though it is uncertain when he completed the *Mitākṣarā*, it was patently the product of decades of study and labor, and there is no reason to doubt that this was in fact accomplished in Vikramāditya VI's capital.

[1] The surviving record, the so-called Nīrugunda plates, is dated in the forty-eighth year of Vikrama's regnal era (1123 CE), but sets out to record, confirm, and extend the donation made in his twelfth year. This inscription was first edited and published by L. D. Barnett in 1913 (EI 12.19); that it closely follows the general draft of the documents produced in Vikramāditya VI's chancellery can be seen by a comparison with the Kallasāmbi plates edited in Ramesan (1962).

In this chapter, I will take this imagined tableau of Vijñāneśvara and Bilhaṇa, with their king and patron set figuratively between them, as an entry into the question of the relation between the making of law and the making of literary art in medieval India. The certainty with which we know these two men to be contemporaries, even acquaintances, is very rare indeed in early India, where all too often the assignment of date and provenance to even major authors relies on a tissue of guesswork and wishful thinking. But this serendipity of their shared location in the Cālukya court aside, there is much to recommend Vijñāneśvara and Bilhaṇa as exemplary figures within their respective fields. Vijñāneśvara, the scholar of *dharma*, expressly sought to make his *Mitākṣarā* into a totalizing explanation of moral and legal knowledge, citing masses of other works to amplify or modify Yājñavalkya's teachings. His work was thus a testament to both the breadth and the vitality of the science of *dharma*; it represented one of the most significant syntheses in the long history of Indic legal and ethical thought.[2] And while Bilhaṇa was a creative and even innovative poet, his long poem reveals a deeply self-conscious attempt to relate to earlier poets and to the whole genre of royal panegyric.

We may take these two works as symptomatic of the wider trends within the creation of literature and of legal theory in South Asia early in the second millennium CE. As Donald Davis notices in this volume, there is a striking congruity between the creation of a new, self-aware body of codified *dharma* treatises like the *Laws of Manu* and the use of literary Sanskrit for purposes of political expression.[3] It is thus worth paying attention to the subsequent history of interrelation between these discourses, linked together both in their historical origins and in their shared and enduring problems and foci. The late eleventh century and the court of Kalyāṇa present an especially fruitful time and place to examine this continued relationship, in the midst of the transformations that S. Pollock has described as the later phase of cosmopolitan life in South Asia, in which Sanskrit as a properly elevated medium of discourse was joined by the emergent vernacular languages along with Persian and Arabic (with their own juridico-moral and literary heritages), and the cosmocratic imperial polities of earlier centuries began to give way to more circumscribed and more intensely imagined regional worlds (2006: 380–423).[4]

[2] Compare Kane's judgment, who likens Vijñāneśvara to the epochal figure of Patañjali in the field of grammar.

[3] Critically extending the ideas of Olivelle (2006a) and S. Pollock (2006).

[4] Pollock's understanding of the later history of Sanskrit literature may be supplemented by the suggestive study of Bronner and Shulman (2006: 5–10, 27–9, and *passim*).

Juxtaposing these two works raises many questions, but the most salient such question is one of form. How are these two texts put together as complex and sustained works of language, and what does their construction tell us about their authors, their chosen genres, and what they intended to communicate? On the surface, the two texts are formally quite different. Bilhaṇa's long work is in verse, and – while tied to the actual events of Vikramāditya VI's life as prince and young ruler – a work of the imagination. By contrast, Vijñāneśvara's work is largely in prose, and is a specimen of the forensic and anthological techniques of *śāstra* or systematic thought. Despite these differences in surface texture, there is nevertheless a deeper affinity between the texts and, we may presume, their authors, an affinity that rests on their shared focus on the complex moral fact of kingship.

In the *VDC*, the reflection on the means and ends of kingship depends explicitly on the public career of Bilhaṇa's patron. The long poem (*mahākāvya*) begins with a partly mythical genealogy of the kings of the Cālukya house, from the birth of their eponymous ancestor from the hand of the god Brahmā to the reign of Vikramāditya's father Someśvara I. The birth of Vikramāditya, the second of his three sons, is heralded by propitious omens and prophetic dreams. While acting as his father's marshal, the young prince conducts two successive extensive and successful campaigns to the south of the Cālukya realm. With the death of his elderly father and the accession of his elder brother as Someśvara II, the fortunes of the royal house appear secure. Vikramāditya, who had earlier convinced his father not to pass over his elder brother in his favor, returns to his martial duties under the new king. Someśvara II quickly warps under the pressures of rule, until his ambitions demand Vikramāditya's destruction. The hero flees to the south in the company of his younger brother Jayasiṃha, while Someśvara turns to an alliance with the Cōḻa king – the Cālukyas' perennial enemy – only to be defeated and ultimately deposed. The family troubles of the newly crowned Vikramāditya VI did not end there, as later, in another act of power-blind madness, Jayasiṃha would also turn on him, and have to be defeated on the battlefield. Before this, however, the king makes a fitting and auspicious marriage match in the beautiful daughter of the king of Karahāṭa, Candralekhā, and spends many happy hours making love to her, as described in great detail by Bilhaṇa. By the poem's end, Vikramāditya VI reigns indisputably over a kingdom free from the travails of fortune, a country so famous as to draw poets like Bilhaṇa himself from all over the civilized world.

The *Mitākṣarā* lacks the narrative flair of Bilhaṇa's *kāvya*: Vijñāneśvara sets out to speak of the permanent verities of *dharma*, not of just a single if exceptional king. But within this very wide ambit, the figure of the king occupies a key node. In the order of presentation in the Yājñavalkya text, which begins with a description of the licit behavior (*ācāra*) of the men of the three highest estates, the king is introduced as a special case of the wider class of householders. As Vijñāneśvara understands it, kings possess all the ordinary rights and prerogatives of an independent man, along with the bundle of additional functions and responsibilities peculiar to them. Among these is the paramount task of legal adjudication (*vyavahāradarśana*): this forms the next section of the Yājñavalkya text and a topic of great interest to legal theorists like Vijñāneśvara and his fellow *dharmaśāstrin*s. The king also serves as the supervising guarantor of the acts of penance (*prāyaścitta*) that provide the subject of the text's third and final section. The king is thus literally the pivotal figure for the major divisions of the *smṛti*, the point of transition from the duties incumbent upon the regulated moral life to the public occasions of the actual practice of law and of expiation. The rest of the text follows from this central transition: Without a king at the center and apex of the realm, the maintenance of *dharma*, and so of the whole human and natural order, would become untenable.

POWER, REPRESENTATION, AND POLITICS

Starkly put, the creation of both Dharmaśāstra and courtly poetry can thus be seen to be centrally concerned with the ideology of power in medieval India. The opinions of learned jurists and the imaginations of skilled poets both explored the moral underpinnings of power, especially that of kings, and in the process provided elaborate and compelling defences for why a certain family or a certain segment of the population had the ineluctable right to hold sway over others. For many a poet and *dharmaśāstrin*, the rule of a righteous king was all that separated the human world from degenerating into criminality and utter chaos, and both were seriously – and by no means merely cynically – engaged in explicating why this was so. Both law and literature aimed to represent the way that power should work in a properly constituted social order and conversely with its pathologies, with the ways that the moral universe could be impinged upon by its unlawful, excessive, or otherwise deranged exercise. Poets and jurists in early India thought and wrote about other things than just the power of kings, of course. Poets wrote about love, about the beauties of nature and the mysteries of the divine; and writers on *dharma* were concerned with everything from the course of the ideal human life to how one should properly clean one's teeth in the morning. Yet questions of royal power were fundamental to poets like Bilhaṇa and jurists like Vijñāneśvara.

But it is here that our problems begin. For all that *kāvya* and Dharmaśāstra were centrally concerned with questions of power and of kingship, they present the historian with a fundamentally skewed picture of the actual workings of power, royal or otherwise, in the historical societies of early South Asia. And this is due to both fields' ambiguous relationship to politics. If we may define power as the ability to control and allocate material and symbolic resources, and so then may define politics as the effort to control the apportionment of power within a given social order, then it is politics or the political that is missing from the works of Bilhaṇa and Vijñāneśvara, and other authors like them.[5] This is not to say that poets and jurists were ignorant or willfully blind to this thoroughgoing feature of human life; instead, I would suggest that the problem of the political is handled in both domains through a pattern of characteristic displacement, of substituting the contents of the political with something else. It is in this process of displacement or substitution that the formal work of *kāvya* and Dharmaśāstra takes place.[6]

Historians of medieval India have not tended to read *kāvya* and Dharmaśāstra in this way. Earlier historians have tended to take these sources at their word, either as a simple reflection of historical states of affairs or as a pathological misapprehension of a reality from which their creators were deeply alienated. The centrality accorded to the king by the *kavi* or "poet" and the *dharmaśāstrin* or (roughly) "jurist" – a centrality that often approached divinity – has been put in the service of many different theories of the state and society in medieval India. Taken literally, this has been taken as evidence that Indian kings possessed totalitarian control over their subjects; others following this same train of thought have tried to

[5] These definitions of "power" and "politics" are necessarily very broad, and no doubt unsatisfying to specialists. I take as the point of departure here Weber's definition of politics as "the striving to share power or striving to influence the distribution of power, either among states or among groups within a state" (1946a: 78). This may be supplemented by Runciman's definition of power, "the capacity of persons to affect either through inducements or sanctions what is thought, felt, said, or done by other persons, subject to that capacity deriving from institutional, not personal attributes" (1989: 2).

[6] Compare here S. Pollock's classic article (1989b), which argues for a related evacuation of the historical-referential content from Sanskrit learned and literary discourse. On this view, "politics" could be thought to be just a double for history. And, in fact, this has a certain attraction: The necessary role of contingency in any tenable form of historical explanation includes an *a priori* acknowledgment of the political working-out of the distribution and maintenance of social and institutional power. However, as will be argued below, it does some violence to both Vijñāneśvara and Bilhaṇa to simply understand their respective textual projects as solely committed to "[naturalizing] the present and its asymmetrical relations of power," as is subserved by the suppression of historical referentiality in Pollock's view (p. 610).

sympathetically reconstruct this as a benevolent system of divine kingship, where politics was subordinated to a sacral ideal. Taken as a misapprehension, the focus on kingly power has been understood as subserving a largely ceremonial, "ritual" idiom of essentially powerless sovereignty or as a massive historical wrong turn in Indian history, where royal power ended up complicit in its own feudal abnegation.[7]

It is only quite recently that the actual substance of the history of public power in medieval India has emerged from the shadow of these caricatures. There is much that is subject to still-ongoing debate, but a growing consensus has emerged that may be briefly and uncontroversially characterized here. Unsurprisingly, perhaps, the consensus centers on the politics of the medieval Indian state. The king and his court, on this view, were not the sole locus of power in the medieval Indic states; instead, the royal court was a nodal point in a network of other centers of authority. These other centers ranged upward from the head of an individual household, through to the lineage leader of dominant caste-communities, cutting across the collective assemblies that governed commercial markets and Brahmanical enclaves. Seen from the perspective of the court, these individuals and groups had to be marshaled so that taxes could be gathered, irrigation works renewed, and armies raised. Much of the work of the king, his royal household, and his bureaucratic apparatus was thus strictly speaking intensely political, negotiating with these shifting constellations of actors across a disparate, internally heterogeneous territory, one that resembled less the demarcations of the contemporary nation-state than the discontinuous and adventitious groupings of an archipelago. Such a complex mixture of negotiation, coercion, and arbitration that governed the internal relations of kingdoms was, if anything, seen in intensified form in the affairs between royal courts, or between courts and the groups of pastoralists, peddlers, tribal societies, and independent cultivators that ranged alongside and within the archipelagan networks of their territory.[8]

Politics, then, was something both intensive and extensive in medieval India: intensive, in that the continuity of the polity depended on the creation and maintenance of alliances between the royal court and any of a number of regional and local figures within the kingdom, and extensive, in that the different greater and lesser courts of southern Asia were linked by

[7] See the historiographical survey found in Inden (1990: 162–211).

[8] Among the recent scholarship with which I would associate this interpretative sketch would be Ali (2004), Chattopadhyaya (1994b), Heitzman (1997), Ludden (1999: 69–87) (from whom I borrow the image of an archipelago), and Talbot (2001). Especially notable in the present context is D. R. Davis (2005), which seeks to integrate this historical picture with the evidence from Dharmaśāstra.

far-flung networks of affiliation and potential fissure, by marriage, compact, embassy, and war. The Cālukya house of Vikramāditya VI's time presents an extraordinary case of this. Kings claiming a common descent with the lord of Kalyāṇa ruled to his north in Gujarat and to his east in Veṅgī; his greatest rival, Kulottuṅga Cōḻa, was in this sense his distant cousin. The intricately linked royal families of Europe at the beginning of the twentieth century present the modern reader with the closest analog to this situation, with all the same potential for affinal back-door diplomacy and explosive conflict.

But presuming that Vijñāneśvara and Bilhaṇa were participants in this court society, how are we to characterize their understanding of the solsticial court at Kalyāṇa? Our knowledge that this event even took place is, as mentioned earlier, based on a public record of it that was drawn up and copied onto copper plates, a record that begins with an elaborate eulogy in Sanskrit verse to the Cālukya family and concludes with a punctilious legal accounting of the terms of the donation solicited by Palatapāṇḍya and granted by the king. This document, therefore, was drawn up by men very much like our poet and jurist-renouncer, as were all such records that survive from medieval India. Why is it then that Vijñāneśvara and Bilhaṇa's works take so little seeming cognizance of the politics of power?

POLITICS AS PROCEDURE: *MITĀKṢARĀ* ON THE CONSTITUTION OF ROYAL POWER

Vijñāneśvara's work, as mentioned earlier, forms an extended commentary on the *Yājñavalkya Smṛti*, one of the most significant of the classical *dharmaśāstras*. Although he is a strong reader with his own systematic agenda, Vijñāneśvara reliably grounded his presentation in the *smṛti* text, something that is especially clear in his theory of royal power. While the Yājñavalkya text does not describe kingship in what we would think of as realistic terms – there is no account of royal succession and no attempt to argue for the legitimacy of the institution or its incumbents – it is free of the theophanic defense of kingship that Manu famously provides in his seventh *adhyāya*.[9] Showing a decidedly pragmatic streak, the *YSm* is not even especially concerned with whether a king be of the Kṣatriya order.[10] Kings

[9] *MDh* 7.4–9 (see Olivelle's chapter in this volume for a description of this and other Dharmaśāstra texts). See also Kane (1968–75, vol. III: 23 ff.).

[10] The opening verse on *rājadharma* (1.309) stipulates that the king must be *kulīnaḥ* ("of good family"), which Vijñāneśvara interprets as simply meaning "of high birth on both his father's and mother's sides" ("*mātṛtaḥ pitṛtaś cābhijanavān*"). Compare here Vijñāneśvara's comment on the word "*nṛpaḥ*"

simply *are*, and as such need to be thought about and are good for thinking through the question of *dharma*, its limits, and its norms.

This can clearly be seen in Vijñāneśvara's unpacking of *rājadharma*, the law of kings, which the *YSm* makes a subset of the general rules incumbent on all twice-born men. Introducing this discussion, he writes, "Having taught the collectively held *dharmas* of [adult, male] householders, Yājñavalkya now teaches the particular *dharmas* of the householder who has been invested with such virtues as royal consecration," that is, the king.[11] This minimal definition of what type of man is suited to be king is not found in the *YSm* text, though it does accord with its rhetorically subdued vision of royal power. It is the more or less mechanical fact of being processed through a ritual consecration that makes a man a king: This sort of formalism is representative of Vijñāneśvara's thinking in general. This becomes especially acute in his understanding of the root text's second major division, on *vyavahāra* or the practice of law. As he begins the second *adhyāya*, he writes:

> The king, who has been invested with such virtues as the royal consecration, has as his highest *dharma* the protection of his subjects. And this is not possible in the absence of the subjugation of wicked people. Further, an understanding of wicked people is impossible absent supervision of legal transaction. It follows that, as has already been taught earlier, the supervision of legal transactions [*vyavahāradarśanam*] should be practiced on a daily basis.

It is here that Vijñāneśvara's interests in a jurist's practical work comes to the fore: The discussion of the procedures of *vyavahāra* is much richer and more carefully structured in the *YSm* than in many other *smṛtis*; the procedures of actual legal casework forms the key structural concern, something that may have contributed to Vijñāneśvara's decision to comment upon it in the first place, instead of the enormously more prestigious text associated with Manu.[12] Vijñāneśvara's main exegetical task in commenting on this section is directed toward a systematic, rationalized end product, a comprehensive theory of the institutions and processes of jurisprudence, as centered on the king.

In his discussion and interpretation of the logic underlying *vyavahāra*, Vijñāneśvara is concerned with an exercise of model building, of providing

("king"), as it occurs in the opening verse of the second *adhyāya*: "By the word 'king' it is not meant that this is a property solely of a member of the Kṣatriya order; rather it refers to anyone charged with the task of the people's protection."

11 Introduction to 1.309; "of the householder…" ("*rājyābhiṣekādiguṇasya gṛhasthasya*").

12 On the "evident technical progress" that can be seen in the *YSm*'s presentation of legal procedure, compare Lingat (1973: 99 ff.); on the prestige of the *Mānava Dharmaśāstra* by Vijñāneśvara's period, see Olivelle (2005a: 1–2), and McCrea's chapter in this volume.

the basic conditions to ensure the legitimate operation of a recognized set of social practices.[13] It is here that Vijñāneśvara's formalism is at its most evident.[14] By formalism, I mean the set of norms and governing restrictions meant to grant efficacy and legitimacy to a given practice: By the successful realization of these formal conditions, the everyday chaos of social interaction and collective behavior is regimented into performance, indeed into ritual.[15] In the domain of *vyavahāra* generally, this can be seen above all in the eliciting and recording in documentary form of the verbal testimony of parties to a dispute. It has long been recognized that the place accorded to written documents in the *YSm* marks an innovation on the sole reliance on verbal testimony found in the earlier *Arthaśāstra* and *Mānava Dharmaśāstra*.[16] In Vijñāneśvara's hands, this is systematized into an elaborate body of procedural and evidentiary rules for the production and use of written documentation, marked by the highly ritualized eliciting and recording of verbal text that obeys a systematically organized protocol for ensuring an appropriately rule-bounded text from each of the two disputing parties.[17] All of this fine-grained structuring of these social performances – the details of which are beyond the scope of this chapter – is made without any reference whatsoever to the actual case at hand, or to the social identities of the participants beyond the minimal definitions of the king and his Brahmin advisers. Instead, Vijñāneśvara's description is an essay in the pragmatics of pure social form, awaiting inflection by particular social content.

Especially evident in these discussions, but at work throughout the *Mitākṣarā*, is an attempt to provide a textually grounded rationale for an ideally functioning royal institutional order, where the king is utterly central and yet endlessly substitutable. The content of politics – of what kings and others *do* on a day-to-day basis – is evacuated in favor of a set of overlapping,

[13] This can most clearly be seen in two extended passages where Vijñāneśvara introduces independent procedural essays based on the *YSm* text. These essays, which he terms "*mātṛkā*s" ("outlines" or "aide-mémoire"), address the theory of legal transactions in general (*vyavahāramātṛkā*, based on *YSm* 2.1–8) and the special conditions for the performance of ordeals (*divyamātṛkā*, based on 2.95–9).

[14] My use of the term "formalism" here is indebted to Stephen Greenblatt's thought-provoking essay on the rites of territorial possession performed by Christopher Columbus upon his arrival in the New World of the Western hemisphere (1991: 60–2).

[15] See Yelle (2002) and his chapter in this volume.

[16] See Michaels's chapter in this volume.

[17] Here Vijñāneśvara takes care to note that the verbal text so elicited is not necessarily in Sanskrit, and includes a careful accounting of the ways in which the interpretability and felicity of the text is to be ensured. In speaking of "felicity" here, I obliquely invoke the Austinian doctrine of infelicity, the conditions that might potentially make a given speech-act "misfire" or fail to carry out its social function (Austin 1975: 14–24). I nevertheless readily accept Yelle's (2002) critique of the limited applicability of Austin's theory to descriptions of ritual practice, especially Indic ritual.

interlinked protocols, models for how they might go about what it is they do. Politics is here encompassed within ritual: The procedural, formalist standards of practice that Vijñāneśvara lays down for the king, his advisers, and the agents who jointly produce the text of *vyavahāra* can in principle be remounted in any context where the rules of the interaction are tacitly accepted by all parties. The potentially messy world of reality is not ignored in this theory; rather it is abstracted away from, in much the same way as the rules of grammar abstract away from real usage.

Vijñāneśvara thus presents perhaps the most detailed theory of the constitution of the premodern Indian royal state that we have. Like other constitutional theorists in other times and places, his work is not to be condemned for its abstraction. Above all else, he is a theorist of procedure: The *Mitākṣarā* is concerned to present a processural model of power, one that focuses on the king as the principal transactional agent in all the business of the kingdom, from building a council of advisers and overseeing religious gifts to Brahmins to making war on neighboring kingdoms and administering punishment for legal and moral infractions within his own domain. Perhaps the jurist's greatest achievement is the way that he sought to create a morally intelligible paradigm by which the day-to-day activities of the premodern royal state could be modeled and could be evaluated. Since the *Mitākṣarā*'s constitutional theory was to remain salient from its own time and place all the way up to Banaras at the dawn of the nineteenth century,[18] Vijñāneśvara's work was to provide an intellectual framework and an authority of final appeal for matters of jurisprudential reason.

POLITICS AS SENTIMENT: NARRATIVE, *RASA*, AND THE *VIKRAMĀṄKADEVACARITA*

There is a basic sense in which the world of the poet and the world of the jurist intersected in medieval India: Dharmaśāstra, along with much else, was an important part of the omnivorous literary education of the aspiring *kavi*. But there is a larger affinity between the two domains: From its earliest mature articulation, poetry was thought to be somehow inherently bound up with the maintenance of the moral order. It is only through the work of a poet that a report of a king's great deeds can be transmitted to future generations. As the late seventh-century poet and critic Daṇḍin put it (*Kāvyādarśa* 1.5):

[18] See Rocher's chapter in this volume.

Look: though the ancient kings are gone,
it is only their reflected glory,
caught for all time in the mirror made of language,
that does not fade away.

Poetry was also thought to be a reliable (because pleasant) means for the moral education of future rulers. The classic case for this is found in the frame story to the *Pañcatantra*, where a king, frustrated by his callow sons, retains the help of a learned Brahmin to teach them edifying yet entertaining stories about the world. This theory of moral amelioration, however, was taken to encompass the whole range of literary texts: Through reading Valmīki's *Rāmāyaṇa*, it is said, one learns to act like the god-king Rāma, and not like his archenemy, the prideful and lusty demon Rāvaṇa.

Alongside this focus on the inculcation and transmission of *dharma*, however, there was another dominant understanding of literary art, in which the purpose of poetry is above all else to elicit pleasure, especially through the representation of a restricted set of refined, aestheticized emotional states. In this understanding, what differentiates poetry from any other form of language is its ability to communicate through objective means the subjective depths of experience. This form of emotive communication, what from the earliest times literary thinkers in Sanskrit termed "*rasa*" or "flavor," had by Bilhaṇa's time become the acme of literary value, the result of a theoretical revolution in the study of Sanskrit literature. In Kashmir in the middle decades of the ninth century, the poet and critic Ānandavardhana had reconceptualized the mechanisms of emotional communication within the realm of language analysis: The perception of *rasa* occurs because of the workings of the intra-linguistic mechanism of suggestion (*dhvani*), the presence of which differentiates literary art from all other uses of language. As a result of this theory of the process of *rasa*-cognition, the creation and critical evaluation of poetry both took a strongly sentimentalist turn, as the individual sophisticated consumer of literature – the *sahṛdaya* – became its prime subject.[19] The depth of feeling that a poem or song summoned in the heart of the *sahṛdaya* became the real measure of aesthetic success: All of the details of a work of art were thought to be ultimately subordinate to that emotional outcome. A further tenet of this theory held that a work must possess one and only one *rasa*, one structure of feeling as it were, as its key note. Other sentiments may be present, but only insofar as they subserve this single aesthetic end. Bilhaṇa, himself a Kashmiri, explicitly endorsed his understanding of the means and ends of

[19] See McCrea's foundational study of the transformation of Kashmirian *alaṃkāraśāstra* (2009).

poetry. But in this theory of literature there lurked a problem: If the highest aim for poetry was to produce an emotional representation that definitionally transcended the mundane conditions of time, place, and person, then the moral knowledge of *dharma* would be in danger of losing its place within the literary order.

In the *VDC*, Bilhaṇa adapts the demands of a *rasa* poetics to the needs of his narrative and focuses in on the king's leading affective or moral relationships. Within the heroic framework dictated by the poem's genre, the great public occurrences of Vikramāditya's life are all cast as fundamentally and deeply personal events by the poet. It is here, in the affective life of the king, where Bilhaṇa's version of politics may be found. For all that it is concerned with statecraft, alliance, and war, Bilhaṇa's poem depicts a surprisingly intimate world centered on its hero, a series of miniaturist details of the prince's inner life. When, for instance, he learns of his father Someśvara's sudden illness and death from the mouth of a messenger (4.39 ff.), Vikramāditya collapses into apoplexy. That this happens to the poem's hero and patron who a few verses earlier was figured as an unstoppable warrior is totally in keeping with the rhetorical style of *rasa* poetry. The narrative structure of this episode is significant: A man arrives bearing news for Vikrama, and the audience is privy to the message and to the hero's response and reaction. This is repeated at every significant narrative juncture in Bilhaṇa's long poem. Vikrama is never the inciter of the narrative's action; instead, he is its reactive recipient. This too is congruent with the poetics of *rasa* – it provides an occasion to see the central figure's reaction, with all its attendant triggers of affect – but it also connects up however obliquely with the figure of the arbitrating king seen in the *Mitākṣarā*, handing down judgment based on the properly structured verbal performances of the two parties to *vyavahāra*. But – and this is a very telling difference – while the *Mitākṣarā* is concerned with setting the king's audiences in their wider circuits of courtiers and advisers, the meetings that Bilhaṇa describes are always tête-à-tête, seemingly private conversations. And while the *Mitākṣarā*'s procedural logic centers on the appropriateness and felicity of these performances on a formal level, in the *VDC* the speeches of the king and his interlocutors are delivered with all the eloquent embellishment made possible by classical Sanskrit poetics at its height. This typifies Bilhaṇa's style of narration: In peacetime, it is in the miniaturist detail of personal interaction that the substance of events takes shape. Even on the battlefield, when this scope widens to a panoramic view of immense armies, the figure of the king remains in the foreground. Taken together, these two poles to the narrative – private intimacy and cataclysmic display of public violence – come together into the affective whole of *vīrarasa*, the poem's sublimated vision of the substance of statecraft.

JURIST AND POET, SEEN TOGETHER

If we return to the opening tableau of Vijñāneśvara, Bilhaṇa, and Vikramāditya, we are now in a position to see that there is a certain asymmetry between the three figures. While both jurist and poet can be seen in relationship to the real political power that the king embodies, this relationship is not one of perfectly arrayed, triptych-like balance. The substance of the political is that from which the constitutional theory of the *Mitākṣarā* departs; in turn, it can (and demonstrably did) "feed back" onto the practices of politics, while itself retaining its abstract character. The *Mitākṣarā*'s abstract model provides, moveover, a publicly held group of norms that are available to a poet like Bilhaṇa as he portrays his patron through poetic, narrative means. It is not so much that our poet and jurist are ranged on either side of their patron-king, but that the poet is representing – whether truthfully or not – the king as held against the standard that the *dharmaśāstrin* supplies, as if Vijñāneśvara fell obliquely within Bilhaṇa's gaze.

The difference once again amounts to a question of textual form. Vijñāneśvara's model of royal institutions sought quite deliberately to empty the figure of the king of all particular content and so make the king the most important node in an interlocking set of unspecified social actors. The work can be (and was) judged successful insofar as it provided a constitutional standard, a procedurally and ethically competent rendition of the royal practice of juridical oversight and executive authority. By contrast, Bilhaṇa's poem was meant to fill in the details of the king's existence that had been emptied by the juridical theory, to make the smallest details of his public life filled with detail and incident. In the poem, Vikramāditya's worldly life is determined above all else by just a handful of his relationships: his father and brothers, his wife, a couple of friends and a couple of enemies. In this, he is not very different from anyone else, then or now, and so resembles the *Mitākṣarā*'s basic definition of a king: just another man, surcharged with the qualities and burdens of his office.

This is in line with the expressive, transformative effects of Sanskrit *kāvya* more generally, its power to "make reality more real by making it more noticeable, more complex, more beautiful," as S. Pollock has elegantly put it (2006: 255). But this is turned to surprising ends by Bilhaṇa, who shows himself to be more than a little disgusted with what power leads men to do.[20] In exploring the moral and affective fault lines of kingship using all the resources made available by this expressive power, Bilhaṇa is able to formulate a skeptical, ironic view of the politics of kingship, which, while not unprecedented,[21] distinguishes him from the ranks of other court eulogists. It is a remarkable feat of Bilhaṇa as a court poet that he manages to lay bare this thoroughgoing cynicism about what it is that kings do, only to pull back, and reestablish the figure of his patron. Many are the wicked kings in this world; isn't it lucky to be ruled by one who isn't?

In describing the relationship between the *Mitākṣarā* and the *VDC* in this way – with law tending toward a methodical abstraction away from the concrete and evaluative particular that is the preserve of literature – I have been influenced by the study of these two domains in the contemporary world, especially the comparative study of law and literature. In her influential description of the relationship between these two discourses, Martha Nussbaum finds the literary imagination to be "subversive" of the normative claims of the law; adapting Whitman, she describes a judge who can encompass both the norm and its subversive supplement as one who judges "'as the sun falling round a helpless thing,' . . . with rich human concreteness, not with quasi-scientific abstraction but with a vision of the human world" (1995: 2, 81). It is in the modern social novel that she finds the most perspicacious means to this end, as "present[ing] persistent forms of human need and desire realized in specific social situations," that call out for empathetic response in the sensitive and morally alert reader (Nussbaum 1994: 7).[22]

Of course, the differences between a royal court in eleventh-century Karnataka and the late modern, capitalist West are so great as to caution us against seeing too strong a correspondence here. Vijñāneśvara's *dharma* is as dissimilar to the Constitution of the United States or the US Code as Bilhaṇa's long Sanskrit poem is to the modern novel.

[20] Here, and throughout my reading of the *VDC*, I am very much indebted to an unpublished essay by Yigal Bronner (Bronner 2009), whom I would like to thank.

[21] In his skepticism, Bilhaṇa may perhaps be thought heir to the paradigmatic cynic of Sanskrit literature, the epigrammatist Bhartṛhari. See the adroit if idiosyncratic judgments of Kosambi (1948: 80–1 and 2002).

[22] Compare here Crotty's perceptive remarks (2001: 88–9), apropos a reading of the *Oresteia* from a perspective similar to Nussbaum's:

> In drawing attention to concrete particulars, works of literature implicitly question – or, more precisely, should lead us to question – the ability of any political institution to capture and reflect its members in all their intricacy . . . by banning tragedies like the *Oresteia*, Plato would have excluded a vision of legal institutions as emerging from the passions, and never quite leaving them behind – especially the passionate demand for justice and the polysemous, thickly opaque language in which this demand finds expression.

Yet even the contrast here is instructive: Bilhaṇa's classicizing poem studiously maintains a unity of tone and of authorial voice that is in direct contrast to the insistent polyphony of the novels championed by Nussbaum; but this itself serves his skepticism, lending a timeless, nomic quality to his condemnation of the desperate acts men will commit in order to become kings, and to the ruinous and self-destructive ends that kings come to. Here, as Bilhaṇa speaks in a language that approaches the decontextualized norms of Dharmaśāstra, he creates a new and morally charged space from which certain of the Sanskrit poets who were to follow him could base their own searching explorations of public life; of these inheritors, the most significant is surely his fellow Kashmirian Kalhaṇa whose *Rājataraṅginī* is throughout imbued with a similar spirit of critique, and who tells his reader that a true poet's language must, like a judge's, speak of the facts in a way that is free of passion (1.7; Stein 1988). A poet can best serve his art, we learn, through learning to see and to speak more like the *dharmaśāstrin*, a fascinating inversion of Nussbaum's humanistic model.

These two Kalyāṇa Brahmins, jurist and poet, were at once emblematic of the wider dynamics of their fields and men who set forth singular, indissolubly particular understandings. Through their works we can see that the politics of power in medieval India could not be reduced to a univocal, simplified understanding. Instead, the science of *dharma* and the theory and practice of literature both possessed powerful intellectual and moral resources for interpreting the political order in which they existed, and – when read carefully, sympathetically, and above all historically – can contribute inestimably to our understanding of the social realities of premodern South Asia.

CHAPTER 11

Hindu law as performance: ritual and poetic elements in Dharmaśāstra

Robert A. Yelle

Every system of law is, at the same time, a semiotics: a set of rhetorical techniques designed to communicate the law's commands, persuade that these commands are just, and impress them on the popular memory. Although this is as true of modern law as it is of ancient, the semiotics of some older legal systems such as Hindu Dharmaśāstra is markedly different from that of our contemporary legal system. Dharmaśāstra deploys numerous rituals and poetic and other literary devices in both its textual structures and its depictions of legal practice. Examples are oaths, trials by ordeal, penances, and symbolic punishments that resemble and coordinate with the operations of the cosmic law of karma. Such devices have inspired the classification of Dharmaśāstra as "primitive" or "religious" law, a characterization that, although not entirely inaccurate, serves mainly to defer explanation.

The present chapter attempts to account for some of these curious features of Dharmaśāstra by describing their semiotic function. In doing so, it borrows from the growing field of legal semiotics which, sometimes under the rubric of "law and literature," in recent decades has made significant progress in illuminating the symbolic, narrative, and rhetorical dimensions of both modern and ancient legal systems (compare D. R. Davis 2007). This approach to Dharmaśāstra is informed in particular by recent semiotic analyses of ancient Jewish law (Douglas 1999; Jackson 2002a, 2006; Sawyer and Douglas 1996). There are significant parallels between these two ancient legal systems, particularly in terms of their semiotic properties. As in the case of Jewish law, some of the more distinctive features of Dharmaśāstra may best be understood in terms of their contribution to rhetorical performance: as aesthetic and communicative activity, rather than merely a set of substantive rules or a "code" in the modern sense. "Performance" denotes the entire range of communicative and expressive functions served by cultural forms, including "intersubjective communication, cultural transmission, social influence, and rhetorical persuasion"

(Yelle 2006: 379; compare Bell 1998; Tambiah 1985). An analysis of performance attends to the work done or effects achieved by ritual and other expressive forms of behavior in situated social contexts, and emphasizes the pragmatic dimensions of such behaviors rather than merely their semantic contents. Such an approach holds significant promise for the interpretation of the symbolic and ritual dimensions of legal systems such as Dharmaśāstra and, as we shall see, represents an advance over earlier views that either dismissed these rituals as superstitious nonsense or attempted to account for them in naturalistic terms.

The ritual and symbolic features of ancient law have often been criticized as a form of "primitive" or even "magical thinking" which exaggerates the perennial lawyerly sin of formalism, meaning the rigid attachment to certain prescribed words or legal procedures. In contrast, modern law emphasizes the value of substantive law and of legal realism over formalism. In the early twentieth century, the legal historian Frederick Pollock recognized that in some cases formalism served the "rational" purpose of providing "a hard and fast rule" (F. Pollock 1912: 14–16). However, the excessive formalism of ancient law stemmed from "the oldest form of superstition ... the prehistoric belief in symbolic magic ... [which] assumed that words have in themselves an operative virtue which is lost if any one word is substituted for any other." Pollock allowed the human instinct "to clothe ... collective action in dramatic and rhythmical shapes ... [which] are both impressive at the time and easily remembered." Yet he declined to follow any further the inquiry into "the aesthetic history of ritual."

Nowadays, such biases have begun to abate, and we find more attention being paid precisely to the symbolic and ritual dimensions of ancient law, as well as to the performative function of such devices in their original social contexts. Poetry, ceremony, and vivid narrative images may serve to call attention to the "message" of the law, produce a sense of symmetry, or make the law more memorable (Douglas 1999; Jackson 1991, 1998, 2002a, 2002b). As described below, these were especially important features in primarily oral cultures before the wide distribution of literacy or printing.

OATHS, ORDEALS, ASCETICISM, AND THE PRODUCTION OF RITUAL CERTAINTY

Let us begin with the oaths and ordeals in Hindu Dharmaśāstra, which are surely one of that tradition's most interesting features, and which serve to distinguish it from modern law as well as to reinforce its resemblance to other ancient legal systems where such forms of adjudication were widely used. These ordeals are described in the *Divyatattva* (hereafter *DT*) authored by the sixteenth-century Bengali Raghunandana Bhaṭṭācārya (Lariviere 1981a). The most common reaction to these rituals has been to declare them a species of superstition that reflects a belief in the supernatural and its power to suspend the natural order. However, a minority opinion has sought to uphold the rationality of these rituals through naturalistic, scientific principles (e.g., Pendse 1985: 93). For example, according to Derrett (1978b), in the Hindu trial by fire (*DT* 214–20), an innocent person supposedly perspires less and escapes blisters; in the water ordeal (*DT* 248–50), an innocent person will have a lower rate of pulse and respiration, and may remain submerged longer; and in the ordeal of chewing uncooked dry rice without bleeding (*DT* 285–9), the dry mouth of a guilty person will "make failure inevitable."

Such attempts to rationalize ordeals appear strained. One can imagine them being extended with some plausibility to certain cases, such as the ordeals of taking the oath (*DT* 332–50) or drinking holy water (*DT* 283–4), each of which was followed by a prescribed waiting period following which, if no calamity befell the accused, he was pronounced innocent. In these cases, the guilty mind might eventually break down and suffer psychosomatic illness or, perhaps, produce a confession. However, in the case of other ordeals – such as drinking poison (*DT* 265–8) or drawing lots (*DT* 330–1) – no physiological explanation appears adequate.

Moreover, the Dharmaśāstra texts declare explicitly that the basis of the ordeals' efficacy is supernatural, and that in the ritual context of the ordeal natural substances may work contrary to their ordinary physical properties. The ordeals depended on a belief in "immanent justice" or a connection between the human and divine realms (Lariviere 1981b: 348). Attempts to reinterpret them in scientific terms are blatantly anachronistic. Ordeals were supposed to work automatically if performed according to the prescribed procedures (Lariviere 1981a: xii; compare Medhātithi, commentary on *MDh* 8.116, in G. Jha 1920–9, vol. VI: 145). The anticipated result might not occur, as a result of the accused's good or bad karma, but this would not call into question the justice and efficacy of the ordeal as a mode of adjudication.

What did the formal features of the ordeals contribute to the belief in their efficacy? A performative or semiotic approach may provide a partial answer. First of all, it should be noted that the ordeals employ various forms of repetition, involving either ritual gestures – heating the iron ball (*DT* 214), drinking the holy water (*DT* 284), and spitting out the dry rice after chewing it (*DT* 287) are all supposed to be done three times – or the use of alliteration and other poetic devices in some of the accompanying invocations:

paraṃ pavitram amṛtaṃ ghṛta tvaṃ yajñakarmasu
"O Butter, you are the best purifier, ambrosia in sacrificial acts" (*DT* 301).
pāpaṃ punāsi vai yasmāt tasmāt pāvaka ucyate
"You [Fire] are called 'purifier' because you purify sin" (*DT* 216).
dhakārād dharmamūrtis tvaṃ ṭakārāt kuṭilaṃ naram |
dhṛto dhārayase yasmād dhaṭas tenābhidhīyate ||
"From the letter *dha*, you [the Balance] are the embodiment of justice [*dharma*]; from the letter *ṭa*, when raised [*dhṛta*], you raise [*dhārayase*] the dishonest [*kuṭilaṃ*] man, therefore you are called *dhaṭa*" (*DT* 169–70).

Poetic repetition was by no means limited to the invocations found in ordeals. Some of the accounts of karmic punishments in the afterlife or next life, as described below, employed similarly poetic and alliterative formulas. Indeed, such devices are frequently found in the ritual languages of many cultures, where they serve to make such formulas more impressive and memorable, and to reinforce the rhetorical associations among the ideas they express (Yelle 2002). As Douglas puts it, "to be convincing, what is true must chime with justice" (1999: 27). Poetry contributes to the appearance of the "naturalness" of these associations: For example, the fire is intrinsically connected with purity, and the balance with fairness. Such rhetorical reinforcement of the conviction in the efficacy of ritual would appear to be especially important in the case of ordeals, which are, generally speaking, a remedy of last resort, a method of proof employed only when other sources of evidence are lacking. In this situation, it is particularly crucial to avoid the appearance of partiality, and to displace the decision of guilt or innocence onto some supernatural or, at any rate, non-human entity or process. If the semiotic function of the ordeal is to produce a clear verdict – a yes-or-no, either-or answer – the function of the ritual and poetic dimensions of the ordeal is to provide rhetorical cover for the correctness or justice of that verdict. Such a semiotic interpretation of the ordeal's function is, of course, directly at odds with naturalistic explanations.

It would be just as vain to search for a naturalistic explanation for most of the dietary prescriptions and expiations of Dharmaśāstra. The rationale of many of these is often manifestly symbolic. For example, the consumption of the *pañcagavya* (five excretions of the cow) as a form of penance refers to the belief in that animal's special purity and holiness. Other penances, like some punishments described below, bear some symbolic relationship to the offense committed, for instance a twice-born man who drinks liquor must drink boiling liquor (*MDh* 11.91); a man who sleeps with his elder's wife must lie down on a red-hot iron bed or castrate himself (*MDh* 11.104–5). There is even a kind of poetry in the word "*prāyaścitta*" ("penance") itself, in the following etymologies quoted in *Prāyaścittaviveka* (vol. 11; Misra 1982):

prāyo nāma tapaḥ proktaṃ cittaṃ niścaya ucyate |
taponiścayasaṃyuktaṃ prāyaścittam iti smṛtam ||

> "Going forth [*prāyaḥ*] indeed is asceticism [*tapas*], and *cittam* is explained as resolve; [thus] asceticism joined with resolve is known as *prāyaścittam*."

prayatatvād vopacitam aśubhaṃ nāśayatīti prāyaścittam

> "Or through effort [*prayatatvād*] it destroys [*nāśayati*] the accumulated [*upacitam*] evil [*aśubham*]: thus, *prāyaścittam*."

Although many of the ascetic practices prescribed in Dharmaśāstra appear to consist of arbitrary prescriptions, which have meaning only in terms of a cultural system (compare Valantasis 1995: 548), the prevailing view from within this system is that such prescriptions constitute a form of "natural law," in a strong sense. Various forms of symbolism are deployed to support this view.

KARMA, CHIASMUS, AND COMMUNICATION

One of the clearest illustrations of this principle is the various representations in Dharmaśāstra of the law of karma and of symbolic punishments that follow this cosmic law. Karma follows a broader cross-cultural pattern of representing justice – especially divine justice – symbolically. Often described under their Roman name as the *lex talionis* or law of talion (Yelle 2001), such punishments use resemblance or an indexical connection to reinforce the symmetry between crime and punishment: for example, burning an arsonist or cutting off the hand of a thief. Rhyme, alliteration, and other poetic devices are also used to reinforce the connection between crime and punishment, making the latter serve as a rhyming ending or, as Douglas put it, making it "chime with justice." Depictions of karma, as of symbolic punishments elsewhere, employ not only substantive analogies but even various forms of linguistic parallelism and chiasmus, meaning the inversion of letter, word, or sentence order, a literary device similar to, but less exacting than, the palindrome.

The list of karmic punishments at *MDh* 12.61–7 (compare 11.48–53) includes a number that are clearly analogical in nature (L. Rocher 1980: 68–9). Several of these analogies are substantive – a thief of grain will be reborn as a rat (12.62), and so on – while others are purely formal and poetic. Thus, *MDh* 12.63 (following Olivelle 2005a) reads in part "*tailaṃ tailapakaḥ khagaḥ*" – "by stealing oil [*tailaṃ*], [one becomes] a cockroach [*tailapakaḥ*]" – and 12.64 reads "*godhā gāṃ vāggudo guḍam*" – "by stealing a cow [*gāṃ*], [one becomes] a monitor lizard [*godhā*]; by stealing molasses [*guḍam*], a flying fox [*vāgguda*]." When both phrases are read together, the degree of alliteration appears even more pronounced. It is unclear in these cases what, if any, substantive analogy might obtain between the sin and the karmic punishment imposed, yet the poetic analogy emerges clearly from the Sanskrit. A further example is the retribution for eating meat described at *MDh* 5.55:

māṃ sa bhakṣayitāmutra yasya māṃsam ihādmy aham
etan māṃsasya māṃsatvaṃ pravadanti manīṣiṇaḥ
"Me he [*māṃ sa*] will eat in the next world, whose meat
[*māṃsa*] I eat in this world."
This, the wise declare, is what gave the name to and discloses the true nature of "meat" (*māṃsa*). (Olivelle 2005a)

The karmic punishment expressed in this verse is in the form of a folk etymology, where the word for a thing is supposed to disclose the true nature of that thing. Like other examples of this genre, such as the definitions of "fire" and "the balance" in the invocations of the *DT* quoted above, it relies on alliteration. There is also a parallelism between the first and second halves of the first line: "*māṃ sa . . . yasya māṃsam.*" Substantively, this has the logical form of an inverted "if . . . then" proposition, in which the consequence is spelled out first, followed by its condition of occurrence. This indexical relationship is reinforced and rendered more symmetrical by the addition of a pair of indexical phrases marking spatiotemporal location ("in the next world" vs. "in this world").

Examples can be found in other cultures where poetic inversion or chiasmus is used to depict retribution, as in the Hebrew Bible's formulations of the law of talion. As many scholars have noted, Leviticus 24.13–23 encloses the basic talionic formula ("eye for eye, tooth for tooth") within an elaborate chiasmus (Boys 1825; Jackson 1996; 1998: 133–4; 2002a: 291 ff.; 2002b: 25–8; 2006: 202–8). As Welch notes, "the talionic formula stands squarely at the physical and conceptual center" of the chiasmus, which "lends itself formally to the substantive content of talionic justice" (1999: 162, 165). Such literary forms appear to serve both a rhetorical and a mnemonic function, by simultaneously reinforcing the idea of retribution and making it more memorable. Both persuasion and memorability, however, are only specialized aspects of a more general function that might best be termed "communication." In Leviticus 24, God lays down the law, in the form of a verbal command, and at the end of the passage, what God has commanded is performed. This is an instance of successful communication between the divine and human realms. The same appears to be true of *MDh* 5.55, which also uses parallelism to depict a reciprocity between this world and the next.

Far from being confined to literary texts, chiasmus is often employed in situations in which the act of communication or dialogue is itself highlighted. The inversion of word order is quite common, not only in English but in many other languages as well, to denote the form of a question. This inversion calls forth an answer that reverses the word order of the question:

> Will you wash the dishes?
>   I will wash the dishes.
> What sort of dog does Lucinda have?
>   Lucinda has a toy dog.

The dialogical rhythm of question-and-answer is reinforced by the inversion of word order. Similar inversions characterize and help to define the "pair-part" structure of some other communicative acts, such as call-and-response, as in the following English and Arabic greetings:

> How are you?
>   I am fine.
> *as-salām ʿalē-kum* (Peace be upon you.)
>   *wa ʿalē-kum as-salām* (And upon you be peace.)

The reciprocal relationship between the person giving and the one receiving the latter greeting is mirrored in the palindromic form of the greeting itself (Caton 1986: 297).

The use of similar-sounding words to describe the crime (or sin) and punishment (or retribution) is another way of reinforcing the apparent fitness or causal (indexical) relationship between these two. The legal philosopher Jeremy Bentham argued that such "characteristical" or analogical punishments as the law of talion strengthen the connection between the ideas of crime and punishment, and make punishment more "popular" by appealing to our intuitions of justice (Yelle 2001: 637, 641). Chiastic representations of the law of talion may similarly reinforce the popularity of such punishments. Like related symbolic forms, chiasmus employs imitation to establish a reciprocity or symmetry between two qualities. Such forms of imitation are basic to human communication, cognition, and recognition.

These comparative cases suggest that the examples of karmic punishments based on analogy reflected a belief in immanent justice common to many traditional cultures, and employed devices similar to those used in those cultures to reinforce the apparent association between deeds and their consequences. In addition to substantive analogies between crime and punishment, Dharmaśāstra texts such as Manu used poetic analogies to reinforce the perception of symmetry between the human and divine realms; to heighten the "message" or warning of the law of karma and make it more memorable; and to provide a guide to the king or other executor of temporal justice. As such, they contributed a religious sanction to the force of law.

ORAL PERFORMANCE AND LITERARY STYLE

The talionic formula appearing in the Hebrew Bible may have developed originally in a culture in which law was transmitted orally and administered in a decentralized fashion by individuals or local bodies (Jackson 2002a, 2002b). The conditions of legal performance determined the appropriateness of such formulas, which served a narrative function: They suggested but did not mandate a perfect symmetry between crime and punishment; they established a flexible standard in the absence of a more fully elaborated code; and they provided an analogical model that could be adapted as necessary. The law of talion deployed evocative and exemplary images such as "an eye for an eye," which were intended to be taken as illustrations rather than as rigid and abstract rules. The subsequent view that the talionic formula was to be interpreted literally reflected the mistaken imposition of a semantic model of meaning, which reflected the biases of literate and abstract cultures such as our own (Jackson 2002a: 283–6). Some apparent contradictions in biblical law were a by-product of the imposition of a literalist reading on the record of fluid oral custom.

Like ancient Jewish law, Dharmaśāstra originated as an oral tradition, the provisions of which circulated, and changed, as maxims or proverbs before being compiled and written down in texts such as Manu's (L. Rocher 1994; compare Lariviere 1996: 181; Maine 1883: 9–10). Legal rules varied according to locality, and were applied variably and informally, being quoted as occasion required. Nor were such customary traditions entirely displaced by the Dharmaśāstra texts, despite the well-known European colonial bias toward the interpretation of these texts as equivalent to a legal code. This may explain some of the contradictions that occasionally appear when we attempt to derive a single legal rule from a text such as Manu (L. Rocher 1994: 27–8).

As with the talionic formula (compare Jackson 2002b), the transition from orality to literacy appears to have contributed to the decline of various poetic devices in ancient law. Parallelism, alliteration, and chiasmus promote the memorability of legal rules, a necessary function in an oral culture. With the development of a written legal tradition, the need for such formulas abated accordingly.

The use of poetic devices such as parallelism and chiasmus is, however, not confined to oral traditions. Even if many of the provisions of ancient Jewish and Hindu law began their life as oral maxims, they evolved within increasingly specialized and literate legal traditions. It is unlikely that the chiasmus in Leviticus 24.13–23 was an oral formula, as the text is too long, and the chiasmus too elaborate, being revealed only by backward scanning of the written text (Jackson 2006: 203 n. 170; *pace* Welch 1981: 12). In such cases, we assume that poetic devices served primarily a rhetorical rather than a mnemonic function: They made punishment appear more just or "fitting," as well as more impressive.

Despite such qualifications, there does appear to have been a close association between the poetic form of many ancient laws and their function in an oral culture. Some of the more obviously poetic formulas in Dharmaśāstra, such as the invocations in the ordeals of the *DT*, occurred in instances of direct speech, and even of ritual "speech acts."[1] Although prescribed in written texts, these formulas were meant to be spoken. As such, their poetry would have served to make them more impressive to an audience that must have consisted of literate and illiterate alike.

CONCLUSION

Although the need for law to communicate its rules and make them more persuasive and impressive has not changed since ancient times, the semiotic techniques employed by law to fulfill these functions have changed to accord with the very different social, cultural, and material conditions of modernity. As just noted, one of the primary reasons for the demise of legal poetry, such as we find in Dharmaśāstra, was the rise of print culture, which rendered the mnemonic function of such devices largely obsolete. Yet it would be too simplistic to attribute the more prosaic character of modern legal language solely to the invention of movable type. The poetry of ancient law, as we have seen in the case of ordeals and karmic punishments in Dharmaśāstra, also reinforced the idea that law reflected the natural order of

[1] On speech acts, see also the chapter by Malik in this volume.

the cosmos. Various currents of thought that we refer to for convenience as the "Reformation" and the "Enlightenment" combined in European culture to discredit such views. Like language, laws and punishments are now regarded as arbitrary social conventions, and the social and natural domains have been "disenchanted," so that the belief in immanent justice has declined. These developments – a discussion of which is beyond the scope of the present chapter – mark a shift in legal consciousness that separates modernity from the world of the Dharmaśāstra texts.

PART III

Law and modern Hinduism

CHAPTER 12

Temples, deities, and the law

Richard H. Davis

"Sueing Shiva Dismays Dealers," read the headline in the *Sunday Times* of London, February 21, 1988. The Hindu god Śiva, it appeared, had come to the old imperial capital to bring a suit before the Queen's Bench for the return of his stolen property. It seemed to be a classic man-bites-dog story, and the *Times* reporter Alison Beckett emphasized the exotic quality of the court case.

> The case was a bizarre enough event in itself. It was brought by the God Shiva against the Metropolitan Police and the Bumper Development Corporation of Alberta, Canada, for the return of an eleventh century bronze dancing figure of the god. Since he could not actually appear, Shiva was represented by the Indian government and, on paper, by the Shiva Lingam, a cylindrical stone phallus, the deity's main physical manifestation in any Shiva temple – although the phallus was not produced in court. (Beckett 1988: 9C)

The object in question, the Pathur Naṭarāja, had been accidentally dug up in 1976 in a small hamlet in southern India by a landless laborer, sold to a local buyer for about Rs. 200 (about US$15 at the exchange rate of the time), and then transmitted through an underground network of clandestine antiquities dealers until it reached London. There a Canadian businessman and art collector, Robert Borden, purchased the Naṭarāja for something around £250,000. Before the image went on to Canada, however, it was sent over to the British Museum for cleaning. There, suspicions were raised that the Naṭarāja was in fact a stolen art object, and Scotland Yard impounded the Pathur Naṭarāja.

At this point, Borden's firm issued a writ for return of the sculpture, on the grounds that he had purchased it in good faith. The Indian government then joined in with a counterclaim. The Union of India alleged that the Naṭarāja that Borden had purchased was in fact one stolen from Pathur and illegally smuggled to London. They became the plaintiff seeking return of stolen property, while the Bumper Corporation headed by Borden was the defendant seeking to maintain possession of it. But there was a legal problem here. Did the Indian government in fact have any legal claim to this object? Here is where the god Śiva entered into the case. He would appear as the former "owner" of his own property, namely the Naṭarāja icon depicting one of his many manifest forms, and act as plaintiff, with the Indian government serving only as "technical plaintiff." The Indian case identified Śiva as a "juristic personality" who could own property and seek its lawful return when expropriated. And with the decision of Justice Anthony Kennedy, Śiva's claim was affirmed.

The legal victory of Śiva and the Indian government in a British court caused consternation among the art dealers and museums of the United Kingdom, as Beckett reported. She quoted Anthony Gardner, an Indian specialist at Spinks, on the new anxieties: "Anyone contemplating buying a Shiva Nataraja in the future is going to think very carefully about its history, or else risk a writ from Shiva."[1]

In the twenty years since Śiva's successful suit, the cultural politics of the international art market have certainly become hotly contested. Every week, it seems, newspapers report on another case involving illegally smuggled art works and claims for their repatriation. In this essay, however, I wish to focus on the most distinctive element of the Pathur Naṭarāja case: Śiva's appearance in court as a juristic agent. The *Times* report highlighted the "bizarre" quality of this, but I will argue that Śiva's actions here provide a valuable point of departure for exploring the intricate and conflictual interrelations of medieval South Indian temple practices, the classical Indian legal discourse of the Dharmaśāstra tradition, and the efforts of British and Indian jurists of the colonial period to articulate appropriate legal principles to govern Hindu religious institutions.

TEMPLE WORSHIP AND IMAGES: PREMISES AND PRACTICES

A medieval bronze image like the Pathur Naṭarāja, fabricated in the twelfth century for a small Hindu Śaiva temple in southern India, would have served primarily as a processional icon. The main object of worship in the Pathur temple would have been a *Śivaliṅga*, a non-anthropomorphic stone icon fixed at the center of the inner sanctum of the temple. (By the 1970s, when the Pathur Naṭarāja was disinterred, the temple had fallen into

[1] Beckett (1988: 9C). For an extended account of this case, with discussion of the pertinent issues it raised, see Richard Davis (1997: 222–59).

disrepair. Fragments of the original stone *liṅga* were found in the ground near the temple ruins, but it was no longer usable for ritual purposes.) As the principal cultic object, the *Śivaliṅga* would have received daily offerings of worship, known as *pūjā*, performed by priests on behalf of the entire local community. It is important to emphasize that the *Śivaliṅga* was not simply a symbolic object of worship. According to local Śaiva premises as articulated in priestly guidebooks (or *āgamas*), the *liṅga* should be regarded and treated as a living instantiation of the god Śiva. Local devotees considered the *liṅga* to be the god himself, as he made himself present in this particular community, for the benefit of his votaries. Śiva was a universal god who also made himself manifest in many local temples throughout southern India and beyond, in the form of icons fabricated by humans to receive his divine presence.[2]

As well as being a manifestation of the universal god, the local embodiment of Śiva was regarded as the "lord" and "owner" (Skt. *svāmin*, Tamil *uḍaiyār*) of the temple and all its properties. In the medieval South Indian context, these properties might be quite extensive, for the temples acted as economic centers within their society. They received gifts of money, goods, and land; they leased or sold land to receive commodities needed for ritual; they employed persons to supply provisions and carry out all necessary ceremonial activities. The properties of the temple owned by the deity could include also the various additional icons, such as the images taken in procession during the regular temple festivals. In this sense it is appropriate to imagine that the Pathur Naṭarāja would once have been considered a "property" belonging to the central *Śivaliṅga* of the Pathur temple.

We can construct a clearer picture of medieval temple practices and their underlying cultural presuppositions from inscriptions. On the walls of most old temples in southern India may be found numerous epigraphs carved permanently into the stone. These inscriptional texts deal predominantly with the affairs of the temple. This profuse corpus of documents can tell us a great deal about the presuppositions and practices of the medieval South Indians who originally composed them.[3]

The key tenet that lies at the foundation of the great corpus of medieval South Indian inscriptions is that the central images or icons of Hindu temples were identified as living deities. The inscriptional texts regularly

[2] For a general treatment of medieval South Indian Śaiva understandings and practices of image worship as portrayed in the *Śaiva-āgamas* (medieval ritual texts), see Richard Davis (1991).

[3] See Orr (2006) for an excellent general discussion of inscriptions as sources. There is an enormous body of inscriptions, most still unpublished, and an ever-growing historical literature employing these inscriptions for the reconstruction of the political, social, and religious history of medieval South India.

refer to and address these divine persons by name. Usually the deity's name includes the location of the deity, as the "Lord of such-and-such a place," or alternatively the name of the temple itself. In the common phrasing, the god "is pleased to dwell" in the earthly temple. There are no locutions that might suggest a distinction between the icon and the deity. Rather, the inscriptions consider the enlivened icon to be a living personal deity, a localized instantiation of a universal god (whether Śiva, Viṣṇu, the Goddess, or some other divine figure) who also lives in many other places, in other localized manifestations.

The Śrīvaiṣṇava school of medieval South India articulated this tenet as Viṣṇu's "icon incarnations" (*arcā-avatāra*). For the Śrīvaiṣṇava theologians, the god Viṣṇu makes himself present and accessible to human worshipers through various incarnations. They identify several types or categories of incarnations. At times he becomes incarnate in the anthropomorphic and zoomorphic forms we know as Rāma, Kṛṣṇa, the Tortoise, the Boar, and others. He manifests himself as an "inner controller" (*antaryāmin*) in the hearts of his human devotees. And Viṣṇu also enters into and enlivens the naturally occurring and human-fabricated icons that serve as the supports for his divine presence in shrines and temples.[4] These are Viṣṇu's icon incarnations, just as real and animate as any other.

As a living being, the central deity of a temple acts as recipient of all the gifts (*devadāna*) that devotees donate to the institution. These gifts begin with the temple itself, as the palatial habitation fabricated to house the deity, and they include the ancillary images that share the residence. The gifts would also include grants of land whose revenue would be used to provide the material support for the ritual ceremonies of honoring and celebrating the iconic deity at the center of all temple transactions.

The recipient of all these gifts also becomes their proprietor or owner. The inscriptions generally take for granted the god's ownership of the temple and its properties. The deity, like any lord or property owner, need not always administer his or her properties directly.[5]

In some inscriptions from Śaiva temples, another semi-divinity in image form, Caṇḍeśa, acts as the assigned administrator (*nibandhana*) for the temple possessions of his lord and master, Śiva. More practically, various human agents take care of the material transactions involved in the

[4] Vasudha Narayanan (1985) provides a valuable summary of the Śrīvaiṣṇava theology of Viṣṇu's five incarnation types. For the parallel theology in the medieval Śaiva Siddhānta school directed toward Śiva, see Davis (1991: 112–36).

[5] For parallel assumptions about presence and ownership among Indian Buddhists during the same period, see Schopen (1990).

administration of temple properties. These might include priests, temple trustees, village assemblies, local elites, or members of the royal family. The multiple activities of these human agents, as reflected in the prolix temple inscriptions, have enabled social historians to learn a great deal about South Indian society during medieval times.[6] However, for our purposes, the most important underlying cultural fact is that the administrators of temple properties organized their transactions as agents dealing with possessions that belonged ultimately to the divine beings residing in the central sanctuaries of Hindu temples.

As Leslie Orr observes, these inscriptions were meant "to serve as legal documents, sanctioning the transfer of property, the undertaking of various responsibilities, and the acquisition of rights and privileges" (2006: xiii). The exhortations and avowals regularly included in the inscriptions, she points out, give the texts "the force of a charter, if not a contract." The inscriptions point to arrangements that are to be maintained, ideally, "as long as the sun and moon endure." But in the realm of human beings, all sorts of departures from the ideal may ensue. Properties of the gods may be mismanaged or expropriated, just as any other property. A number of inscriptions record such misappropriations and the efforts made to restore the proper order. We do not hear of temple gods suing in court in medieval South India, but there are many indications that the deities found agents among human political authorities, such as officers of the king or local authorities, to act on their behalf.

DHARMAŚĀSTRAS AND DIVINITY

Not everyone in classical or medieval India agreed with the South Indian perspective on divine images articulated in medieval inscriptions. The primary legal literature of medieval India grows out of a different tradition of religious practice and reflects an uneasy accommodation with, or more strongly a critical skepticism toward, the conceptual bases of Hindu temple practice. Dharmaśāstra literature recognizes the Vedas as the fundamental textual source of authority, and it considers *yajña*, fire offerings made to immaterial divine figures, as the paradigmatic ritual means by which humans ought best to interact with the divine.

[6] The model of the temple deity as the center of a transactional network is most effectively formulated in Appadurai and Breckenridge (1976), though the authors there are dealing with a later period of South Indian history. For useful references to much of the social historical literature on medieval South India, see Orr (2006).

Dharmaśāstra authors and commentators certainly were aware of the common practices of Hindu image worship. A few passages in the Dharmaśāstra literature acknowledge the worship of images as a positive practice, and even set forth procedures for proper worship. For example, the *Viṣṇu Smṛti* prescribes the worship of Viṣṇu Vāsudeva in the form of a divine image (*devārcā*) as one of the regular daily duties of a householder (*VDh* 65).[7] Likewise the *Baudhāyana Gṛhya Pariśiṣṭa Sūtra*, an appendix to the text of the Baudhāyana school on household rites, provides instructions for installing and worshiping images of Viṣṇu, Śiva, and other deities (Harting 1922). While some Vedic schools evidently accepted the theistic practices of image worship and selectively incorporated these rites into their own rules of conduct, other Brahmin schools were clearly not so accommodating. Indeed, in the Dharmaśāstra literature, the predominant attitude toward worship of images was hostile. And there was good reason for this hostility, since image worship and the growing cult of temple Hinduism were supplanting the Vedic sacrificial system as the dominant form of public Hindu ritual practice in India. As Heinrich von Stietencron has argued, this shift involved a conflict within the Brahmin class, with "bitter feuds between traditionalists and innovators."[8]

An excellent example of a "traditionalist" perspective may be seen in the most influential of the *dharmaśāstras*, the *Mānava Dharmaśāstra*, composed around the second century CE. In his instructions for Brahmin householders, Manu does not provide any guidelines for the worship of images. However, he does take note of a new category of ritual specialist, the *devalaka*, a priest who attends images in a shrine or temple. He recommends that Brahmins concerned with their personal purity shun the temple priest. For instance, in the monthly ancestral offerings (*śrāddha*), a good Brahmin householder maintains the continuity and status of his own lineage. Therefore, Manu recommends, it is important to exclude from these rites anyone who might detract from the purity of the ritual or of the person offering it. Among those to be shunned are the *devalaka*s: "Physicians, temple priests, meat sellers, and those who live by trade – these should be avoided at divine and ancestral offerings" (*MDh* 3.152).[9] Manu cites these among a larger set of the disinvited: not only doctors and butchers, but also

[7] See Jolly (1880, 1881) and Krishnamacharya (1964). Inden (1992) discusses important shifts within orthodox Vedic schools, as does Bakker (2004).

[8] Von Stietencron (1977: 126). While this historical shift has not received as much scholarly attention as its cultural significance warrants, see Inden (1992) and R. Davis (2001), as well as von Stietencron's valuable essay (1977), for further detail.

[9] I have used the translation of Patrick Olivelle throughout this chapter.

men with deformed nails or black teeth, people with one eye, actors, singers, gamblers, drunks, Buddhists (*nāstikas*), and many others should be avoided at the ceremonies of ancestral solidarity (*MDh* 3.150–66). In the end, Manu concludes, wise Brahmins "should avoid those lowest of the twice-born, men of despicable conduct alongside whom it is unfit to eat" (*MDh* 3.167).

Manu's later commentator Kullūka gives a further reason for excluding temple priests from the *śrāddha* ceremonies. Kullūka glosses the term "*devalaka*" as "an attendant of images" (*pratimā-paricāraka*), and explains that they obtain their livelihood from god's treasures. Food given to the temple deities ends up in the bellies of temple priests. Like physicians, butchers, and merchants, they act for the sake of profit, Kullūka says, not for the sake of *dharma*. It is noteworthy that Kullūka here accepts the tenet that gifts to a temple ought to be considered the property of the presiding deity. In this light, *devalakas* can be viewed as thieves who appropriate the donations given to gods to satisfy their own needs.[10]

Later in his *dharmaśāstra*, Manu explains what will happen to the greedy temple priests: "If a man seizes what belongs to a god [*devasva*] or a Brahmin out of greed, in the next world that evil man will live on the leftovers of vultures" (*MDh* 11.26). Here Manu also seems to accept the theistic principle that what is given to a temple belongs to the god of that temple. For Manu's commentators, though, it was not so simple, for the concept of *deva*, "god," was itself problematic.

Manu and other Dharmaśāstra authors might seek to exclude temple priests from the ceremonies of pious Brahmins, but a more subtle and far-reaching critique of the practices of Hindu temple worship came in the definitional struggle over the category of divinity. Here we need to consider another branch of orthodox exegetical literature concerned with *dharma*, the Pūrva Mīmāṃsā school of Jaimini and his successors. As Robert Lingat (1973) (and McCrea, in this volume) have observed, the Mīmāṃsā school provided the Dharmaśāstra commentators with their basic interpretive principles.

The Vedic exegesis of Mīmāṃsā starts from the axiom that *dharma* has been established completely and authoritatively in the Vedas. The task is therefore one of interpretation. If proper human action follows directly

[10] The temple priests and theistic schools had a different view of food-offerings to images, not involving theft. Gifts of food would first be presented to the image-deity, who consumed the subtle portion of the food. The remaining matter was god's leftovers, transfigured by contact with the divine into a substantial form of god's grace (*prasāda*). These consecrated leftovers would then be enjoyed by temple priests and other devotees. See R. Davis (1991: 154–7) for a brief résumé of this viewpoint, and its Śaiva Siddhānta variant.

from the words of the Vedas, the question is: Which of those words possess an injunctive force (*vidhi*), and which are simply rhetorical (*arthavāda*). The Vedas clearly enjoin humans to perform sacrifice, but what is the basis for the efficacy of this ritual practice?

The key passage here is found in Jaimini's *Pūrva Mīmāṃsā Sūtra*s (9.1.6–10), where the Mīmāṃsā master articulates two principal views of sacrificial efficacy.[11] In the first, the "preliminary view" (*pūrvapakṣa*), one should sacrifice to gods like Indra and Agni in order to please them with offerings. According to this viewpoint, the gods have bodies and thus are able to enjoy the material offering conveyed to them through the sacrificial fire. The powerful gods are also able to compensate those humans whose tokens of respect have pleased them. The efficacy of sacrifice, in this perspective, depends on divinities who exist outside the sacrificial action itself, and the purpose of sacrifice is to place oneself in a beneficial exchange relationship with those gods.

This reciprocal-exchange theory may well reflect the common or worldly understanding of sacrifice. However, in his second or "conclusive view" (*siddhānta*), Jaimini argues against it. Sacrifice does not require any outside intervention to attain its effects. Rather, sacrifice is inherently efficacious. That is, by obeying the injunction of the Veda to perform sacrifice, one attains the "intrinsic self-completion of the sacrifice," which Mīmāṃsā authors call the *apūrva*. If the sacrifice fulfills itself and accomplishes *dharma*, then there is no need to be concerned with divine agency.

The problem with excluding the Vedic gods from a role in Vedic sacrifice is that this appears to go against the contents of the Vedic texts. The hymns of the Vedas repeatedly address the gods as if they have bodies, eat and drink the sacrificial offerings, enjoy their meals, and reward the human hosts accordingly. But this, the Mīmāṃsā exegetes reply, is a mistaken view. The gods do not have bodies, argues the Mīmāṃsā scholar Śabara in his commentary on Jaimini's earlier work. If they lack bodies, then they do not need the sacrificial sustenance, nor do they have the ability to reward their votaries. Śabara interprets all Vedic passages that offer anthropomorphic images of the gods as figurative or inconclusive. When the *Ṛg Veda* says "we have taken hold of Indra's hand," says Śabara, it means only "we depend on Indra." This, he goes on, is just a rhetorical reinforcement (*arthavāda*) to the injunction (*vidhi*) that one should offer sacrifice to Indra. What then is left of the god Indra? In Śabara's austere hermeneutics,

[11] For a more complete exploration of this passage and its Mīmāṃsā context, see the works of Francis X. Clooney (1988, 1997). Colas (2004) also traces aspects of the Mīmāṃsā critique of divine images.

the only reliable existence of the gods lies in the sound (*śabda*) of their names or the mantras addressed to them. "Divinity is only sound," proclaims the Mīmāṃsā school. The god Indra has no necessary existence apart from the name "Indra" and its usage in sacrificial activities compelled by the Veda and performed by humans.

The Mīmāṃsā masters Jaimini and Śabara argue against a theistic understanding of the Vedic sacrifice, but their rigorous interpretation can easily be extended against the premises of Hindu image worship as well. Writing in the fifth century, Śabara was certainly aware of the growing popularity of the Hindu gods Viṣṇu and Śiva and their expanding temples. If the worship of icons depends on the assumption that gods exist as autonomous beings and enter into physical forms like images to receive the offerings of their devotees, then Śabara's denial of divine embodiment subverts this practice at its most fundamental level. Further, the Mīmāṃsā restriction of divine agency reappears in the writings of Dharmaśāstra commentators like Medhātithi, the ninth-century Kashmiri author whose explication of Manu, the *Manubhāṣya*, is one of the preeminent authorities in the genre.[12]

We have seen already that Manu mentions the "property of the gods" (*devasva*) in the context of theft and its consequences. One who seizes the property of the gods or Brahmins, says Manu, is liable for severe punishment in the next world (*MDh* 11.26). Medhātithi informs us, however, that this "property of the gods" in fact belongs to humans of the three twice-born classes. *Devasva* denotes the wealth that has been set aside for the purpose of rituals like sacrifice directed toward the gods. But it must belong in fact to human proprietors, for it is not possible for gods to have direct ownership (*sva-svāmin*) of property. Divinity cannot make volitional use of wealth, nor can it exercise protection over it.

Medhātithi does recognize the more common viewpoint, that in ordinary or worldly usage (*loka*), *devasva* may indicate the property connected with four-armed images (*pratimā*) of the gods. However, he rejoins, the fact that one refers to the four-armed icon as an "image" indicates already that it is not itself divine. Further, there is no definition of god that can be applied to such an image. Therefore, as he has argued previously (in his comments on *MDh* 2.189), one must take Manu's reference to "god's property" as figurative (*guṇavāda*), just as the Vedic passages referring to Indra's hand and the like are to be understood as figurative expressions.

[12] Ganganatha Jha edited and translated the *Manubhāṣya* in several volumes. See Jha (1920–9). For an assessment and appreciation of Medhātithi, see Derrett (1976).

After surveying several Dharmaśāstra works, Günther-Dietz Sontheimer has summarized the position of the commentators succinctly: "We can see from the texts which we have cited above that the main argument against the corporality of a *devatā* and its capacity to hold property is derived from the *pūrvamīmāṃsā* doctrines according to which deities are purely hypothetical entities, posited to assist in the performance of a sacrifice and subordinate to it" (1964: 68). At the same time, as Sontheimer recognizes, this placed the legal perspective of the Dharmaśāstra masters at odds with the broader public practices of Hindu temple worship: "It appears that in practice there existed no difficulty in the donor's dedicating property to the deity, whose servants appropriated the property on behalf of the deity and used the property for the benefit of the deity. The property in the eyes of the public belonged to the deity" (1964: 69). It is difficult to know if the constrictive orthodox Dharmaśāstra interpretation of divine agency made any impact on South Indian temple practices of the medieval period. Inscriptions generally indicate that the icon-deities continued to act as lords and proprietors of the temple properties, despite the Mīmāṃsā view. However, the discrepancy between Dharmaśāstra principle and public practice did pose a problem for legal theory in the colonial period. This led to the new concept of the deity as a "juristic person."

ANGLO-INDIAN LAW AND THE HINDU GODS

As the British began to assume direct political rule over territories in India, starting in the mid-eighteenth century, they faced a series of practical administrative and legal quandaries. One fundamental decision was taken by Governor-General Warren Hastings, when he chose to establish the legal system of British India, as far as possible, on indigenous or Indian principles. "We have endeavoured to adapt our Regulations," he explained to the East India Company directors in 1772, "to the Manners and Understandings of the People, and the Exigencies of the Country, adhering as closely as we are able to their ancient uses and institutions."[13] In the sphere of law, this required the British to seek out, and seek to understand, the existing legal codes of India. For the Hindu population, they identified the Dharmaśāstra genre as the most pertinent legal literature. The result was an extensive effort of collaborative scholarship on Dharmaśāstra literature

[13] Letter from the governor-general and Council to the Court of Directors, November 3, 1772, printed in "Reports from Committees of the House of Commons" (1772–3), quoted in Bernard Cohn (1996b: 26).

by British administrators and Brahmin Sanskrit pandits, aimed at developing a usable "Hindu law" from the great mass of Dharmaśāstra literature.[14] This label is not really accurate, since the legal system that grew out of British administrative application of Dharmaśāstra principles was in fact a complex colonial-period hybrid. Not just Dharmaśāstra, but also Roman, British, and Muslim legal concepts were drawn on by both British and Indian jurists, in new institutional settings created by British rulers, resulting in something altogether different from anything Manu and Medhātithi could have imagined.

Early juristic decisions of the British colonial period involving temple properties tended to allow the deities their agency and their ownership, as Sontheimer has shown (1964: 78–80). The judges of the early nineteenth century appear to have supported what they considered popular Hindu understandings and practices. However, by the late nineteenth century, Indian jurists began to revise this legal view and to grant greater weight to the Dharmaśāstra perspective. Specifically they divested the icons of their claims to full identity. Following the Dharmaśāstra notion of "figurative" divinity, they introduced the Roman legal concept of "juristic personhood" as a way to accept the religious intentions of a donor who gave property to a temple image without accepting the donor's theological premise that god was embodied in that image. The deity, they argued, holds property only in an "ideal sense," since it, as a "merely artificial person," only personifies the pious motivation of the donor. Thus they ruled out the idea underlying South Indian temple practice that deities could become embodied in physical icons, and shifted the legal focus to the intentions or motivations of human benefactors of religious institutions.

Sontheimer expertly traces the development of this new legal doctrine through a series of court cases and decisions (1964: 80–97). The results can be found in twentieth-century legal compendia of Hindu law by learned jurists like Dinshah Fardunji Mulla (*Principles of Hindu Law*, 1929), Satish Chandra Bagchi (*Juristic Personality of Hindu Deities*, 1933), and Bijan Kumar Mukherjea (*The Hindu Law of Religious and Charitable Trust*, 1952). Mukherjea summarizes the resulting legal status of divine images in several propositions. First, neither God nor any supernatural being can be a person in law. This means that the Supreme Being which an icon represents cannot own property in a legal sense. If it did, Mukherjea explains, then the Supreme Being of one temple icon might be able to make a claim against the Supreme Being of another. Second, the property given to a temple by its

[14] For valuable accounts of this intellectual collaborative effort, see Cohn (1996a) and R. Rocher (1989).

founder is disposed for the pious spiritual purposes of the donor. And third, that pious aim of the founder continues to reside in the physical icon, which represents or symbolizes that intention. Echoing Medhātithi, Mukherjea cautions that a deity can be said to exercise ownership only in a secondary or ideal sense. "The deity as owner represents nothing else but the intentions of the founder" (Mukherjea 1952: 46). This is in briefest form what is meant by the juristic personhood of the divine icon.

Mukherjea's propositions bring the economic activities of Hindu temples as "endowments and charitable trusts" within the scope of a state administrative and legal system that does not recognize the claims of gods and other supernatural beings.[15] Through the notion of a god's juristic personality, the human administrators of a temple may conduct its affairs as if the deity embodied in the icon were the actual proprietor of all its properties. The "popular view" of a divine icon's agency may not cohere with the more restricted legal perspective of its juristic personality, but the two viewpoints can accommodate one another.

When the bronze image of dancing Śiva from Pathur, Tamil Nadu, appeared in the UK High Court in London, the Indian legal formulation of Śiva's juristic personality reached beyond the national boundaries of India. Quoting Mukherjea's authoritative propositions, Justice Kennedy held that Śiva, embodied in the *Śivaliṅga* at the ruined Pathur temple, could act as a plaintiff, as a juristic personality embodying the pious intention of the anonymous twelfth-century founder of the temple. Further, Śiva's claim on the bronze processional image was superior to that of Robert Borden, the Canadian collector who had purchased it in London. The image would be returned to India.

For Justice Kennedy and the lawyers directly involved in the Pathur Naṭarāja case, the role of the god Śiva in recovering the Naṭarāja as his property may have been limited to the purely symbolic role of an embodiment of a past donor's pious intentions. Modern-day Hindus in southern India, however, understood the dynamics of the case differently. As one Tamil Nadu state official put it, "I can only say that lord Naṭarāja himself won the case appearing before courts in the form of the idol" (Vidyasagar 1991).

[15] The best overview of the postcolonial administration of Hindu temples in the southern Indian state of Tamilnad is Pressler (1987).

CHAPTER 13

In the divine court of appeals: vows before the god of justice

Aditya Malik

This chapter discusses the place of law and justice within the context of "folk" Hinduism by referring to the practice of social justice from the perspective of the religious cult of Goludev, a widely venerated regional, "folk" deity in the recently formed central Himalayan state of Uttarakhand. While the nature and content of "Hindu law" has been discussed at relative length from the perspective of classical textual sources as well as on the basis of evidence provided by inscriptions,[1] scant attention has been paid to the conceptual understanding and actual practice of law in non-classical, contemporary "folk" traditions within the broader framework of Hinduism. Thus, for example, what does it mean to imagine temples as legal courts in which the deity receives legal (and other) petitions? In what ways do rituals of divine embodiment (or "possession") enact and articulate concepts of social justice?

Goludev presides explicitly over matters of justice (*nyāy*) and is known in the Himalayan district of Kumaon as the "god of justice" (*nyāy kā devtā*). Kumaon is a mountainous region bordering on Nepal in the east and Tibet in the north. Together with Garhwal, a region that lies to its west, Kumaon forms the state of Uttarakhand. Goludev is worshiped by both high-ranked and low-ranked communities (Thakurs, Brahmans, Dalits). Goludev's devotees perceive him to be a manifestation or incarnation of Bhairav, the wild and terrifying aspect of Śiva.[2] In Kumaon, the juristic authority of Goludev is considered greater than the authority of civil courts in the region. In several instances, for example, if someone involved in a civil suit threatened to take a petition to Goludev, the party in the wrong would quickly back down and admit to being in the wrong rather than have Goludev deal with the "case."

[1] See the chapters by Michaels, Lubin, and R. H. Davis in this volume.

[2] As an incarnation of Bhairav, Goludev can be considered to be a "split" deity in the sense that he is perceived to be peaceful and benevolent, whereas his principal guardian and "henchman," Kalua Masān, or Kāl Bhairav, is wild and dangerous.

Goludev is the most important of several folk deities in Kumaon. Kumaonis often refer to their province as "*Dev Bhūmī*" ("Land of Gods" or "Divine Earth"). Indeed many powerful gods and goddesses reside here, and in Garhwal, along the banks of sacred rivers and on snow-covered mountain peaks. These regional deities are also located in hillside shrines in villages, and manifest in rituals of embodiment in which they enter and speak through the bodies of sensitive mediums during intense ceremonies of "awakening" (*jāgar*). There are other long religious processions and rituals in which gods and goddesses are appeased, awakened, and made present so that devotees can participate in their divine power and resolve problems that they face. Each god and goddess has his or her own story of how he or she "originated" and came to reside at a particular place, and of why he or she is particularly potent when dealing with specific concerns. The particular connection that Goludev has to justice is derived from his own experience of injustice as a child, as it is described in the oral and written narratives of his life.[3] Goludev was the only son of a king and his eighth queen, whose seven barren stepmothers attempted unsuccessfully to kill him several times. Finally, abandoned by them to float down a river in a box, he is caught by a childless fisher couple in their net. Raised by these humble foster parents, Goludev as a young boy confronts his stepmothers, proving to the king that he is his son. The stepmothers are punished and Goludev and his biological mother, the queen, are given their rightful place in the kingdom. When he ascends the throne he visits all the villages and towns in his kingdom making sure that his subjects' concerns are heard and that justice is established in the kingdom of Kumaon.[4]

There are two primary channels for soliciting Goludev's power in matters of justice. The first way of requesting his mediation is through the submission of written petitions (*manautī*) in his main temples at Chittai (near Almora), Ghoda Khal (near Bhavali), and in Champavat (in Pitthoragarh District). The second manner of soliciting his advice and intervention is through an oracular trance or ritual of divine embodiment (*jāgar*). These forms of mediation have a direct bearing on popular conceptions of the juristic personality of a divinity, and of ritual acts of devotion as forms of legal practice.[5]

[3] The narrative of Goludev's life is told during the *jāgar* ritual (see below). In the concluding sections of the narrative, villages and subregions of Kumaon are mentioned which Goludev visits in order to attend to injustices. The establishment of justice sometimes involves the defeat of other divine, demonic, or human forces.

[4] See Agrawal (1992: 22–7) for a more extensive account of Goludev's life-story.

[5] See the chapters by R. H. Davis (on juristic personality of deities) and Yelle (on ritual acts) in this volume.

FOLK HINDUISM

These and other forms of worship associated with Goludev's cult fall within the practices of "folk" or "popular" Hinduism. Broadly speaking, in the South Asian context, the term "folk" indicates a set of practices and discourses that do not necessarily derive from or rest on Brahmanical practices and discourses, that is, those deriving from the authority of classical texts and rituals handed down by Brahmins. In conceptual terms, folk religion or folk Hinduism "occupies an eccentric status . . . it forms a kind of residual supplementary category . . . of a different kind than e.g., renunciation (sanyas), bhakti or even Brahmanism (priesthood)" (Fuchs 1994). Scholars argue for the autonomous status of folk or "popular" Hinduism: "popular Hinduism is an authentic religion, equal in standing to any other . . . In particular, the view that popular Hinduism is degenerate textual Hinduism . . . is completely indefensible in the light of ethnographic evidence" (Fuller 1994: 6). Although, as Fuller points out, ethnographic reality clearly shows the existence of "folk" Hinduism, the conceptual and material contents of this category remain tenuous. G. D. Sontheimer (1997) links folk Hinduism to four other "components" that, according to him, constitute Hinduism: the teaching of Brahmins, *bhakti*, renunciation, and tribal religion. For each of these four components he supplies a descriptive outline while positing the interconnectedness – both historical and in contemporary religious practice – of the components. Similar to the case of the other four components, Sontheimer attempts to provide a preliminary "checklist" that outlines the characteristic features of folk Hinduism. In his summary statement of the components of folk religion,[6] he points out that "a crucial ingredient in folk religion is the immediate presence and access to a god or a goddess in the form of a *mūrti* [image] . . . The god exists 'here and now', is earthbound, and does not live in some puranic *svarga* [heaven]" (1997: 315).

The "immediate presence," and, indeed, corporeality of a folk deity is expressed, for example, in terms of the deity's "possessing" the body of a devotee or medium, the deity's "play" or participation in ritual performances and processions, and also through the fact that the deity is considered "alive, attentive, heedful and responsive" to devotees' needs (Sontheimer 1997: 316). Thus, the deity responds to the material concerns or wishes of his or her devotees by way of granting offspring, cattle, and healing.

[6] His conclusions are based on his magisterial studies of folk Hinduism in the Deccan.

Importantly, in the context of this essay, an "attentive" deity is also one who responds to issues of jurisprudence facing his or her devotees by deciding on legal cases.[7] Again, while these legal cases may refer to matters of criminal or civil justice, the deity may also preside over issues concerning marital relations, financial prosperity, child-bearing, misfortune, calamity, disease, employment, travel, and so on. These and other possible life concerns are equally subsumed under the category of justice, as are more straightforward criminal or civil issues such as theft, bodily injury, or property disputes.

GOD OF JUSTICE

The Kumaoni and Hindi term "*nyāy*" that is used in Goludev's title has, in both scholarly and popular discourse, been translated as "justice" or sometimes as "equity." However, the classical meaning of the parallel Sanskrit term "*nyāya*" can also refer to "a process of reasoning which facilitates a choice." Hence it may apply to an abstract formulation of logic or "to the administration of justice where the king or his delegate, the deciding judge, is free to take into account the circumstances surrounding the matter before him" (Lingat 1973: 161, n. 40). "*Nyāya*" therefore refers to the enactment of law through a person invested with the authority to decide on matters of justice. The materials in this essay will make it clear, however, that the range of issues included under the category of "*nyāy*" in the case of Goludev is extremely diverse. They do not always refer to matters of litigation or judicial decisions, but to "life concerns" such as material prosperity, health, bearing children, passing examinations, gaining employment, and so on (Agrawal 1992: 53).

TEMPLES AS COURTS

The first two temples of Goludev in Chittai and Ghoda Khal are administered by Brahmin priests of the Panth and Joshi lineages respectively,[8] while a third temple in Champavat is administered by householders of the Nath lineage. These temples are referred to as "courts of justice" (*kacahrī*). The first temple is described by devotees as Goludev's "supreme court," the

[7] There is ample historical evidence for the "juristic personality" of folk deities in the form of inscriptions from the precolonial period and written documents from the nineteenth century originating from the Deccan. See Sontheimer (1964, 1997) and Wagle (2005).

[8] According to priests of these temples, the lineages have their origin in Maharashtra, and have involved migration from that region going back several generations.

second as "high court," and the third as "district court," thus adopting a terminology from the secular judicial system to rank the relative importance of the temples. The temple at Ghoda Khal has also become the location for marriage ceremonies, particularly for couples not having the endorsement of their families, for example, on account of belonging to different castes or different religious communities (e.g., Hindu and Sikh). On such occasions the priest is able to issue a marriage certificate for the bride and bridegroom, for which Goludev acts as witness. The certificate issued by the priest is legally binding, and once handed over to a civil court, a valid marriage certificate must be issued by civil authorities.

PETITIONS TO THE DEITY

The petitions or appeals are termed "*manautī*" or "*fariyād*" and are usually in the form of handwritten documents, some of which are composed on official stamp paper. *Manautī*, meaning "surety, pledge," is a contractual pledge in which a devotee vows to offer the deity a material object in return for the deity's fulfillment of the wish expressed in the petition. In the case of Goludev, this may involve the gifting of a brass bell or the sacrifice of a goat. Although written petitions are the most tangible and visible forms of *manautī*s, petitions or requests can also be made in an interior manner in the form of a prayer. "*Fariyād*," used interchangeably with "*manautī*," is a Persian loan-word meaning "complaint, grievance, cry for help," suggesting the urgency of the devotee's appeal to the god.

The satisfactory resolution of these requests through the divine and royal authority of Goludev who is both god and king suggests an emphasis on the administration of *nyāya* ("justice, equity, fair ruling") rather than on *dharma* ("righteousness, piety, duty"). It is within the jurisdiction, so to speak, of Goludev to decide on the merit of the requests put forward to him. The transactional nature of *manautī*, however, places the juristic act of granting a hearing to devotees within the context of giving and taking gifts, as well as that of sacrifice, since goats and other domestic animals may be slaughtered in keeping with a devotee's vow. Acts of gift giving and sacrifice extend the understanding of justice itself as a transactional, substantive concept that revolves around divine agency and power while involving reciprocal practices expressing gratitude, reverence, and appeasement. These practices are in line with the transactional nature of the relationship between deity and devotee in general in India, with regard to forms of ritual and worship that emphasize reciprocity – for example, in the keeping of religious vows by devotees in return for the granting of specific requests, wishes, or even demands on a deity, or the enactment of justice through the ascertainment of truth in legal or criminal matters through the rendering of an oath in front of a deity and its response.

RITUALS OF DIVINE EMBODIMENT

The second important manner, besides petitions or appeals, in which Goludev deals with matters of justice (and indeed healing in a broader sense) is through what may, in conventional terms, be described as an oracular trance ritual, but what I will refer to here as a ritual of divine embodiment called "*jāgar*."

"*Jāgar*" means "waking," "staying awake," and can also be translated as "night vigil." The *jāgar* can therefore be described as an intense ritual of "awakening" for both deity and devotees. Monika Krengel (1999: 281) in her essay on the *jāgar* notes its complex nature:

> It is not possible to single out one aspect, e.g., curing, healing, psychological effects, without taking others, such as integration, dealing with uncertainties, and the definition of justice and responsibility into account. All relevant memories, rules, deviations and expectations are encapsulated in the institution of jagar, which potentially affords a bird's eye view of being that transcends present social and political action.

The *jāgar* has two main actors: a singer or bard called the "*jagariyā*" (literally "awakener") and the person entering into a so-called trance who is called the "*ḍaṅgariyā*" or "nacnevālā" (dancer). Both *jagariyā* and *ḍaṅgariyā*, in contrast to the high-caste priests of the two main temples of Goludev, often (although not always) belong to low-caste Dalit communities. Similar to the case of written petitions handed to the god in his temples, the concerns of devotees here can vary, though a *jāgar* is most often used to establish the hidden cause of illness, misfortune, or injustice (Krengel 1999; Leavitt 1997). *Jāgar*s are usually performed in a devotee's home, into which the singer and dancer are invited. Immediate family members but also a wider public from the village participate as the audience. The *jāgar* usually has four sequential parts. In the first, which is called "*sandhyā*" ("evensong"), several regional and supra-regional deities are mentioned and praised. In the second section, Goludev is invoked by narrating his life-story. This second section is also specially referred to as the *jāgar* since it involves the most potent awakening of the deity. Thus, even though the deity is manifest from the very commencement of the ritual, it is only after this second "phase" of the *jāgar* that the deity is in a position to articulate the insights and responses that he will provide to the gathering of devotees. In the third section, the deity responds to the questions and concerns that are put to him by devotees gathered for the ritual. The fourth and final section involves the "release" of the deity and the conclusion of the ritual. Here again, as in the case of written petitions but perhaps even in a stronger sense, justice is negotiated or transacted in a dialogic process involving the deity, the singer, and the family or community that is hosting the ritual. Even though the ritual involves the divine speech of the deity, this is not uttered as a single pronouncement, but through a series of divine insights into the nature and cause of the issue facing the host family or community. The appropriate resolution of these issues – for example, through the establishment of a shrine to the deity or through the sacrifice of an animal or other substantive means – is ascertained through interpretation of and deliberation on the deity's words, uttered by the medium in what becomes a conversation between deity, devotee, and singer.

The representation of Goludev's temples as courts of law, and the rendering of justice during rituals of divine embodiment, offer a counterpoint to the temporal power wielded in the secular legal institutions in the state of Uttarakhand. In fact, the active pursuit of these "folk" forms of justice by devotees implies that divine agency is considered more potent and powerful than secular forms of institutional agency. Furthermore, the concept of justice in this context also appears to depart from classical notions of law embedded in the idea of duty or *dharma*.[9] It does, however, reflect the historical practice of juristic decision-making on the basis of the authority of the king or his legal representative.

APPENDIX: EXAMPLES OF PETITIONS

Petition 1 *(on ten-rupee non-judicial stamp paper)*

[In Hindi:]

Most venerable Goludevta,

[In English:]

Kindly consider my name i.e. SUSHIL KUMAR JAIN for the Post of ASJ [Additional Sessions Judge] Delhi High Court, Delhi.

[signature with date, 8.2.08]

S. K. Jain [with address and phone numbers]

[9] See Lubin's chapter in this volume.

Petition 2

[In Hindi:]

Victory to Goludevta

at Chatai Temple – my salutations to you.

I heard your name and I am present in your court. I have heard that you resolve everyone's (issues), resolve my (issues) too. I was told at the Jageshvar Temple about the Chittai Golu Temple. You remove everyone's problems, remove mine as well.

My problems:

[In English:]

Divorce.

Health.

Financial situation.

Father's health.

Love & affection amongst the two brothers.

Job which would follow the divorce or as you wish.

When all the samasyas [problems] are resolved I will return from Delhi and sacrifice a goat as liked by you, and hand a bell, and give a shell. 6 months. First I will come to Jageshwar where I will complete the Mahamritunja I will come to your temple. If I don't come after 6 months after completion of my work my witness is Rajesh Chand.

Anand Sharma

[address in New Delhi] [signature of witness]

25.2.08

Petition 3

[In Hindi:]

O Lord,

Please evict Jagdish alias Rakesh quickly from our land, and make the

court case go in our favor. Thank you.

[signature]

CHAPTER 14

Contemporary caste discrimination and affirmative action

Laura Dudley Jenkins

In the spring of 2006, medical students at the elite All India Institute of Medical Sciences (AIIMS) in Delhi, dressed in their white coats, took up brooms and swept the streets. They were protesting against affirmative-action policies by suggesting that they would become untouchable "sweepers" if proposals to increase lower-caste student admissions were implemented. In 2007, the government-sponsored Thorat Committee report on the All India Institute of Medical Sciences documented continuing casteism, including denial of promotions to low-caste faculty, segregation of low-caste students in distinct hostels (dorms), and blatant harassment of low-caste students (Mitta 2007). In 2008, the Supreme Court of India upheld the expansion of affirmative action in higher education, noting the "duty of the State to promote positive measures to remove barriers of inequality and enable diverse communities to enjoy the freedoms and share the benefits guaranteed by the Constitution" (*Ashoka Kumar Thakur* v. *Union of India and Others* [2008], SCCL.COM 436).

Caste discrimination in India continues. Affirmative-action laws, known as "reservations" and based on caste and socioeconomic categories, are an important legal means to offset this discrimination. India's affirmative-action policies are among the oldest and most far-reaching affirmative-action policies in the world, but the future of these policies is the subject of ongoing societal and legal controversy and debate. This chapter will introduce the problem of contemporary caste discrimination, the affirmative-action policies to combat it, and three contemporary developments: classification controversies, international activism, and growing attention to other disadvantages, in addition to caste, in Indian affirmative action.

CONTEMPORARY CASTE DISCRIMINATION

Caste continues to be an organizing principle of social life in India, although the practices associated with "untouchability" are no longer legal. Caste is rooted in ancient religious laws and codified in texts written before, during, and after the colonial period.[1] A four-part social hierarchy of *varṇa*s (classes) was canonized in the subcontinent beginning with *Ṛg Veda* 10.90 (*c.* 1200 BCE) and later elaborated in ritual manuals and the Dharmaśāstra literature. These *varṇa*s were associated with different occupations, rules of behavior, and standards of ritual purity. Legal texts of the period between 1550 and 1680 CE went into even more depth about the roles and duties of the lowest *varṇa*, the Śūdras, than the frequently cited code of Manu, and the caste society that developed includes "axes of ritual status, occupation, endogamy, power."[2] "The Laws of Manu" became a contemporary "lightning rod" and has been burned by activists as a symbol of both caste and gender oppression (Olivelle 2004a: xvii–xviii, xxxv; Zelliot 1996).

Such legal texts on caste preceded a colonial obsession with classification that has received much scholarly attention (Cohn 1987, 1996a; Metcalf 1995). The British appropriated the Portuguese term "*casta*" (referring to lineage or race), applying the word "caste" to South Asian social structures in the colonial era. The term "caste" persists in contemporary legal and administrative jargon: The so-called "Untouchable" groups officially listed (or "scheduled") as eligible for affirmative action are still known as the "Scheduled Castes." Thus the word "caste" is still widely used by South Asians today. "Caste" is a rough translation of the indigenous terms "*jāti*" (referring to countless birth groups that vary depending on context and region) and "*varṇa*" (which refers to an idealized hierarchy of Brahmins, Kṣatriyas, Vaiśyas, Śūdras, and, below all of these, the *avarṇa* – castes outside the *varṇa* system – sometimes referred to as "Untouchables"). "Dalit," which means "oppressed" or "ground down," is the label currently preferred by many in these lowest, or "Untouchable," castes.

In practice, caste divisions are more ambiguous and regionally varied than any of the legal caste codifications (ancient, colonial, or contemporary) would suggest; nevertheless, caste continues to shape the life chances of many people in terms of residence, social interaction, marriage, education, and occupation. Occupational and educational discrimination are the forms most explicitly targeted via affirmative action.

Unequal opportunities in employment are due to both past discrimination and contemporary discrimination. The economist Narendra Jadhav argues that past exclusion and discrimination have "impacted Dalit access to capital assets and employment opportunities. This has meant a greater

[1] See the chapters by Donald Davis and Vajpeyi in this volume.
[2] See Vajpeyi's chapter in this volume p. 161.

incidence of poverty and deprivation among Dalits" (Jadhav 2007: 9). A recent study in the sphere of private-sector hiring, modeled on a US study of racial discrimination, vividly illustrates the persistence of discrimination in India. A striking study of name-based racial discrimination in the United States ("Are Emily and Greg more employable than Latisha and Jamal?") was replicated in India (Bertrand and Mullainathan 2003). Because caste affiliations are sometimes identifiable by surnames, this type of study proved to be quite revealing within the Indian context of discrimination. Researchers in India sent 4,808 applications from fictional, equally qualified male graduates to 548 private-sector employers in response to advertisements, using surnames associated with different communities: high-caste Hindu names, Dalit ("Untouchable") names, or Muslim names. A Dalit's odds of progressing to the next stage in the hiring process were only two-thirds of that of a high-caste Hindu "applicant." A Muslim's odds were one-third of that of a high-caste Hindu (Thorat and Attewell 2007). Such discrimination in the private sector has inspired increasing demands for affirmative action in this sector.

Dalit students continue to face discrimination in both school education and higher education. A recent human-rights report described "discrimination, discouragement, exclusion, alienation, physical and psychological abuse, and even segregation, from both their teachers and their fellow students" due to ongoing casteism in some Indian schools (Human Rights Watch and Center for Human Rights and Global Justice 2007: 92). Discrimination at educational institutions persists even in urban areas and at the highest levels of higher education. In 2006 Dalit medical students at India's premier medical school, the AIIMS, filed a complaint about intimidation and discrimination, accompanied by a memorandum from forty other students reporting similar incidents. One student wrote: "I have been subjected to mental and physical torture from my very first day at this institute . . . I was abused on my caste and, in the last few days my room had been locked from outside because of which I was unable to attend classes" (Human Rights Watch and Center for Human Rights and Global Justice 2007: 92, n. 429). A young Dalit activist described how caste discrimination persisted through postgraduate studies in Mumbai (Bombay), even when external faculty came to participate in the evaluation of students. One such faculty member routinely put a hand across the backs of male students, a seemingly friendly gesture, to feel for the sacred thread worn by many Brahmin men (interview, October 2006).

Although many Dalit students have excelled in academic and professional spheres, caste discrimination in India continues to thwart many citizens, keeping them from achieving their full potential. Narendra Jadhav, former chief economist of the Reserve Bank of India and vice chancellor of the University of Pune, is an inspiring example of a person who overcame caste, yet he himself recognizes the continuing social and economic costs of caste: "When you meet a person in India today, even as you introduce yourself, your caste will quickly be assessed from your family name. Consciously or subconsciously, Indians, whether in their own country or abroad, still make judgments based on caste. Over the years, the caste system has taken on sophisticated dimensions; it has become subtler, though no less pernicious" (Jadhav 2007: 3).

CASTE-BASED AFFIRMATIVE ACTION

The Constitution of India abolished untouchability and discrimination on the basis of caste (Article 15), but caste categories continue to be politically salient (Jaffrelot 2003, 2007) and legally recognized for purposes of affirmative action in the form of reservations, a system of quotas regulating access to government employment, university admissions, and legislative seats (Galanter 1984). In fact, one must declare one's caste and even prove it with an official caste certificate to receive the benefits of reservations. Such affirmative action based on legally recognized caste categories offsets but does not solve the problem of past and current discrimination. More fundamental changes, particularly the consistent enforcement of laws relating to education for all and human rights, would augment low-caste advancement, but affirmative action remains an important legal means to increase opportunities for lower castes.

Colonial-era reservations were most developed in the south, notably in the Madras Presidency and some princely states: "In 1902 the Kolhapur ruler adopted one of the earliest examples of an official caste-based 'reservations' scheme, decreeing that 50 per cent of all administrative vacancies were to be reserved for those of 'non-Brahman' birth. A similar measure had been enacted in Mysore state in 1895" (Bayly 1999: 242). Reserved legislative seats for non-Brahmins in Madras from 1919 resulted in a government that created a 48-percent quota for non-Brahmins in administrative posts (Jaffrelot 2005). Classifying the lowest of the groups within the larger non-Brahmin category, the British colonial government officially recognized the so-called "Untouchable" castes, previously known as "depressed classes," by listing them in 1936 as the Scheduled Castes in order to implement the 1935 Government of India Act. This act gave special electoral representation to various minority groups.

Legal recognition and rights for the lowest castes were a key point of disagreement between nationalist leader Mohandas Gandhi and Dr. B. R. Ambedkar, a member of the depressed classes who returned to India from advanced study in Britain and the United States to work for the rights of India's lowest castes.[3] Although both Dr. Ambedkar and Mohandas Gandhi fought for the rights of "Untouchables," their divergent approaches in debates and negotiations over constitutional reforms in the last decades of British rule reflected their different ideas about Hinduism, law, and the Indian nation. "Fundamentally, this debate was about the place that social difference would have in the context of an emergent Indian identity" (Tejani 2007: 58).

Gandhi hoped to further lower-caste rights by reforming Hinduism and worried that distinct legal rights for lower castes or large-scale conversions from Hinduism by lower castes would splinter Indians during the anticolonial struggle. He even fasted to protest against Dr. Ambedkar's proposals to give the "depressed classes" reserved seats and separate electorates. Reserved seats would mean only candidates from the depressed classes could run for a certain percentage of seats. Separate electorates would mean only voters from the depressed classes could vote in elections for those particular seats. Although Dr. Ambedkar gave up his proposal for separate electorates to end Gandhi's fast, the depressed classes gained reserved legislative seats as "Scheduled Castes" prior to Independence. Dr. Ambedkar insisted that such group rights for the depressed classes were necessary and criticized both Hinduism and Gandhi's reformist approach. Dr. Ambedkar eventually led a mass conversion to Buddhism in 1956 (Jenkins 2008).

After Independence in 1947, the Scheduled Caste list was reenacted with the Scheduled Caste Order of 1950, prepared for the purpose of compensatory discrimination policies and other programs and protections for these groups. Dr. B. R. Ambedkar became independent India's first law minister and the principal architect of India's 1950 Constitution, which, in amended form, is still in use today. India's Constitution prohibits discrimination on the grounds of religion, race, caste, sex, or place of birth (Article 15). An early amendment in 1951 stated that this article should not prevent the government from "making any special provision for the advancement of any socially and educationally backward classes of citizens or for the Scheduled Castes or Scheduled Tribes" (Article 15, Clause 4).

[3] See the chapter by Williams in this volume.

The Scheduled Tribes are listed by the government based on cultural and geographic distinctiveness and disadvantaged socioeconomic status. The Scheduled Tribes, also known as Adivasis, are "those groups distinguished by 'tribal characteristics' and by their spatial and cultural isolation from the bulk of the population" (Galanter 1984: 147). Like the Scheduled Castes, groups to be included in this category were initially listed as a protected minority in the 1935 Government of India Act and later recognized in the Indian Constitution for policy purposes, including affirmative action. The Constitution leaves the contents of the schedules of tribes and castes up to the president, in consultation with the governors; the Parliament can by law include or exclude groups from the list (Constitution of India, Articles 341 and 342). Based on the constitutional commitment to these groups, Indian federal law and many state laws have long included reservations of government jobs, public university admissions, and legislative seats for Scheduled Castes and Tribes. Unlike members of the Scheduled Castes, who must be either Hindu, Sikh, or Buddhist to maintain eligibility for affirmative action, Scheduled Tribe members may be of any religion and keep their ST designation.

Yet another affirmative-action beneficiary group, with a curious label drawn from the 1951 constitutional amendment cited above (Article 15, Clause 4), is the category officially known as the Socially and Educationally Backward Classes (SEBCs) or, more commonly, the "Other Backward Classes" (OBCs). The OBCs include low, but not "Untouchable," castes and various similarly disadvantaged castes or groups within non-Hindu religions, including Islam and Christianity. Some groups in this category benefited from reservations as non-Brahmins in parts of India before Independence. After Independence Backward Classes Commissions chaired by K. Kalelkar (Backward Classes Commission 1955) and B. P. Mandal (Backward Classes Commission 1980) developed social and economic criteria for the Other Backward Classes. The Mandal Commission report, including a list of OBC communities, eventually became the basis for national-level reservations for OBCs in government jobs, instituted in the early 1990s (Galanter 2002). The Indian Supreme Court upheld these politically controversial reservations, with some restrictions, in the landmark case *Sawhney* v. *Union of India*. In this case, the court capped the overall percentage of reserved seats and insisted that socioeconomically advanced individuals from OBC communities (dubbed the "creamy layer") be skimmed from the pool of people eligible for reservations (*Indra Sawhney* v. *Union of India*, 1992 SCALE 1: 68) The Other Backward Classes are now eligible for new reservations in higher education.

The affirmative-action system in India is a quota or reservation system, although in practice these quotas are not always filled, especially in the higher ranks of the civil service or in the most competitive degree programs. Thus the difference, at a practical level, between quotas and the looser "goals" used in other countries, such as the United States, may not be as great as the terminology implies; a rigorously enforced system of goals may achieve more advancement for disadvantaged communities than a less enthusiastically enforced quota system (interview with Delhi University sociology professor Satishe Deshpande, January 7, 2008). Nevertheless, Indian quotas do not face the legal hurdles they would elsewhere, as long as the overall quotas remain below 50% (although even this limit is currently being ignored in some Indian states). In central-government jobs, for example, the Scheduled Caste quota is 15%, and the Scheduled Tribe quota is 7.5%, based roughly on their percentages in the population. The central-government job reservations for OBCs are limited to 27%, so as not to exceed the 50% limit (*Indra Sawhney* v. *Union of India* 1992: 68).

In addition to being eligible for affirmative action, low-caste victims of discrimination, violence, and other crimes can bring claims under the Protection of Civil Rights Act of 1955, enforcing Article 17 of the Constitution, which abolished untouchability, or the Scheduled Castes and Scheduled Tribes (Prevention of Atrocities) Act of 1989. These far-reaching but unevenly implemented provisions have provided some recourse for individuals confronting significant continuing problems of caste-based discrimination, ranging from socioeconomic barriers to violent attacks (Narula 1999a: 39–41).

With economic liberalization, opportunities in the once dominant public sector are being overshadowed by the growing private sector, so demands for affirmative action in private-sector jobs are escalating. Private-sector affirmative action is, so far, very limited and the product of voluntary efforts or conditions placed on public/private initiatives, as in the state of Uttar Pradesh under Chief Minister Mayawati, herself of Dalit origin. Indian industries have proposed their own affirmative-action plans to dissuade the government from enacting mandatory reservations in the private sector. For example, the Confederation of Indian Industries has published a report detailing their plans for "voluntary and self-regulated" affirmative action for the lowest castes and tribes (Confederation of Indian Industry 2007). Even if private-sector affirmative action became the law, the large informal economy in India would complicate implementation because "a large and increasing percentage of workers are in the 'unorganized sector' in which reservations, let alone affirmative action, are not applicable because they are inoperable" (Wright 2007).

RECENT CONTROVERSIES AND DEBATES OVER AFFIRMATIVE ACTION

By simultaneously abolishing the worst forms of caste-based discrimination and recognizing official caste categories to achieve social justice, the government of India has sparked legal and societal battles over the future of affirmative-action policies. Recent developments related to caste-based affirmative action include (1) classification controversies, (2) international activism on caste discrimination, and (3) growing attention to affirmative action rationales and policies based on disadvantage rather than caste *per se*.

Classification controversies

Although sometimes assumed to be fixed, caste is complex and ever changing, leading to controversies over the classifications of castes and the appropriate uses of these classifications to achieve social justice. The bench of Supreme Court justices staying the implementation of the Central Educational Institution (Reservation in Admission) Act of 2006 lamented that "Nowhere else in the world do castes, classes or communities queue up for the sake of gaining backward status . . . Nowhere else in the world is there competition to assert backwardness and then to claim we are more backward than you" ("SC Stays OBC Quota" 2007). Controversies over which groups should be eligible for which reservations and which individuals should be included in those groups demonstrate the complexity of using caste as a legal or policy category.

In May 2007, fourteen people died in clashes with police when thousands of protestors from the Gujjar community demanded that their entire community be recognized as a Scheduled Tribe rather than an "Other Backward Class," their official category, which is eligible for fewer benefits than the Scheduled Tribes (Reuters 2007). Their claim was referred to the Justice Jasraj Chopra Committee, which drew on their tours of 147 villages, 35,000 affidavits, and nearly 200 video discs of Gujjar habitations, which were submitted to local collectors (Rajalakshmi 2008a). The committee suggested that rather than reclassify the Gujjars using the "obsolete and outdated" criteria used to define Scheduled Tribes, the government should invest in infrastructure, education, and health to benefit the disadvantaged populations within the Gujjar community ("Justice Chopra Committee

Rejects Gujjars' Demand for ST Status" 2007). The committee recommended revamping the Scheduled Tribe criteria, but not waiting for this revision to be completed before infusing remote Gujjar areas with some resources to aid their development.

To assess whether Gujjars are a Scheduled Tribe, the committee was supposed to use criteria that are throwbacks to an era of oversimplified and stereotypical views of tribal identity. These include the following anachronistic (and difficult to measure) criteria: "primitive traits, distinctive culture, geographical isolation, shyness of contact and backwardness" (Rajalakshmi 2008a). In addition to critiquing these criteria, the Justice Jasraj Chopra Committee questioned the fundamental premise of organizing affirmative action on the basis of communities such as castes or tribes. They found it "difficult to take caste as the basis for favoured treatment. It is the geography of caste that defines the sociology of deprivation. Replacement of caste by an area-based strategy seems to be the only way out" (quoted in Rajalakshmi 2008a). Proposals such as this, to replace group classifications with other indicators of disadvantage, are part of a broader affirmative-action debate that will be explored in more depth below.

Ultimately the state government of Rajasthan responded to the committee's recommendations by denying support for the Gujjars' claim to be a Scheduled Tribe, but also by proposing a special, 5% Backward Class reservation category for Gujjars, in addition to the existing reservations in the state for Scheduled Castes, Scheduled Tribes, and Other Backward Classes. At the same time, the state government proposed a 14% reservation for economically backward higher castes in the state (Rajalakshmi 2008b). By bringing the total reservations in Rajasthan above 50%, and by basing additional reservations on purely economic criteria, this scheme has faced legal challenges based on the Supreme Court's decision in *Indra Sawhney* v. *Union of India* (1992).

Such disputes over the proper designation for groups such as the Gujjars are only one form of classification controversy. Even if the group in question is clearly on the official list of groups eligible for affirmative action, and satisfied with their current category, individuals' identities can remain ambiguous. Caste classification becomes particularly unclear for people who have shifted identities through religious conversion, intercaste marriage, or migration (Jenkins 2003). The Indian Supreme Court has, for example, grappled with a case in which a child of converts to Christianity reconverted to Hinduism and applied for a reserved job for Scheduled Castes (*S. Swvigaradoss* v. *Zonal Manager, F.C.I.* (1996), RD-SC 137, 1996 AIR 1,182, 1,196 SCC (3) 100 JT, 1996 (2) 182, 1996 SCALE (2) 11; Jenkins

2003: 35–8). A Presidential Order in 1950 restricted Scheduled Caste reservations to Hindu Scheduled Castes but was later amended to include Sikh Scheduled Castes in 1956 and Buddhist Scheduled Castes in 1990. Christians and Muslims have argued that they too face caste discrimination in India, but the Supreme Court has postponed considering whether Christians or Muslims of Scheduled Caste origins should benefit from reservations. There is no such religious restriction on Scheduled Tribe or Other Backward Class status.

Intercaste marriage also complicates individuals' identities, resulting in legal challenges when, for example, the upper-caste wife of a lower-caste man applied for a job reserved for OBCs (*Valsamma Paul* v. *Cochin University* [1996], 3 SCC 545; Jenkins 2003: 31–4). Migration also blurs legal identities because communities on a list of "backward classes" in one state may not be on the list in another. A case in 2008 involved a migrant in a local election, competing for a seat reserved for OBC candidates. She claimed to be in a "carpenter" caste that had two different names in two bordering states, "Badhai" in Madhya Pradesh and "Sutar" in Maharashtra. The movement of people and even the movement of state boundaries during the reorganization of Indian states became issues in this case (*Sau Kusum* v. *State of Maharashtra and Others*, 2008 INDLAW SC 1,994).

A final form of classification controversy results from the use of caste certificates to prove individual identities in order to apply for reserved opportunities. The Supreme Court has pondered cases about what could be characterized as identity fraud, as in their decision that some "social-status certificates" verifying Scheduled Tribe identity, furnished to a medical school as part of the admissions process, were "false." In this case the students in question had their Scheduled Tribe status revoked and were demoted (in terms of priority for reserved admissions) to the less "backward" category of "Other Backward Classes" (*Kumari Madhuri Patil* v. *Additional Commissioner of Tribal Development* [1994], 6 SCC 241, discussed in more detail in Jenkins 2004). Concerns about fake certificates continue, as in a recent exposé of a certificate racket in Amritsar (S. P. Jha 2008).

A 2008 Supreme Court Case dealt with several of these definitional challenges associated with deciding who is in a reserved category, in a case involving a bogus certificate, the blurred line between "caste" and "tribe," geographical complications, and disagreements between different arms of the government (*Union of India and Others* v. *S. Krishnan and Another*, 2008 INDLAW SC 156). A government employee, hired under a Scheduled Tribe quota, was found to have been hired using a bogus caste certificate. He then claimed to be in another caste (Lambadi caste), which he claimed was a Scheduled Tribe in the state of Tamil Nadu. A letter from a Director of District Welfare stated that the Lambadi caste was considered a Scheduled Tribe in most districts in the state, evidence that was given greater weight in the state High Court, yet the Supreme Court found that the official state Scheduled Tribe list did not include the Lambadi group. The Supreme Court denied his Scheduled Tribe status. Categorization controversies involving groups claiming a more "backward" status, individuals crossing social lines via conversion, marriage, or migration, and the process of certifying identities will continue to pose legal and administrative challenges.

International activism

Activists are increasingly recognizing caste as a global phenomenon and participating in international legal debates, as in efforts to unite oppressed populations from countries ranging from Japan to Nepal to Senegal in a call to declare casteism a form of racism at the 2001 UN World Conference against Racism. Such appeals to international law have not convinced the government of India to equate caste and race or to submit meaningful reports to international entities such as the UN Committee on the Elimination of Racial Discrimination. On the other hand, caste is getting more recognition internationally; activists are gaining publicity and energy from international collaborations; and nongovernmental organizations have created excellent "shadow reports" documenting ongoing problems related to discrimination and the implementation of affirmative action.

The Convention on the Elimination of All Forms of Racial Discrimination (CERD) refers to discrimination based on "descent," making this convention the focus of activists challenging caste at the international level. Activism sparked by the United Nations World Conference against Racism, Racial Discrimination, Xenophobia and Related Intolerance, held in Durban in 2001, drew new attention to "work and descent-based discrimination" such as caste discrimination. The draft documents for this conference included caste discrimination, but the participating governments did not adopt the caste paragraph in the official Declaration and Programme of Action.

The simultaneous Non-Governmental Organization (NGO) Forum Declaration and Programme of Action, however, did recognize caste-based discrimination as a form of racism and devoted several paragraphs to it. NGO interaction and activism at the forum publicized and internationalized the struggle against caste discrimination as practiced not only in South Asia, including India, Pakistan, Sri Lanka, Nepal, and Bangladesh, but also in Japan and in several African countries, such as Nigeria, Senegal, and Mauritania (Bob 2009).

In the following year, the United Nations Committee on the Elimination of Racial Discrimination "expanded the meaning of the term 'descent' in Article 1 of the International Convention on the Elimination of All Forms of Racial Discrimination (ICERD), to include discrimination based on caste" (Sengupta 2008). The Indian government had earlier ratified this convention but persistently argues that caste is not race. The Indian government submitted a report in 2006 to the Committee on the Elimination of Racial Discrimination, arguing that the Indian Constitution lists caste and race as distinct categories, in Article 15, which prohibits discrimination on the basis of either. The Committee on the Elimination of Racial Discrimination, in its "observations," challenged the Indian government's arguments: "Discrimination based on 'descent' includes discrimination against members of communities based on forms of social stratification such as caste and analogous systems of inherited status which nullify or impair their equal enjoyment of human rights" (quoted in Sengupta 2008).

The UN Committee on the Elimination of Racial Discrimination receives and offers such "observations" about the predictably self-serving and political reports from national governments. This process lacks "teeth," although it arguably publicizes problems of discrimination. Another recent attempt by the UN to publicize "Untouchables" (as well as to laud private-sector clinics for low castes and to draw attention to the International Year of Sanitation) brought several Dalit women, whose previous employment was manually cleaning septic systems, to the UN in New York, where they walked down a runway in UN-blue saris, accompanied by professional models in chiffon (Hughes 2008). This kind of publicity is not likely to solve problems of caste discrimination.

On the other hand, bringing the issue of caste discrimination to the attention of the UN has inspired many other organizations to contribute substantive, documented "shadow reports" to the Committee on the Elimination of Racial Discrimination, reports that can be much more revealing than government reports or special events in New York City. One such report from Human Rights Watch and the Centre for Human Rights and Global Justice, *Hidden Apartheid* (2007) is a comprehensive overview documenting ongoing discrimination on the basis of caste. Such documentation is a major benefit of the internationalization of caste struggles.

Moreover, despite the refusal of official Indian UN delegations to recognize casteism as racism, Prime Minister Manmohan Singh, at a conference in Delhi in 2006, drew parallels between discrimination against Dalits and apartheid (Rahman 2006). In addition, Indian justices in affirmative-action decisions often take a more global view of the parallels between caste and race. The Supreme Court of India routinely refers to American case law on affirmative action. Their most recent decision on affirmative action in higher education includes the following argument: "Of the classifications on which there is case law, the one that most closely resembles caste is race. This is because both are immutable traits. They are used by the powerful, or those seeking power, to justify oppression. Racism and casteism have long haunted both nations" (*Ashoka Kumar Thakur* v. *Union of India and Others*, writ petition [civil], paragraph 192, decided on April 10, 2008). This decision goes on to cite two US Supreme Court decisions from 2003 on affirmative action at the University of Michigan (*Grutter* v. *Bollinger* [2003], 539 US 244 and *Gratz* v. *Bollinger* [2003], 539 US 306), as well as several older US cases, and even a (US-based) Cato Institute study entitled "The Affirmative Action Myth" and a *New York Times* article entitled "The New Affirmative Action." The Indian Supreme Court notes that US cases are "not binding" but "have great persuasive value and they may provide broad guidelines as to how we should tackle our prevailing condition" (*Ashoka Kumar Thakur* v. *Union of India and Others*, paragraph 183). Likewise, caste-based affirmative action in India has gained some international attention as a potential model for similar policies elsewhere (Ginsburg and Merritt 1999; Cunningham, Loury, and Skrentny 2002).

Caste versus disadvantage

In India, longstanding policies of caste-based quotas are increasingly shifting toward policies and proposals targeting beneficiaries based on more multifaceted indicators of disadvantage. Blending caste and other criteria is not new in India but these other criteria are an increasingly important aspect of reservation policies. The shift toward recognizing "multiple discrimination" in affirmative action may primarily be inspired by legal developments, but it follows longstanding feminist and sociological theorizing on the "intersectionality" of identities and the importance of tracing the effects of multiple axes of discrimination based on race, caste, class, gender, religion, and so on. At a practical level, however, a move toward policies based on disadvantage or diversity could dilute affirmative action for specific caste and racial minorities that still face discrimination. Given ongoing discrimination on the basis of categories such as caste and race, a shift away from policies that recognize race and caste as legitimate and primary indicators of disadvantage could make affirmative action a much weaker tool to combat discrimination against low castes or racial minorities.

The Other Backward Classes category is based on a complicated blend of caste and other socioeconomic criteria. The Mandal Commission on Backward Classes developed criteria for OBC status based on social, educational and economic indicators of "backwardness" (Backward Classes Commission 1980). As discussed above, *Sawhney* v. *Union of India* upheld central-government job reservations that were largely based on the Mandal Commission's recommendations, but recalibrated the definition of beneficiaries. The Supreme Court insisted that governmental classifications of Other Backward Classes must take into account both caste *and* economic status, which necessitates attention to both group *and* individual criteria (Jenkins 2001, 2003). This means that purely economic quotas, for poor individuals within upper castes, are not allowed, and that socioeconomically advantaged individuals from an Other Backward Class, officially known as the "creamy layer," cannot benefit from OBC reservations, despite the "backwardness" of their caste as a whole.

What is the "creamy layer"? People are in the creamy layer when they or their parents have reached specified levels in high government posts, the civil service, the armed forces, or public-sector undertakings, or have surpassed an income/wealth ceiling. This ceiling was originally Rs. 100,000 rupees per year, but it was raised to Rs. 250,000 per year in 2004 and subsequently in 2008 to Rs. 450,000 per year. People with "professional class" jobs, property owners, or those in trade, business, or industry can also be excluded based on property ownership and/or income or wealth (National Commission for Backward Classes 2008). For caste certificates to be provided by OBC candidates for reserved opportunities, local officials must not only certify that the candidate is a member of an Other Backward Class but also that he or she is not in the creamy layer.

A subsequent policy development in Other Backward Class reservations renewed debate over the appropriate beneficiaries of affirmative action and sparked protests by medical students, described above, and others: The Central Educational Institution (Reservation in Admission) Act of 2006 increased quotas to 49.5 percent of seats in national public universities, including the renowned and fiercely competitive All India Institute of Medical Sciences and the Indian Institutes of Technology (IITs). In response to protestors, the government agreed to increase the overall number of seats in these institutions, so that the number of unreserved seats would remain constant. In the face of numerous legal challenges, this expansion was approved by the Supreme Court in April 2008. The 49.5

percent quota in central universities remains controversial because it increases the quota and broadens the eligible groups beyond the most disadvantaged castes and tribes to include the less disadvantaged and more numerous Other Backward Classes.

The expansion of OBC reservations to higher education precipitated the resignation, in 2006, of prominent scholars Andre Beteille (sociology) and Pratap Bhanu Mehta (law and politics) from the government's National Knowledge Commission, which was trying to rethink and improve the Indian education system. In his letter of resignation, Mehta argued for more nuanced affirmative action: "What we needed, Honorable Prime Minister, was space to design more effective mechanisms of targeting groups that need to be targeted for affirmative action." More effective targeting of affirmative action combined with more comprehensive reforms reaching everyone would be better than quotas, he argued: "As a society we focus on reservations largely because it is a way of avoiding doing the things that really create access. Increasing the supply of good quality institutions at all levels (not to be confused with numerical increases), more robust scholarship and support programmes will go much further than numerically mandated quotas" (P. B. Mehta 2006). Mehta has also critiqued the Indian Supreme Court's political "balancing acts" in its decisions on reservations and other issues (P. B. Mehta 2007: 112–13).

The Supreme Court decision on Other Backward Class reservations in higher education includes approving references to the United States Supreme Court decisions in the University of Michigan cases, which have moved colleges and universities in the US to retool admissions policies away from race (particularly racial point systems) and toward a variety of indicators of socioeconomic status or disadvantages. In his judgment in the Indian case, Justice Dalveer Bhandari notes that "Justice Sandra Day O'Connor opined that there may be a time-limit to promoting diversity via preferential treatment for certain races" (*Ashoka Kumar Thakur* v. *Union of India and Others*, paragraph 248). Although recognizing that the nine-judge holding in *Sawhney* necessitates that a combination of caste and economic criteria continue to define Other Backward Castes, Bhandari urges the government to move toward a more economically based system of affirmative action: He laments that *Sawhney* "rejects purely economic criteria (occupation / income / property holdings / or similar measures of economic power) with respect to classification ... It also precludes us from forcing the government to wean itself off caste-based reservations by a certain date in order to achieve a casteless and classless society," but the judge advocates that "after a lapse of ten years, special preference or reservation should be granted only on the basis of economic criteria as long as grave disparity and inequality persist" (*Ashoka Kumar Thakur* v. *Union of India and Others*, paragraph 248).

As the court pushes for less focus on caste and more attention to economic indicators of disadvantage, the current government has proposed the creation of an Equal Opportunity Commission. As political scientist Suhas Palshikar envisages, "the proposed commission of equal opportunity permits the government to comprehend the complex networks of diversity, disadvantage and discrimination instead of remaining entangled in the avoidable path of attending to only one community or focusing on only one axis of this complex phenomenon" (Palshikar 2008: 84). Several voluntary affirmative-action programs in Indian higher education are possible models for policies based on complex calculations of disadvantage. Examples include the admissions policy at Jawaharlal Nehru University (a public, postgraduate institution) and the selection process for the Ford Foundation's international fellowship program in India.

At Jawaharlal Nehru University (JNU) in Delhi, the admissions system included "deprivation points" to give a boost to potential students who are disadvantaged but not eligible for current government mandated reservations for Scheduled Castes or Tribes or the physically handicapped. This sort of voluntary affirmative action scheme has been in place at JNU on and off since the 1970s. Under the JNU policy, applicants from backward districts got an additional three to five marks ("regional deprivation marks"). JNU's own geography and regional-development professors designated districts, giving them three to five marks depending on their degree of "backwardness." The JNU geography professor in charge of the "index of regional backwardness" described three aspects of the district-level index: rural parameters using agricultural productivity data from the Ministry of Agriculture, educational parameters using census literacy data (male and female), and workforce participation parameters (male) also from the census. They divided districts into four quartiles, which determine the number of points applicants got, if any (interview with Professor Sachidanand Sinha, January 16, 2008).

JNU also voluntarily used the existing government OBC category. For OBC applicants, if the applicant was not from the "creamy layer" (at JNU this simply meant parents had enough income to have to pay income tax), female OBCs got ten points and male OBCs five, but there was a cap at ten total deprivation points, so a female OBC from a backward district could not get fifteen points (interview with JNU Registrar/Director of Admissions Professor K. C. Upadhyaya, January 4, 2008). JNU became subject to the new government policy to provide quotas to OBCs in central universities. Geography Professor Sinha argues that JNU's existing policy was reaching a large percentage of OBCs while targeting the most disadvantaged and creating less controversy due to its nonreliance on caste alone (interview with Professor Sinha, January 16, 2008).

In a related approach using points based on various indicators of disadvantage, Delhi-based social scientists Yogendra Yadav (Centre for the Study of Developing Societies) and Satishe Deshpande (Sociology Department, Delhi School of Economics) helped design the Ford Foundation's international fellowship program selection procedures and published their ideas as an alternative to the government's proposed expansion of OBC reservations in higher education (Deshpande and Yadav 2006). Professor Deshpande opposes purely income-based affirmative action in favor of their multifaceted approach that retains caste/community as a key target. "We need a variety of policies rather than a single policy . . . in higher education economic reservations could be against the very goal of reservations . . . If income alone [is used], you could be excluding the only segment of a group that can get into higher education at all" (interview with Professor Deshpande, January 7, 2008).

Professor Yadav argues that reservation policies "should target" and should "be seen to be targeting" the "most disadvantaged." The former is good policy, he notes, and the latter is good politics (interview with Professor Yadav, January 12, 2008). Complicating the already complicated OBC category, Yadav would like to design policies that reflect this "varied group." The "best scheme" in his view "has exactly the map of all these gradations [of disadvantage] and reverses that." The best (and most "non-fudgeable") of the many indicators of educational disadvantage in their scheme is the "school from which you did your matriculation." He states, "You simply do not go to a government school in a village if you can afford not to." From a social-science perspective, indicators such as mother and father's literacy are very telling, he said, but from a practical-policy perspective, you cannot prove parental illiteracy. "Crude but robust indicators" he has worked into his proposal still feature caste and community, but also gender and type of school (based on the type of town, region, type of school, medium of instruction, etc.) (interview with Professor Yadav, January 12, 2008). One small-scale implementation of their vision, the selection process for the Ford Foundation International Fellows from India, uses, in the words of the head of that program, a "rather detailed matrix" including literacy, rural location, primary and secondary education levels in locality, number of family members and number of earners in family, whether the applicant went to government school, and even health standards (all indicators included in the application form itself) (interview with Vivek Mansukhani, Ford Foundation, India, January 17, 2008).

By allowing Other Backward Class reservations and embracing the concept of the "creamy layer," the Supreme Court has reinforced the need for complex designations of disadvantage for affirmative action. Jawaharlal Nehru University, by implementing affirmative action based on both government categories and geographical and gender indices of their own design, offers one model for the future of affirmative action, although their innovative approach may be homogenized by national-level OBC reservations in higher education. Complicating rather than abandoning caste categories, Professor Yadav and Professor Deshpande would include other cross-cutting indicators of social, economic, and, especially, educational disadvantages, while retaining the centrality of caste. Because both Yadav and Deshpande were on the government's committee to design a new Equal Opportunity Commission, their ideas should continue to have an impact on the future shape of affirmative action.

DIRECTIONS FOR FUTURE RESEARCH

Opportunities for future research abound for those interested in the study of contemporary connections between caste and the law. Research could fruitfully center on the most recent permutations of caste and tribal classifications, on international legal strategies of low-caste groups, or on the potential globalization of legal rationales for continuing affirmative action based on disadvantage or diversity rather than group categories such as caste or race. More broadly, the linkages between caste, religion, and the law shed light on the varied meanings and philosophies of secularism in different legal and cultural contexts (Needham and Rajan 2007). The impact of religious and legal categories on the lives of women has inspired rich critiques and commentaries capturing the intersections of religion, caste, gender, and the law in women's lives (Ray and Basu 1999).[4] The potential expansion of affirmative action in the private sector in India, and the challenges of affirmative action or anti-discrimination policies in unorganized or informal economic sectors, are timely topics for further study.

Laws based on caste or religious identities highlight the complex, contingent nature of social and legal groups, as individual and group identities change over time through conversion (Robinson and Clarke 2003;

[4] See also Sturman's chapter in this volume.

Viswanathan 1998) or through social mobility up the caste hierarchy (Srinivas 1962).[5] Assigned and asserted identities interact, as legal definitions of who is a Scheduled Caste, a Scheduled Tribe, or an Other Backward Class shape, but do not determine, the identities claimed by individuals or groups. Indeed some groups claim identity categories explicitly rejected by the government, such as the Dalit activists asserting that they face "racial" discrimination. Caste as a basis for both discrimination and affirmative action has taken on new and unexpected forms in contemporary India and continues to be a salient social, political, and legal category.

[5] Vajpeyi's chapter in this volume is also pertinent here.

CHAPTER 15

Law and Hindu nationalist movements

Smita Narula

INTRODUCTION

The opening of the Indian Constitution proudly proclaims its resolve to constitute India into a "secular democratic republic" and to secure to all its citizens "liberty of thought, expression, belief, faith and worship" and "equality of status and of opportunity." Though the country's constitutional vision may be clear, the appropriateness of such a vision for a society as deeply religious and socially stratified as India is continuously subject to social and political challenge.

The task of securing religious liberty while upholding secular aspirations in a deeply religious society is a daunting one. Hinduism, the professed religion of over 80 percent of Indians, is often described as a "way of life," highlighting the "profound tension that penetrates to the core of Indian constitutionalism, where 'the State is secular . . . but the people are not'" (Jacobsohn 2003: 35–6). On one side of what is often a very polemical debate are those who advocate for equal treatment of religious groups in India, where the language of equal treatment may disguise a quest for assimilation through subordination. On the other side of the debate are those who argue that neutrality toward religion is a prescription for majoritarian rule, adding that minorities must be protected against the dominance of the majority Hindu culture.

Hindu nationalism therefore poses a dual challenge to secularism in India: as a movement that seeks to mobilize support on the basis of advocating for a Hindu nation, thereby challenging secular ideals; and as a movement that purports to defend secular values through its admonition of "pseudo-secularists" and the "minority appeasement" of Muslims. Both sets of challenges have found their way to the Supreme Court: the first in

The author acknowledges with great appreciation the research assistance provided by Nishanth Chari, Dennis Hermreck, Munia Jabbar, and Tara Mikkilineni.

cases involving the prosecution of elected representatives of Hindu nationalist political parties for corrupt practices, and in cases following the aftermath of large-scale episodes of communal violence fomented and led by militant Hindu nationalist groups; and the second in cases involving Muslim personal law and the associated endeavor to create a uniform civil code.

This paper provides an overview of the key areas of intersection between Hindu nationalism and the law, as set against the backdrop of the origins, organization, and tactics of the Hindu nationalist movement. A journey into this heated terrain quickly reveals that the Supreme Court's interpretation of the Constitution's secular vision is highly contextual and highly contested. Case law related to secularism oscillates between the twin poles of emphasizing the rights and sensibilities of religious minorities, and conflating Hindu religion with Indian culture, all the while frustrating the achievement of equal treatment among religions.

HINDU NATIONALISM: ORIGINS, ORGANIZATION, AND OBJECTIVES

Any inquiry into the influence of Hindu nationalism on the law, as well as the challenge it poses to India's secular aspirations, must begin with a brief examination of the origins, organization, and objectives of Hindu nationalist groups. The ideology of Hindutva, or a movement for "Hindu awakening," is a political strategy rooted in the teachings of the founders of the Rashtriya Swayamsevak Sangh ("RSS," National Volunteer Corps). The RSS was founded in the city of Nagpur in 1925 by Keshav Baliram Hedgewar with the mission of creating a Hindu state. Since its founding, it has promulgated a form of Hindu nationalism as the dominant basis for national identity in India (Tamminen 1996).

According to the RSS, both the leaders of India's nationalist movement and those of post-Independence India failed to create a nation based on Hindu culture. The role of the RSS in the nationalist struggle for independence was defined in opposition to its ideological differences with the Indian National Congress. While the latter sought to end British rule, the RSS argued that the restoration of Hinduism should be the cornerstone of the movement. In particular, the RSS was critical of what it termed the Congress's policy of "appeasement of Muslims" and opposed the partition of India and the creation of Pakistan as a separate Muslim state (Tamminen 1996). The RSS wanted "the entire gamut of social life" to be designed "on the rock-bed of Hindu nationalism" (Rashtriya Swayamsevak Sangh n.d.: Part VII), a goal that inspired the creation of the political, social, and educational wings of the RSS, a family of organizations that is now referred to collectively as the Sangh Parivar, or "family" of Hindu nationalist organizations.

Although different from one another in many respects, Sangh Parivar–affiliated groups have collectively promoted the argument – in political, cultural, and social spheres – that India should be a Hindu state because Hindus constitute the majority of Indians (Narula 2007: 367). The following organizations are among the more prominent Sangh Parivar–affiliated groups. The Jana Sangh Party was formed in 1951 as the political wing of the RSS, and was later replaced in 1980 by the Bharatiya Janata Party (BJP). The BJP – which has emerged as a national party alternative to the Congress Party – claims to be an inclusive political party (Nussbaum 2007: 67) and has attempted to portray itself as a party devoted to economic reform and battling corruption (Nussbaum 2007: 179). Still, it continues to "derive ... its support in part from its religious roots, not only from its political values" (Nussbaum 2007: 138).

The Vishwa Hindu Parishad (VHP) was formed in 1964 to cover the social aspects of the RSS activities. It organizes and communicates the RSS message to Hindus living outside India and holds conferences for Hindu religious leaders from across the country. The Bajrang Dal is the militant youth wing of the VHP and was formed in 1984. The Vidya Bharati (or the Vidya Bharati Akhil Bharatiya Shiksha Sansthan) was established in 1978 with the objective of organizing the activities of the RSS in education. Similar organizations at the state and regional levels have existed since the 1940s (Narula 2003a: 45). The RSS and the VHP/Bajrang Dal, whose membership is exclusively male, have set up counterpart women's organizations – namely the Rashtriya Sevika Samiti and the Durga Vahini, respectively. Like the Bajrang Dal, the Durga Vahini plays a paramilitary role (Sarkar and Butalia 1995). Collectively, these groups focus on restoring what they see as women's traditional roles in the family as mothers and wives (Cossman and Kapur 1995: 92–102).

What began as a fringe movement has over time become a formidable force whose members are well represented in the wide spectrum of Indian political, social, and cultural life. Sangh Parivar–affiliated groups have also proliferated overseas in countries with large Hindu diaspora populations. Moreover, what was initially envisioned as a long-term project in which state power was subordinated to the primacy of organizing society around Hindu ideals (Jaffrelot 1996: 77) now has its sights firmly trained on the goal of capturing political power. In the process, Hindu nationalist leaders have pushed the boundaries of the law in their electioneering while militant allied groups have been accused of trampling human rights in the Sangh Parivar's collective quest for sociopolitical dominance.

The law has proved a malleable ally in such an undertaking. As noted below, Hindu nationalist groups have made ample and effective use of the legal space afforded by the Constitution, the courts, and the legislature to advance their agenda, and have in the process co-opted members of the law-enforcement machinery for wholly unlawful ends. In many respects, the law operates in the context of Hindu nationalism and not the other way around. More than six decades after Independence, Hindu nationalists continue to see themselves as the antidote to the "erosion of the nation's integrity in the name of secularism" (Rashtriya Swayamsevak Sangh n.d.: Part 11). And all the while, their call for a restoration of that integrity seamlessly manages to cloak itself in secular liberal terms. The Constitution's own internal contradictions have proven ripe for such manipulation.

SECULARISM IN THE INDIAN CONTEXT

Secularism in the Indian context has long been the focus of academic inquiry, most notably as a curious alternative to the Western liberal democratic brand of secularism as separation of religion and state.[1] The Indian Constitution, which is "determinedly secular" (Galanter 1984: 305), guarantees an expansive vision of religious freedom that embodies religious thought, beliefs, and rituals, and freedom from discrimination on religious, racial, or caste-related grounds (Dhavan 2001: 311). The Supreme Court has also "consistently defined the limits of state power in terms of constitutional secularism" (Baxi 2000: 891). But in sharp contrast to Western conceptions of secularism, religion in India can never truly be separate from the state (Jacobsohn 2003: 10). Indian society does not lend itself to such an interpretation, nor does the Constitution require it of the state (Sathe 2002: 161). Rather, the state is charged with the arduous project of guaranteeing freedom of religion while reforming the Indian citizenry away from religion-based practices that offend liberal sensibilities. The Indian Constitution not only makes room for state intervention, but implicitly invites it; as a result "the two can, and often do, interact and intervene in each other's affairs within the legally prescribed and judicially settled parameters" (Mahmood 2006: 756–7).

India's constitutional commitment to secularism is therefore neither indifferent nor impartial to religion; rather, it seeks to ensure that all religions are accorded equal treatment (Sripati 1998: 413) while simultaneously subjugating

[1] For a recent analytical overview of this topic, see R. Sen 2007.

religious freedom to the project of social reform. Article 25 of the Indian Constitution, which guarantees individuals the right to freely "profess, practise and propagate religion," explicitly invites this project of social reform by stipulating that the right is "subject to public order, morality and health and to the other provisions" of the Fundamental Rights section of the Constitution. Article 25 adds that nothing in the article shall "prevent the State from making any law … providing for social welfare and reform." A number of provisions of the Indian Constitution, under the headings of Fundamental Rights and Directive Principles, underscore these reformist intentions. These include provisions calling on the state to "endeavour to secure for the citizens a uniform civil code" subjecting all religions to the same set of personal laws (Article 44); to abolish the caste-based practice of untouchability (Article 17); and to protect Scheduled Castes (so-called "Untouchables") and Scheduled Tribes from social injustice (Article 46), to name a few. The Constitution additionally empowers the state to make special provisions, including through reservations or quotas, for the advancement of any socially and educationally backward classes of citizens, or for Scheduled Castes and Scheduled Tribes (for instance in Articles 15[4], 16[4], 330, 332). Such "compensatory discrimination" programs "permit departure from formal equality for the purpose of favoring specialized groups" in order to protect them from exploitation and injustice (Galanter 1984: 41–2).

The Constitution's dual commitments to social reform and the preservation of religious group identity can and do come into conflict. The Hindu nationalist movement has strategically stepped into this disharmonic context to position itself as a defender of secularism whenever the state acts to preserve the group identity of religious minorities. The Hindu nationalists' claim of upholding secularism has been characterized as a distortion of the dominant understanding of secularism, from one of equal respect of all religions to a majoritarianist strategy whereby the Hindu majority sets the norm by which religious minorities must abide (Cossman and Kapur 1997: 115). Perhaps nowhere is this distortion more pronounced than in the Hindu nationalists' support for the development of a secular uniform civil code (UCC), which would apply with equal force to all religious communities, and in particular to the Muslim community whose practices, they argue, discriminate against women.

PERSONAL LAWS VERSUS THE UNIFORM CIVIL CODE

Article 44 of the Indian Constitution calls upon the state to *endeavor* to establish a uniform civil code (UCC) that would subject the Indian citizenry to a uniform set of personal laws. Such an endeavor, however, is fraught with tension. Compelling India's Muslim community to abandon their religious practices (in the areas of marriage, divorce, inheritance, and maintenance) risks imposing majoritarian values on a minority community, while the ongoing failure to enact the UCC undermines the project of liberal constitutionalism and institutionalizes differential treatment based on religion (Narula 2006).

These tensions have given rise to a peculiar anomaly in India wherein both proponents and opponents of the UCC can lay claim to the mantle of secularism when making arguments in defense of their position. Those opposed to the UCC, including dominant members of the Muslim community, view the code as a threat to their cultural and religious identity that they claim must be protected as part of their constitutional right to religious freedom. Enacting the UCC would elevate secular laws while trivializing the importance of culturally anchored personal laws as a basis for law-making in India (Menski 2008: 227). Support for the UCC, or more generally for the equal treatment of religions, can be born of two very different motives: one that comes out of a "principled commitment to procedural liberalism" and another that "recognize[s] the utility of this position because it facilitates a desirable political objective, namely the subordination of minorities to majoritarian Hindu norms" (Jacobsohn 2003: 148).

The call for a uniform civil code has, as a result, made strange bedfellows of women's rights advocates (who support the UCC as beneficial to the rights of Muslim women who are significantly disadvantaged under Muslim personal law) and Hindu nationalists (who extract considerable political mileage from supporting the UCC as a counterweight to minority appeasement or the extending of special privileges to the Muslim minority) (Narula 2006). The BJP, for instance, has criticized "pseudo-secularism" as inadequately protecting the interests of Hindu communities (Baxi 2000: 891).

Though argued in *ameliorative* terms (i.e., as supportive of Muslim women's rights) the rights discourse deployed by the Hindu nationalist movement is said to be in furtherance of its *assimilationist* strategy that demands that religious minorities "owe allegiance to Hindu symbols of identity because these were the embodiment of the Indian nation" and because of "the conviction that Hindu culture contains within it the essence of Indian identity" (Jaffrelot 1996: 57). The Hindu nationalists' distortion of the dominant understanding of secularism has been compounded by the Supreme Court's problematic engagement with the issue, as seen in cases concerning the relationship between secular law and religious law as associated with the rights under Articles 25 and 26 of the Constitution to profess and practice religion and manage religious affairs. The issue of whether an allegedly secular right could be claimed despite conflicting provisions of religious personal law was explored in the landmark case of *Mohammed Ahmed Khan* v. *Shah Bano Begum* (AIR 1985 SC 945) (Basu 1999: 271; Engineer 1987). There, the Supreme Court addressed this relationship in the context of a possible conflict between the Muslim personal law and Section 125(1)(a) of the Code of Criminal Procedure. Section 125(1)(a) allows a destitute wife to sue her divorced husband for monthly maintenance (financial support), provided that the husband has sufficient means and has neglected or refused to support his former wife. Under Muslim personal law, a Muslim man is required only to provide maintenance to his divorced wife during the period of *iddat* – the obligatory three-month period following a divorce during which marriage is prohibited.

In a highly controversial ruling, the Supreme Court first asserted the primacy of secular law over religious law in cases of conflict, holding that religion "cannot have any repercussion on the applicability of such laws," as Section 125 "cut across the barriers of religion" (*Shah Bano* 948–9). The Court went on to find no such conflict in the instant case, despite the accepted interpretation of the Muslim personal law as limiting a husband's liability to maintain his divorced wife to the period of *iddat*. Instead, the Court noted that the "true position" of the Muslim personal law distinguished between divorced wives able to maintain themselves, in which case the husband's liability would cease with the expiration of the *iddat* period, and divorced wives left destitute, who would be "entitled to take recourse to section 125" (*Shah Bano* 950–1).

The Court reached this conclusion based upon its own analysis of the Quran and other Islamic texts, which left "no doubt that the Quran imposes an obligation on the Muslim husband to make provision for or to provide maintenance to the divorced wife." Submissions by the All India Muslim Personal Board arguing otherwise were dismissed as "facile" or as "a shuffling plea" (*Shah Bano* 951–2, 954). The Court evinced a clear preference for secular law on the grounds that "a common Civil Code will help the cause of national integration by removing disparate loyalties in laws which have conflicting ideologies" (*Shah Bano* 954). While the case served in part to advance Muslim women's rights, the language of "national integration" and the disapproval of citizens' "loyalties" to their personal laws were deeply troubling for India's minority groups.

The ruling sparked an outcry from the Muslim right and the Ulema (scholar clerics) issued a widely publicized proclamation condemning the judgment as contrary to Islamic teachings (Kumar 1994: 84). The anger was in part directed at the fact that a presumably Hindu judge issued the judgment's commentary on *iddat* and its Quranic origins (Basu 1999: 272–3). Soon after the ruling, the Congress Party, presumably fearing a loss of Muslim votes following their endorsement of the *Shah Bano* decision, passed the Muslim Women (Protection of Rights on Divorce) Act (1986), which declared that Section 125 of the criminal code was not applicable to Muslims, thereby nullifying the judgment. In response, Hindu nationalists engaged in acts of hostility and violence toward Muslims, claiming the bill was proof of Muslim domination. Playing on this fear, the Hindu nationalist movement acquired unprecedented support by framing the bill as "minority appeasement" and as a crisis revealing secularism to be inimical to national integrity (Hasan 1998: 81).

The *Shah Bano* controversy enabled the Hindu nationalist movement to spin the recognition of cultural difference as a vehicle of Muslim minority privilege and unfair oppression of the Hindu majority. In so doing, the Hindu nationalists effectively oriented the political discourse to incite mass outrage toward symbolic edifices such as the sixteenth-century Babri Masjid (mosque) in Ayodhya, Uttar Pradesh (Panikkar 1993: 67). The VHP claimed that the Babri Masjid was built on a site that was the birthplace of the Hindu Lord Ram, and that a temple at that site had been destroyed in order to build the mosque. The Bajrang Dal – the militant youth wing of the VHP – was formed in order to mobilize youth for the campaign to build a temple to Lord Ram at the site of the mosque (Narula 2003a: 47), a campaign that has led to much violence and legal wrangling.

The Sangh Parivar's strategy was to portray the alleged destruction of the temple as an act of aggression against Hindus for which the entire Muslim community – as descendants of the Muslim rulers accused of the destruction – must be held responsible. This symbolic meaning of Ayodhya was communicated to the masses through a series of organized public interventions and through political campaigns that made Ayodhya "a powerful mobilizing force" (Panikkar 1993: 67). The Ram temple campaign also enabled the rapid expansion of the BJP's electoral base (Panikkar 1993: 63) as it was easily folded into their electioneering strategy described below. The ultimate result – a toxic mix of violence and feelings of Hindu inferiority aroused by portraying Muslims as a formidable threat – led ultimately to the destruction of the Babri Masjid, also described below.

A decade after the *Shah Bano* decision, the Court once again reiterated the need for a uniform civil code. In *Sarla Mudgal* v. *Union of India* (AIR 1995 SC 1,531) the Court considered the legal validity of second marriages by Hindu men after they had converted to Islam, holding that such marriages were void (*Sarla Mudgal* 1,537). The Court did not limit itself, however, to answering the specific legal question presented; instead, it called for a uniform personal law to supersede the Muslim marriage laws on the ground that the Constitution mandated "the establishment of a 'common civil Code' for the whole of India" (*Sarla Mudgal* 1,538). In so doing, the Court implied that the Muslim practice of bigamous marriage ran counter not only to "the cause of the national unity and integration," but to the Constitution itself. Specifically, the Court stated that "The Hindus along with Sikhs, Buddhists and Jains have forsaken their sentiments in the cause of the national unity and integration, some other communities would not, though the Constitution enjoins the establishment of a 'common civil Code' for the whole of India" (*Sarla Mudgal* 1,538).

According to Ahmad, in cases such as *Sarla Mudgal*, the question of what it means to be "un-Indian" is usually defined in opposition to a nationalist, monolithic, and static notion of what constitutes the "true Indian" identity – which often coincides with the identity of the Hindu majority (Ahmad 1996: 330–5). The Court's reasoning reflects to some extent the success of the Hindu nationalist project to recast Indian identity as one that is synonymous with being Hindu. The language of the decision did little to camouflage this perspective; it noted that "[w]hen more than 80% of the citizens have already been brought under the codified [Hindu] personal law there is no justification whatsoever to keep in abeyance, any more, the introduction of 'uniform civil code' for all citizens," in effect assuming that Hindu law, being the majority law, should apply to all (*Sarla Mudgal* 1,531–2; cf. Ahmad 1996: 330–2). Such a conflation of identity, culture, and religion was also on display in the so-called Hindutva cases described below.

In 2001, the Supreme Court revisited the maintenance issue in *Danial Latifi* v. *Union of India* ([2001], 7 SCC 740) and found *Shah Bano* to be good law (*Danial Latifi*, paragraph 44). The Court interpreted the Muslim Women (Protection of Rights on Divorce) Act – passed after the *Shah Bano* ruling ostensibly to exempt Muslims from Section 125 – as codifying rather than nullifying the *Shah Bano* holding (*Danial Latifi*, paragraph 44). The Court drew on the language of the act that mandates "reasonable and fair provision and maintenance" for Muslim ex-wives (*Danial Latifi*, paragraph 44) and noted that a reading of the act that deprived Muslim women the protections of Section 125 would discriminate on the basis of religion and would therefore be unconstitutional (*Danial Latifi*, paragraph 46). Relying explicitly on the interpretation of Muslim personal law in the *Shah Bano* decision (*Danial Latifi*, paragraph 46), the Court found that under Section 125 of the Criminal Procedure Code, Muslim women were entitled to "reasonable and fair" maintenance from their husband beyond the *iddat* period (*Danial Latifi*, paragraph 48). Though there continues to be no uniform civil code at least one commentator argues that the current system manages to achieve a measure of legal uniformity stemming in part from the harmonization of the personal law system through both legislation and judicial interpretation (Menski 2008: 213, 220).

REPRESENTATION OF THE PEOPLE ACT OF 1951

As the goal of capturing political power took center stage in the Hindu nationalist movement so too did religion-based electioneering. The nature of such electioneering came to light in the Hindutva cases whereby the Court erroneously accepted the "secular" nature of election speeches by Hindu nationalist leaders and failed to interrogate the "anti-secular vision of secularism" that such speeches represent (Cossman and Kapur 1997: 114–15). The case of *Ramesh Yeshwant Prabhoo* v. *Prabhakar Kasinath Kunte* (AIR 1996 SC 1,113) involved the prosecution of elected representatives of the BJP–Shiv Sena alliance government in the western state of Maharashtra for corrupt practices under the Representation of the People Act of 1951. (The Shiv Sena is a Maharashtra-based Hindu nationalist political party.) The act prohibits and defines as a corrupt practice the use of religion or religious symbols, *inter alia*, to promote one's candidacy or to adversely affect the election of another candidate. The BJP–Shiv Sena candidate Ramesh Yeshwant Prabhoo appealed a Bombay High Court judgment that pronounced Prabhoo and Shiv Sena leader Bal Thackeray (as Prabhoo's agent) guilty of violating the act.

Thackeray addressed several meetings during the course of Prabhoo's 1987 election. During one such meeting he stated, "We are fighting this election for the protection of Hinduism. Therefore, we do not care for the votes of the Muslims. This country belongs to Hindus and will remain so" (*Prabhoo*, paragraph 6). Soon thereafter at another election meeting, Thackeray stated:

> Hinduism will triumph in this election and we must become hon'ble recipients of this victory to ward off the danger on Hinduism, elect Ramesh Prabhoo to join with Chhagan Bhujbal who is already there. You will find Hindu temples underneath if all the mosques are dug out ... A candidate by [the] name [of] Prabhoo should be led to victory in the name of religion. (Prabhoo, paragraph 11)

Prabhoo argued that the election campaign speeches made by Thackeray, which were the basis of the High Court's decision, "did not amount to appeal for votes on the ground of his religion [as] the substance and main thrust thereof was 'Hindutava' which means the Indian culture and not merely the Hindu religion" (*Prabhoo*, paragraph 15). Although the Supreme Court upheld the High Court's conviction, it agreed with Prabhoo that Hindutva "is related more to the way of life of the people in the subcontinent [and] is not to be equated with, or understood as religious Hindu fundamentalism" (*Prabhoo*, paragraph 60). Rather, the Court found, the term "is used and understood as a synonym of 'Indianisation', i.e., development of uniform culture by obliterating the differences between all the cultures co-existing in the country."

In *Manohar Joshi* v. *Nitin Bhaurao Patil* (AIR 1996 SC 796), Joshi, a candidate of the BJP–Shiv Sena alliance, appealed to the Supreme Court after the Bombay High Court declared the election result void under the Representation of the People Act of 1951, finding that speeches given by Joshi and other leaders of the BJP–Shiv Sena alliance constituted "corrupt practices" under the act. The Supreme Court reversed the decision, dismissing much of the election petition on essentially procedural grounds. With regard to Joshi's own statements, the Court reiterated that "the word 'Hindutva' by itself does not invariably mean Hindu religion" (*Joshi*, paragraph 58). Without much explanation, the Court added that Joshi's declaration that "the first Hindu State will be established in Maharashtra" did not constitute an appeal for votes on the basis of religion, but merely an "expression, at best, of such a hope" (*Joshi*, paragraph 73).

In contrast to the Court's understanding of "Hindutva," the term "Hindutva" was developed by early leaders of the Hindu right as a political conceptualization of the Hindu nation that was centered around religion (Cossman and Kapur 1997: 129–34). As noted above, the Hindutva movement is at its core a political strategy that aspires toward the creation of a Hindu state and the subordination and assimilation of religious minorities therein. The Court's conflation of Hindutva with "Indian culture" also assumed a level of cultural homogeneity that in reality does not exist. The Hindu nationalist movement is both led by, and protects the interests of, a small minority of India's "upper" castes and classes. The success of the movement, however, relies on its ability to lay claim to the majority mantle and develop a collective consciousness that in many ways defies the "essential characteristics of Hinduism" (Jaffrelot 1996: 1) and the caste system's rigid and hierarchical social stratification.

Jaffrelot sees Hindu nationalism as a modern sociocultural and political phenomenon "which took place despite the original characteristics of Hinduism" (Jaffrelot 1996: 5) and sketches a "process of cultural reorganisation launched in reaction to external threats, real and/or imagined, in the form of proselytisation by Christian missionaries, the impact of British rule and the militancy of the Muslim minority" (Jaffrelot 1996: 6). This process of cultural reorganization includes a deliberate strategy to recast traditionally marginalized groups – such as Dalits (so-called "Untouchables") and Adivasis (tribal community members) – into a Hindu identity and deploy them in opposition to the Christian/Muslim Other. Politically, the vilification of Christians and Muslims is also a synthesizing feature of Hindutva that helps to consolidate the Hindu vote bank while stemming the tide of defecting Dalit and Adivasi voters to other parties (Narula 2003a: 52).[2]

The Hindutva decision was seen as a victory for the "upper-caste" dominated Hindu right. Citing the *Prabhoo* decision, the BJP's 1999 manifesto declared Hindutva to be compatible with secularism (Jacobsohn 2003: 201). The Sangh Parivar's overall political strategy has led to electoral success on both the state and the central level, which in turn has given rise to the introduction of legislation in a number of states to ban religious conversions under the pretext of "protecting" Dalits and Adivasis from Christian missionaries. A spate of attacks on members of the Christian community since 1998 in BJP-dominant states has also been blamed on the violent activities and hate propaganda of Sangh Parivar–affiliated groups, as has the forcible "reconversion" of Dalits and Adivasis to Hinduism (Narula 2007: 367). The movement's turn to violence is not a recent phenomenon, however. Numerous commissions of inquiry officially appointed to investigate communal riots between Hindus and Muslims in India since the partition of India and Pakistan have indicted Hindu nationalist groups for their role in violent crimes against India's minorities. The two most prominent episodes of violence related directly to the Ram temple campaign.

HINDU NATIONALIST GROUPS AND COMMUNAL VIOLENCE

Ayodhya and its aftermath

On December 6, 1992, following years of political propaganda and incitements to violence, the Babri Masjid was demolished by a frenzied mob of Hindu nationalist supporters (Human Rights Watch 1996). In the months preceding the demolition, the BJP, the RSS, the VHP, and the Shiv Sena

[2] For more on Dalits see Jenkins's chapter in this volume.

had amplified their call for the construction of a temple on the site of the mosque as integral to their struggle to achieve Hindu rule in India. The movement for the destruction of the mosque was also strategically timed to divert attention away from the 1990 Mandal Commission recommendation to extend reservations (or government quotas) to "Other Backward Castes" "which not only set Hindu castes against each other, but also threatened high caste dominance" (Upadhyaya 1992: 823).

Communal violence swept the country in the days that followed the mosque's destruction, reaching its peak in the city of Bombay – the capital of Maharashtra state and a Shiv Sena stronghold – where violence directed at Muslims claimed hundreds of lives, the vast majority of them Muslim. Police fired on Muslim demonstrators, entered and burned Muslim homes, and fired on their residents. Hindus marching in support of the destruction of the mosque were left alone. In the latter days of the violence, members of the Shiv Sena attacked Muslim households alongside the police (Narula 2003a: 47–8).

Following the demolition of the mosque, and the subsequent anti-Muslim violence that engulfed many parts of the country, President's Rule was imposed in the states of Madhya Pradesh, Himachal Pradesh, and Rajasthan on the grounds that these state governments had failed to uphold the constitutional commitment to secularism. The government's decision to impose President's Rule was seen as political in nature: A Congress Party-led central government dismissed three BJP-led state governments but did not dismiss the Congress-led government of Maharashtra where the post-Ayodhya violence was at its worst (Jacobsohn 2003: 130). In the landmark case of *S. R. Bommai* v. *Union of India* (AIR 1994 SC 1,918) the Supreme Court of India upheld the dismissal of the three state governments by the central government pursuant to Article 356 of the Constitution, and held that secularism was a "basic feature" of the Indian Constitution. While in the past the Court would examine laws with reference to religion-related constitutional provisions, such as Article 25, in *Bommai* the Court went a step further to examine the "validity of actions with reference to secularism" (Sathe 2002: 57). Efforts to hold individual culprits responsible for the post-Ayodhya violence, however, found little traction.

Senior officials of Hindu nationalist political parties were implicated in instigating the anti-Muslim violence in 1992. The Maharashtra government–appointed Srikrishna Commission, which presented its report more than five years after the 1992–3 Bombay violence took place, determined that the violence was the result of a systematic and deliberate effort to incite violence against Muslims. Specifically, the report singled out Shiv Sena leader Bal Thackeray and Manohar Joshi (who went on to become chief minister of Maharashtra) for their role in inciting the violence. The state government led by the Shiv Sena and the BJP refused to adopt the Commission's recommendations and labeled the report "anti-Hindu" (Srikrishna 1998).

The question of what to do with the disputed religious site in Ayodhya also remained unresolved. The Court soon found itself once again delving into the murky territory of what constituted essential religious practices, and therefore entitled to protection under Article 25 of the Indian Constitution. In a case challenging the validity of a law enacted for the purposes of state acquisition of the disputed site of land in Ayodhya (*Faruqui* v. *Union of India*, AIR 1995 SC 605) the Court held that offering prayers in a mosque was not "essential" to the practice of Islam. The Court upheld the constitutionality of The Acquisition of Certain Area at Ayodhya Act of 1993, which froze the status quo at the disputed site and thus allowed Hindu worship to continue while forbidding Muslim worship nearby. Though the Court employed the rhetoric of secularism, it interpreted the meaning of secularism and ruled on the legal questions in a manner that favored the Hindu nationalist claim (Parikh 2005: 98). Subsequent developments, however, reaffirmed the Court's commitment to secularism. In *Mohd. Aslam @ Buhre* v. *Union of India* (AIR 2003 SC 3,413), it prohibited all religious activity on the disputed site, voicing concern for the rights of the Muslim minority; since then, it has allowed the national government to establish a trust comprised of Hindu and Muslim trustees responsible for proposing amicable solutions to the dispute (Parikh 2005: 102). The *Buhre* judgment followed on the heels of the 2002 anti-Muslim massacres in the BJP-led western state of Gujarat for which Hindu nationalist groups were most responsible.

Godhra and its aftermath

The violence in Gujarat began on February 27, 2002 in the town of Godhra where two carriages of a train carrying Hindu activists were set on fire killing at least fifty-eight people, many of them women and children. The activists were returning from Ayodhya, where they supported the VHP-led campaign to construct a temple on the site of the destroyed mosque. Because the fire was immediately preceded by a skirmish between the Hindu passengers and Muslims at the train station, the police – despite a lack of hard evidence – proceeded on the assumption that the fire was the result of a Muslim conspiracy (Nussbaum 2007: 19). In the days that followed,

Muslims were branded as terrorists by government officials and the local media while armed gangs set out on a four-day retaliatory killing spree directed at the broader Muslim population in Gujarat. The attackers, shouting Hindu-right slogans, destroyed Muslim homes, businesses, and places of worship (Nussbaum 2007: 20). Scores of women and girls were brutally raped and sexually mutilated before being burned to death. In the weeks that followed the massacres, Muslims destroyed Hindu homes and businesses in continued retaliatory violence. Over 2,000 people were killed and close to 100,000 were displaced by the violence, an overwhelming majority of whom were Muslim (Narula 2002: 4–6). The Gujarat massacres were a testament to the success of the Hindu nationalist strategy to recast marginalized groups into a Hindu identity and deploy them against religious minorities; Dalits and Adivasis were implicated in some of the attacks against Muslims.

According to eyewitnesses, state officials of the BJP were directly involved in the Gujarat attacks. In many instances – as was the case in Bombay in 1992 – the police sided with the attackers and participated in the violence (Narula 2002: 4–5). Investigations by the Concerned Citizens' Tribunal, headed by former Indian Supreme Court judges, pointed the finger at senior ministers from Gujarat Chief Minister Narendra Modi's cabinet who allegedly held a meeting just hours after the attack in Godhra to draw up and disseminate plans to carry out the attacks on Muslims (Narula 2003a: 5). Modi also allegedly met with top police officials and gave oral directives not to interfere with the Hindu retaliation against Muslims (Narula 2003a: 34).

Both the magnitude of the Gujarat violence and the widespread impunity in its aftermath have been attributed to the success of the Hindu nationalist movement's infiltration of key state agencies and institutions, including the police and the judiciary. Since the BJP first assumed power in the state in 1995, it has stacked its inner ranks with VHP and RSS members as well as others who share and actively promote the Sangh Parivar's policies and programs (Narula 2002: 41). The violence has also proved a useful election strategy: The BJP-led government has twice been re-elected to office since the 2002 massacres. In the December 2002 elections, using posters and videotapes of the Godhra train attack, and rhetoric that depicted Muslims as terrorists intent on destroying the Hindu community, the party gained the most seats in areas affected by the communal violence. A number of winning candidates were implicated by eyewitnesses in the attacks (Narula 2003a: 6–7). The election results, in turn, also helped ensure impunity from prosecution for those who orchestrated the attacks (Narula 2003a: 52).

After more than two years of repeated acquittals in Gujarat – and following the sabotaging of cases through, *inter alia*, evidence tampering, witness intimidation, and the removal of names of state officials and other perpetrators allegedly involved in the violence from First Information Reports (Narula 2003a: 5) – the Supreme Court stepped in to transfer key cases from the jurisdiction of Gujarat courts to the Bombay High Court, and later ordered the reopening of over 2,000 cases that had been prematurely closed by the police. Citing "collusion between the government and prosecution," the Supreme Court lambasted the Gujarat government as "modern day 'Neros'" who "were looking elsewhere when ... innocent children and helpless women were burning, and were probably deliberating how the perpetrators of the crime can be protected" (*Zahira Habibullah Sheikh* v. *State of Gujarat*, AIR 2004 SC 3,146, paragraph 69). The transferring of cases outside of Gujarat led ultimately to a handful of convictions but widespread problems with investigations remained.

In March 2008, the Court ordered the setting up of a Special Investigation Team (SIT) chaired by former Central Bureau of Investigation Chief Inspector R. Raghavan. The SIT was mandated to reinvestigate and examine witnesses in relation to the Godhra train-burning case and a number of key post-Godhra violence cases. The order – made in response to a 2003 plea by the National Human Rights Commission to transfer several high-profile massacre cases out of Gujarat – stopped short of moving the cases outside the state but empowered the SIT to conduct further investigations and file supplementary charge-sheets (*National Human Rights Commission* v. *State of Gujarat & Others*, writ petition 109/2003, order 03/26/2008).

In September 2008, the Gujarat government-appointed Commission of Inquiry for the Godhra incident and subsequent violence released Part 1 of its findings. Under the guidance of its chairman, Justice G. T. Nanavati, the Commission was in part tasked with investigating "the adequacy of administrative measures taken" to prevent the post-Godhra crime wave (Nanavati and Mehta 2008: 3). According to the report, the Commission reached three major conclusions. First, it found no connection between the Godhra train fire and the subsequent wave of violence against Muslims (Nanavati and Mehta 2008: 10). Second, the Commission concluded that the attack was the result of "a conspiracy to burn ... [the] train coming from Ayodhya and to cause harm to the [Hindu activists] travelling in that coach" (Nanavati and Mehta 2008: 172) but found "no evidence regarding involvement of any definite religious or political organization in the conspiracy" (Nanavati and Mehta 2008: 175–6). Third, though the Commission's findings regarding the post-Godhra violence against Muslims had not been released at this writing, the Commission dismissed the possibility that any ministers or police officers lapsed in providing protection to the victims of the subsequent "communal riots" (Nanavati and Mehta 2008: 176) despite a mountain of evidence to the contrary.

Some have sharply criticized the Nanavati report for not holding Gujarat's Chief Minister Narendra Modi accountable for his role in the post-Godhra violence. For example, one organization noted that the Nanavati Commission quickly brushed off the possibility of government complicity, ignoring requests for the cross-examination of several high-level Gujarati ministers (Jan Sangharsh Manch 2008: preamble no. 3). The group additionally criticized the Commission for ignoring several key pieces of testimony before reaching the conclusion that there was a conspiracy behind the Godhra attack (Jan Sangharsh Manch: no. 3f, no. 3l).

Large-scale episodes of anti-Muslim violence following the destruction of the Babri Masjid in Ayodhya and the burning of the train carrying Hindu activists in Godhra reveal the dangers of Hindu nationalist militancy and the ease with which Hindu nationalist rhetoric has been deployed to incite popular fear and garner electoral support. The police–politician–criminal nexus in Maharashtra and Gujarat, among other states, has all but guaranteed impunity for these crimes; at the time of writing, none of the political leaders and officials implicated in either episode of violence had been brought to justice and only a handful of the thousands of cases registered had resulted in convictions. The infiltration of the police, prosecutors, and in some cases the lower judiciary by members of the Sangh Parivar is a significant part of the impunity equation and has led to a selective and biased application of the law. Both the episodes and their aftermath also testify to the undue influence of Hindu nationalist groups on India's criminal-justice system.

CONCLUSION

The tension inherent in the Indian Constitution's dual commitment to ensuring equal treatment of all religions while subjugating religious freedom to the project of social reform has proven ripe for manipulation by the Hindu nationalist movement. The movement's majoritarian strain of secularism has served as a vehicle to oppose religious-minority interests under the guise of equal treatment, co-opting the rhetoric of secularism to legitimize Hindu primacy. The Supreme Court's record on issues concerning secularism has been mixed at best. The Court's decisions in *Shah Bano* and *Sarla Mudgal*, while serving in part to advance Muslim women's rights, did so through assimilationist language that called for national unity and disapproved of citizens' "loyalties" to their personal laws. While the Court was lauded for reaffirming the principle of secularism in cases such as *Bommai*, its subsequent decisions in the Hindutva cases were heavily critiqued for failing to protect secularism from the threat of the Hindutva agenda.

Despite the Court's problematic engagement with personal laws and its mixed record on issues concerning the challenge posed to secularism by Hindu nationalists, it has stepped in to provide much-needed accountability checks in the face of grave episodes of communal violence. The Court's actions following the post-Godhra violence were, for example, seen as a scathing rebuke of the government of Gujarat. But while these procedural interventions helped stem the tide of acquittals, the Court fell short of holding the state and its institutions responsible for the violence itself, revealing once again the extent to which the law operates in the context of Hindu nationalism, and not the other way around.

The Sangh Parivar's success in capturing political power and infiltrating the machinery of law enforcement in a number of states has also led to a selective application of the law and to the passing of legislation that harms minority interests. Ultimately, while civil society has attempted to use the courts and the Constitution to provide a stalwart defense against the rise of Hindu nationalism, as noted throughout this chapter, the law itself has been unduly influenced by the power of the movement.

CHAPTER 16

Legally and politically layered identities: a thumbnail survey of selected Hindu migration patterns from South Asia

Jayanth K. Krishnan

INTRODUCTION

This chapter will survey the several historic centers of the Hindu diaspora and the circumstances that led to these migrations, offering a brief discussion of the legal and political issues encountered by the Hindu communities in their adopted homelands, and the responses these communities have offered in order to solidify or improve their position within their respective societies. In addition, illustrative case studies will be interspersed that shed light on how the Hindu communities in their environments have asserted their legal and political status, which routinely has involved claiming not simply a Hindu identity, but multiple, or layered, identities instead.

DEFINING "DIASPORA" AND MAPPING WHO WENT WHERE

The use of the term "diaspora" has been a matter of debate among scholars (see, e.g., Brown 2006: 4; Chander 2001: 1,006; Rukmani 2001: xi; Vertovec 2000: 141–59). Here we will adopt Brown's proposal to apply the word "diaspora" to:

> groups of people with a common ethnicity; who have left their original homeland for prolonged periods of time and often permanently; who retain a particular sense of cultural identity and often close kinship links with other scattered members of their group, thus acknowledging their shared physical and cultural origins; and who maintain links with that homeland and a sense of its role in their present identity. (Brown 2006: 4)

The value of Brown's definition is that it allows for considering a range of factors – from flight from persecution to voluntary migration – in modeling a South Asian Hindu diaspora.

Signs of a Hindu presence beyond the Indian subcontinent date back at least to the early centuries of the Common Era. Indian merchants controlled trade in the Bay of Bengal and the Indian Ocean as far east as the Straits of Malacca. Indian trading communities also appear to have emerged along the coasts of mainland Southeast Asia and Sumatra (Cœdès 1968; Kulke 1993). It is important to note, however, that these diaspora sailors who clustered around the region's coastal markets were a tiny population compared to the indigenous rulers and subjects who inhabited these territories. To be sure, there were those artisans, scribes, Brahmins, and monks from India who were brought to the upland capitals to serve the courts but, even with the addition of these groups, Hindus from the subcontinent were but a fraction of the overall population (Kulke 1993). Nevertheless, emulating Indian royal states, the indigenous rulers of this area actively imported Indic religious, political, and legal practices, including aspects of the Dharmaśāstra. An "interplay" (Lubin in press) between these imports and local customs and institutions resulted in distinctive forms of Hinduism and legal traditions influenced by Hindu law in Cambodia up to 1431, and even to the early 1500s in Indonesia (Ricklefs 1991). And although Islam eventually displaced Hinduism as the primary religion of this region, a Hindu culture persists in Bali and in the highlands of Java to this day, and in what is today Malaysia where there are presently over 1.5 million Hindus.

The movement of Hindus beyond South Asia in the ancient and medieval period was on a small scale, mainly in connection with trade and diplomacy. In the modern era, the numbers of South Asians living abroad rose dramatically. Vertovec describes how "large-scale migration and settlement of South Asian people abroad can be divided into two major periods" (2000: 15). The first of these waves began when the British outlawed slavery in their domains in the first part of the nineteenth century; indentured servitude came to replace it as a means of supplying inexpensive labor. During the 1800s and into the early 1900s the British transported indentured laborers to other parts of the world, including "Mauritius, Guyana, Surinam, Trinidad, Jamaica, and other British and French West Indian islands, South Africa, East Africa and Fiji, . . . and Burma and Malaysia" (2000: 15).

The second major wave took place after World War II. Because of new educational and employment opportunities and more favorable governmental policies in many potential host countries, South Asians (mainly Hindu) began migrating to the United Kingdom, the United States, Canada, Australia, New Zealand, continental Europe, and the Arab Gulf region (Baumann 2001; Bilimoria 2001; Brown 2006; Menski 1999, 2007; Pearson 2001; Vertovec 2000). Moreover, during the past couple of decades, for different political or socioeconomic reasons, there has been a growth in what are referred to as "twice migrants" (Vertovec 2000: 15) – members of the Hindu diaspora in one adopted country who have relocated to another.

While previous research has addressed how Hindus have adjusted (or failed to adjust) to their different environments socially, culturally, linguistically, and economically, the questions of import for this chapter are: What legal and political problems has this diaspora faced over time in the various settings; and how have these encounters shaped this community's legal and political identities in their respective places of residence? We turn to these issues next.

THE "FIRST WAVE" OF MIGRATION

Africa

In eastern Africa, while there is evidence that "small settlements of coastal traders" (Morris 1956: 194) date their South Asian ancestry back nearly 2,000 years, the main influx of immigration came in the nineteenth century. On the island of Zanzibar, for example, the Sultan of Oman, working with the British, brought over various communities from western India in an effort to strengthen his hold over the international slave and ivory trade in which he was engaged. Although many of these Indians included Muslims, Christians, and Jains, Hindus were prominent, including the Bhatia family, which became the Sultan's main custom and tax collectors (Younger 2001: 367–8).

By the late 1800s, the British had consolidated their hold over Zanzibar, Uganda, Kenya, and Tanganyika. They set about building a railroad which would run from the coastline to Lake Victoria (Morris 1956: 195; Younger 2001: 368). Initially, Punjabis were sent by the British to work on the rail project, but "more than 90 percent returned ... at the end of their contracts" (Morris 1956: 195). Once this infrastructure was built, though, a new set of entrepreneurial, commercially oriented Indians – mostly Gujaratis of diverse castes and religions – traveled to East Africa and by 1910 firmly established themselves as the region's preeminent artisans, traders, and merchants (Pocock 1957; Vertovec 2000: 91; Younger 2001: 368). In addition, a new cohort of workers from Punjab arrived (Muslims, Sikhs, and Hindus) to pursue employment in the textile sector (D. Kapur 2006; Younger 2001: 368–9). Thus, "By about 1910 the [Indian demographic] scene in East Africa was more or less set" (Morris 1956: 195).

One important factor that helped shape the legal identity of these Indians in East Africa was the way in which family (or "personal") law regimes were administered by the British between the late 1800s and the early 1960s. The British had established a general state court system that covered the jurisdictions of Tanganyika, Zanzibar, Kenya, and Uganda (Derrett 1963: 535; also see Menski 2006: 450–1). Within this setting though, as Menski has observed, a "plural system of laws" (2006: 451) existed, whereby in addition to these courts the British delegated certain amounts of legal and political authority to local Africans and also accepted the presence of indigenous law, some of which "could be extensively manipulated and turned into official customary law, while many other customs remained in the unofficial realm" (Menski 2006: 451). In terms of personal-law disputes, the state courts attempted to apply the religious law, which for Hindus were laws statutorily codified by the British in each of the four territories (Derrett 1963: 536). There was no uniformity in these four sets of laws (likely because of demographic differences in each of the territories) and, perhaps not surprisingly, how these statutes were then applied varied from jurisdiction to jurisdiction (Derrett 1962b: 396–7).

For example, in Zanzibar there had been virtually no updating of Hindu law by the British during the twentieth century. The Hindu population who lived in this territory were governed by the Anglo-Hindu law developed in India by the British during the eighteenth and nineteenth centuries and interpreted primarily by the Bombay High Court (Derrett 1963: 537, 554–5). Furthermore, despite the changes made to the Anglo-Hindu law by the post-Independence Indian government's enactment of the 1955–6 Hindu Code, which included abandoning the *varṇa* distinctions, the indissolubility of marriage, the preference for the extended joint family, and inheritance only by males and those who could confer spiritual benefit (see Galanter and Krishnan 2000: 108), there is little evidence to suggest that Zanzibar took into account this modernizing evolution. In Tanganyika though, the British gave "scope for the personal law ... to be wider" (Derrett 1963: 549), statutorily codifying a great deal of deference to the Hindu community in matters of marriage, succession, and the like.

But in the cases of Kenya and Uganda, a very different situation arose. In certain instances, the codified Hindu personal laws here were more conservative than their African counterparts or the 1955–6 Indian Hindu Code (for example, in fixing the conditions under which Hindus could marry, divorce, or serve as guardians). There were then those times when the Kenyan and Ugandan laws essentially incorporated what the reformed Indian Hindu Code stated, for example when it came to how marriage ceremonies were to be conducted. And between Kenya and Uganda differences sometimes existed in how each addressed certain types of Hindu personal law issues in their own respective jurisdiction (Derrett 1962b: 398–403). In sum, while it may have seemed logical for Hindus in East Africa to have been treated by the British uniformly, this did not occur, and consequently, as Derrett has observed, the status of one's Hindu identity in personal-law matters was squarely affected by the jurisdiction where that individual lived, which ultimately led to both "ineffectiveness" and "inefficiency" (Derrett 1962b: 397) in the overall administration of this legal regime.

Yet the best-known episodes that affected the legal standing of Hindus in East Africa took place following the British departure from the region in the 1960s. Although they made up no more than 3 percent of the population in newly independent Kenya, Uganda, or Tanzania (which comprised the former Tanganyika and Zanzibar), many Hindus had come to thrive economically and professionally in these countries. But even with this economic privilege, Hindus in these environments often kept to themselves, not interacting with the local African population (Brown 2006: 46). Furthermore, because they had not participated vigorously in the independence efforts and frequently were perceived as sympathizing with the British – a perception confirmed when Hindus in large numbers opted for British citizenship rather than the citizenship in the new nation-states – resentment toward this diaspora only intensified among the indigenous populations as well as among government leaders (Brown 2006: 46).

Given mounting political and economic pressure, politicians in each of these countries often used South Asians as scapegoats for the problems that were present. Kenya, Tanzania, and Uganda all passed statutes that restricted several public-sector and lucrative private-sector posts only to indigenous Africans. In addition, South Asians' assets were frozen by the East African states to prevent money transfers out of the country (Brown 2006: 46–8). The response by the unwanted communities was not surprising. Between 1965 and the early part of 1968 some 35,000 left Kenya for Britain; and in Dar-es-Salaam, the Tanzanian capital, there was a drop of nearly two-thirds in the number of South Asians present by the end of the 1960s (Brown 2006: 47). Worst of all, though, was that in Uganda, under the brutal leadership of Idi

Amin, the 80,000 Hindu "bloodsuckers" (as they were derisively called; Somerville 2002), were ordered out of the country, a mandate with which most complied (Brown 2006: 46; Twaddle 1975).

The result was an identity crisis in these diasporic communities. On the one hand, because they rarely integrated with the local population and occasionally sympathized (or were perceived as sympathizing) with the British, Hindus and other South Asians identified themselves (and were identified by the locals and the colonial power) as politically, legally, religiously, economically, and socially distinct from the majority population. At the same time, many of them had up to three generations of family who had lived in East Africa; their ties to India were minimal and for all intents and purposes their physical and emotional connections were to Africa. Leaving the only home they ever knew was thus devastating and a complete betrayal by the respective environments to which they felt they had given so much.

This identity dilemma was present in other parts of the continent as well. In South Africa, for example, there had been a demand by Hindus and other South Asians during the late nineteenth and early twentieth centuries for greater rights under the British Crown. Mohandas Gandhi, a Hindu from the Bania caste who had been educated in England as a lawyer and traveled to South Africa to establish a legal career, was one of the architects of this movement. In his autobiography, Gandhi conceded that while he was concerned about the plight of the local African population, his efforts and energy centered on uplifting the rights of those from his own community and South Asians at large (Gandhi 1966). In part, this was because he "did not want to impose his leadership on" the local Africans (Anbarasan 2004).

But there is evidence that at least in Natal and Transvaal, where Gandhi spent much of his time, identity politics clearly influenced Gandhi's priorities and perspective on advancing the agenda of those within his community. For example, in one petition to the British, Gandhi "successfully demanded that ... authorities should provide three entrances instead of two in public buildings, so that Indians would have their own and would not have to share one with Africans" (Power 1969: 445). He also believed that, while his community should not be required to meet constant and demeaning registration and identification requirements, enforcing such measures against Africans might not be problematic (Power 1969: 445–6). During this same time as well, Gandhi had urged many of his constituents to join ambulance teams to help injured British soldiers fighting first in the Boer War (1899–1902) and then in the suppression by the British of a Zulu rebellion in 1906, with the hopes that such participation might yield better treatment from the colonial elite (Power 1969: 442). And he initially did not seek to expand voting rights universally for all people of color in this territory – attempting instead to preserve the limited franchise on behalf of those he was championing (Power 1969: 448–9).

By taking these positions, the perception was reinforced that Hindus and other South Asians were at best apathetic to the majority black population. Beginning in 1906, Gandhi and other leaders in his movement turned away from tactics of accommodation to tactics of engagement and confrontation, including politically lobbying, litigating, promoting grassroots awareness campaigns, and organizing civil disobedience protests. (Indeed Gandhi's conceptualization and reliance on *satyāgraha*, which he would later use in India as part of his tactical arsenal to oust the British, was first employed at this time [Power 1969: 452, 455].) This shift in strategy came as the British delegated increasing amounts of governing responsibilities to the Dutch Afrikaner authorities, who in turn sought to consolidate their power by passing a spate of legally repressive statutes. Subsequently, as Gandhi and his colleagues ratcheted up their fight against the racial discrimination perpetuated by the British and Afrikaners in a land which, although foreign, they (the Hindus and other South Asians) still considered home, they continued to do so in a type of vacuum, more or less independent of the local African population who of course faced institutional bigotry from the same colonial regime. In fact, years later Gandhi remained unapologetic for pursuing this course of action, believing the norms and circumstances of the day required "that Africans should carry out their own struggle" against colonialism (Anbarasan 2004; also see Power 1969: 447–9).

We thus see that these Asians in South Africa sought to secure a discrete legal identity within this multicultural society. Let us move to another country where Hindu identity politics also emerged during this first wave of migration: Fiji.

Fiji

The nation-state of Fiji is located in the South Pacific Ocean and comprises a chain of islands with a population of over 850,000. Approximately one-third are Hindus, mainly of Indo-Fijian ethnic origin. Large numbers of Hindus began arriving in Fiji during the last quarter of the nineteenth century, transported by the British as indentured servants. From 1876 to 1919, some 60,000 Indians from both North and South India came to Fiji, 85 percent of them Hindu (Kelly 1991: 1–2). Indentured labor ended in Fiji in 1919 and within a decade Hindus began politically mobilizing for representation in the colonial government (Kelly 1991: 2–6), although they had difficulty making headway in the legislative assembly during the late 1920s and 1930s. At the same time, there was an ongoing struggle within this religious group as to the direction in which Fijian Hinduism would move. According to both Kelly (Kelly 1991: 6) and Gillion (1977), a clash between the reformist Arya Samaj and the more conservative Sanatan Dharm occurred, with the latter eventually able to convince the Fijian courts and legislature to declare the Arya Samaj's interpretation of Hinduism illegal. Today, three-quarters of Fijian Hindus are adherents of Sanatan Dharm.

In addition to this intra-Hindu discord, there has also been tension between religious and ethnic groups – particularly between the Hindu Indo-Fijians and the Christian indigenous community – before (but especially since) independence from Britain in 1970. Arguably, the main legal and political issue that has dominated the public landscape in Fiji has been how much representation these ethnic and religious groups would be given in government (B. Lal 1998). A compromise brokered by the Crown upon its departure in 1970 divided up seats in the national Parliament on the basis of ethno-religious ties (B. Lal 1998; Lawson 1991). Still, there has been debate over how great a role Hindus may play in politics; consider that as late as 1997 only indigenous (Christian) Fijians could hold the office of Prime Minister.[1] Since the late 1980s, there have been four military coups, including the toppling of the country's first Hindu Prime Minister, Mahendra Chaudhry, in 2000. The military continues to dominate the political establishment to this day and of major concern to the Hindu community of late has been the promotion of Christianity as the state religion as well as a series of desecrations against various Hindu temples by vandals.[2]

The Caribbean

The role of religion in the public square has also been of significance in different Caribbean states which experienced an influx of Hindu migration during the nineteenth and early part of the twentieth century. Between 1838 and the end of World War 1, about half a million Indians – 85 percent of

[1] This was changed in 1997 after an amendment was added to the Constitution allowing for Indo-Fijians, including Hindus, to serve as Prime Minister. (The Hindu American Foundation [2007: 30–4] has published a study documenting this and other points as well.)

[2] See Hindu American Foundation (2007); also note that the Hindu community's grievances have been voiced in particular by the Fiji Labor Party which is headed up by the former Prime Minister, Mahendra Chaudhry.

whom were Hindus – had been hired as indentured laborers to work in this region (Vertovec 2000: 43–4). What are now the countries of Guyana, Surinam, and Trinidad were among the places with the highest number of laborers who came from India.[3] It is important to remember that, while Trinidad and Guyana were British colonies until 1962 and 1966 respectively, Surinam was under Dutch control until 1975. Migrants from India came to Surinam as a result of a nineteenth-century treaty signed between Britain and the Netherlands in which the former provided laborers to this Dutch colony (Ramsoedh and Bloemberg 2001: 125). And while clearly each of these nation-states has had its own distinct historical, cultural, demographic, and linguistic traditions, there are some definite similarities in how the Hindu diaspora in each setting has asserted itself (Vertovec 1994).

For example, because Caribbean Hindus were "thrust together on plantations far from India, [this] militated against any such successful continuity" of living in a segregated manner as they might have done in their homeland (Vertovec 2000: 49). Moreover, upon their arrival, Hindus in this region created their own version of Hinduism which, although still very much a minority religion, managed to serve as a competitor in the public square to the other existing faiths, including missionary-fueled Christianity (Vertovec 2000: 52). Interestingly, however, this plural group of Hindus who had come together despite their differences in each context turned to Brahmins to consolidate and lead their community into the twentieth century (van der Burg and van der Veer 1986; Ramsoedh and Bloemberg 2001; Vertovec 2000: 52–7). Even though caste divisions were not as stark as they were in India, Brahmins continued to possess legitimacy and influence which helped shape how this Caribbean form of Hinduism was practiced (Vertovec 2000: 53).

The power and influence of these Caribbean Brahmins, who promoted a more traditional vision of the faith, was further solidified after they successfully defeated challenges from those of the Arya Samaj sect – the same group that had unsuccessfully advocated for reforms in Fiji (Vertovec 2000: 55–7). Space constraints limit discussion of this fascinating development during the 1900s, but this point has been explored elsewhere in detail (see Vertovec 2000 for literature review). Perhaps the most noteworthy finding from these accounts, for our purposes, was that several orthodox Hindu "interest groups" in Guyana, Surinam, and Trinidad turned their attention to politics. Certain political parties crystallized around the religious tenets

[3] Vertovec (2000: 44) notes that the "net immigration," after taking into account Indians who came and then returned to their original homes, was: 153,362 in Guyana (between 1838 and 1917), 110,645 in Trinidad (between 1845 and 1917), and 22,745 in Surinam (between 1873 and 1916).

espoused by these Brahmanical leaders and, although in recent years some younger Caribbean Hindus have broken from their orthodox roots, politics in each of these nation-states remains influenced by the demands of those who practice this conservative brand of Hinduism (Vertovec 2000: 58–62).

MIGRATION TO "SECOND-WAVE" NATION-STATES

We thus far have briefly sketched parts of the first major modern-day migration patterns of Hindus who traveled from South Asia during the last part of the nineteenth century through the early parts of the twentieth century. In this section, we examine what has been referred to as the second wave.

Noticeable Hindu migration to different parts of the globe also came after World War II (Brown 2006: 39; Jensen 1988; Vertovec 2000: 15). Included, perhaps most prominently, among the places where Hindus landed during this period was the United Kingdom (Menski 1993, 1999, 2007). Immediately after the British scaled back the colonial empire, Hindus and others who had been "[c]itizens of Commonwealth countries[,] . . . had free right of access into Britain at this stage" (Brown 2006: 40). Therefore, Hindus of all skill-sets and backgrounds entered, leading today to their population being nearly 750,000 (Hindu Forum of Britain 2008). For example, there were Hindus from South Asia who immigrated to the UK; there were also those from East Africa who had been driven out by the regimes mentioned above. In addition, with their legal and political status in a precarious position after their respective countries had received independence, South African and Caribbean Hindus began migrating to the UK in the late 1960s and into the 1970s (Brown 2006: 49–50). These twice-migrants (Baumann 2001: 61; Bhachu 1985; Brown 2006: 45) brought with them great diversity which subsequently made the needs and demands of the Hindu community congregating in the UK quite diverse as well.

Consider the growth in temples alone in the UK in just one decade. To accommodate the different belief structures of this heterogeneous community, the number went from about 100 in 1982 to over 300 ten years later (Baumann 2001: 61). And the number is thought to be even higher as of 2008. Furthermore, given the changes in demographics over the past four decades – from a situation at first where it was primarily men who migrated and sent remittances home[4] to one where whole families immigrated – there

[4] Remittances – and more largely the subject of how emigration affects the economies of home countries (in particular, India) – have been importantly explored in a sophisticated fashion by the social scientist

has correspondingly been a proliferation of different Hindu-focused social, educational, and cultural groups located in various parts of the country (Baumann 2001: 61–2; Vertovec 2000).

With this increase in the population of Hindus in the UK, it should not be surprising that the courts too have encountered legal and political issues involving this community, often adjudicating procedural and jurisdictional questions. For example, in a case where a Hindu temple in the Indian state of Tamil Nadu sought to regain possession of a stolen idol from a British purchaser who had bought the deity under the belief that the transaction was legitimate, the British Court of Appeal deferred to the lower court's "researches into Hindu law" in finding that there was no public-policy reason for why the temple should not be afforded standing in the British courts (*Bumper Dev. Corp.* v. *Commission of Police of the Metropolis and Others* [1991], 1 WLR 1,362).[5] In another case published in 2004, however, where a Kenyan Hindu sought to gain standing in order to pursue an inheritance claim against a party residing in England, the Privy Council refused to entertain such a motion, ruling that the Kenyan courts were better able to handle Hindu family-law disputes (*Hindocha and Others* v. *Geewala and Others* [2004], 1 CLC 502). There have been other types of cases as well. Hindu law has been referenced in a range of immigration matters, including, for example, a well-known case where an adoption by British parents of a Hindu child in India, in accordance with the Indian Hindu Adoptions and Maintenance Act (1956), was not recognized as sufficient in the eyes of the British courts for the purposes of admitting the child into the country (*MN [India]* v. *Entry Clearance Officer [New Delhi], Secretary of State for the Home Department* [2008], WL 45,600). And in a petition by the Anglo-Asian Friendship Society, an administrative law judge recently ruled that the country should consider allowing Hindus to have open-air funeral pyre ceremonies, which currently are banned under British law (Ekklesia 2007). (Notably, the largest umbrella organization of Hindu temples and Hindu cultural groups, the Hindu Council of the UK, came out against the order arguing that the practice would be "unsuited to the British climate" [Ekklesia 2007].)

But perhaps the most publicized case in recent years centered around the slaughter of a cow deemed sacred by a Hindu community in Wales. Shambo (the cow) was found to have bovine tuberculosis, and as such was ordered by the Welsh legislative assembly to be destroyed. After stays

Devesh Kapur (see e.g., 2004; 2006). D. Kapur's latest book (2010) examines this topic as well and, while it is not yet available for review at the time of writing, its subject matter promises to be most rewarding.

[5] See Richard Davis's chapter in this volume.

were issued by lower-court judges, the Court of Appeal ultimately agreed with the government (*Surayanda* v. *The Welsh Ministers* 2007), and despite public pleas and protests, Shambo was put down in mid-2007.

The case of Shambo made national and international headlines, resulting in outrage from Hindus in India and from diaspora Hindus around the world. In Canada, for instance, where there are approximately 375,000 Hindus, that country's national Hindu Conference stated its "shock and dismay at the insensitive and unwarranted decision on the part of the Welsh government" (Banerjee 2007). Indeed in Canada and the United States, another country to which Hindus have migrated heavily since the 1960s, Hindu communities have participated in similar types of salient legal and political cases. Although Hindu presence on American soil dates back to the eighteenth century, the first mass migration of Hindus to the US came in 1965 after the federal government loosened immigration restrictions into the country. While the Hindu population was initially (and continues to be) stereotyped as focusing their skills in the medical, science, and high-tech fields (as well as in the hotel, convenience store, and taxicab sectors), in fact Hindus have long been involved in substantive questions of law and politics in American society (V. Lal 2008).

As early as the 1910s, federal courts were split as to whether Hindus from South Asia could be granted US citizenship. An existing federal statute dating back to 1790 allowed for the naturalization of citizenship for "free white persons," and at issue in these cases was how Congress intended these particular words to be defined. One judicial approach was that, since South Asian Hindus derived their ancestry from Aryans, who were Caucasian or white, Hindus qualified under the law for citizenship (*In Re Mohan Singh* [1919], 257 F. 209). A contrasting position was that the racial color of Hindus simply precluded them from claiming that they were white (*In Re Sardar Bhagwab Singh* [1917], 246 F. 496). In 1923 the US Supreme Court stepped in and resolved the dispute. In *United States* v. *Bhagat Singh Thindi* ([1923], 261 US 204), the Court held that individuals from South Asia – whether they were Hindus, Sikhs (a population that lower courts often misclassified as Hindus), or Muslims – were Asians and not Caucasian or white. The Court then went on to hold that, because there was a federal law prohibiting Asians from citizenship, people from South Asia too fell under this preclusion. The aftermath of the Court's decision resulted in the federal government targeting those Hindus (and other South Asians) who had become Americans and affirmatively stripping them of their citizenship (see, e.g., *United States* v. *Akhay Kumar Mozumdar* [1923], 296 F. 173; *United States* v. *Ali* [1925], 7 F. 2nd 728).

The *Thind* decision remained in effect for over two decades until President Harry Truman signed the Luce–Cellar Act of 1946. This law lifted the ban on South Asians naturalizing. Then in 1965 President Lyndon Johnson further enhanced all immigrants' rights, including those from South Asia, by signing into law the Immigration and Nationality Act, which allowed for greater immigration into the United States from countries previously discriminated against. In the years that followed, there was a massive growth in the number of Hindu immigrants (Nussbaum 2007: 302–29), and correspondingly their claims in American courts grew as well. The issues that American courts have adjudicated include:

- ruling that no immunity exists for one seeking to avoid testifying at a grand jury hearing on the claim that Hinduism prohibits it (*People* v. *Woodruff* [1966], 26 AD 2nd 236);
- ruling that under the first amendment preaching about Hinduism is permissible at a state fair (*International Society for Krishna Consciousness* v. *State Fair of Texas* [1979], 480 F. Supp. 67);
- ruling that Hindu inmates can have access to their religious texts and to Hindu meals (*Karmasu* v. *Tate* [1994], 95 Ohio App. 3d 399; *Widmer* v. *Moore* [2001], 776 So. 2nd 324; *Patel* v. *Wooten* [2001], 15 Fed. Appx. 647);
- ruling that Hindu-performed weddings can be binding (*Persad* v. *Balram* [2001], 724 NYS 2d 560);
- ruling that a mother who has primary custody of her child does not have to assent to the father's wish to perform *cūḍākaraṇa*, a Hindu life-cycle rite for a child (*Sagar* v. *Sagar* [2003], App. Ct. MA, 02-P-89);
- ruling against a Hindu couple who sought to challenge a local ordinance that banned housing cows on private property (*Village of Angelica* v. *Voith and Voith* [2006], 28 A.D.3d 1,193); and
- ruling on a case involving whether a Hindu organization could challenge proposed revisions to public-school textbooks that, in the group's view, unfairly depicted the practices and tenets of the faith (*Hindu American Foundation* v. *California State Board of Education* [2006], Case no. 06 CS 00386).

Other second-wave countries have not experienced the volume of Hindu-based litigation found in the United States and Britain. However, it is important not to discount the activity in which Hindus have been engaging in these other contexts. For example, in the Netherlands, where there are more than 215,000 Hindus, many of whom migrated from Surinam to escape the "Creole domination" (Brown 2006: 49) that was occurring in the

1970s and 1980s, there has been the emergence of various temples and social and cultural nongovernmental organizations; there has even been an ideological split between those who follow the above-mentioned Sanatan Dharm branch of Hinduism and those who adhere to the Arya Samaj movement (Brown 2006: 49–50). Australia and New Zealand are two other countries that have seen an influx of Hindus since the 1990s. For both these countries, a significant percentage has come from Fiji, but Hindus have also arrived from Singapore, Malaysia, Indonesia, and from different areas within India (Bilimoria 2001; Brown 2006: 51–2). Indeed in Australia there are now estimated to be nearly 150,000 Hindus and several Hindu-advocacy organizations as well, including the Hindu Council of Australia that attempts to serve as the "umbrella organization for the purpose of bringing together various [Australian] Hindu Associations ... [in order] to act as the representative of the Australian Hindu Community in dealings with the federal, state, and local governments" (Hindu Council of Australia 2008).

With the case of Australia, as in the other second-wave countries, we see Hindu communities increasingly calling for space, recognition, and protection to exercise their religion peaceably. The purpose of this short survey has been to trace the migratory patterns of Hindus over the course of time to demonstrate not only where they have traveled to, but also briefly to shed light on the challenges they have faced in their different environments. As Vertovec (2000) has argued, there is no one Hinduism for the diaspora; each community in its respective context develops its own practices, tenets, and belief structures to fit what is most workable for its constituents. Quite obviously, this chapter only scratches the surface of the different legal and political issues that need to be further fleshed out by future researchers. The hope is that this preliminary study will spur more in-depth inquiry into these sorts of specific issues. Only then will we have a better understanding of how Hindu communities around the world are attempting to preserve their faith while negotiating around the multitude of norms they invariably face within their adopted environments.

Glossary

Note on pronunciation: In romanized Indic-language names and italicized terms, short *a* is pronounced like the *u* in "but"; the other vowels have roughly the same values as in Spanish or Italian; *ṣ* and *ś* are pronounced like English *sh*; *c* is pronounced like English *ch*; and *h* after any other consonant simply adds extra breath, without changing the sound of the preceding consonant (thus, not *ph* as in "physics" or *th* as in "thin"). Other letters may be given their usual English values.

E = English; H = Hindi (or related North Indian language); L = Latin; S = Sanskrit

Most Sanskrit terms can be used in Hindi (usually dropping final *-a*).

ācāra	(S) custom, practice; customary rule; local law
adhikāra	(S) competence, qualification; authorization; responsibility
āśrama	(S) at first, a way of life (such as that of a married householder or ascetic); the *Mānava Dharmaśāstra* canonized the ideal of four sequential *āśrama*s (hence, "life-stages": student, householder, hermit, and homeless ascetic [*yati*; later, *saṃnyāsin*]; see Olivelle 1993)
bhakti	(S) devotion experienced as a direct personal contact or union with God; a largely vernacular devotional movement originating in seventh-century South India
bhāṣya	(S) "commentary," a prose text structured as a running explication or interpretation of a *sūtra* or *śāstra*
communis error facit ius	(L) "A common error makes law"

Dalit	(E < H) "oppressed," label often used to denote castes formerly known as "low caste" or "Untouchable," and often adopted today by members of such castes
daṇḍa	(S) "staff; royal scepter"; punishment, symbol of the king's authority to punish the guilty
deśadharma	(S) law peculiar to a region
dharma	(S) righteousness, duty, law; (H) religion
dharmādhikārin, -kārī	(S, H) state-appointed official, properly an expert in Dharmaśāstra, concerned especially with the enforcement of *prāyaścitta* and caste penalties
dharmaśāstra	(S) canonical treatise on *dharma*; *dharma* literature in general (capitalized in this sense); compare *śāstra*
dharmaśāstrin, -śāstrī	(S, H) expert in Dharmaśāstra
diaspora	(E) the dispersal or spread of people of a common religion or ethnicity due to political or economic pressures, leading to their long-term or permanent resettlement abroad; collectively, the people thus dispersed
divya	(S) "divine" proof, i.e., oath or ordeal
diwani (*dīvānī*)	(E < H) revenue collection under Islamic or colonial administration
jayapattra	(S) document recording success in a legal suit
kacahrī	(H) court of law, cutchery
kāvya	(S) ornate courtly poetry in Sanskrit
laukika	(S) "of this world; customary" (as opposed to "divine" or "sacred")
lekha, lekhya	(S) written document
manautī	(H) pledge, votive petition
Mandal Commission	a committee created in 1979, chaired by B. P. Mandal, to reassess government policies intended to benefit "backward classes," i.e., those socially or economically disadvantaged because of their caste status

mantrin	(S) minister, appointed high official of the state
mūla	(S) "root" or source (e.g., of *dharma*)
nibandha	(S) topically organized digest of quotations from various *smṛtis*
nyāya	(S) logic; legal reasoning; a judicial ruling (*nyāya-vāda*); by extension, "justice" in a legal proceeding
Other Backward Classes	(E) category used in Article 340 of the Indian Constitution to designate a roster of castes other than the Scheduled Castes and Scheduled Tribes and women as beneficiaries of reservations under Indian law; commonly abbreviated "OBCs"
pañcagavya	(S) the five pure products of the cow: milk, curd, butter, urine, manure
pandit (*paṇḍita*)	(E < S, H) learned man; expert in traditional learning
pramāṇa	(S) criterion or means of correct knowledge; authoritativeness; proof
prāmāṇya	(S) authority
prāyaścitta	(S) penance, ritual expiation according to Brahmanical Hindu ritual and Dharmaśāstra
purohita	(S) chief Brahmin priest of a king, responsible for performing his consecration and other rites of state
quod fieri non debuit factum valet	(L) "What ought not to have been done is valid, once done"
rājadharma	(S) the *dharma* of a king according to Dharmaśāstra
rājan	(S) king
reservations	(E) legally mandated quotas for lower castes and women in the public sphere, a form of compensatory discrimination or "affirmative action"
sabhā	(S) council of Brahmins constituted to make decisions or hear cases
sabhya	(S) appointed member of a *sabhā*

samaya	(S) established convention, sometimes recorded in a document (*pattra* / *patra* / *pātra*)
śapatha	(S) oath, an appeal to divine authority when used in court
śāsana	(S) command, especially a written royal decree, grant, or ruling
śāstra	(S) canonical treatise, composed mainly in verse, with any commentary thereon; field of scholastic expertise
śāstrin / *śāstrī*	(S/H) expert in *śāstra*
satī	(S) devoted wife who immolates herself on her husband's funeral pyre; in British usage ("suttee"), the (ostensibly voluntary) act itself
Scheduled Castes and Scheduled Tribes	(E) the categories used in Indian law to designate specifically enumerated castes and tribes to whom the policy of reservations applies; abbreviated SCs and STs
smṛti	(S) "memory" of Vedic precepts as recorded in *sūtra*s, *dharmaśāstra*s, and other Sanskrit works; often used as a synonym of "*dharmaśāstra*"
śruti	(S) the "audible" Vedic scriptures as preserved orally through rote memorization, held in Mīmāṃsā and Dharmaśāstra to have the highest authority of all sources of knowledge (*pramāṇa*s); contrasted with *smṛti*, which is considered second to *śruti* in authority
stare decisis	(L) "Stand by prior decisions"
sthiti	(S) rule based on customary norms (*ācāra*), sometimes recorded in a document (*pattra* / *patra* / *pātra*)
sūtra	(S) code of rules composed in compressed, aphoristic style in Sanskrit, generally one of the older canonical texts of tradition; the *dharmasūtra*s were the earliest works devoted to the rules of *dharma*
suttee	see *satī*

svadharma	(S) the *dharma* appropriate to oneself
twice migrants	(E) members of the Hindu diaspora of one adopted country who relocate to another
varṇa	(S) caste category in the fourfold hierarchy taught in Brahmanical doctrine: Brahmin, Kṣatriya, Vaiśya, Śūdra
varṇāśramadharma	(S) *dharma* defined in relation to caste (*varṇa*) and stage of life (*āśrama*), a concept established in the *Mānava Dharmaśāstra*
vijaya	(S) victory, success in litigation, sometimes recorded in a document (*pattra / patra / pātra*)
vyavahāra	(S) in general: social intercourse, commerce; in the *Arthaśāstra*: legally recognized transaction; in Dharmaśāstra: lawsuit, legal procedure
vyavasthā	(S) ruling, decision, determination of a case by a pandit serving as law officer to a court, sometimes recorded in a document (*pattra / patra / pātra*)

Bibliography

CASES

Anandi Pai v. *Hari Suba Pai* (1909), ILR 33 Bom 404.
Ashoka Kumar Thakur v. *Union of India and Others* (2008), SCCL.COM 436.
Babubhai Girdharlal v. *Girdharlal Hargovandas* (1937), 61 Bom 708.
Bhagirthibai v. *Kahnujirav* (1886), ILR 11 Bom 285.
Bumper Dev. Corp. v. *Commission of Police of the Metropolis and Others* (1991), 1 WLR 1,362.
Collector of Madura v. *Moottoo Ramalinga* (1868), 12 MIA 397.
Danial Latifi v. *Union of India* (2001), 7 SCC 740.
Faruqui v. *Union of India* (1995), AIR 1995 SC 605.
Gratz v. *Bollinger* (2003), 539 US 244.
Grutter v. *Bollinger* (2003), 539 US 306.
Hindocha and Others v. *Geewala and Others* (2004), 1 CLC 502.
Hindu American Foundation v. *California State Board of Education* (2006), Case no. 06 CS 00386.
In Re Mohan Singh (1919), 257 F. 209.
In Re Sardar Bhagwab Singh (1917), 246 F. 496.
Indra Sawhney v. *Union of India* (1992), 1992 SCALE 1.
International Society for Krishna Consciousness v. *State Fair of Texas* (1979), 480 F. Supp. 67.
Jagannath Raghunath v. *Narayan Shethe* (1910), ILR 34 Bom 553.
Jugmohandas Mangaldas v. *Sir Mangaldas Nathubhoy* (1886), ILR 10 Bom 528.
Karmasu v. *Tate* (1994), 95 Ohio App. 3d 399.
Kumari Madhuri Patil v. *Additional Commissioner of Tribal Development* (1994), 6 SCC 241.
Lakshmibai v. *Ramchandra* (1896), ILR 22 Bom 590.
Manohar Joshi v. *Nitin Bhaurao Patil* (1996), AIR 1996 SC 796.
Mathura Naikin v. *Esu Naikin* (1880), ILR 4 Bom 545.
MN (India) v. *Entry Clearance Officer (New Delhi), Secretary of State for the Home Department* (2008), WL 45,600.
Mohammed Ahmed Khan v. *Shah Bano Begum* (1985), AIR 1985 SC 945.
Mohd. Aslam @ Buhre v. *Union of India* (2003), AIR 2003 SC 3,413.

National Human Rights Commission v. *State of Gujarat & Others*, writ petition 109/2003, order 03/26/2008, http://judis.nic.in/temp/1092003426320o8p.txt.
Patel v. *Wooten* (2001), 15 Fed. Appx. 647.
People v. *Woodruff* (1966), 26 AD 2nd 236.
Persad v. *Balram* (2001), 724 NYS 2d 560.
Pranjivandas Tulsidas v. *Devkuvarbai* (1859), 1 Bom HCR 130.
Ramesh Yeshwant Prabhoo v. *Prabhakar Kasinath Kunte* (1996), AIR 1996 SC 1,113.
Reg. v. *Sambhu Raghu* (1876), ILR 1 Bom 347.
S. R. Bommai v. *Union of India* (1994), AIR 1994 SC 1,918.
S. Swvigaradoss v. *Zonal Manager, F.C.I.* (1996), RD-SC 137, 1996 AIR 1,182, 1,196 SCC (3) 100 JT, 1996 (2) 182, 1996 SCALE (2) 11.
Sagar v. *Sagar* (2003), App. Ct. MA, 02-P-89.
Sarla Mudgal v. *Union of India* (1995), AIR 1995 SC 1,531.
Sau Kusum v. *State of Maharashtra and Others* (2008), 2008 INDLAW SC 1,994.
Surayanda v. *The Welsh Ministers* (2007), WL 2041877.
Tara v. *Krishna* (1907), ILR 31 Bom 495.
Union of India and Others v. *S. Krishnan and Another* (2008), 2008 INDLAW SC 156.
United States v. *Akhay Kumar Mozumdar* (1923), 296 F. 173.
United States v. *Ali* (1925), 7 F. 2nd 728.
United States v. *Bhagat Singh Thind* (1923), 261 US 204.
Valsamma Paul v. *Cochin University* (1996), 3 SCC 545.
Village of Angelica v. *Voith and Voith* (2006), 28 A.D.3d 1,193.
Widmer v. *Moore* (2001), 776 So. 2nd 324.
Zahira Habibullah Sheikh v. *State of Gujarat* (2004), AIR 2004 SC 3,114.

REFERENCES

Abhyankar, Vasudeva Shastri, and Ganeshashastri Joshi (eds.). 1970–7. *Mīmāṃsādarśanam*. Ānandāśrama Sanskrit Series, 97. Pune: Ānandāśramamudraṇālaya.
Acharya, Narayana Rama (ed.). 1991. *Nirṇayasindhu*. Vidyabhavana Pracyavidya Granthamala, 31. Varanasi: Chowkhamba Vidyabhavana.
Agarwal, Bina. 1994. *A Field of One's Own: Gender and Land Rights in South Asia*. New York: Cambridge University Press.
Agnes, Flavia. 1996. "The Hidden Agenda beneath the Rhetoric of Women's Rights." In Madhushree Dutta, Flavia Agnes, and Neera Adarakar (eds.), *The Nation, the State and Indian Identity*. Calcutta: Samya, 68–94.
1999. *Law and Gender Inequality: The Politics of Women's Rights in India*. Delhi: Oxford University Press.
Agrawal, C. M. 1992. *Golu Devata: The God of Justice of Kumaun Himalayas*. Shree Almora Book Depot.
Ahmad, Sara. 1996. "Judicial Complicity with Communal Violence in India." *Northwestern Journal of International Law and Business* 17(1): 320–50.
Alam, Muzaffar. 2004. *The Languages of Political Islam: India 1200–1800*. Delhi: Permanent Black.

Ali, Daud. 2004. *Courtly Culture and Political Life in Early Medieval India*. Cambridge University Press.

Anbarasan, Ethirajan. 2004. "Restoring Gandhi's African Legacy." *BBC News*, September 3. http://news.bbc.co.uk/2/hi/south_asia/3576420.stm, accessed May 6, 2010.

Annoussamy, David. 2005. *L'intermède français en Inde: Secousses politiques et mutations juridiques*. Pondicherry: Institut français de Pondichéry / L'Harmattan.

Appadurai, Arjun, and Carol Appadurai Breckenridge. 1976. "The South Indian Temple: Authority, Honour and Redistribution." *Contributions to Indian Sociology* 10(2): 187–211.

Arunima, G. 2003. *There Comes Papa: Colonialism and the Transformation of Matriliny in Kerala, Malabar c. 1850–1940*. Hyderabad: Orient Longman.

Asher, Catherine, and Cynthia Talbot. 2006. *India before Europe*. New York: Cambridge University Press.

Austin, J. L. 1975. *How to Do Things with Words*, 2nd edn. Cambridge: Harvard University Press.

Backward Classes Commission (K. Kalelkar, chair). 1955. *Report*. Delhi: Manager of Publications.

(B. P. Mandal, chair). 1980. *Report*. New Delhi: Controller of Publications.

Bagchi, Satish Chandra. 1933. *Juristic Personality of Hindu Deities*. Calcutta: University of Calcutta.

Bakker, Hans. 2004. "At the Right Side of the Teacher: Imagination, Imagery, and the Image in Vedic and Śaiva Initiation." In Phyllis Granoff and Koichi Shinohara (eds.), *Images in Asian Religions: Texts and Contexts*. Asian Religions and Society Series. Vancouver: UBC Press, 117–48.

Banerjee, Ron. 2007. "Hindu Conference of Canada Letter." *Skanda Vale*, August 6. www.skandavale.org/shambo.htm, accessed May 6, 2010.

Basu, Srimati. 1999. *She Comes to Take Her Rights: Indian Women, Property, and Propriety*. Albany, NY: State University of New York Press.

2001. "The Personal and the Political: Indian Women and Inheritance Law." In Gerald James Larson (ed.), *Religion and Personal Law in Secular India: A Call to Judgment*. Bloomington, IN: Indiana University Press, 163–83.

Baumann, Martin. 2001. "The Hindu Diasporas in Europe and an Analysis of Key Diasporic Patterns." In T. S. Rukmani (ed.), *Hindu Diaspora: Global Perspectives*. New Delhi: Munshiram Manoharlal Publishers, 59–80.

Baxi, Upendra. 2000. "Kar Seva of the Indian Constitution? Reflections on Proposals for Review of the Constitution." *Economic and Political Weekly* 35(11): 891–5.

Bayly, Susan. 1999. *Caste, Society and Politics in India: From the Eighteenth Century to the Modern Age*. The New Cambridge History of India, Part IV, vol. III. Cambridge University Press.

Beckett, Alison. 1988. "Sueing Shiva Dismays Dealers." *Sunday Times*, February 12, 9C.

Bell, Catherine. 1998. "Performance." In Mark C. Taylor (ed.), *Critical Terms for Religious Studies*. University of Chicago Press, 205–24.

Bendrey, V. S. (ed.). 1960. *Coronation of Shivaji the Great: Gāgābhaṭṭakṛtaḥ Śrīśivarājābhiṣekaprayogaḥ*. Bombay: P. P. H. Bookstall.

Benke, Theodore. 2010. "The *Śūdrācāraśiromaṇi* of *Kṛṣṇa Śeṣa*: A 16th Century Manual of Dharma for Śūdras." Doctoral dissertation, University of Pennsylvania.

Benton, Lauren. 2002. *Law and Colonial Cultures: Legal Regimes in World History, 1400–1900*. Cambridge University Press.

Bertrand, Marianne, and Sendhil Mullainathan. 2003. "Are Emily and Greg More Employable than Lakisha and Jamal? A Field Experiment on Labor Market Discrimination." Working paper series WP 03–22, Massachusetts Institute of Technology, Department of Economics. http://papers.ssrn.com/sol3/papers.cfm?abstract_id=422902, accessed May 6, 2010.

Bhachu, Parminder. 1985. *Twice Migrants: East African Sikh Settlers in Britain*. London: Tavistock.

Bhatt, Govardhan P. 1962. *The Epistemology of the Bhāṭṭa School of Pūrva Mīmāṃsā*. Chowkhamba Sanskrit Studies, 17. Varanasi: Chowkhamba.

Bilimoria, Purushottama. 2001. "The Making of the Hindu in Australia: A Diasporic Narrative." In T. S. Rukmani (ed.), *Hindu Diaspora: Global Perspectives*. New Delhi: Munshiram Manoharlal Publishers, 3–34.

Bob, Clifford. 2009. "'Dalit Rights Are Human Rights': Untouchables, NGOs and the Indian State." In Clifford Bob (ed.), *The International Struggle for New Human Rights*. Philadelphia, PA: University of Pennsylvania Press, 30–51.

Bonnan, Jean-Claude. 1999. *Jugements du tribunal de la chaudrie de Pondichéry, 1766–1817*, 2 vols. Pondicherry: Institut français de Pondichéry / École française d'Extrême-Orient.

[Borradaile, H.] 1825. *Reports of Civil Causes Adjudged by the Court of Sudur Udalat for the Presidency of Bombay*, 2 vols. Bombay: Courier Press.

Bouchet, Jean Venant. 1843. "Lettre du P. Bouchet à M. Cochet de Saint-Vallier, Président du Palais, à Paris." In M. L. Aimé-Martin (ed.), *Lettres édifiantes et curieuses concernant l'Asie, l'Afrique et l'Amérique*, 4 vols. Paris: Société du Panthéon Littéraire, vol. II, 485–99.

Boys, Thomas. 1825. *Key to the Book of Psalms*. London: L. B. Seeley.

Brereton, J. 2004. "*Dhárman* in the *Ṛgveda*." In Olivelle 2004a: 449–89.

Brick, David. 2006. "Transforming Tradition into Texts: The Early Development of *Smṛti*." *Journal of Indian Philosophy* 34(3): 287–302.

Bronner, Yigal. 2009. "Ambivalence and Alienation in Bilhaṇa's *Vikramāṅkadevacarita*." Paper presented at the 38th Annual Conference on South Asia, October 23.

Bronner, Yigal, and David Shulman. 2006. "'A Cloud Turned Goose': Sanskrit in the Vernacular Millennium." *The Indian Economic and Social History Review* 43(1): 1–30.

Brown, Judith M. 2006. *Global South Asians: Introducing the Modern Diaspora*. Cambridge University Press.

Bühler, Georg (ed.). 1875. *Vikramāṅkadevacarita*. Bombay Sanskrit Series, 14. Bombay: Central Government Book Depot.

van der Burg, C., and P. van der Veer. 1986. "Pandits, Power, and Profit: Religious Organization and the Construction of Identity among Surinamese Hindus." *Ethnic and Racial Studies* 9: 514–29.

Burnell, A. 1878. "The Intellectual Tendencies of South India as Shown by Current Publications." *The Academy* 14: 603–4.

Caland, Willem (ed.). 1927. *Vaikhānasasmārtasūtram*. Calcutta: Asiatic Society.

(trans.). 1929. *Vaikhānasasmārtasūtram*. Calcutta: Asiatic Society.

Cannon, Garland. 1970. *The Letters of Sir William Jones*, 2 vols. Oxford: Clarendon Press.

Carroll, Lucy. 1983. "Law, Custom and Statutory Social Reform: The Hindu Widows Remarriage Act of 1856." *Indian Economic and Social History Review* 20(4): 363–88.

Caton, Steven. 1986. "*Salām Taḥīyah*: Greetings from the Highlands of Yemen." *American Ethnologist* 13: 290–308.

Chakravarti, Uma. 1998. *Rewriting History: The Life and Times of Pandita Ramabai*. Delhi: Kali for Women.

Chander, Anupam. 2001. "Diaspora Bonds." *New York University Law Review* 76: 1,005–99.

Chatterjee, Indrani. 1999. *Gender, Slavery and Law in Colonial India*. Delhi: Oxford University Press.

(ed.). 2004. *Unfamiliar Relations: Family and History in South Asia*. New Brunswick, NJ: Rutgers University Press.

Chatterjee, Partha. 1990. "The Nationalist Resolution of the 'Women's Question.'" In Kumkum Sangari and Sudesh Vaid (eds.), *Recasting Women: Essays in Indian Colonial History*. New Brunswick, NJ: Rutgers University Press, 233–53.

1996. *The Nation and Its Fragments: Colonial and Postcolonial Histories*. Princeton University Press.

Chattopadhyaya, Brajadulal. 1994a. *The Making of Early Medieval India*. Delhi: Oxford University Press.

1994b. "Political Processes and the Structure of Polity in Early Medieval India." In Chattopadhyaya 1994a, 183–222.

Chinnaswami Sastri, A. (ed.). 1936. *Tāṇḍyamahābrāhmaṇa with the Commentary of Sāyaṇācārya*. Kashi Sanskrit Series, 105. Varanasi: Chowkhamba.

Clooney, Francis X. 1988. "Devatādhikaraṇa: A Theological Debate in the Mimamsa-Vedanta Tradition." *Journal of Indian Philosophy* 16: 277–98.

1997. "What's a God? The Quest for the Right Understanding of *Devatā* in Brahmanical Ritual Theory (Mīmāṃsā)." *International Journal of Hindu Studies* 1: 337–85.

2005. *Fr. Bouchet's India – An 18th Century Jesuit's Encounter with Hinduism*. Chennai: Satya Nilayam Publications.

Cœdès, George. 1968. *The Indianized States of Southeast Asia*. Honolulu: East-West Center Press.

Cohn, Bernard S. 1952–4. "Anthropological Notes on Disputes and Law in India." *American Anthropologist* 6–7: 148–68.

1959. "Some Notes on Law and Change in North India." *Economic Development and Cultural Change* 8(1): 79–93.

1987. *An Anthropologist among the Historians and Other Essays*. New Delhi: Oxford University Press.

1996a. *Colonialism and Its Forms of Knowledge: The British in India.* Princeton University Press.

1996b. "The Command of Language and the Language of Command." In Cohn 1996a: 16–56.

1996c. "Law and the Colonial State in India." In Cohn 1996a: 57–75.

Coke, Sir Edward. 1777. "Bonham's Case." In *The Reports of Sir Edward Coke, Knt.*, 8 vols. London: J. Rivington.

Colas, Gérard. 2004. "The Competing Hermeneutics of Image Worship in Hinduism (Fifth to Eleventh Century AD)." In Phyllis Granoff and Koichi Shinohara (eds.), *Images in Asian Religions: Texts and Contexts.* Asian Religions and Society Series. Vancouver: UBC Press, 149–79.

Colebrooke, H. T. 1798. *A Digest of Hindu Law on Contracts and Successions*, 4 vols. Calcutta: Honourable Company's Press.

1810. *Two Treatises on the Hindu Law of Inheritance.* Calcutta: Hindoostanee Press.

Concerned Citizens' Tribunal. 2002a. "Crime against Humanity, vol. II: Findings and Recommendations." Mumbai: Citizens for Justice and Peace. www.sabrang.com/tribunal/tribunal2.pdf, accessed May 6, 2010.

2002b. "Crime against Humanity, vol. III: List of Annexures." Mumbai: Citizens for Justice and Peace, 262–5. www.sabrang.com/tribunal/tribunal3.pdf, accessed May 6, 2010.

Confederation of Indian Industry. 2007. "Affirmative Action: Empowering Society for a Brighter Tomorrow." www.cii.in/documents/Report%20on%20AA.pdf (last updated September 26), accessed February 12, 2009.

Cossman, Brenda, and Ratna Kapur. 1995. "Communalising Gender Engendering Community: Women, Legal Discourse and the Saffron Agenda." In Tanika Sarkar and Urvashi Butalia (eds.), *Women and the Hindu Right: A Collection of Essays.* Delhi: Kali for Women, 82–120.

1997. "Secularism's Last Sigh?: The Hindu Right, the Courts, and India's Struggle for Democracy." *Harvard International Law Journal* 38(1): 113–70.

Cotterrell, Roger. 1983. "Legality and Political Legitimacy in the Sociology of Max Weber." In David Sugarman (ed.), *Legality, Ideology and the State.* New York: Academic Press, 69–93.

Crotty, Kevin M. 2001. *Law's Interior: Legal and Literary Constructions of the Self.* Ithaca, NY: Cornell University Press.

Cunningham, Clark D., Glenn C. Loury, and John David Skrentny. 2002. "Passing Strict Scrutiny: Using Social Science to Design Affirmative Action Programs." *Georgetown Law Journal* 90: 835–82.

Dalmia, Vasudha. 1996. "Sanskrit Scholars and Pandits of the Old School: The Benares Sanskrit College and the Constitution of Authority in the Late Nineteenth Century." *Journal of Indian Philosophy* 24: 321–37.

Dangol, B. D. (ed.). 1991–2. *Catalogue of the 'Guthi Papers'*, 2 vols. Kathmandu: H. M. G. Nepal, National Archives.

Davis, Donald R., Jr. 1999. "Recovering the Indigenous Legal Traditions of India: Classical Hindu Law in Practice in Late Medieval Kerala." *Journal of Indian Philosophy* 27: 159–213.

2002. "*Dharma, Maryāda*, and Law in Early British Malabar: Remarks on Words for 'Law' in the Tellicherry Records." *Studien zur Indologie und Iranistik* 23: 51–70.

2004a. *The Boundaries of Hindu Law Tradition, Custom and Politics in Medieval Kerala*. Corpus Iuris Sanscriticum, 5. Turin: CESMEO.

2004b. "Dharma in Practice: Ācāra and Authority in Medieval Dharmaśāstra." *Journal of Indian Philosophy* 32(1): 813–30.

2005. "Intermediate Realms of Law: Corporate Groups and Rulers in Medieval India." *Journal of the Economic and Social History of the Orient* 48(1): 92–117.

2007. "Hinduism as a Legal Tradition." *Journal of the American Academy of Religion* 75: 241–67.

2008. "Law." In Gene Thursby and Sushil Mittal (eds.), *Studying Hinduism: Key Concepts and Methods*. London: Routledge, 218–29.

Davis, Richard H. 1991. *Ritual in an Oscillating Universe: Worshiping Siva in Medieval India*. Princeton University Press.

1997. *Lives of Indian Images*. Princeton University Press.

2001. "Indian Image-Worship and Its Discontents." In Jan Assmann and Albert I. Baumgarten (eds.), *Representation in Religion: Studies in Honor of Moshe Barasch*. Studies in the History of Religions. Leiden: Brill, 107–32.

Derrett, J. Duncan M. 1957. *Hindu Law: Past and Present*. Calcutta: A. Mukherjee & Co.

1962a. "The Development of the Concept of Property in India c. AD 800–1800." *Zeitschrift für vergleichende Rechtsgeschichte* 64: 15–130.

1962b. "East Africa: Recent Legislation for Hindus." *The American Journal of Comparative Law* 11(3): 396–403.

1963. *Introduction to Modern Hindu Law*. Oxford University Press.

1967. "A Jurist and His Sources: Medhātithi's Use of Bhāruci." *Adyar Library Bulletin* 30: 1–22.

1968. *Religion, Law and the State in India*. London: Faber and Faber.

1975. *Bhāruci's Commentary on the Manusmṛti (The Manu-Śāstra-Vivaraṇa, Books 6–12)*, 2 vols. Wiesbaden: Steiner.

1976. "The Concept of Law according to Medhatithi, a Pre-Islamic Indian Jurist." In Derrett 1976–8: 174–97.

1976–8. *Essays in Classical and Modern Hindu Law*, 4 vols. Leiden: E. J. Brill.

1978a. *The Death of a Marriage Law: Epitaph for the Rishis*. New Delhi: Vikas.

1978b. "Ancient Indian 'Nonsense' Vindicated." *Journal of the American Oriental Society* 98: 100–6.

1979. *Beiträge zu indischem Rechtsdenken*. Wiesbaden: Franz Steiner Verlag.

Deshpande, Madhav. 2006. "Changing Perspectives in the Sanskrit Grammatical Tradition and the Changing Political Configurations in Ancient India." In Olivelle 2006a: 215–25.

Deshpande, Satishe, and Yogendra Yadav. 2006. "Redesigning Affirmative Action." *Economic and Political Weekly*, June 17, 2,419.

Dhavan, Rajeev. 2001. "The Road to Xanadu: India's Quest for Secularism." In Gerald James Larson (ed.), *Religion and Personal Law in Secular India: A Call to Judgment*. Bloomington, IN: Indiana University Press, 301–29.

Douglas, Mary. 1999. *Leviticus as Literature*. Oxford University Press.

Dow, Alexander. 1770–2. *The History of Hindostan*, 2nd edn., 3 vols. London: T. Becket and P. A. de Hondt.

Dubois, J. A. 1897. *Hindu Manners, Customs and Ceremonies*, annotated edn., trans. Henry K. Beauchamp. Oxford: Clarendon Press.

Eaton, Richard M. 1993. *The Rise of Islam and the Bengal Frontier, 1204–1760*. Berkeley, CA: University of California Press.

2005. *A Social History of the Deccan, 1300–1761: Eight Indian Lives*. The New Cambridge History of India, Part 1, vol. VIII. Cambridge University Press.

Ekklesia. 2007. "Debate Continues about UK Hindu Funeral Rites." April 20. www.ekklesia.co.uk/node/5098, accessed May 6, 2010.

Ellis, F. W. 1827. "On the Law Books of the Hindoos." *Transactions of the Madras Literary Society* 1: 1–25.

Elphinstone, Mountstuart. 1821. *Report on the Territories, Conquered from the Paishwa*. Calcutta: Government Gazette Press. Reprinted New Delhi: Oriental Publishers, 1973.

Engineer, Asghar Ali. 1987. "Introduction." In Asghar Ali Engineer (ed.), *The Shah Bano Controversy*. Hyderabad: Orient Longman Limited, 1–19.

Fallers, Lloyd A. 1969. *Law without Precedent: Legal Ideas in Action in the Courts of Colonial Busoga*. University of Chicago Press.

Fezas, Jean (ed.). 2000. *Le code népalais (Ain)*, 2 vols. Corpus Juris Sanscriticum, 2. Turin: CESMEO.

Finnis, John. 1980. *Natural Law and Natural Rights*. Oxford: Clarendon Press.

2007. "Natural Law Theories." In Edward N. Zalta (ed.), *The Stanford Encyclopedia of Philosophy (Spring 2007 Edition)*. http://plato.stanford.edu/archives/spr2007/entries/natural-law-theories, accessed November 10, 2008.

Fitzgerald, James L. 2004. *The Mahabharata: Book 11: The Book of the Women; Book 12: The Book of Peace, Part* 1. University of Chicago Press.

Foucault, Michel. 1991. "Governmentality." In Graham Burchell, Colin Gordon, and Peter Miller (eds.), *The Foucault Effect: Studies in Governmentality, with Two Lectures by and an Interview with Michel Foucault*. University of Chicago Press, 87–104.

Fuchs, Martin. 1994. "Discursive Practices and Experiential Attitudes: Difficulties in Conceptualising Folk Religion." Paper presented at the 13th European Conference on Modern South Asian Studies, Panel on "Folk Religion Reconsidered," Toulouse.

Fuller, Christopher J. 1994. *The Camphor Flame: Popular Hinduism and Society in India*. Princeton University Press.

Gajendragadkar, Pralhad Balacharya. 1951. *The Hindu Code Bill*. Dharwar: Karnatak University Extension Lectures Series.

Galanter, Marc. 1965. "The Aborted Restoration of 'Indigenous' Law in India." *Comparative Studies in Society and History* 14: 53–70.

1984. *Competing Equalities: Law and the Backward Classes in India.* Delhi: Oxford University Press.
1989. *Law and Society in Modern India*, ed. with an introduction by Rajeev Dhavan. Delhi: Oxford University Press.
2002. "The Long Half-Life of Reservations." In Zoya Hasa, E. Sridharan, and R. Sudarshan (eds.), *India's Living Constitution: Ideas, Practices, Controversies.* Delhi: Permanent Black, 306–18.
Galanter, Marc, and Jayanth K. Krishnan. 2000. "Personal Law and Human Rights in India and Israel." *Israel Law Review* 34: 98–133.
Ganapati Sastri, T. (ed.). 1921–2. *Yājñavalkyasmṛti with the Commentary Balakrīḍā of Viśvarūpācārya.* Trivandrum Sanskrit Series, 74 and 81. Trivandrum: Government Press.
Gandhi, Mohandas K. 1966. *An Autobiography: The Story of My Experiments with Truth*, 2nd edn. London: Jonathan Cape.
Gharpure, J. R. (ed.). 1943. *Dharma Dwaita Nirṇaya or Alternatives Solved.* Collection of Hindu Law Texts, 28. Bombay: Aryabhushan Press.
(trans.). 1948. *The Smṛtichandrikā*, 2 vols. Bombay: Office of the Collection of Hindu Law Texts.
Gillion, Kenneth L. 1977. *The Fiji Indians: A Challenge to European Dominance.* Canberra: Australian National University Press.
Ginsburg, Ruth Bader, and Deborah Jones Merritt. 1999. "Affirmative Action: An International Human Rights Dialogue." *Cardozo Law Review* 21 (October): 253–82.
Greenblatt, Stephen. 1991. *Marvelous Possessions: The Wonder of the New World.* University of Chicago Press.
Griffiths, John. 1986. "What Is Legal Pluralism?" *Journal of Legal Pluralism* 24: 1–55.
1991. "Legal Pluralism and the Social Working of Law." In A. Soeteman, W. van der Velden, and A. de Wild (eds.), *Coherence and Conflicts concerning the Law.* Zwolle: Tjeenk Willink, 151–76.
1995. "Legal Pluralism and the Theory of Legislation." In H. Petersen and H. Zahle (eds.), *Legal Polycentricity: Consequences of Pluralism in Law.* Aldershot: Dartmouth, 201–34.
Guha, Ranajit. 1998. *Dominance without Hegemony: History and Power in Colonial India.* Cambridge, MA: Harvard University Press.
Guha, Sumit. 1995. "An Indian Penal Regime: Maharasthra in the Eighteenth Century." *Past and Present* 147: 101–26.
Gune, Vithal Trimbak. 1953. *The Judicial System of the Marathas: A Detailed Study of the Judicial Institutions in Maharashtra from 1600–1818* AD, *Based on Original Decisions called Mazhars, Nivadpatras and Official Orders.* Deccan College Dissertation Series, 12. Pune: Deccan College.
[Halhed, Nathaniel Brassey]. 1776. *A Code of Gentoo Laws, or Ordinations of the Pundits, from a Persian Translation Made from the Original, Written in the Shanscrit Language.* London: [East India Company].
Hara, Minoru. 2009. "Divine Witness." *Journal of Indian Philosophy* 37: 253–72.
Hart, H. L. A. 1961. *The Concept of Law.* Oxford: Clarendon Press.

Harting, Pieter Nicolaas Ubbo. 1922. *Selections from the Baudhāyana-Gṛhyapariśiṣṭasūtra*. Amersfoort: J. Valkhoff & Co.

Hasan, Zoya. 1998. "Gender Politics, Legal Reform, and the Muslim Community in India." In Patricia Jeffery and Amrita Basu (eds.), *Appropriating Gender: Women's Activism and Politicized Religion in South Asia*. New York: Routledge, 71–88.

Heitzman, James. 1997. *Gifts of Power: Lordship in an Early Indian State*. Delhi: Oxford University Press.

Hiltebeitel, A. 2001. *Rethinking the Mahābhārata: A Reader's Guide to the Education of the Dharma King*. University of Chicago Press.

Hindu American Foundation. 2007. "Hindus in South Asia and the Diaspora: A Survey of Human Rights 2007." www.hinduamericanfoundation.org/pdf/HHR2007.pdf, accessed May 6, 2010.

Hindu Council of Australia. 2008. www.hinducouncil.com.au/index.html, accessed May 6, 2010.

Hindu Forum of Britain. 2008. www.hinduforum.org, accessed May 6, 2010.

Holden, Livia S. 2003. "Custom and Law Practices in Central India: Some Case Studies." *South Asia Research* 23(2): 115–34.

Hooker, M. B. 1975. *Legal Pluralism: An Introduction to Colonial and Neo-Colonial Laws*. Oxford: Clarendon Press.

Horsch, Paul. 2004. "From Creation Myth to World Law: The Early History of *dharma*." In Olivelle 2004a: 423–48. Originally published in German in 1967.

Horstmann, Monika. 1998. "The Preambles of Official Letters from Rajasthan: Towards a Stylistic Typology." *The Indian Historical Review* 15(1): 29–44.

Hughes, C. J. 2008. "'Untouchable' Women Enjoy a Night of Fashion at the UN." *New York Times*, July 4, C9.

Human Rights Watch. 1996. "Communal Violence and the Denial of Justice." *Human Rights Watch* 8(2).

Human Rights Watch and Center for Human Rights and Global Justice. 2007. "Hidden Apartheid: Caste Discrimination against India's 'Untouchables.'" *Human Rights Watch* 19(3c).

Hussain, Nasser. 2003. *The Jurisprudence of Emergency: Colonialism and the Rule of Law*. Ann Arbor, MI: University of Michigan Press.

Hutchins, Francis G. 1967. *The Illusion of Permanence: British Imperialism in India*. Princeton University Press.

Ilbert, Courtenay. 1915. *The Government of India: Being a Digest of the Statute Law Relating Thereto*, 3rd edn. Oxford: Clarendon Press. Reprinted Delhi: Neeraj Publishing House, 1984.

Inden, Ronald. 1990. *Imagining India*. Oxford: Blackwell.

1992. "Changes in the Vedic Priesthood." In A. W. van den Hoek, D. H. A. Kolff, and M. S. Oort (eds.), *Ritual, State and History in South Asia: Essays in Honour of J. C. Heesterman*. Memoirs of the Kern Institute, 5. Leiden: Brill, 556–77.

2006. *Text and Practice: Essays on South Asian History*. Delhi: Oxford University Press.

Innes, L. C. 1882. *Examination of Mr. Nelson's Views of Hindu Law, in a Letter to the Right Hon. Mountstuart Elphinstone Grant Duff, Governor of Madras*. Madras: Higginbotham.

Ishwaran, K. 1964. "Customary Law in Village India." *International Journal of Comparative Sociology* 5: 228–43.

Jackson, Bernard. 1991. "Law and Language: A Metaphor in Maine, A Model for his Successors?" In Alan Diamond (ed.), *The Victorian Achievement of Sir Henry Maine: A Centennial Reappraisal*. Cambridge University Press, 256–93.

1996. "Talion and Purity." In John F. A. Sawyer and Mary Douglas (eds.), *Reading Leviticus: A Conversation with Mary Douglas*. Sheffield Academic Press, 119–21.

1998. "An Aye for an I: The Semiotics of *Lex Talionis* in the Bible." In Roberta Kevelson, William Pencak, and J. Ralph Lindgren (eds.), *New Approaches to Semiotics and the Human Sciences: Essays in Honor of Roberta Kevelson*. New York: Peter Lang, 127–49.

2002a. *Studies in the Semiotics of Biblical Law*. Sheffield Academic Press.

2002b. "Models in Legal History." *Journal of Law and Religion* 18: 1–30.

2006. *Wisdom-Laws: A Study of the Mishpatim of Exodus 21:1–22:16*. Oxford University Press.

Jacobsohn, Gary J. 2003. *The Wheel of Law: India's Secularism in Comparative Constitutional Context*. Princeton University Press.

2004. "The Permeability of Constitutional Borders." *Texas Law Review* 82(7): 1,763–818.

Jadhav, Narendra. 2007. *Untouchables: My Family's Triumphant Escape from India's Caste System*. Berkeley, CA: University of California Press.

Jaffrelot, Christophe. 1996. *The Hindu Nationalist Movement in India*. New York: Columbia University Press.

2003. *India's Silent Revolution: The Rise of Lower Castes in North India*. New York: Columbia University Press.

2005. "The Politics of OBCs." *Seminar* 549 (May): 41–6.

2007. "Caste and the Rise of Marginalized Groups." In Sumit Ganguly, Larry Diamond, and Marc F. Plattner (eds.), *The State of India's Democracy*. Baltimore, MD: The Johns Hopkins University Press, 67–88.

Jan Sangharsh Manch. 2008. "The Derailed Report of Sabarmati Express." http://nsm.org.in/2008/09/29/jan-sangharsh-manch-comments-on-nanavati-commission-report, accessed May 7, 2010.

Jayaswal, Kashi Prasad. 1920. "A Judgment of a Hindu Court in Sanskrit." *Journal of the Bihar and Orissa Research Society* 6: 246–53.

Jenkins, Laura Dudley. 2001. "Becoming Backward: Preferential Policies and Religious Minorities in India." *Commonwealth and Comparative Politics* 39(2): 32–50.

2003. *Identity and Identification in India: Defining the Disadvantaged*. London and New York: RoutledgeCurzon.

2004. "Race, Caste and Justice: Social Science Categories and Antidiscrimination Policies in India and the United States." *Connecticut Law Review* 2004 (spring): 747–85.

2008. "Women's Empowerment through Religious Conversion: Voices of Buddhists in Nagpur, India." In Manu Bhagavan and Anne Feldhaus (eds.), *"Speaking Truth to Power": Religion, Caste and the Subaltern Question in India*. New Delhi: Oxford University Press, 153–64.

Jensen, J. M. 1988. *Passage from India: Asian Indian Immigrants in North America*. New Haven, CT: Yale University Press.

Jha, Ganganath (ed. and trans.). 1920–9. *Manusmṛti with the "Manubhāṣya" of Medhātithi*, 10 vols. Bibliotheca Indica, 256. Calcutta: Indian Press. Reprinted Delhi: Motilal Banarsidass, 1999.

1930. *Hindu Law and Its Sources*. Allahabad: Indian Press.

Jha, I. (ed.). 1969. *Likhanāvalī by Vidyāpati*. Patna: Indrālaya Prakāśana.

Jha, Shiv Pujan. 2008. "CNN-IBN Expose: Procuring Fake Caste Certificates Easy." *IBN Live*, April 11. http://ibnlive.in.com/news/cnnibn-expos-procuring-fake-caste-certificates-easy/63088-3.html, accessed July 4, 2008.

Jolly, Julius. 1880. *The Institutes of Vishnu*. Sacred Books of the East, 7. Oxford: Clarendon Press.

1881. *Viṣṇusmṛti*. Bibliotheca Indica, 91. Calcutta: The Asiatic Society.

1889. *The Minor Law-Books: Nārada, Brihaspati*. Sacred Books of the East, 33. Oxford: Clarendon Press.

1896. *Recht und Sitte*. Strasbourg: Karl J. Trübner.

[Jones, Sir William.] 1794. *Institutes of Hindu Law: or, the Ordinances of Menu, according to the Gloss of Cullúca ... Verbally Translated from the Original Sanscrit*. [Calcutta: Government].

Joshi, Lakshman Sastri (ed.). 1937–41. *Dharmakośa*, vol. 1: *Vyavahārakāṇḍa*, 3 parts. Wai: Prājñapāṭhaśālā.

"Justice Chopra Committee Rejects Gujjars' Demand for ST Status." 2007. Online article, December 18. www.rediff.com/news/2007/dec/18rajriot.htm, accessed May 13, 2010.

Kane, Pandurang Vaman. 1933. *Kātyāyanasmṛtisāroddhāra*. Pune: Oriental Book Agency.

1950. *Hindu Customs and Modern Law*. University of Bombay.

1968–75. *History of Dharmaśāstra*, 2nd edn., 5 vols. in 8 parts. Pune: Bhandarkar Oriental Research Institute.

Kangle, R. P. (ed. and trans.). 1969. *The Kauṭilīya Arthaśāstra*, 2nd edn., 3 vols. Bombay University. Reprinted Delhi: Motilal Banarsidass, 1988.

Kapur, Devesh. 2004. "Ideas and Economic Reforms in India: The Role of International Migration and Indian Diaspora." *India Review* 3(4): 364–84.

2006. "Leveraging the Diaspora." *Seminar* 567: 54–7.

2010. *Diaspora, Development, and Democracy: The Domestic Impact of International Migration from India*. Princeton University Press.

Kapur, Ratna, and Brenda Cossman. 1996. *Subversive Sites: Feminist Engagements with Law in India*. New Delhi: Sage Press.

Kelly, John D. 1991. *A Politics of Virtue: Hinduism, Sexuality, and Countercolonial Discourse in Fiji*. University of Chicago Press.

Kielhorn, F. (ed.). 1880–5. *The Vyâkaraṇa-Mahâbhâshya of Patanjali*, 3 vols. Bombay: Government Central Book Depot.

Kishwar, Madhu, and Ruth Vanita. 1990. "Inheritance Rights for Women" and "What the Law Says." *Manushi* 57: 2–15.

Kölver, Bernhard (ed.). 1997. *Recht, Staat und Verwaltung im klassischen Indien / The State, the Law, and Administration in Classical India*. Schriften des Historischen Kollegs, 30. Munich: Oldenbourg Wissenschaftsverlag.

Kölver, Bernhard, and Hemrāj Śākya (eds.). 1985. *Documents from the Rudravarṇa-Mahāvihāra, Pāṭan 1: Sales and Mortgages*. Sankt Augustin: VGH Wissenschaftsverlag.

Kosambi, D. D. (ed.). 1948. *The Epigrams Attributed to Bhartṛhari*. Singhi Jain Series, 23. Mumbai: Bharatiya Vidya Bhavan.

2002. *Combined Methods in Indology and Other Writings*, ed. B. D. Chattopadhyaya. Delhi: Oxford University Press.

Krengel, Monika. 1999. "Spirit Possession in the Central Himalayas. Jagar-Rituals: An Expression of Customs and Rights." In J. Assayag and G. Tarabout (eds.), *Possession in South Asia: Speech, Body, Territory*. Collection Purusartha, 21. Paris: Éditions de l'École des Hautes Études en Sciences Sociales, 265–88.

Krishna Ayyar, K. V. 1938. *The Zamorins of Calicut*. Calicut: Norman Printing.

Krishna Varier, N. V. (ed.). 1979. "Peruvanaṃ Kṣetra Granthavari." In *Peruvanaṃ Mahākṣetra Kalasopahāraṃ*. [Kerala.]

Krishnamacharya, V. (ed.). 1964. *Viṣṇusmṛti with the commentary Keśavavaijayantī of Nandapaṇḍita*, 2 vols. Adyar Library Series, 93. Madras: Adyar Library and Research Centre.

Kulke, Hermann. 1978. "Royal Temple Policy and the Structure of Medieval Hindu Kingdoms." In A. Eschmann, H. Kulke, and G. C. Tripathi (eds.), *The Cult of Jagannath and the Regional Tradition of Orissa*. New Delhi: Manohar, 125–37.

1993. *Kings and Cults: State Formation and Legitimation in India and Southeast Asia*. Delhi: Manohar.

Kumar, Radha. 1994. "Feminism Faces Fundamentalism in India." *Agenda: Focus and Education* 21: 81–92.

1999. "From Chipko to Sati: The Contemporary Indian Women's Movement." In Nivedita Menon (ed.), *Gender and Politics in India*. Delhi: Oxford University Press, 342–69.

Kurup, K. K. N. (ed.). 1995. *Koodali Granthavari*. Calicut University Historical Series, 4. University of Calicut.

Lal, Brij V. 1998. *Another Way: The Politics of Constitutional Reform in Post-Coup Fiji*. Canberra: Asia Pacific Press.

Lal, Vinay. 2008. "The Indian Diaspora." *Manas*. www.sscnet.ucla.edu/southasia/Diaspora/diaspora.html, accessed December 9, 2008.

Lariviere, Richard W. (ed. and trans.). 1981a. *The Divyatattva of Raghunandana Bhaṭṭācārya: Ordeals in Classical Hindu Law*. Delhi: Manohar.

1981b. "Ordeals in Europe and India." *Journal of the American Oriental Society* 101: 347–9.

1984. "A Sanskrit Jayapattra from Eighteenth Century Mithilā." In Richard W. Lariviere (ed.), *Studies in Dharmaśāstra*. Calcutta: Firma KLM, 49–80.

1988. "Adhikāra – Right and Responsibility." In M. A. Jazayery and W. Winter (eds.), *Languages and Cultures: Studies in Honor of E. C. Polomé*. Trends in Linguistics: Studies and Monographs, 36. Berlin: Walter de Gruyter, 359–64.

(ed. and trans.). 1989a. *The Nāradasmṛti*, 2 vols. Philadelphia, PA: University of Pennsylvania, Department of South Asia Regional Studies.

1989b. "Justices and *Panditas*: Some Ironies in Contemporary Readings of the Hindu Legal Past." *Journal of Asian Studies* 48(4): 757–69.

1996. "Dharmaśāstra: Its Present Value and Relevance." In K. Satchidananda Murty and Amit Dasgupta (eds.), *The Perennial Tree: Select Papers of the International Symposium on India Studies*. New Delhi: Indian Council for Cultural Relations, 176–89.

1997. "Dharmaśāstra, Custom, 'Real Law' and Apocryphal Smṛtis." In Bernhard Kölver (ed.), *Recht, Staat und Verwaltung im klassischen Indien / The State, the Law, and Administration in Classical India*. Munich: Oldenbourg Wissenschaftsverlag, 97–110. Reprinted in Olivelle 2004a: 611–27.

Larson, Gerald James (ed.). 2001. *Religion and Personal Law in Secular India: A Call to Judgment*. Bloomington, IN: University of Indiana Press.

Lawson, Stephanie. 1991. *The Failure of Democratic Politics in Fiji*. Oxford: Clarendon Press.

Leavitt, John (ed.). 1997. *Poetry and Prophecy: The Anthropology of Inspiration*. Ann Arbor, MI: University of Michigan Press.

Levy, Harold Lewis. 1973. "Indian Modernization by Legislation: The Hindu Code Bill." Doctoral dissertation, University of Chicago.

Lingat, Robert. 1962. "Les 'quatre pieds du procès.'" *Journal asiatique* 250: 489–503.

1973. *The Classical Law of India*, trans. J. Duncan M. Derrett. Berkeley, CA: University of California Press.

Logan, William. 1887. *Malabar*, 2 vols. Madras Government Press.

Lubin, Timothy. 2007. "Punishment and Expiation: Overlapping Domains in Brahmanical Law." *Indologica Taurinensia* 33: 91–120.

in press. "Legal Diglossia: Modeling Discursive Practices in Premodern Indic Law." In Vincenzo Vergiani and Whitney Cox (eds.), *Bilingual Discourse and Cross-Cultural Fertilisation: Sanskrit and Tamil in Mediaeval India*. Cambridge University Press.

Ludden, David. 1999. *An Agrarian History of South Asia*. The New Cambridge History of India, Part IV, vol. IV. Cambridge University Press.

Luschinsky, Mildred Stroop. 1963. "The Impact of Some Recent Indian Government Legislation on the Women of an Indian Village." *Asian Survey* 3(12): 573–83.

Macnaghten, Francis Workman. 1824. *Considerations on the Hindoo Law, as It Is Current in Bengal*. Serampore: Mission Press.

Macnaghten, William Hay. 1827–35. *Reports of Cases Determined in the Court of Sudder Dewanny Adawlut*, 4 vols. Calcutta: Bishop's College Press.

1828–9. *Principles and Precedents of Hindu Law*, 2 vols. Calcutta: Baptist Mission Press.

Mahadeva Sastri, A., and K. Rangacarya (eds.). 1985. *Taittirīya Āraṇyaka, with the Commentary of Bhaṭṭa Bhāskara Miśra*. Delhi: Motilal Banarsidass.

Maheshwaran Nair, K. (ed.). n.d. *The Chronicles of the Trivandrum Pagoda*, vol. 1. Trivandrum: R. Syamala Devi.

Mahmood, Tahir. 2006. "Religion, Law, and Judiciary in Modern India." *Brigham Young University Law Review* 2006(3): 755–76.

Maine, Henry Sumner. 1861. *Ancient Law: Its Connection with the Early History of Society and Its Relation to Modern Ideas*. London: John Murray.

1871. *Village Communities in the East and West: Six Lectures Delivered at Oxford*. London: John Murray. Reprinted, with other lectures, addresses, and essays, New York: Henry Holt & Co., 1876.

1883. "The Sacred Laws of the Hindus." In *Dissertations on Early Law and Custom*. London: John Murray, 1–25.

Majumdar, R. C. 1969. *Corporate Life in Ancient India*, 3rd edn. Calcutta: K. L. Mukhopadhyay.

Malinowski, Bronislaw. 1926. *Crime and Custom in Savage Society*. London: K. Paul, Trench, and Trubner.

Mandalik, V. N. (ed.). 1886. *Mānavadharmaśāstra with the Commentaries of Medātithi, Sarvajñanārāyaṇa, Kullūka, Rāghavānanda, Nandana and Rāmacandra*. Bombay: A. Kanoba.

Mani, Lata. 1998. *Contentious Traditions: The Debate on Sati in Colonial India*. Berkeley, CA: University of California Press.

Mathur, Ashutosh Dayal. 2007. *Medieval Hindu Law: Historical Evolution and Enlightened Rebellion*. New Delhi: Oxford University Press.

McCrea, Lawrence. 2009. *The Teleology of Poetics in Medieval Kashmir*. Harvard Oriental Series. Cambridge, MA: Harvard University Press.

McKeon, Michael. 2005. *The Secret History of Domesticity: Public, Private, and the Division of Knowledge*. Baltimore, MD: The Johns Hopkins University Press.

Mehta, Pratap Banu. 2006. "Dear Prime Minister." *Indian Express*, May, 22. www.indianexpress.com/news/Dear-Prime-Minister/4916/, accessed February 12, 2009.

2007. "The Rise of Judicial Sovereignty." In Sumit Ganguly, Larry Diamond, and Marc F. Plattner (eds.), *The State of India's Democracy*. Baltimore, MD: The Johns Hopkins University Press, 105–20.

Mehta, Uday. 1999. *Liberalism and Empire: A Study in Nineteenth Century British Political Thought*. University of Chicago.

Menon, Nivedita. 2000. "State, Community and the Debate on the Uniform Civil Code in India." In Mahmood Mamdani (ed.), *Beyond Rights Talk and Culture Talk*. New York: St. Martin's Press, 75–95.

Menski, Werner. 1993. "Asians in Britain and the Question of Adaptation to a New Legal Order: Asian Laws in Britain?" In Milton Israel and N. K. Wagle (eds.), *Ethnicity, Identity, Migration: The South Asian Context*. University of Toronto Press, 238–68.

1999. "South Asian Women in Britain, Family Integrity and the Primary Purpose Rule." In Harriet Bradley, Steve Fenton, and Rohit Barot (eds.), *Ethnicity, Gender and Social Change*. Lewiston, NY: Edwin Mellen Press, 81–98.

2003. *Hindu Law: Beyond Tradition and Modernity*. New York: Oxford University Press.

2006. *Comparative Law in a Global Context: The Legal Systems of Asia and Africa*, 2nd edn. Cambridge University Press.

2007. "Law, Religion and South Asians in Diaspora." In John Hinnells (ed.), *Religious Reconstruction in the South Asian Diaspora: From One Generation to Another*. New York: Palgrave Macmillan, 243–64.

2008. "Recent Developments in the Uniform Civil Code debates in India." *German Law Journal* 9(3): 212–50.

Merry, Sally Engle. 1988. "Legal Pluralism." *Law & Society Review* 22(5): 869–96.

Mesquita, Roque. 1997. *Madhva und seine unbekannten literarischen Quellen: Einige Beobachtungen*. Vienna: de Nobili Research Library.

Metcalf, Thomas. 1995. *Ideologies of the Raj*. New Delhi: Cambridge University Press.

Michaels, Axel. 1994. *Die Reisen der Götter – Der nepalische Pashupatinatha-Tempel und sein rituelles Umfeld*, 2 vols. Bonn: VGH Wissenschaftsverlag.

2001. "The Pandit as a Legal Adviser: *Rājguru, rājpurohita* and *dharmādhikārin*." In Axel Michaels (ed.), *The Pandit: Traditional Scholarship in India*. South Asian Studies, 38. New Delhi: Manohar, 61–78.

2005. *The Price of Purity: The Religious Judge in 19th Century Nepal. Containing the Edition and Translation of the Chapters on the Dharmādhikārin in Two (Mulukī) Ains*. Corpus Juris Sanscriticum et fontes iuris Asiae Meridianae et Centralis, 6. Turin: CESMEO.

2009. "Nepal." In Stanley N. Katz (ed.), *The Oxford Encyclopedia of Legal History*, vol. v. New York: Oxford University Press.

Misra, Kulamani (ed.). 1982. *Prāyaścittaviveka*, 2 vols. Puri: Utkala.

Mitra, Subrata, and Alexander Fischer. 2002. "Sacred Laws and the Secular State: An Analytical Narrative of the Controversy over Personal Laws in India." *India Review* 1(3): 99–130.

Mitta, Manoj. 2007. "Diagnosis: Casteism." *Times of India*, May 13. http://timesofindia.indiatimes.com/articleshow/2039283.cms, accessed May 13, 2010.

Moghe, S. G. 1984. *Studies in the Pūrva-Mīmāṃsā*. Delhi: Ajanta Publications.

1991. *Studies in the Dharma-śāstra*. Delhi: Ajanta Publications.

1998. *Studies in Applied Pūrva-Mīmāṃsā*. Delhi: Ajanta Publications.

Moore, Sally Falk. 1973. "Law and Social Change: The Semi-Autonomous Social Field as an Appropriate Subject of Study." *Law & Society Review* 7(4): 719–46.

Morris, Stephen. 1956. "Indians in East Africa: A Study of a Plural Society." *The British Journal of Sociology* 7(3): 194–211.

Mukherjea, Bijan Kumar. 1952. *The Hindu Law of Religious and Charitable Trust*. Calcutta: Eastern Law House Ltd.

Mulla, Dinshah Fardunji. 1901. *Jurisdiction of Courts in Matters Relating to the Rights and Powers of Castes*. Bombay: Caxton Printing Works.

1929. *Principles of Hindu Law*, 6th edn. Bombay: J.M. Pandia.

Nanavati, G. T., and Akshay H. Mehta. 2008. "Report by the Commission of Inquiry, Part 1: Sabarmati Express Train Incident at Godhra." www.home.gujarat.gov.in/homedepartment/downloads/godharaincident.pdf, accessed May 7, 2010.

Nanda, Ved P., and Surya Prakash Sinha (eds.). 1997. *Hindu Law and Legal Theory*. International Library of Essays in Law and Legal Theory; Legal Cultures, 12. New York University Press.

Narayana Rao, Velcheru, David Shulman, and Sanjay Subrahmanyam. 1992. *Symbols of Substance: Court and State in Nāyaka Period Tamilnadu*. Delhi: Oxford University Press.

Narayanan, M. G. S. (ed.). 1987. *Vanjeri Grandhavari*. Calicut University Historical Series, 1. University of Calicut.

Narayanan, Vasudha. 1985. "Arcāvatāra: On Earth as He Is in Heaven." In Joanne Punzo Waghorne and Norman Cutler (eds.), *Gods of Flesh / Gods of Stone: The Embodiment of Divinity in India*. Chambersburg, PA: Anima Publications, 53–66.

Narula, Smita. 1999a. *Broken People: Caste Violence against India's "Untouchables."* New York: Human Rights Watch.

1999b. "Politics by Other Means: Attacks against Christians in India." *Human Rights Watch* 11(6).

2002. "We Have No Orders to Save You: State Participation and Complicity in Communal Violence in Gujarat." *Human Rights Watch* 14(3).

2003a. "Compounding Injustice: The Government's Failure to Redress Massacres in Gujarat." *Human Rights Watch* 15(3).

2003b. "Overlooked Danger: The Security and Rights Implications of Hindu Nationalism in India." *Harvard Human Rights Journal* 16(1): 41–68.

2006. "Review of Gary Jefferson Jacobsohn, *The Wheel of Law: India's Secularism in Comparative Constitutional Context*." *International Journal of Constitutional Law* 4(4): 741–51.

2007. "Criminal Injustice: Impunity for Communal Violence in India." In C. Raj Kumar and K. Chockalingam (eds.), *Human Rights, Criminal Justice and Constitutional Empowerment*. Delhi: Oxford University Press, 363–90.

National Commission for Backward Classes. 2008. "Persons/Sections Excluded from Reservation which Constitute Creamy Layer of the Society." Annual report 2007–8, Appendix 1 to Annexure IV, pp. 37–42. New Delhi: National Commission for Backward Classes. http://ncbc.nic.in/html/creamylayer.htm, accessed February 10, 2009.

Needham, Anuradha Dingwaney, and Rajeswari Sundar Rajan (eds.). 2007. *The Crisis of Secularism in India*. Durham, NC: Duke University Press.

Nehru, Jawaharlal. 1990. *Letters to Chief Ministers (1947–64)*, ed. G. Parthasarathi, vol. IV. Delhi: Oxford University Press.

Nelson, J. H. 1877. *A View of the Hindū Law as Administered by the High Court of Judicature at Madras*. Madras: Higginbotham.

1881. *A Prospectus of the Scientific Study of the Hindu Law*. London: Kegan Paul.

1882. *A Letter to Mr Justice Innes, Touching His Attack on Nelson's View of Hindû Law*. Madras: Higginbotham.

1887. *Indian Usage and Judge Made Law in Madras*. London: Kegan Paul.

Nicholls, George. 1907. *Sketch of the Rise and Progress of the Benares Patshalla or Sanskrit College, Now Forming the Sanskrit Department of the Benares College*. Allahabad: Government Press.

Njammasch, Marlene. 1984. *Untersuchung zur Genesis des Feudalismus in Indien*. Berlin: Akademie Verlag.

Nussbaum, Martha C. 1995. *Poetic Justice: The Literary Imagination and Public Life*. Boston: Beacon Press.

2007. *The Clash Within: Democracy, Religious Violence, and India's Future*. Cambridge, MA: Belknap Press.

O'Hanlon, Rosalind. 2009. "Narratives of Penance and Purification in Western India, c. 1650–1850." *The Journal of Hindu Studies* 2: 48–75.

Oldenburg, Veena Talwar. 2002. *Dowry Murder: The Imperial Origins of a Cultural Crime*. New York: Oxford University Press.

Olivelle, Patrick (trans.). 1992. *The Saṃnyāsa Upaniṣads: Hindu Scriptures on Asceticism and Renunciation*. New York: Oxford University Press.

1993. *The Āśrama System: History and Hermeneutics of a Religious Institution*. New York: Oxford University Press.

(ed. and trans.) 2000. *Dharmasūtras: The Law Codes of Āpastamba, Gautama, Baudhāyana, and Vasiṣṭha*. Delhi: Motilal Banarsidass.

(ed.). 2004a. *Dharma: Studies in Its Semantic, Cultural, and Religious History*. Special double issue of the *Journal of Indian Philosophy* 32.

2004b. "The Semantic History of *Dharma*: The Middle and Late Vedic Periods." In Olivelle 2004a: 491–511.

(ed. and trans.) 2005a. *Manu's Code of Law: A Critical Edition and Translation of the Mānava-Dharmaśāstra*, with the editorial assistance of Suman Olivelle. New York: Oxford University Press.

2005b. "Power of Words: The Ascetic Appropriation and the Semantic Evolution of Dharma." In *Language, Texts, and Society: Explorations in Ancient Indian Culture and Religion*. Florence: University of Firenze Press, 121–35.

2005c. *Dharmasūtra Parallels*. Delhi: Motilal Banarsidass.

(ed.). 2006a. *Between the Empires: Society in India 300 BCE to 400 CE*. New York: Oxford University Press.

2006b. "Explorations in the Early History of Dharmaśāstra." In Olivelle 2006a: 169–90.

2007. "Manu and Gautama: A Study in Śāstric Intertextuality." In K. Preisendanz (ed.), *Expanding and Merging Horizons: Contributions to South Asian and Cross-Cultural Studies in Commemoration of Wilhelm Halbfass*. Österreichische Akademie der Wissenschaften. Vienna: Austrian Academy of Sciences Press, 681–92.

(ed. and trans.) 2009. *The Law Code of Viṣṇu: A Critical Edition and Annotated Translation of the Vaiṣṇava-Dharmaśāstra*. Harvard Oriental Series, 73. Cambridge, MA: Harvard University Press.

Orr, Leslie C. 2006. "Preface." In G. Vijayavenugopal (ed.), *Pondicherry Inscriptions / Putuccēri mānilak kalveṭṭukaḷ*, vol. 1. Collection Indologie, 83, no. 1. Pondicherry: École française d'Extrême-Orient / Institut français de Pondichéry, i–xxvii.

Palshikar, Suhas. 2008. "Of Democracy and Diversity." *Seminar* 581: 83–7.

Pandey, Umesh Chandra (ed.). 1967. *Yājñavalkyasmṛti, with the Mitākṣarā Commentary of Vijñāneśvara*, 4th edn. Kashi Sanskrit Series, 178. Varanasi: Chowkhamba Sanskrit Series Office. Reprinted 1990.

Panikkar, K. N. 1993. "Religious Symbols and Political Mobilization: The Agitation for a Mandir at Ayodhya." *Social Scientist* 21(7/8): 63–78.

Pant, Mahes Raj. 1997. "Six 15th- and 16th-Century Deeds from Tirhut Recording the Purchase of Slaves." In Bernhard Kölver (ed.), *Recht, Staat und Verwaltung im klassischen Indien / The State, the Law, and Administration in Classical India*. Munich: Oldenbourg Wissenschaftsverlag, 159–94.

2002. "Documents from the Regmi Research Collection 1." *Ādarśa* (Kathmandu) 2: 61–152.

Parikh, Sheetal. 2005. "Enshrining a Secular Idol: A Judicial Response to the Violent Aftermath of Ayodhya." *Case Western Reserve Journal of International Law* 37(1): 85–109.

Pearson, Anne M. 2001. "Mothers and Daughters: The Transmission of Religious Practice and the Formation of Hindu Identity among Hindu Immigrant Women in Ontario." In T. S. Rukmani (ed.), *Hindu Diaspora: Global Perspectives*. New Delhi: Munshiram Manoharlal, 427–42.

Pendse, S. N. 1985. *Oaths and Ordeals in Dharmasastra*. Vadodara: University of Baroda Press.

Pocock, David F. 1957. "'Difference' in East Africa: A Study of Caste and Religion in Modern Indian Society." *Southwestern Journal of Anthropology* 13: 285–300.

Pollock, Frederick. 1912. *The Genius of the Common Law*. New York: Columbia University Press. Reprinted New York: AMS Press, 1967.

Pollock, Sheldon. 1985. "The Theory of Practice and the Practice of Theory in Indian Intellectual History." *Journal of the American Oriental Society* 105: 499–519.

1989a. "The Idea of Śāstra in Traditional India." In A. L. Dallapiccola and S. Zingel-Avé Lallemant (eds.), *The Śāstric Tradition in the Indian Arts*. Beiträge zur Südasienforschung. Wiesbaden: Steiner, 17–26.

1989b. "Mīmāṃsā and the Problem of History in Traditional India." *Journal of the American Oriental Society* 109(4): 603–10.

1990. "From Discourse of Ritual to Discourse of Power in Sanskrit Culture." *Journal of Ritual Studies* 4(2): 315–45.

1993. "Deep Orientalism? Notes on Sanskrit and Power beyond the Raj." In Carol A. Breckenridge and Peter van de Veer (eds.), *Orientalism and the Postcolonial Predicament*. Philadelphia, PA: University of Pennsylvania Press, 76–133.

2001a. "The Death of Sanskrit." *Comparative Studies in History and Society* 43(2): 392–426.

2001b. "New Intellectuals in Seventeenth-Century India." *The Indian Economic and Social History Review* 38(1): 3–31.

2006. *The Language of the Gods in the World of Men: Sanskrit, Culture and Power in Premodern India*. Berkeley, CA: University of California Press.

Povinelli, Elizabeth. 2002. *The Cunning of Recognition: Indigenous Alterities and the Making of Australian Multiculturalism*. Durham, NC: Duke University Press.

Power, Paul F., 1969. "Gandhi in South Africa." *The Journal of Modern African Studies* 7(3): 441–55.

Prasad, Pushpa. 2007. *Lekhapaddhati: Documents of State and Everyday Life from Ancient and Early Medieval Gujarat*. New Delhi: Oxford University Press.

Prasad, Rajendra. 1984–95. *Dr. Rajendra Prasad: Correspondence and Select Documents*, ed. Valmiki Chaudhary, vols. XV–XVIII. New Delhi: Allied.

Pressler, Franklin A. 1987. *Religion under Bureaucracy: Policy and Administration for Hindu Temples in South India*. South Asian Studies, 38. Cambridge University Press.

Rahman, Masech. 2006. "Indian Leader Likens Caste System to Apartheid Regime." *The Guardian*, December 28. www.guardian.co.uk/world/2006/dec/28/india.mainsection, accessed July 4, 2008.

Rajagopalan, P. (ed.). 1960. *Śrī Aḻakiṉ Perumāḷ avarkaḷ pāṭiyaruḷiya Maṉu viññaṉēcuvarium eṉṉum Mitāṣrattin vaḻi nūl*. Ceṉṉai: Makāmakōpātyāya Ṭākṭar U. Vē. Cāminātaiyar Nūl Nilaiyam.

Rajalakshmi, T. K. 2008a. "Passing the Buck." *Frontline* 25(1): 120–2.

2008b. "Deal and Discontent." *Frontline* 25(14): 33–5.

Rāmajaya Tarkālaṅkāra. 1827. *Dāyakaumudī evaṃ Dattakakaumudī evaṃ Vyavasthāsaṃgrahaḥ*. Calcutta: Church Mission Press.

Ramesan, N. (ed.). 1962. *Copper Plate Inscriptions of Andhra Pradesh Government Museum*. Hyderabad: Government of Andhra Pradesh.

Ramsoedh, Hans, and Lucie Bloemberg, 2001. "The Institutionalization of Hinduism in Suriname and Guyana." In T. S. Rukmani (ed.), *Hindu Diaspora: Global Perspectives*. New Delhi: Munshiram Manoharlal Publishers, 123–64.

Ranbaore, M. R. 1974. "Hindu Law in Medieval Deccan." In H. K. Sherwani and P. M. Joshi (eds.), *History of Medieval Deccan (1295–1724)*, vol. II. Hyderabad: Government of Andhra Pradesh, 521–37.

Rangaswami Aiyangar, K. V. 1941a. *Bṛhaspatismṛti (Reconstructed)*. Gaekwad's Oriental Series, 85. Baroda: Oriental Institute.

1941b. "Additional Verses of Kātyāyana on Vyavahāra." In S. M. Katre and P. K. Goode (eds.), *A Volume of Studies in Indology* (presented to P. V. Kane on his 61st birthday. Pune: Oriental Book Agency, 7–11.

Rao, Anupama (ed.). 2003. *Gender & Caste*. Issues in Contemporary Indian Feminism, 1. New Delhi: Kali for Women.

Rashtriya Swayamsevak Sangh. n.d. "Widening Horizons." www.hindubooks.org/WideningHorizons, accessed May 7, 2010.

Ray, Bharati, and Aparna Basu (eds.). 1999. *From Independence towards Freedom: Indian Women since 1947*. New Delhi: Oxford University Press.
Raz, Joseph. 1986. *The Morality of Freedom*. Oxford University Press.
(ed.). 1990. *Authority*. New York University Press.
Regmi, D. R. 1965–6. *Medieval Nepal*, 4 vols. Calcutta: K. L. Mukhopadhyay.
Reuters. 2007. "14 Die in Clashes between Police and Protesters in Western India." *New York Times* May 30, A4.
Ricklefs, M. C. 2009. *A History of Modern Indonesia since c. 1200*, 3rd edn. Stanford University Press.
Robinson, Rowena, and Sathianathan Clarke. 2003. *Religious Conversions in India: Modes, Motivations, and Meanings*. New Delhi: Oxford University Press.
Rocher, Ludo. 1972a. "Schools of Hindu Law." In J. Ensink and P. Gaeffke (eds.), *India Maior: Congratulatory Volume Presented to J. Gonda*. Leiden: Brill, 167–76.
1972b. "Indian Response to Anglo-Hindu Law." *Journal of the American Oriental Society* 92: 419–24.
1978. "Hindu Conceptions of Law." *Hastings Law Journal* 29: 1,283–305. Reprinted in V. P. Nanda and S. P. Sinha (eds.), *Hindu Law and Legal Theory*. Hants: Dartmouth Publishing Company, 1996, 3–26.
1979. "Caritraṃ Pustakaraṇe." *Indologica Taurinensia* 7: 345–50.
1980. "*Karma* and Rebirth in the *Dharmaśāstras*." In Wendy Doniger (ed.), *Karma and Rebirth in Classical Indian Traditions*. Berkeley, CA: University of California Press, 61–89.
1984a. "Changing Patterns of Diversification in Hindu Law." *Proceedings of the South Asia Seminar, University of Pennsylvania (Identity and Diversification in Cults and Sects in South Asia)*, 31–44.
1984b. "Father Bouchet's Letter on the Administration of Hindu Law." In Richard W. Lariviere (ed.), *Studies in Dharmaśāstra*. Calcutta: Firma KLM, 15–48.
1993. "Law Books in an Oral Culture: The Indian *Dharmaśāstras*." *Proceedings of the American Philosophical Society* 137: 254–67.
1994. "Orality and Textuality in the Indian Context." *Sino-Platonic Papers* 49.
1995. "Jīmūtavāhana's *Dāyabhāga* and the Maxim *factum valet*." *Brahmavidyā: Adyar Library Bulletin* 59: 83–96.
unpublished. *Studies in Hindu Law and Dharmaśāstra*, ed. Donald R. Davis, Jr.
Rocher, Rosane. 1983. *Orientalism, Poetry, and the Millennium: The Checkered Life of Nathaniel Brassey Halhed 1751–1830*. Delhi: Motilal Banarsidass.
1989. "The Career of Rādhākānta Tarkavāgīśa, an Eighteenth-Century Pandit in British Employ." *Journal of the American Oriental Society* 109(4): 627–33.
2007. "Henry Thomas Colebrooke and the Marginalization of Indian Pandits." In Birgit Kellner et al. (eds.), *Pramāṇakīrtiḥ: Papers Dedicated to Ernst Steinkellner on the Occasion of his 70th Birthday*, vol. II. Wiener Studien zur Tibetologie und Buddhismuskunde. Vienna: Arbeitskreis für Tibetische und Buddhistische Studien, Universität Wien, 735–56.

Rocher, Rosane, and Ludo Rocher. 2010. *The Making of European Indology: Henry Thomas Colebrooke and the East India Company*. Royal Asiatic Society Books. London: RoutledgeCurzon.

Roebuck, Thomas. 1819. *The Annals of the College of Fort William*. Calcutta: Hindoostanee Press.

Rosen, Lawrence. 1989. *The Anthropology of Justice: Law as Culture in Islamic Society*. Cambridge University Press.

Rukmani, T. S. 2001. *Hindu Diaspora: Global Perspectives*. New Delhi: Munshiram Manoharlal.

Runciman, W. G. 1989. *A Treatise on Social Theory*, vol. II*: Substantive Social Theory*. Cambridge University Press.

Salomon, Richard. 1998. *Indian Epigraphy. A Guide to the Study of Inscriptions in Sanskrit, Prakrit, and Other Indo-Aryan Languages*. Oxford University Press.

Sarkar, B. K. (ed. and trans.). 1923. *Śukranīti*, 2nd edn. Allahabad: Panini Office.

Sarkar, Tanika. 2001. *Hindu Wife, Hindu Nation: Community, Religion, and Cultural Nationalism*. Bloomington, IN: Indiana University Press.

Sarkar, Tanika, and Urvashi Butalia (eds.). 1995. *Women and the Hindu Right: A Collection of Essays*. Delhi: Kali for Women.

Sarkar, U. C. 1958. *Epochs in Hindu Legal History*. Hoshiarpur: Vishveshvaranand Vedic Research Institute.

Sarkāra, Śrī 5-ko [H. M. G.]. [1965]. *(Mulukī) Ain : Śrī 5 Surendra Bikram Śāhadevakā Śāsanakālamā Baneko Mulukī Ain*. Kathmandu: Kānūna tathā Nyāya Mantrālaya, VS 2022.

Śarmā, Nityānanda, Viṣṇuprasāda Bhāṇḍārī, and Padmaprasāda Upadhyāya Bhaṭṭa (eds.). 1916. *Vīramitrodaya of Mitramiśra*, vol. I [Paribhāṣā-Prakāśa]. Chowkhamba Sanskrit Series, 103. Calcutta: Chowkhamba Sanskrit Series Office.

Sarma, Rani Siva Sankara. 2007. *The Last Brahmin: Life and Reflections of a Modern-day Sanskrit Pandit*, translated from the Telugu by D. Venkat Rao. Delhi: Permanent Black.

Śarmā, Viṣṇu Kānta (ed.). 2000. *Sūcipatra (Aithāsik Ciṭhṭhipatra Saṃgraha)*. Kathmandu: H. M. G. Nepal, National Archives, VS 2057.

Sathe, S. P. 2002. *Judicial Activism in India*. New Delhi: Oxford University Press.

Sawyer, John F. A., and Mary Douglas (eds.). 1996. *Reading Leviticus: A Conversation with Mary Douglas*. Sheffield Academic Press.

"SC Stays OBC Quota." 2007. *Statesman (India)*, March 30. www.accessmylibrary.com/, accessed May 13, 2010.

Schopen, Gregory. 1990. "The Buddha as Owner of Property and Permanent Resident in Medieval Indian Monasteries." *Journal of Indian Philosophy* 18: 181–217.

Scott, Joan. 1996. *Only Paradoxes to Offer: French Feminists and the Rights of Man*. Cambridge, MA: Harvard University Press.

Sen, Ronojoy. 2007. *Legalizing Religion: The Indian Supreme Court and Secularism*. Policy Studies, 30. Washington: East-West Center.

Sen, Surendranath, and Umesha Mishra (eds.). 1951. *Sanskrit Documents Being Sanskrit Letters and Other Documents Preserved in the Oriental Collection at the National Archives of India*. Allahabad: Ganganatha Jha Research Institute.

Sengupta, Ipshita. 2008. "Caste as Race." *India Together*, June 8 (digital edition). www.indiatogether.org/2008/jun/soc-casterace.htm, accessed October 16, 2009.

Sharma, Ram Sharan. 1966. *Light on Early Indian Society and Economy*. Bombay: Manaktalas.

Shama Shastry, R. (ed.). 1927. *Sarasvatīvilāsa. Vyavahārakāṇḍa*. Mysore: Government Branch Press.

Sinha, Mrinalini. 1995. *Colonial Masculinity: The "Manly Englishman" and the "Effeminate Bengali" in the Late Nineteenth Century*. New York: St. Martin's Press.

2006. *Specters of Mother India: The Global Restructuring of an Empire*. Durham, NC: Duke University Press.

Sircar, D. C. 1953–4. "No. 30 – Charter of Vishnushena, Samvat 649" [= 592 CE]. *Epigraphia Indica* 30: 163–81.

1965. *Indian Epigraphy*. Delhi: Motilal Banarsidass.

1966. *Indian Epigraphical Glossary*. Delhi. Motilal Banarsidass.

1974. *Studies in the Political and Administrative Systems in Ancient and Medieval India*. Delhi: Motilal Banarsidass.

1984. "Glimpses of Ācāra and Vyavahāra in Early Indian Literary and Epigraphic Records." In Richard W. Lariviere (ed.), *Studies in Dharmaśāstra*. Calcutta: Firma KLM, 3–14.

Skariah, Joseph (ed.). 1996. *Talaśśēri Rêkhakaḷ*. Tübingen University Library Malayalam Manuscript Series, 5. Kottayam: DC Books.

Somerville, Keith. 2002. "Ugandan Asians: Successful Refugees." *BBC News*, November 8. http://news.bbc.co.uk/2/low/in_depth/2399549.stm, accessed May 7, 2010.

Sontheimer, Günther-Dietz. 1964. "Religious Endowments in India: The Juristic Personality of Hindu Deities." *Zeitschrift für vergleichende Rechtswissenschaft* 67(1): 45–100.

1997. "Hinduism: The Five Components and their Interaction." In Günther-Dietz Sontheimer and Hermann Kulke (eds.), *Hinduism Reconsidered*. New Delhi: Manohar, 305–24.

Spivak, Gayatri. 1988. "Can the Subaltern Speak?" In Cary Nelson and Lawrence Grossberg (eds.), *Marxism and the Interpretation of Culture*. Urbana, IL: University of Illinois Press, 271–316.

Sreenivas, Mytheli. 2004. "Conjugality and Capital: Gender, Families and Property under Colonial Law in India." *Journal of Asian Studies* 63(4): 937–60.

Srikrishna, B. N. 1998. "Srikrishna Commission Report." www.sabrang.com/srikrish/sri%20main.htm, accessed May 7, 2010.

Srinivas, M. N. 1962. *Caste in Modern India and Other Essays*. Bombay: Asia Publishing House.

Srinivasacharya, L. (ed.), 1914–21. *Smṛticandrikā / Smritichandrika by Devana-Bhatta*, 5 vols. Mysore: Government Branch Press.

Sripati, Vijayashri. 1998. "Toward Fifty Years of Constitutionalism and Fundamental Rights in India: Looking Back to See Ahead (1950–2000)." *American University International Law Review* 14(2): 413–96.

Steele, Arthur. 1827. *Summary of the Law and Custom of Hindoo Castes within the Dekhun Provinces Subject to the Presidency of Bombay, Chiefly Affecting Civil Suits*. Bombay: Courier Press.

Stein, Marc Aurel (ed. and trans.). 1988 [1892, 1900]. *Kalhaṇa's Rājataraṅginī, or, Chronicle of the Kings of Kashmir*, 3 vols. Delhi: Motilal Barnasidass.

Stenzler, Adolf Friedrich (ed. and trans.). 1849. *Yâjnavalkya's Gesetzbuch. Sanskrit und Deutsch*, 2 vols. Berlin: Ferd. Dümmler.

von Stietencron, Heinrich. 1977. "Orthodox Attitudes towards Temple Service and Image Worship in Ancient India." *Central Asiatic Journal* 21(2): 126–38.

Strange, Thomas Andrew Lumisden. 1816. *Notes of Cases in the Court of the Recorder and in the Supreme Court of Judicature at Madras*, 3 vols. Madras: Asylum Press.

1825. *Elements of Hindu Law; Referable to British Judicature in India*, 2 vols. London: Payne & Foss.

Strauch, Ingo (ed. and trans.). 2002. *Die Lekhapaddhati–Lekhapañcāśikā. Briefe und Urkunden im mittelalterlichen Gujarat. Text, Übersetzung, Kommentar*. Berlin: Dietrich Reimer.

Sturman, Rachel. 2005. "Property and Attachments: Defining Autonomy and the Claims of Family in Nineteenth-Century Western India." *Comparative Studies in Society and History* 47(3): 611–37.

2006. "Marriage and the Morality of Exchange: Defining the Terrain of Law in Late Nineteenth Century Western India." In Durba Ghosh and Dane Kennedy (eds.), *Decentering Empire: Britain, India, and the Transcolonial World*. Hyderabad: Orient Longman, 51–75.

Subrahmanya Aiyar, K. V. 1954–5. "Largest Provincial Assemblies in Ancient India." *Quarterly Journal of the Mythic Society* 45(4): 270–86, and 46(1): 8–22.

Subrahmanyam, Sanjay. 1997. "Connected Histories: Notes toward a Reconfiguration of Early Modern Eurasia." *Modern Asian Studies* 31(3): 735–62.

2005. *Explorations in Connected History: From the Tagus to the Ganges*. Delhi: Oxford University Press.

Taber, John. 1992. "What Did Kumārila Bhaṭṭa Mean by *Svataḥprāmāṇya*?" *Journal of the American Oriental Society* 112(2): 204–21.

Talbot, Cynthia. 2001. *Precolonial India in Practice: Society, Region, and Identity in Medieval Andhra*. Delhi: Oxford University Press.

Tamanaha, Brian Z. 2001. *A General Jurisprudence of Law and Society*. New York: Oxford University Press.

Tambiah, Stanley. 1985. "A Performative Approach to Ritual." In *Culture, Thought, and Social Action*. Cambridge, MA: Harvard University Press, 123–66.

Tamminen, Tapio. 1996. "Hindu Revivalism and the Hindutva Movement." *Temenos* 32(1996): 221–38. www.abo.fi/comprel/temenos/temeno32/tamminen.htm, accessed May 7, 2010.

Tarkalankara, Chandrakanta (ed.). 1893. *Parāśarasmṛti with the Commentary of Mādhava*. Calcutta: Bibliotheca Indica.

Tejani, Shabnum. 2007. "Reflections on the Category of Secularism in India: Gandhi, Ambedkar, and the Ethics of Communal Representation, c. 1931." In Anuradha Dingwaney Needham and Rajeswari Sundar Rajan (eds.), *The Crisis of Secularism in India*. Durham, NC: Duke University Press, 45–65.

Telang, K. T. 1900. "Gleanings from the Maráthá Chronicles." Appendix in Mahadeo Govind Ranade, *Rise of the Maratha Power*. Bombay: Punalekar, 255–324. Reprinted Delhi: Ministry of Information and Broadcasting, 1961, 117–46.

Teubner, Gunther. 1992. "The Two Faces of Janus: Rethinking Legal Pluralism." *Cardozo Law Review* 13: 1,443–62.

Thakur, Anantalal. 1927–8. "Documents in Ancient India." *Annals of the Bhandarkar Oriental Research Institute* 9, 49–81.

Thakur, Anantalal, and Upendra Jha (eds.). 1957. *Kāvyalakaṇa with the Ratnaśrī of Ratnaśrījñāna*. Darbhanga: Mithila Institute of Post-Graduate Studies and Research in Sanskrit Learning.

Thorat, Sukhadeo, and Paul Attewell. 2007. "The Legacy of Social Exclusion: A Correspondence Study of Job Discrimination in India." *Economic and Political Weekly*, October 13, 4,141–5. www.epw.org.in/uploads/articles/11135.pdf, accessed May 7, 2010.

Trautmann, Thomas R. 2006. *Languages and Nations: The Dravidian Proof in Colonial Madras*. Berkeley, CA: University of California Press.

Tubb, Gary, and Emery Boose. 2007. *Scholastic Sanskrit: A Manual for Students*. New York: American Institute of Buddhist Studies.

Twaddle, Michael. 1975. *Expulsion of a Minority: Essays on Ugandan Asians*. London: Athlone Press.

Unni, N. P. (ed.). 2003. *Laghudharmaprakāśikā (*alias *Śāṅkarasmṛti)*. Corpus Iuris Sanscriticum, 4. Turin: CESMEO.

Upadhyaya, Prakash Chandra. 1992. "The Politics of Indian Secularism." *Modern Asian Studies* 26(4): 815–53.

Vajpeyi, Ananya. 2004. "Politics of Complicity, Poetics of Contempt: A History of the Śūdra in Maharashtra, 1650–1950 CE." Doctoral dissertation, University of Chicago.

2005. "Excavating Identity through Tradition: Who Was Shivaji?" In Satish Saberwal and Supriya Varma (eds.), *Traditions in Motion: Religion in Society and History*. New Delhi: Oxford University Press, 240–71.

in press. "The *Śūdra* in History: From Scripture to Segregation." In Y. Bronner, L. McCrea, and W. Cox (eds.), *Festschrift for Sheldon Pollock on his 60th Birthday*.

Valantasis, Richard L. 1995. "A Theory of the Social Function of Asceticism." In Vincent Wimbush and Richard L. Valantasis (eds.), *Asceticism*. New York: Oxford University Press, 544–52.

Vasundhara, C. 1989. *Vijñānēśvaramu of Mūlaghaṭika Kētana: Telugulō toli dharmaśāstra grantham̩*. Nellūru: Mānasa Pablikēṣans.

Velu Pillai, T. K. (ed.). 1940. *Travancore State Manual*, 4 vols. Trivandrum: Government Press.

Venkasawmy Row, T. A. 1911–16. *Indian Decisions (Old Series)*, 17 vols. Madras: Law Printing House.

Vertovec, Steven. 1994. "'Official' and 'Popular' Hinduism in the Caribbean: Historical and Contemporary Trends in Surinam, Trinidad, and Guyana." *Contributions to Indian Sociology* 28(1): 123–47.

2000. *Hindu Diaspora: Comparative Patterns*. London: Routledge.

Vidyasagar, N. 1991. "Back Home – but Not Yet." *Aside*, August 31.

Vidyasagara, Jivananda. 1874. *Manusaṃhitā, with the Ṭīkā of Kullūkabhaṭṭa*. Calcutta: Viḍan Yantre.

Viswanathan, Gauri. 1998. *Outside the Fold: Conversion, Modernity and Belief*. Princeton University Press.

Voltaire. 1880. "Commentaire sur l'Esprit des lois (1777)." In *Œuvres complètes de Voltaire*, vol. xxx: *Mélanges*. Paris: Garnier Frères, Part ix, 405–64.

Wagle, N. K. 1970. "The History and Social Organization of the Gauda Sarasvata Brahmanas of the West Coast of India." *Journal of Indian History* 48(1): 7–25.

1980. "A Dispute between the Pancal Devajna Sonars and the Brahmans of Pune regarding Social Rank and Ritual Privileges: A Case Study of the British Administration of Jati Laws in Maharashtra, 1822–1825." In N. K. Wagle (ed.), *Images of Maharashtra: A Regional Profile of India*. London: Curzon Press, 129–59.

1982. "The Candraseniya Kayastha Prabhus and the Brahmans: Ritual, Law and Politics in Pune: 1789–90." In G. D. Sontheimer and P. Aithal (eds.), *Indology and Law: Studies in Honour of Professor J. Duncan M. Derrett*. Wiesbaden: Franz Steiner, 303–28.

1987. "Ritual and Change in Early Nineteenth Century Society in Maharashtra: *Vedokta* Disputes in Baroda, Pune and Satara, 1824–1838." In Milton Israel and N. K. Wagle (eds.), *Religion and Society in Maharashtra*. University of Toronto, 145–81.

1995. "On Relations amongst Bhūts, Gods, and Men: Aspects of Folk Religion and Law in Pre-British Maharashtra." In Günther-Dietz Sontheimer (ed.), *Folk Culture, Folk Religion, and Oral Traditions as a Component in Culture and Society*. New Delhi: Manohar, 181–220.

1998. "Women in the Kotwal's Papers, Pune, 1767–1791." In Anne Feldhaus (ed.), *Images of Women in Maharashtrian Society*. New York: SUNY Press, 15–60.

2005. "Customary Laws among the Non-Brahman *Jātis* of Puṇe, 1824–1826." In Aditya Malik, Anne Feldhaus, and Heidrun Brueckner (eds.), *In the Company of Gods: Essays in Memory of Günther-Dietz Sontheimer*. New Delhi: Manohar, 283–328.

Washbrook, David. 1981. "Law, State, and Agrarian Society in British India." *Modern Asian Studies* 15(3): 649–741.

Weber, Max. 1946a. "Politics as a Vocation." In *From Max Weber: Essays in Sociology*, trans. and ed. H. H. Gerth and C. Wright Mills. New York: Oxford University Press, 77–128.

1946b. "The Social Psychology of the World Religions." In *From Max Weber: Essays in Sociology*, trans. and ed. H. H. Gerth and C. Wright Mills. New York: Oxford University Press, 267–301.

Weintraub, Jeff. 1997. "The Theory and Politics of the Public / Private Distinction." In Jeff Weintraub and Krishan Kumar (eds.), *Public and Private in Thought and Practice: Perspectives on a Grand Dichotomy*. University of Chicago Press, 1–42.

Welch, John W. (ed.). 1981. *Chiasmus in Antiquity: Structures, Analyses, Exegesis*. Hildesheim: Gerstenberg.

(ed.). 1999. "Criteria for Identifying and Evaluating the Presence of Chiasmus." In John W. Welch and Daniel B. McKinlay (eds.), *Chiasmus Bibliography*. Provo, UT: Research Press, 157–74.

West, Raymond, and Johann Georg Bühler. 1878. *A Digest of the Hindu Law of Inheritance and Partition: From the Replies of the Śâstris in the Several Courts of the Bombay Presidency*, 2nd edn. Bombay: Education Society's Press. (The 1st edn. was published in 2 vols. in 1867–9 under the title *A Digest of Hindu Law*.)

Wezler, Albrecht. 1985. "Dharma und Deśadharma." In H. Kulke and D. Rothermund (eds.), *Regionale Traditionen in Südasien*. Wiesbaden: Franz Steiner Verlag, 1–22.

2004. "Dharma in the Veda and the Dharmaśāstras." In Olivelle 2004a: 629–54.

Williams, Rina Verma. 2005. "Gender, Nation, Religion: Political Discourse and the Personal Laws in India, 1952–1956." *Journal of the Southwest Conference of Asian Studies* 5: 52–84.

2006. *Postcolonial Politics and Personal Laws: Colonial Legal Legacies and the Indian State*. Delhi: Oxford University Press.

Witte, John, Jr. (ed.). 2008. *Christianity and Law: An Introduction*. Cambridge University Press.

Wright, Theodore. 2007. "Affirmative Action vs. Reservations in the Private Sector: The United States and India." *The IUP Journal of Governance and Public Policy* 2(2): 19–26.

Yelle, Robert A. 2001. "Rhetorics of Law and Ritual: A Semiotic Comparison of the Law of Talion and Sympathetic Magic." *Journal of the American Academy of Religion* 69: 627–47.

2002. "Poetic Justice: Rhetoric in Hindu Ordeals and Legal Formulas." *Religion* 32: 259–72.

2006. "To Perform or Not to Perform? A Theory of Ritual Performance versus Cognitive Theories of Religious Transmission." *Method & Theory in the Study of Religion* 18: 372–91.

Younger, Paul. 2001. "Behind Closed Doors: The Practice of Hinduism in East Africa." In T. S. Rukmani (ed.), *Hindu Diaspora: Global Perspectives*. New Delhi: Munshiram Manoharlal Publishers, 367–86.

Zelliot, Eleanor. 1996. *From Untouchable to Dalit*. New Delhi: Manohar.

Index